Young Women in Japan
Transitions to Adulthood

This book examines young women in Japan, focusing in particular on their transitions to adulthood, their conceptions of adulthood and relations with Japanese society more generally. Drawing on detailed primary research including a year-long observation of high schools and subsequent interviews over a 12-year period, it traces the experiences of a group of working-class women from their last year of high-schooling in 1989 through to 2001 as they approached their 30s. It considers important aspects of the transition to adulthood including employment, marriage, divorce, childbirth and custody. It shows how the role and identities of young women changed over the course of the 1990s, exploring the impact of changes within Japanese society and global forces, and explains fully the implications for ordinary young people and their everyday lives. It considers to what extent young women's perceptions of themselves and society are shifting, and how far this can be explained by external constraints and their own experiences and decisions.

Kaori H. Okano is Associate Professor/Reader in the School of Social Sciences, La Trobe University, Melbourne, Australia. Her publications include *Language and Schools in Asia: Globalisation and Local Forces* (2006, as editor); *Education in Contemporary Japan: Inequality and Diversity* (1999, co-authored with M. Tsuchiya) which has been published in Malay as *Pendidikan Moden Jepun* (2004); School to *Work Transition in Japan: An Ethnographic Study* (1993); and articles in leading scholarly journals.

Young Women in Japan

Transitions to Adulthood

Kaori H. Okano

Routledge
Taylor & Francis Group

LONDON AND NEW YORK

First published 2009
by Routledge
2 Park Square, Milton Park, Abingdon, Oxon OX14 4RN

Simultaneously published in the USA and Canada
by Routledge
270 Madison Ave, New York, NY 10016

Routledge is an imprint of the Taylor & Francis Group, an Informa business

Typeset in Times New Roman
by Taylor & Francis Books
Printed and bound in Great Britain
by TJI Digital, Padstow, Cornwall

British Library Cataloguing in Publication Data
A catalogue record for this book is available from the British Library

Library of Congress Cataloging in Publication Data
Okano, Kaori, 1959-
    Young women in Japan : transitions to adulthood / Kaori H. Okano.
        p. cm. – (Women in Asia series)
    Includes bibliographical references.
    1. Young women–Japan. 2. Young women–Japan–Longitudinal studies.
3. Adulthood–Japan. I. Title.
    HQ799.8.J3O36 2009
    305.242'20952–dc22
                            2008034630

ISBN: 978-0-415-46941-8 (hbk)
ISBN: 978-0-203-88237-5 (ebk)

To Tom, Yukiko and David

Contents

Illustrations

Figures

Tables

Acknowledgements

It has been a great privilege to have known the young Japanese women who have participated in this study since 1989 when they were high school students. I cannot express my gratitude sufficiently to these women and their families, who over the years so willingly shared with me their stories of growing up.

I would like to thank the Japan Foundation, the Australian Research Council and La Trobe University for helping to fund my research. Without their generous support, it would have been impossible to undertake such a longitudinal study, which required visits of substantial duration every few years. A fellowship from the Japan Foundation enabled me to spend one year in Japan where I completed the manuscript.

My deliberations and writing have benefited greatly from discussions with my colleagues both in Australia and overseas, and from lively discussions with my students at La Trobe University who were also trying to make sense of young adulthood. I would also like to thank my research assistants, Shoko Hagino, Sonomi Atsuzawa and Nori Sato, for their tireless efforts.

Portions of Chapter 4 appeared as 'Japanese working-class girls in their first employment: transition to adulthood' (2004), *Journal of Education and Work*, 17(4): 421–39. They are reproduced by permission of Taylor & Francis Ltd.

Last but not least I should like to thank my family, Yukiko, Tom and David, for their continuous support.

Introduction

This book presents young women's stories about becoming adults in urban Japan. We will see how they experience and make sense of this process of growing up through to their late 20s. How do young people make transitions to adulthood in Japan? How do they conceive of adulthood? How are their pathways to adulthood shaped by individual decisions and actions on one hand, and by structural conditions on the other? How are their trajectories to, and understanding of, adulthood guided by urban working-class status, and for some, ethnic minority status? These are the questions that underpin this book.

Drawing on a unique set of longitudinal data collected over the course of 12 years, I trace the life experiences of a group of working-class women from the late 1980s and through the start of the twenty-first century when the Japanese economy and society underwent profound changes. In 1989 they were in their last year of high school as 17–18 year olds in Kobe-city in the greater Hanshin conurbation in the western part of Japan. In early 2001 the women were approaching 30 years of age and still living in the region. The book uncovers a hitherto largely unstudied aspect of Japanese society – the processes through which individuals make their transition to adulthood. In focusing on Japan, one of the very few non-Western post-industrial democratic societies, the book provides an important contrast with the extensive work on transitions to adulthood undertaken in the West (e.g. Settersten et al. 2005; Arnett 2004; Mortimer and Larson 2002).

In the following chapters I present extensive biographies based on vivid narratives of individual young adults; and examine how they experienced and made sense of employment, unemployment, relationships, families, marriages and divorce, in charting their individual trajectories to adulthood. After graduating from high school, some quit first jobs, experienced periods of unemployment, and found temporary work or other permanent full-time jobs. Many developed new relationships or interests outside work. Some married, left their parents' homes and bore children. Some underwent a bitter divorce, returned to their parents' home, and resumed another working life. In this process the young people developed more extensive human relationships, formed views of how the society works, came to see themselves as adults, and crafted their identities in relation to class, gender and ethnicity.

These women's transitions occurred against the backdrop of the social conditions of the 1990s, when global trends affected Japanese society in significant ways. In 1990 when these young people entered the workforce, Japan was reaching the end of the bubble economy. The decade of the 1980s was characterised by continuing trade surplus, an unrealistic rise in property prices, full employment and consumerism. In 1990 employment opportunities were still abundant; but signs of upcoming changes were visible. More young people started choosing casual or contract jobs instead of permanent employment, which prompted the emergence of casual job recruitment magazines in the market. At the time teachers at the two schools where I was conducting fieldwork were concerned that their students might be influenced by these trends and attracted to jobs that were presented to young people as being 'glamorous'. The media deplored the phenomenon and coined the term *frîtâ* to describe such casual or contract workers. By 1995 Japan was in the midst of a recession. Job opportunities for new graduates were limited. Companies were forced to cut back on the traditional biannual bonuses and 'restructure' their operations (for example, by reorganising the company structure, employment practices and salary scales), and required employees to work long hours without pay. Companies relocated production offshore, which decreased domestic job opportunities in manufacturing. These trends continued until well into 2000. By then the 1990s were described as Japan's 'lost decade'.

The young women in this study not only experienced the 'lost decade' occupying marginal positions in society; but also survived a large-scale external event, the Hanshin-Awaji earthquake of January 1995, which was the most damaging earthquake Japan had experienced since 1923. Many houses and commercial premises were destroyed, and the city was temporarily immobilised. As we shall see, many of the women in this study were displaced when their homes were damaged or destroyed, and underwent what they described as 'unimaginable' daily routines until they were able to return to normality. We will see how individually they managed these changes imposed upon them in charting trajectories to adulthood, by constantly referring to both nationwide and global trends and debates.

Transitions to adulthood in a global context

Thirty years ago ordinary people took it for granted that everyone eventually grows up to be an 'adult'. There was also a degree of consensus on what adulthood entailed. Recently we have been forced to question these assumptions about young people in the Anglo-West. This is because many young people today seem to face difficulties assuming conventionally defined 'adult roles' and consequently experience prolonged dependent adolescence. Others seem to enjoy a deliberate deferment from taking on adult roles.

Do we see a similar process occurring in Japan? Japan presents an interesting case in that it is one of the very few non-Western democratic societies with a comparable level of industrialisation, affluence and a relatively even wealth distribution. It offers a particular set of institutions, circumstances, and social and cultural norms. These institutions include the link between high schools and employment, employment practice and particular normative expectations of marriage and relationships. In revealing the case of Japan, the book offers readers in the West the opportunity to critically reflect on the Western interpretation of transitions to adulthood; which will in turn advance our understanding of transition to adulthood in the post-industrial era.

Changes in the patterns and subjective understandings of transition to adulthood in Western post-industrial societies have been documented by a large number of studies in the last two decades; but very few of these works refer to non-Western societies. Recent trends in the West depict a somewhat fragmented transition, and a prolonged youth or period between adolescence and adulthood. Young people stay in educational institutions longer; try out different casual jobs before obtaining full-time permanent employment; experience periods of unemployment before or between employment; live in their parents' homes longer; try pre-marital cohabitation; and defer marriage and parenthood. They are less likely to see completing role transitions as the end point to young adulthood. In this situation, young people make adjustments to the normative notion of adulthood, and create their own view. When the media laments 'the young's refusal of adulthood', it suggests that young people are not only refusing the adulthood expected by the older generation, but also offering a critique of the adult world they perceive to exist. Relevant recent books such as Arnett's *Emerging Adulthood* (2004) and Cote's *Arrested Adulthood* (2000), along with earlier works (e.g. Bynner et al. 1997; Irwin 1995), effectively capture changing experiences of transition to adulthood and describe young adults who cite intangible, individualistic and psychological characteristics in their own understanding of what adulthood may entail in North America and the United Kingdom (UK). Edited volumes on transitions to adulthood in the West provide insightful international comparisons with a focus on institutional differences (e.g. Booth et al. 1999; Corijn and Klijzing 2001; Heinz 1999; Settersten et al. 2005; Furstenberg et al. 2002).

Another stream of studies of young adulthood focuses on how individual trajectories are shaped by structural factors such as class, gender and ethnicity; and how this process reinforces the existing social divisions during this fluid period of life (Ball et al. 2000). Studies on working-class females' transitions to adulthood in the United States of America (USA) and UK (Skeggs 1997; Walkerdine et al. 2001) illuminate the complexity involved, and provide a point of comparison for my Japanese study.

Young Japanese women: class and ethnicity

This book enhances our understanding of three areas of Japanese society: (1) transitions to adulthood, the process of growing up and the notion of maturity; (2) youth; and (3) women. Only a few books touch on transition to adulthood in Japan. They are LeTendre (2000), Rohlen (1983), Okano (1993) on adolescence, which are all year-long ethnographic studies of schools, and Plath (1980) on the rhetoric of maturity based on retrospective accounts by middle-aged interviewees. While not specifically focusing on the transitions to adulthood experienced by those in their 20s, all of them are concerned with how human development (personal and social growth) occurs through individuals' experiences of institutions and relationships; and discuss the nature of the 'maturity' that is shaped socially and felt individually. This book is a valuable addition to the above works by illuminating in detail the actors' transitions to adulthood as they occurred, rather than retrospectively, over a 12-year period; and thus provides a fuller understanding of the process of growing up. The existing books on Japanese youth tend to centre on specific groups and teenagers (e.g. Sato 1991; White 1993; Yoder 2004). Mathews and White (2004) in their focus on the generation gap emphasise that young people are 'destroying the adult social order'; but in lacking a comparative perspective do not effectively discuss Japanese young people in the context of global trends.

The book's contributions to the extensive literature on Japanese women are twofold. First, it focuses on working-class women in their 20s, a group which has not to date been studied extensively. Second, it reveals the transition to adulthood as seen in the combination of public and private arenas (rather than studying them separately, as in the existing studies).

The existing literature on contemporary Japanese women illustrates diversity and yet some shared patterns in their concerns and lives, and includes studies of privileged upper-class women (wealthy business families and the late noble families), politicians, farming women in a rural village, full-time housewives, and women in management. The dominant portrait of Japanese women as middle-class full-time housewives (Vogel 1978; Imamura 1987) has been gradually replaced by ones which emphasise diversity and specificity, in terms of class, occupations, generations and regions (e.g. Lebra 1984; Iwao 1993; Rosenberger 2001; Fujimura-Fanselow and Kameda 1995). For example, privileged upper-class women are depicted by Hamabata's study (Hamabata 1990) of wealthy business families and Lebra's (1992) of the late noble families. Women pursuing professional careers are also depicted, by Lam (1992) and Renshaw (1999), who studied business executives, and by Pharr (1981) who focused on female politicians. Taking a rural perspective, Bernstein (1983) describes the life of farming women in a remote village.

We know more about 'ordinary' working women, both blue-collar and white-collar. We can read about the lives of blue-collar workers in family business in Kondo's study (Kondo 1990) of middle-aged workers in a small *shitamachi* confectionery company and in Goldstein-Gidoni's study (Goldstein-Gidoni 1997) of a small beauty salon owner and her part-time workers. We can learn of regular blue-collar female factory workers without tertiary education in Roberts' (1994) and Lo's (1990) respective descriptions of a lingerie manufacturer and a machine factory, and of part-time female factory workers in Roberson's study (1998) of a small manufacturing business. Urban white-collar female workers, both sales and clerical, who have been studied tended to be tertiary-educated, for example, the subjects in Creighton's department store (Creighton 1996) and Matsunaga's supermarket chain store (Matsunaga 2000). Two major studies on female clerical workers, often called 'OLs' (office ladies), almost ten years apart, by Lo (1990) and Ogasawara (1998) suggest that workers in recent years have become more informed about the dynamics of their companies and about how they can derive the most benefit from their marginal positions in their companies.

Among urban working women, there are two distinctive groups – part-time workers who are often older and married, with family responsibilities; and regular full-time workers, many of whom are unmarried (Lo 1990; Ogasawara 1998; Roberts 1994; Matsunaga 2000; Broadbent 2003; Kondo 1990). This creates the well-known 'M-curve' of Japanese female labour participation whereby the rate drops sharply during the child-bearing and rearing period. Different stages in the M-curve (e.g. single women in regular employment, full-time stay-at-home mother and wife, principal home-maker with part-time employment, retirement) are depicted separately in the above-mentioned studies. Rosenberger's volume (Rosenberger 2001), on the other hand, presents different stages of women's lives in the 1970s, 1980s and 1990s, drawing on retrospective interviews with women in their late 30s and older (substantially older than those in this book). Rosenberger explores changes in the women's notion of self over the three decades by interviewing different women in each decade.

The interpretations of women's lives are as diverse as those lives. At one end of the continuum is the popular view that Japanese women are 'victims' of a patriarchal society where women have been oppressed by 'social and cultural norms' and institutions that deprive them of the pursuit of their aspirations. They are said to face barriers to recruitment to desirable companies, and in gaining promotion once employed. This is especially the case when an important period of career development is forsaken for childbirth; or worse, in having to quit work altogether, through either lack of maternity leave or the fear that colleagues would look unfavourably on their taking maternity and child-rearing leave, even when it is offered by the employer. Once leaving regular employment, and with age, it becomes increasingly difficult to enter regular positions, which forces women to take up poorly paid part-time casual work. Even if they find regular employment, married women with children find it impossible to perform the tasks that many regular positions require (e.g. long working hours, lack of flexibility). (I shall discuss this in more detail in Chapters 4 and 5.) At the other end of the continuum is the view that, rather than being oppressed, Japanese women can have healthier and happier lives, and 'better' opportunities for self-fulfilment through non-work channels (such as leisure activities and relationships) than their male counterparts under the current institutional arrangements of Japanese society (Iwao 1993). Men are expected to have no choice but to commit their lives to their jobs in order to be a family provider. Many men internalise, perhaps quite reluctantly, such expectations and perform a corporate warrior role by leaving the responsibilities for household and children to their wives, and are unable to develop meaningful relationships with family members. This view of the corporate warrior and full-time housewife as idealised masculinity and femininity is a post-war construction, and assumes middle-class lifestyles. As we will see, working-class girls are certainly aware of this middle-class view (and indeed some desire it); but they are also aware that the realities of their own upbringings and their current daily lives diverge from this middle-class lifestyle.

When I refer to my actors as 'working-class' girls, I use the term 'class' in a cultural sense. People in a class (or a fraction of a class), being located in similar positions in hierarchical social relations, possess a similar strategy-generating principle or scheme of perceptions, expressions and actions, which enable them to respond to diverse tasks in unforeseen and changing situations. Bourdieu (1977: 72) calls these principles and generating schemes 'habitus', and I found this notion a useful analytical tool for understanding classes in Japan.[1] The women I focus on possess a collective habitus that derives from their shared class-specific experience, and which I consider 'working class' as distinct from dominant middle class. Within this collective habitus there is diversity (Okano 1995b).

While there is a popularly perceived myth that Japan is a mass middle-class society, several studies point to the significance of social classes in contemporary Japanese society (e.g. Ishida 1993; Sugimoto 2003). Roberson (1998) studied working-class culture and identities and vividly depicted blue-collar workers (both male and female, most of the latter aged over 30) in a small urban factory. The working-class young women that I studied differ from Roberson's women in that they are mainly regular white-collar workers (except for three with blue-collar occupations), young (18–29 years old) and mainly work in relatively large companies. In fact, this contrast between the young women in my study and those in Roberson's illustrate the general trend that women shift from white-collar to blue-collar work and from large firms to small firms when they return to work after a break for family responsibilities (Shirahase 1995). Although many women in my study are white-collar workers, I consider them working class as distinct from middle class because of their family backgrounds (discussed in the next chapter) and their past decisions, which have led to their present entry into the workforce via vocational high schools. In contrast, middle-class white-collar female workers, such as those studied by Lo (1990) and Ogasawara (1998), have often received a tertiary education.

Some of the girls in this study are Japan-born Korean nationals, popularly called *zainichi korian* (*zainichi* for short), who were born and grew up in working-class suburbs with a large number of ethnic Koreans. Korean high school students considered their ethnic backgrounds to be the major consideration when deliberating on post-school employment destinations, because of discrimination that *zainichi* often face in recruitment and promotion in the mainstream labour market (Okano 1993, 1997). I argued that while the schools encouraged them to aim at mainstream companies the strategies that these students adopted to counter such restrictions diverged, leading to diverse destinations such as a bank for the ethnic Koreans or a large mainstream Japanese company. A study of these women complements that of young Koreans (of mainly tertiary-educated middle-class backgrounds) portrayed in Fukuoka (2000).

This book then fills a gap in the literature on Japanese women by presenting how working-class non-tertiary-educated women aged between 18 to 29 years experienced the 1990s. Their initial experiences immediately out of high school differed from middle-class late teens (aged 18–20) attending post-secondary private two-year junior colleges, which aim to train 'young ladies' (McVeigh 1997). They also experienced initial employment differently from the tertiary-educated, since they were younger (still in their teens) and had less experience of the 'wider unfamiliar world', and since the work-related expectations placed on them differed from those who are tertiary-educated. The book considers how they differ, and why, in comparison with middle-class tertiary-educated young women in their 20s represented by Lo (1990), Ogasawara (1998), Rosenberger (2001) and Kelsky (2001).

Working-class women becoming adults in Japan: a longitudinal approach

One of the strengths of this book is that it follows a group of the same women from high school to 30 years of age. Building on a year of observing them at high school in 1989–90, the book draws on subsequent interviews (in 1992, 1996–97 and 2000–2001) and correspondence with 21 young women between April 1989 and January 2001, tracing their decisions, actions, resulting consequences and experiences over those almost 12 years. It thus illuminates how their subjective understanding of adulthood altered over time, and allows us to understand these changes in the light of my accumulated knowledge about the women. This approach was also essential in enabling us to understand how an actor's decisions and actions at one historical time had consequences in subsequent years, by creating material conditions and circumstances. Having known the women while in high school helped me gain an insight into the nature of the covert link between schooling and adulthood.

The book has two distinctive parts. Part I takes you to the world of these women as they experienced young adulthood in the 1990s. It includes a short chapter on Kobe-city in order to provide the geographical context for these transitions, and a longer chapter devoted to detailed chronological portraits of eight of the women that I studied. Part II then turns to thematic discussions, introducing the experiences of other women, and involves refer-ence to national trends. It consists of four chapters. The first, Chapter 4, focuses on the initial two years of their experiences after leaving school, a period full of change and anxiety. Chapters 5, 6 and 7 examine four parti-cular domains of experience: employment and further education, relationships and leisure, and marriages and divorce. Chapter 8 integrates the preceding chapters.

The book reveals that young Japanese people understood their transitions to adulthood in terms of intangible aspects or what seemed almost like 'feelings'. This at a glance resembles what has been observed among their middle-class counterparts in the West (e.g. Arnett 2004). These feelings seemed to comprise three distinctive parts. The first was a sense of finding and maintaining a concrete and achievable purpose (*mokuhyō*). It was in concrete, personally significant experiences which gave the young women a sense of achievable goals as well as the motivation required to reach them (*yaruki*) that many recognised their own growth (*seichō*) towards adulthood. The second was a balanced sense of responsibility (*sekinin*), embracing groups of which they were members, significant others (e.g. workplace colleagues, friends, relatives and family members) and personal needs. The third was a sense of independence that they thought would follow from the achievement of realistic personal goals and attainment of a balanced sense of responsi-bility. Independence can be both financial (although there was disagreement on its extent among the women) and in terms of decision-making; and was understood to be a long-term goal that individuals would gradually work towards over the years and eventually achieve at their own pace. The women were discouraged from 'premature independence' by their families, who considered that high school graduates are not ready for economic indepen-dence even with a full-time permanent job and that the young needed further support or guidance under the family umbrella.

The young people's understanding of adulthood involved interpreting immediate circumstances, deciding what was important to them, and acting accordingly. I suggest that, in this process, the women distinguished four domains: (1) employment, (2) further education, (3) family (domestic), and (4) relationships and leisure. Individuals attached varying priorities to respec-tive domains, and these priorities altered over the 12-year period. In making decisions, the women assessed three aspects of each domain: (a) instrumental to the individual, (b) intrinsic to the individual, and (c) human relationships. These aspects were pursued as benefits to the individual at one end of the continuum, or rejected or avoided as losses to the individual at the other end. For example, one woman values most in her job a generous income that allows her to be independent (an instrumental aspect of employment), while another cherishes the intellectual stimulation and sense of achievement that her work bestows (intrinsic aspects). Yet another woman may simply be happy at work because of the close relationships she has with colleagues. These aspects are not mutually exclusive. Some aspects, such as the unexciting nature of the job content, were beyond the actors' control because of external constraints on high school-educated young women; yet they were able to devise strategies to emphasise positive aspects of their jobs in order to make their employment bearable. One woman's assessment of different aspects in one domain often depended on how she perceived the remaining domains. A difficult marriage led a woman to perceive the supportive human relationship aspect as important in the employment and leisure domain.

Drawing on this longitudinal study I argue that priority domains for a particular individual altered over time; and that these working-class women's trajectories to adulthood derive from an interaction of agency and structure. The changes in priority domains were in response to changing external circumstances and conditions (e.g. job opportunities, wishing to accommodate partners, infant children, and the earthquake); but some of these external conditions resulted from the women's own past decisions and actions. The changes also derive from the women gradually developing different ways to perceive and assess immediate circumstances. The women exercised agency in making decisions and acting on them under a set of circumstances and conditions that were beyond their control. They made decisions and acted in the light of their preferences. I suggest that the core of these women's preferences was a sense of 'comfort' (*igokochi no yosa*), and that their preferences were shaped by their past experiences and their place in the social relations of hierarchy. Their decisions and actions in turn had consequence in guiding their subsequent trajectories to adulthood by creating or restricting future opportunities and by influencing their material and social conditions in following years.

The book also demonstrates how working-class background, and in the case of *zainichi* Koreans their ethnic minority background, have guided young women's decisions and actions, leading to trajectories that are distinctive from young middle-class women. A lack of certain parental resources restricted their opportunities for tertiary education (e.g. through not possessing sufficient financial resources, and by being uninformed about the workings of the education system). Lack of tertiary education restricted the range of possible employment and promotion prospects, and deprived them of opportunities for personal exploration as university students without pressure to conform to particular social roles. The young women chose marriage partners with whom they (and their families) felt 'comfortable', and showed little desire to marry someone in pursuit of opportunities for upward social mobility, romantic adventures or alternative lifestyles. Young married couples (some with children) often faced financial constraints in the early stages of marriage due to relatively low levels of income and because they could not count on parental financial support. They devised ways to manage such situations, and subsequently maintained a 'working-class' lifestyle.

I wrote this book with a wide range of readers in mind. For those who work in social science fields (sociology/anthropology/education) dealing with transition to adulthood, the book offers an interesting case of non-Western young adults. For those who study Japan, the book enhances understandings of contemporary Japan as it grapples with the social and economic changes induced by globalisation. But foremost, I would be most pleased if new-comers (e.g. undergraduate students) saw this book as an invitation to explore young adulthood or Japanese society through engagement with vivid biographies representing their contemporaries in Japan.

1 Transitions to adulthood

This chapter presents current discussions on transitions to adulthood in post-industrialised societies. My aim is to provide the global context in which my stories can be understood, and to invite readers to consider some of the questions raised below when reading the following chapters. The chapter argues that industrial societies have experienced diverse patterns in transition to adulthood, at least partly due to the institutional variations (e.g. welfare regime, schooling–employment link) under which transition occurs, but have also shared new trends (e.g. prolonged period of education, casual employment, deferment of marriage). Japanese experience a welfare regime in which families are expected to play a substantial role and where there is a close connection in the education–employment link between individual schools and their network of employers. Both of these features contribute to a context that differs from that of the Anglo-West.

Normative and subjective notions of adulthood

In any society, there is a distinction between a society's dominant notion of adulthood (what it should be), and an individual's subjective understanding of adulthood (how one feels). The normative concept in Western post-industrialised societies assumes that a defining characteristic of the transition from youth to adult status is the progression from partial dependence on parents to independence, and a reliance by individuals on themselves (and their partners) for resourcing their daily living arrangements, often in the family that they create (e.g. Irwin 1995: 2; Kerckhoff 1990: 2). The concept often specifies role transitions or events that young people are expected to achieve, and which are often used as a benchmark to assess how young people are doing. There has been a conventional consensus on major role transitions in these societies: leaving school, being integrated into the labour market by obtaining a full-time job, leaving home, marrying (or living in a de facto relationship) and becoming a parent (e.g. Shanahan 2000: 667; Kerckhoff 1990: 25; Cote 2000: 4). Since a society's normative concept is formed by its history, institutions, and economic and political circumstances, we can expect each society to have a different collective set of expectations of adulthood. Sub-groups within a society (for example, based on gender, ethnicity, locality, sexuality) also attach different meanings to adulthood. At this basic level, Japan and the Western post-industrial societies resemble one another; the transition to adulthood is conceived of in terms of 'events' and 'markers', and this conception is understood to be normative, often created by the older generation, and having internal variations based on class, gender and ethnicity.

It is in the context of society's normative notion of adulthood that popular debate on transition to adulthood takes place when young people's actual experience is discussed. Young people in North America and Europe experience their late teens and their 20s quite differently from their counterparts of three decades ago, and these new trends have attracted research interest in recent years (e.g. Arnett 2004; Settersten et al. 2005; Booth et al. 1999; Furstenberg et al. 2002; Mortimer and Larson 2002; Corijn and Klijzing 2001; Fussell and Gauthier 2005). These studies suggest that young people tend to remain in education longer, try out different casual jobs before settling down in full-time employment (in particular, in Anglophone societies), experience periods of unemployment, live with their parents, and defer marriage and parenthood. They are less likely to see completing role transitions as the end point to adulthood. They may reverse roles (for instance returning to schooling after periods of employment, and to their parents' home after leaving home) in order to respond to, for example, changing circumstances of employment (an outcome of structural changes) and romantic relationships. Some spend time travelling overseas and participate in various voluntary or community services before deciding what they wish to do with their lives. For example, in Australia, where I have lived for over a decade, young people undergo a lengthy process to achieve 'on-going' employment. According to an Australian study 'The Life Patterns Project' (1991–2001), which traced high school graduates of 1991 (conducted over virtually the same period as this Japanese study), only 19 per cent entered the workforce without further study, and eight years after leaving school 47 per cent had made an on-going career for themselves (Dwyer and Wyn 2001: 114–18). While 'having a steady job' was still the first priority in their late 20s, these young people attached increasing importance to private interests because of experiences (e.g. overseas travel, unemployment, trying out various jobs) that had led them to form their priorities (Dwyer and Wyn 2001: 186, 198).

There is a general consensus that such trends have resulted from social changes in recent decades (Bynner et al. 1997; Wyn and Dwyer 2000; Maguire et al. 2001; Morrow and Richards 1996), but divergent views exist as to which aspects of change have been most significant. While some see the changing opportunity structure of the economy (and employment) as most influential (e.g. Booth et al. 1999; Roberts 2003; Bradley and van Hoof 2005), others emphasise the changing cultural dynamic, for example the increasing acceptance of cohabitation without marriage, as an equally key driver of change (Modell 1999).

The new trends in transitions to adulthood, and the society's acknowledgement of and increasing concern about them, at least partially explain the emergence of the term 'young adults' in the media discourse in the West. The term 'young adult' has been in use since the 1960s to describe what psychologists identified as the transition period between adolescence and established adulthood (e.g. Bocknek 1980). It has now entered the administrative vocabulary in continental Europe (EGISR 2001; Cicchelli and Martin 2004). In North America, the terms 'arrested adulthood' (Cote 2000) and 'emerging adulthood' (Arnett 2004) effectively capture not only the experiences of young people but also how they subjectively conceive of their experience of young adulthood.

Do we see a similar debate on young adulthood in contemporary Japan? The equivalent term in the Japanese language for 'young adult' is not frequently used. The media and books for parents and young people have variously presented views on what it means to be an adult (*otona*), such as a biographical account of growing up by a well-known film critic (Sato 1998), advice from counselling psychologists (e.g. Kawai 1996), exploratory accounts by academics (e.g. Kadowaki and Sataka 2001), and a collection of diverse views held by well-known individuals (Kariya 2006). In contrast to the first two examples, which present somewhat normative accounts, the latter two encourage individual initiative and diversity in creating paths to adulthood.

The academic literature on young people tends to centre on the *frîtâ* phenomenon, which Japanese society sees as 'problematic'. Instead of entering the full-time permanent workforce, *frîtâ* hold short-term contract or casual jobs. While it is common for young people in the Anglophone West to pursue a period of personal development partly by undertaking casual employment prior to starting a full-time job, this phenomenon is relatively new in Japan where a linear progression from full-time schooling to full-time work has been considered as a desirable norm. Critics have sought to identify causes for this phenomenon: for example, individual young people who are said to lack self-discipline; changing employment practices, in which employers are less willing to offer permanent jobs; the nature of employment conditions (e.g. long hours and the kind of commitment to employers which many young people seem reluctant to take on); the apparent failure of institutions such as schools and employment–related companies and government agencies to adapt to on-going changes in employment practices and the lifestyle preferences of their young clients (Tachibanaki 2004; Honda 2005a; Miyamoto 2004; Kosugi 2002, 2003; Nihon-Rôdô-Kenkyû-Kikô 2000a, 2000b). While all acknowledge that these factors in combination have resulted in the emergence of increasing number of *frîtâ*, they differ in the weight given to the respective elements. Another phenomenon widely discussed is 'parasite singles' (Yamada 1999), young people who choose to remain in their parents' homes in order to enjoy the convenience of rent-free accommodation and being looked after by their mothers, while enjoying the freedom afforded by relatively sizable disposable incomes. Various possible explanations have been suggested: reluctance on the part of those who grew up in affluence to assume less affluent lifestyles on their own incomes, lack of independence of parents who have spoiled their children in nuclear families, and so forth. What is missing is how young people themselves, regardless of employment status and living arrangements, make sense of becoming an adult.

'Refusal of adulthood' among the young is a phrase frequently heard in recent years. It suggests that young people's experiences often do not conform to the normative notion created by the dominant section of the society and by the older generations. It also signals that young people are questioning and even refusing the 'dominant version of adulthood' (Maguire et al. 2001: 198). If young people are not content with the normative notion of 'adulthood', how do they subjectively conceive of the transition to adulthood, and what 'adulthood' entails?

When asked their views of adulthood, the answers of young people in the West indicate that they construct their own notion more in terms of intangible, individualistic, psychological characteristics (e.g. Arnett 1997; Cote 2000; Westberg 2004). This might be more prevalent among middle-class young people, who do not see completion of adult role transitions as central to survival (since their parents are well resourced to assist and support them), or who are not pressured by their families to fully take on adult roles. A longitudinal study of Dutch youth concluded that those from the 'lower class' tended to perceive adulthood in terms of securing a job and starting a family, while higher-class youth associated adulthood with individual development (Plug et al. 2003). Indeed, studies suggest that experiences of early adulthood are shaped by social class (e.g. Bynner et al. 1997; Maguire et al. 2001; Johnson 2002; Johnson and Elder 2002; Ferri 1993; Morrow and Richards 1996; Plug et al. 2003), ethnic background (Wulff 1995) and gender (e.g. Griffin 1985; Gaskell 1992; Leadbeater and Way 1996; Valli 1986; Thomson et al. 2004; Fussell and Gauthier 2005). Any combination of the three in a specific national or regional context creates a set of experiences that differ from the mainstream privileged (e.g. Connolly et al. 1992; Shorter-Gorden and Washington 1996; Skeggs 1997; Mirza 1992; Walkerdine et al. 2001; Olsen 1996; McRobbie 1978: Mahaffy 2003).

These forces (class, ethnic background, gender, geographical region) shape the transition process, directly by providing a concrete range of opportunities and conditions (social, cultural and material), and indirectly by influencing young people's long-term aspirations, immediate expectations and plans, as well as their daily decision-making. Countering post-modern fluidity and individualisation, Roberts (2003) argues that social origin and structural factors remain crucial for adulthood transitions. People select one course of action from the range of options that they consider to be personally suitable and possible (Okano 1993), which Hodkinson and his colleagues (Hodkinson et al. 1996) call 'horizons for action'. In what ways were the Japanese women's trajectories shaped by individual decisions and external conditions?

International variations: institutional explanations

Beyond shared tendencies, there are variations in the transition paths to adulthood in industrialised societies in the Anglo-West and Europe (Heinz 1999). Comparative studies suggest, for example, that young people in these countries are similar at the age of 15 (when few have left school or entered full-time employment, let alone started their own households and had children) and again at the age of 35 (when many of them have experienced all these transition roles), but the experiences marking the paths between the two ages can vary quite significantly between countries (Cook and Furstenberg 2002).

While young people without tertiary education in Anglophone societies try out jobs in the secondary labour market for a few years before settling on jobs in the primary labour market, German youth experience a more predictable transition via a standardised apprenticeship through the close institutional linkages between schools and the employment system (Heinz 1999). The Swedish welfare system provides a specific youth allowance (generous in comparison to Anglo-Western nations), which means that economic independence is less problematic, and therefore less important, in defining the notion of adulthood (Westberg 2004: 38). In Eastern European nations, which recently adopted the market economy, employment is a prime issue in the transition (Roberts 2003). We see international variations when observing young people's transition to adulthood in France (Cicchelli and Martin 2004), the Netherlands (du Bois-Reymond 1998; Plug et al. 2003), the UK (Raffe et al. 2001; Thomson et al. 2004; MacDonald 1998), North America (Cote 2000; Arnett 2004) and Australia (Dwyer and Wyn 2001). Existing comparative studies have covered Europe, Anglophone Oceania and North America (EGRIS 2001; special issue of *The Annals of the American Academy of Political and Social Science* 580 (Furstenberg et al. 2000)), but none of them includes Japan, one of the few non-Western post-industrial democracies with a wealth distribution comparable to Western countries. Japan offers an institutional linkage between vocational high schools and employers, not akin to the German apprenticeship system but based on a long-term recruitment relationship between schools and employers.

In explaining international variations, Breen and Buchmann's attempt is helpful. Using a comparison of the countries of Western Europe and Anglophone Western countries (North America, Australia and New Zealand), Breen and Buchmann (2002: 303) argue that variations in many aspects of the transition to adulthood derive, at least partially, from institutional variations that provide the context in which the transition takes place. Institutional variations offer a set of opportunities and constraints to which young people and other players (e.g. employers and teachers) respond, and contribute to the development of normatively acceptable modes of behaviour. Their analysis conceives institutional variations in terms of: (1) welfare regime types ('conservative welfare regime', 'liberal welfare regime' and 'social democratic welfare regime'), (2) the nature of educational systems, and (3) labour market regulations. I will explain these in turn.

First, conservative welfare regimes, which exist in the German- and French-speaking countries of continental Europe, try to maintain status differentials and provide occupational- and status-based welfare programmes that differ in their benefit level. Liberal welfare regimes believe in the central role of the market and minimal interference, which leads to means-tested benefits (often applied in cases of market failure). Social democratic welfare regimes, such as those of Scandinavian countries, attempt to maintain universalistic benefit levels and individual entitlements set at average or middle-class levels (Breen and Buchmann 2002: 290–91). Southern European welfare regimes tend to rely on the family to provide welfare for (and to channel any welfare benefits to) individuals through the head of the household, while maintaining a relatively low level of welfare provision by the state. Social democratic welfare regimes take the society's collective responsibility for settlement into adulthood to the greatest extent, while liberal welfare regimes have the minimum involvement in the process.

Second, in education systems, the most important variation, according to Breen and Buchmann, is the nature of the link between education and occupation. Such a link is most direct and specific in societies that strictly maintain both standardisation of educational provision and stratification of the system. At one end of the continuum are societies where educational qualifications signal to employers what capacities a potential employee offers in terms of a particular job, as in Germany, Austria and Switzerland. At the other end specific vocational skills tend not to be taught at higher levels in the formal school system (Breen and Buchmann 2002: 291–92).

Third, in relation to the labour market, job security is considered the most important factor in the transition. Employment protection legislation is strong in social democratic and conservative welfare regimes and weak in Anglophone nations. Southern European countries maintain a secure economic position for the head of the household since the family is assumed to provide welfare for its members. Young people face more difficulties in a labour market with strong employment protection since employers are reluctant to employ new workers whom they cannot easily dismiss (Breen and Buchmann 2002: 292–93). These institutional factors create a set of clusters. In Anglophone societies, what is learned at school is not specifically linked to job demand, and employment tenure is precarious. The opposite is the case in German-speaking countries (Breen and Buchmann 2002: 294). These institutional variations provide a set of conditions (both opportunities and constraints) under which young people navigate their decision-making and actions, and which guide them in planning for the future.

Seen in this scheme, contemporary Japan displays some of the features of Southern European welfare regimes, in that the state wishes families to play significant roles in providing welfare for their family members. Although in Japan unemployment benefits are paid to individuals rather than the household head, receipt of the benefits has conditions, such as a certain length of prior employment, and an extended waiting period (usually three months) before payment starts. The link between what youth learn at school and employment is strong for vocational high schools (which produce 25 per cent of high school graduates), but weak for academic high schools. Academic high schools display diversity, ranging from elite schools which send all graduates to high-ranking universities to those which rank even lower than vocational high schools in terms of entry requirements (Okano and Tsuchiya 1999: 62–74). One of the most important roles that vocational high schools perform for their students is in providing and managing a system of school-based job referral, which is built on long-term relationships between individual schools and their network of employers. Surveys suggest that teenagers at vocational high schools possess clearer post-school occupational plans and less sense of being lost (Honda 2005b). In these institutional settings, how do Japanese working-class young adults make transitions to adulthood, in comparison with their counterparts in Western countries?

Part I
Life stories 1989–2001

2 A longitudinal ethnography

Shino: Of course being a student is easier. Being employed looks demanding. Students can sleep, or take a day off, and you can do what you want if you join a club. You can get teachers to do various things. I guess now that I'm leaving school soon, I can say this. I'd love to be at school another year if I could.

(2 December 1989, three months prior to high school graduation)

People sometimes find themselves unexpectedly in a lasting relationship with a particular town or city. My relationship with Kobe-city has been one of those. More than 17 years ago in early 1989, as a novice researcher I chose the city as the location for my PhD fieldwork for nothing more than pragmatic reasons, to carry out my study on working-class high school students' decision-making about post-school destinations. I was looking for an urban area that offered many employers who absorbed high school graduates, where a relatively large minority population resided (although their presence was not conspicuous to casual observers), and where I could live relatively inexpensively. Since then I have been involved in other projects, and it was one of these projects that again brought me back to this city in 2006 to spend a year on sabbatical. I am extremely pleased that I am writing the final stages of this longitudinal study in Kobe-city where it all started. Just being here brings back fond memories of many encounters and conversations over the last 17 years.

In this chapter, I set out the context for what follows. There are three tasks. I will briefly describe Kobe-city, where I first met the women in this study as high school students and which is the setting for their lives as detailed in this book. This description includes a brief illustration of the 1995 Hanshin–Awaji earthquake that affected the city and these women and their families in many different ways. I shall then explain my relationship with the women, which has evolved gradually over the years, since this is crucial for understanding the nature of the data that I collected and how I interpreted them.

Kobe: a city in the Hanshin conurbation

Kobe is one of the largest cities in the Hanshin conurbation of western Japan. The city originally stood on a long narrow coastal strip bounded by steep mountains running parallel to the coast; but now covers a much more extensive area, having gradually expanded its territory over the mountains. On a clear day, from the top of the mountain, looking seaward you can see the coastline of Osaka Bay and the Seto Island Sea, and looking inland spreading bushland. In winter the mountain tops are often covered by snow and ponds freeze over, while the coastal suburbs hardly ever experience such conditions.

Kobe is typical of coastal cities in the Kansai region. It is home to an extensive range of manufacturing, high-technology and service industries. High-rise office blocks housing local government and company offices and retail outlets concentrate in the city centre. Department stores and shopping malls and streets near major train stations throng with people of all ages. There are numerous temples and shrines, several Christian churches, one mosque, a synagogue and one Chinese temple. High-rise residential complexes, owned either by local governments or by residents, can be seen across the city. Outer suburbs comprise a patchwork of new schools, houses, shopping precincts, residential complexes and parks, often adjacent to farmland. Kobe-city provides many signs and historical monuments that give an insight into what the region has witnessed over the last 2,000 years. Some of the place and street names would be familiar to those who have studied Japanese history.

I went for many leisurely walks in the city and its suburbs and often marvelled at the sight of the legacies that provide a sense of the history of Kobe-city. Grave mounds of powerful local clans from ancient times (the third to fifth centuries) survive in the midst of commercial and residential areas, and some are now used as a children's park. There are numerous Buddhist temples, Shinto shrines and monuments from the periods of aristocratic rule (fifth to tenth centuries); and the hills and beaches where two powerful warring clans (the Genji and the Taira) fought. The major outcome of the war was the transfer of power in the Japanese archipelago from the aristocrats to the samurai class (professional warriors) in the twelfth century. It was the losing clan in this war that consolidated Kobe's port with extensive construction and reclamation works in the eleventh century. During the subsequent feudal periods, Kobe was governed by local lords, as was the case with the rest of Japan, and its port continued to flourish through trade in agricultural products between feudal territories in which sea transport played a significant part.

With the advent of Japan as a modern nation state in the mid-nineteenth century following Japan's opening up to the West after 250 years of isolation policy, Kobe-city and its port suddenly became one of the major points of contact with the foreigners, and in particular, Westerners. Kobe was designated as one of the seven ports for trading with Western powers. Officials and traders of the treaty nations arrived and resided in a designated area where they could exercise their own jurisdiction. Chinese merchants lived in what has now become China Town. The city still retains features of the foreign residential area and other European-style houses from this period. During this time the city also became an engine of industrialisation and modernisation with the establishment of steel and heavy industries. Kobe thus became one of the two major ports for overseas trade in modern Japan.

Burgeoning heavy industry with its key role in rapid industrialisation and the later war-related manufacturing (including ships and trains) brought a large number of unskilled workers to Kobe from other parts of Japan and the Korean Peninsula, then a Japanese colony. Today the descendants of Koreans constitute the largest ethnic minority in the city. These factories and the extensive port facilities made the city a target for numerous bombing raids towards the end of the Second World War. By the time it ended in mid-1945, the city was completely razed. It was 'the sea of fire' across the war-time city that older Kobe residents recalled when large parts of the city were again destroyed by fire in the 1995 earthquake. In the post-war years the city's heavy industries and ports prospered again and drove the reconstruction and economic progress. By 1970 Kobe had rebuilt itself as a modern and prosperous city in Japan's second largest urban conurbation and industrial centre.

The city's population was about 1.5 million in 1989 when I first spent a year observing schools there. It dropped by 100,000 after people moved out of the city following the damage brought by the earthquake in 1995, but returned to the pre-quake level by 2004 (Kobe-shi 2004: 2). The population has been aging over recent decades. As in other cities in Japan, the percentage of elderly people over 65 has increased: from 11.5 per cent of the total population in 1990 to 16.9 per cent in 2000 (Kobe-shi 2004: 7). The city has accommodated a relatively large number of foreign residents in the coastal suburbs where manufacturing industry is located. Ethnic Koreans, descendants of colonial subjects who were brought to work in heavy industrial companies during the war, are concentrated in two coastal suburbs. While ethnic Koreans still remain the largest ethnic minority group in the city, their relative size as a percentage of foreign residents has declined in the last decade (65 per cent in 1990, 60 per cent in 2000, and 53 per cent in 2004), partly because more Koreans have taken up Japanese citizenship (which I shall elaborate on in later chapters) and partly because of increased immigration from China, Vietnam and Brazil (Kobe-shi 1997: 43; 2004: 43). In 1990 foreign residents counted for 2.75 per cent of the city population, and 2.85 per cent in 2000.

People in Kobe-city are employed mainly in manufacturing and service sectors. Conforming to national trends, there has been a shift in employment from manufacturing to service industries in the 1990s. In 1990, when the women in this study entered the workforce, workers in primary, secondary and service industries accounted respectively for 1.0 per cent, 27.0 per cent and 69.7 per cent of the workforce. Ten years later, in 2000, the numbers were 0.8, 23.6 and 73.0 per cent respectively (Kobe-shi 2004: 8). Women's employment in manufacturing, construction and the transport and communication industries was limited in comparison with that of men, and this no doubt determined employment opportunities available to the women I studied.

The types of jobs held changed somewhat over the 1990s. In 1988 the three main types of employment in the city were factory jobs (26.2 per cent), clerical jobs (22.2 per cent) and sales jobs (17.8 per cent) (Kobe-shi 1989: 48–49); and in 2002 factory jobs (22.6 per cent), clerical jobs (22.4 per cent), specialist and professional (15 per cent) and sales jobs (14.9 per cent) (Kobe-shi 2004: 69). In both years the largest percentage of women were engaged in clerical work (33.6 per cent and 32.2 per cent respectively). We continue to see that patterns of women's participation in the Kobe-city workforce differed from those of men; and this must be kept in mind when reading the stories of my actors in the following chapters.

The working-class young women: growing up in the *shitamachi*

I originally studied about 100 final-year high school students in my ethnographic fieldwork at two municipal vocational high schools, during the 1989–90 academic year (Okano 1993). In that year all final-year students at these schools made decisions about their post-school destinations; and the vast majority subsequently entered the workforce instead of proceeding to tertiary education. Among them were the 21 young women that I subsequently followed over the period of 1989 to 2001. I have consistently used the same pseudonymous names for my actors in my previous publications and this book, so that readers can follow the life courses of the actors across publications.Place names within Kobe-city are also fictitious.

These girls came from a particular *shitamachi* (literally, downtown) area of the city. Here small old wooden town houses and family-run shops crowd together with small family-run factories, creating a type of community that exhibits a feeling of neighbourhood solidarity.[1] It is in two *shitamachi* wards that the girls in this study were born and brought up, and from which their high schools received the majority of their students. These wards are also home to ethnic and minority groups – Koreans, the *buraku* people and newcomer Asians.[2] The Kobe-city population included 28,000 Koreans in 1988, around the time of the original fieldwork. If Japanese nationals with a Korean ethnic background had been included, the number would have been larger. The two *shitamachi* wards, where most of the girls resided, included a relatively larger percentage of these minority groups than other wards in the city.

The girls in this study came from modestly resourced families that I would call working class. Among their parents, collectively, only one parent had received a tertiary education, and many either ran small businesses or worked in blue-collar jobs in the small factories that are numerous in the area. Three lived in government housing for lower-income families. Two of the girls' fathers were ill and unable to work. Three were third-generation *zainichi* South Koreans. The girls' direct experience of the world centred on the *shitamachi* neighbourhood and its people. They went to local kindergartens, primary schools and middle schools, maintaining childhood friendships throughout schooling.

The girls attended one of two municipal vocationally oriented high schools, Sasaki High and Imai Technical High. Vocational high schools are generally ranked lower than academic high schools in the high school hierarchy that exists in any school zone, and receive students from relatively less well-resourced families than schools of higher ranking (Rohlen 1983; Okano 1993). They also have distinctive school missions, subcultures and post-school destinations. In 1995 almost 60 per cent of vocational high school graduates entered the full-time workforce, while the equivalent figure for academic schools was 13.4 per cent (Japan-Monbu-shô 1995: 602–3, 608–9). The choice of a particular vocational course (e.g. technical, commercial) is highly gendered. Gender-biased enrolment in these vocational courses directs students to post-school employment destinations that are also gendered. Girls' major destinations are clerical, sales and service jobs, whereas boys tend to be employed in factory and manual jobs (see Table 2.1).

The working lives of these young women over the period 1990–2001 were products of their past experiences and decision-making prior to the entry into the workforce. They faced two major decisions – the first, the choice of a high school at 15 years of age, and the other regarding employment prior to leaving high school. The girls' decisions were constrained by their ascribed status, a result of class, gender and ethnic background, as well as institutional constraints. For instance, in deciding on a vocational high school (rather than an academic one) in their final year of middle school, the majority of these students had already decided to obtain employment immediately after high school, rather than pursue further education. This was partly because few had family members, relatives or neighbourhood acquaintances who had received, and built careers on, a university education. Others mentioned their families' financial constraints. The girls chose commerce-oriented subjects, and showed employment 'preferences' that reflected the jobs that they eventually entered and were consistent with nationwide trends (see Table 2.1). To university graduates, the differences between the types of jobs they aspired to (e.g. clerical, sales, key-puncher) may not seem important; but they were to these girls.[3]

The students then searched for what they considered to be a desirable employer from the list of companies that had sent recruitment cards to their schools. Under the school-based job referral system, an individual school received offers of employment from specific companies, with which the school often had a long-term relationship. These positions and information about them were made available to the students. Since the school could send only one student for each vacancy, it conducted an internal selection meeting to determine the most suitable student from among the applicants for each position. In this process individual students' academic marks, school attendance, club activities and 'suitability' for each position were considered. Applicants with a minority background (e.g. Korean, *buraku*, disabled) received affirmative action

Table 2.1 First occupations of 1990 and 2001 high school graduates according to sex

Occupation	Percentage of all high school graduates who entered employment		Percentage of male high school graduates who entered employment		Percentage of female high school graduates who entered employment	
	1990	2001	1990	2001	1990	2001
Professional and technical	4.3	4.4	5.7	4.4	3.0	4.4
Clerical	29.4	13.3	10.5	3.4	47.7	25.8
Sales	16.0	13.3	13.3	9.6	18.6	18.1
Service	11.1	19.9	8.3	12.3	13.9	29.4
Security	2.0	4.2	3.6	6.6	0.5	1.1
Factory and manual jobs in manufacturing and construction	33.6	39.2	53.1	55.9	14.7	18.1
Transport and communication	1.8	2.4	3.0	3.5	0.7	1.1
Agriculture	0.3	0.9	0.6	1.3	0.1	0.3
Fishing industry	0.1	0.2	0.2	0.4	0.0	0.0
Others	1.2	2.2	1.7	2.6	0.8	1.6

Sources: Japan-Monbu-shô (1991: 631); Japan-Monbukagaku-shô (2002: 741).

treatment in this process. The selected student then sat a recruitment examination and interview set by the particular company. A student who passed the interview and examination could have their employment secured up to almost six months prior to graduation from high school. If the student failed, he or she went through the whole process again until successful in obtaining a job. At the two schools that I studied in 1989–90, almost all of the students had a job before graduation (Okano 1993). Among the 21 women that this study focuses on, only two 'chose' further education. All but one of the remaining girls obtained employment through school-based job referral: 14 took up clerical positions (including one as a bank teller), three obtained sales positions, one became a nurse-trainee, and one went to work in a factory.

Six months prior to graduation, when most students' jobs were finalised, they had mixed feelings. There was a sense of relief to know where they were going; but this was accompanied by a feeling of anxiety. Many in fact preferred the life they had as students, which granted them a carefree existence with minimal responsibility, as shown in Shino's excerpt at the beginning of this chapter.

The January 1995 earthquake

The women all experienced what they described as 'a once-in-a lifetime natural disaster' – a large-scale earthquake hit the region at 5.46 a.m. on 17

January 1995. While a natural disaster is just that, 'natural', in the sense that no one has any control over it, its impact on the population was socially diverse, affected by geographical area of residence, the type of dwelling, family relations at the time, and the level of material, social and cultural resources that individuals could draw on in the post-quake recovery.[4]

When I heard the news of the earthquake on television in Melbourne, I immediately thought of my subject students. I had last met the group of 21 girls three years previously. As the days passed, I felt increasingly uneasy about their plight, since I knew that most of them lived in the wards that were reported to have received the most damage. I could not reach them on the phone. The media reported that all neighbourhood schools had became crisis shelters for local residents, and that their teachers took turns managing the schools 24 hours a day. I imagined Sasaki High and Imai Technical High full of local residents, with teachers mobilised and co-ordinating with local government bodies.

Measuring magnitude 7.2, the quake was the most destructive to hit Japan's urban centres since the Second World War. As of January 2000 (five years after the quake), the official figures record 6,432 deaths (half were elderly people), three missing and 43,792 injured, with 181,799 housing units having collapsed and/or burned down, and 276,166 housing units classed as 'half-damaged' (Matsumoto 2000). Gas, power and water supply were cut across the region. Public transportation stopped completely. Two western long-established inner-city *shitamachi* wards suffered most in terms of damage to housing units and death toll. This was because these wards had a significantly higher percentage of housing units built prior to 1960 (often small wooden structures), the housing lots were small (40 per cent of the single-family houses and terraced houses had a site area of less than 50 square metres) and a substantial number of these old terraced houses were not adjacent to roads of over 4 metres in width (which made it difficult for rescue vehicles to gain access). It was also because these two wards were home to low-income households, the aged and minority groups, who liked inexpensive old-style multi-family rental housing (Hirayama 2000).

Residents initially evacuated themselves from collapsing/burning houses to crisis shelters (*hinansho*) often set up in neighbourhood schools and community centres. At the peak time almost 600 such shelter camps accommodated almost 220,000 displaced evacuees (Hirayama 2000). Since primary schools had large gyms, they became the main shelter providers. Among schools that became shelters, over 60 per cent soon organised self-governing bodies. Most of them were created by the teachers at the school in collaboration with the refugees (Tanayama 1999: 55). A teacher at Sakaki High, Mr Nakane, provides an insight into that time. He was asked by the headmaster to be the co-ordinator of the self-governing body at Sasaki High. When I met him in late 1997 (almost three years after the quake), he vividly recollected his experience.

MR NAKANE: Our school stood unburnt when all surrounding houses were on fire. All the houses around here were old wooden terraces, and the school is concrete. Many residents walked here. By the time I got here there was total chaos – no water, flooded toilets, no food, crying people, the injured, etc. People were distressed, you know, some had just seen neighbours injured or killed ... In a few days, I drew up a roster list for the teachers so that the school was managed by teachers and community representatives around the clock – you know we had hundreds of people sleeping here. We teachers on the roster stayed overnight here. Our home economics room and school canteen were used as a large kitchen. I got community reps to get me young men to carry buckets of water.

(5 November 1997)

Mr Nakane's description resembles what is reported in a case study on an inner-city primary school (Shibata 1999). With a pre-earthquake student population of 270, the school initially accommodated 2,300 refugees. After several days, the deputy-principal took a leadership role and created many *han* (groups) headed by a leader, who communicated with a newly created camp management group. The number of refugees decreased to 1,000 after two weeks when the water system became available, to 700 after five weeks, and 560 after nine weeks, when city gas came back on line. The school started teaching students again one month after the earthquake (Shibata 1999). The teachers' efforts and their commitment to the management of the refugees were widely noted in the media (e.g. staying many nights at school, managing daily routines of food and water distribution, intervening in conflicts and managing sanitation) (Nishida 1999: 79–92).

Some were able to stay with relatives (either locally or in other parts of Japan) while others could afford to rent accommodation outside the affected area. Employees of large companies often moved to accommodation provided by their employers, also located outside the affected area. Those who could not resort to such options remained at shelters and eventually moved to rent-free public temporary housing units (*kasetsu*) that were built by the Ministry of Health and Welfare. Starting in mid-February (one month after the quake), approximately 47,000 temporary units were made available (Ioka 2000). Those still living in crisis shelters, in particular, those considered 'economically weak' (*keizaiteki jakusha*) (e.g. low-income, elderly, lone-household and single-parent families) received priority in moving into these units. These *kasetsu* (where some of my actors stayed, as explained later) were constructed in several locations on the outskirts of the city, and their conditions were far from satisfactory. For example, each unit had only 20–26 square metres of living space and poor insulation. In April 1998 (three years after the quake), the occupation rate was 45 per cent, with almost 14,000 households still living in temporary housing (Hirayama 2000). By March 2000, no one remained in the units, which were later demolished (Ioka 2000).

It is important to note that the earthquake brought the most damaging impact to the least resourced of the city's residents. This occurred in two ways. First, since the inexpensive old wooden houses in the *shitamachi* area were most vulnerable to collapse and destruction by fire, the *shitamachi* residents suffered relatively more deaths and injuries, as well as loss of property. Second, the least-resourced people experienced the most difficulties in rebuilding their lives. As we saw above, the characteristics of the temporary housing unit residents were: elderly, lone-household and low, or no, income (Naitô 1999: 275).

Reconstruction of permanent housing had already started when, several months after the quake, the local government launched a three-year emergency plan for housing reconstruction. A large number of permanent public housing units were built in order to accommodate those still in temporary housing. The central government also agreed to offer subsidies to reduce public housing rents. In the reconstruction 41,000 permanent public housing units were built (Ioka 2000).

Many victims wanted to rebuild their houses on their original plots. Some of them benefited from the city's recovery plans, and were able to access low-interest loans provided by the Housing Loan Corporation, the prefectural and municipal governments, and a system of interest subsidies offered by the Earthquake Restoration Fund. Indeed, families of two of the actors, Sekie and Yayoi, rebuilt houses relying on these benefits. The family of another actor, Yoshie, sold their land to the city, which wanted to purchase many small lots in their neighbourhood to redevelop the inner-city suburb, and bought a newly built larger detached house in an outer suburb, assisted by a special loan and funding. Those who wanted to purchase units also benefited from extremely low interest rates available to the quake victims. Two further individuals, Fumiko and Yayoi, recently divorced and employed full-time, bought units using this system at the age of 26, thinking that the arrangement presented a rare opportunity to own a residence instead of living with their parents.

But there were others who could not rebuild on their land for various reasons (Hirayama 2000). First, those with a precarious financial base (e.g. the unemployed, those in insecure employment, the elderly) did not meet the financial conditions to obtain loans. Second, many housing lots of old wooden terraced housing were extremely small and not adjacent to a road of 4 metres or more in width, and the house occupied over 60 per cent of the land. Although not satisfying the requirements in the Building Standards Act (1960), they had been permitted to remain since they were built prior to the Act. New houses, however, needed to conform to the Act, which made it difficult to build a new house on the existing lot. There were also complexities involved in land ownership, leaseholds and tenants' rights, as shown by the case of another actor, Tomoe, where family members urged her mother to build a house on the existing lot in the belief that she would otherwise lose the leasehold to it. For these reasons many land lots remained vacant after the debris had been cleared away. Another informant, Sekie, claimed that the extent of vacant land near her parents' house made her scared of walking in the neighbourhood at night.

The collective impact of the quake on the economy and industry was significant (Ozawa 2000).[5] Ports were destroyed. The region's manufacturing sector suffered because production stopped because of damage to factories and commercial buildings. In early 2000 the production levels of two major local industries were still at 80 per cent of the pre-quake years; and transactions at Kobe-port remained at around the 80 per cent level (Matsumoto 2000). The service sector also suffered from damage to commercial buildings, consumers' loss of purchasing power, and a decrease of visitors to the city. The vacancy rate of city offices remained at 17 per cent in late 1999, doubling that of the pre-quake period (Ioka 2000).

On the other hand, positive impacts were also noted. Critical evaluation of crisis management at the time led to government and community efforts to devise strategies of crisis management (Sakamoto 2001; Iwasaki 2000). The public and policy makers re-acknowledged the valuable contribution of an unprecedented number of volunteers; and volunteer-based non-profit organisations (NPOs) and non-governmental organisations (NGOs) were established to assist in the long-term recovery of the city (Nishiyama 2005). The quake was also a reminder that the city also comprised groups of people who are particularly vulnerable during natural disasters (e.g. the elderly, the disabled, mothers with infants). A new category to refer to this group of people was coined, *saigai jakusha* (the vulnerable at the time of natural disaster) (Tamaki 2002). Rescue activities by ethnic minority communities (Koreans, Chinese and Vietnamese) revealed how respective ethnic communities and individuals regarded themselves, and were regarded by their Japanese neighbours. It was noted that Japanese rescue efforts extended to ethnic minorities as local citizens, and that the efforts of long-existing Koreans and Chinese communities were inclusive of all local residents, regardless of their ethnic background (Mugikura et al. 1999: 224–47; Asano and Ka 1999).

The quake disrupted individual lives in many significant ways. For the women in this study, such an event is unlikely to recur in their lifetime. They recognised the enormity of the disaster, but quickly got on with their lives. Some were back at work a few days later, walking or cycling for long distances in the absence of public transport. Some carried buckets of water to their flat on the fifteenth floor every day for several months. The quake and its aftermath was thus only one (albeit a major one) of the many events that they experienced in the transition to adulthood.

My 12-year relationship with the young women

Longitudinal studies often focus on changes over a period of considerable length, to effectively illuminate diachronic changes. I follow the lives of a group of young women as they matured from the age of 18 to almost 30 years old, starting from a one-year ethnographic study at their high schools that developed into a 12-year biographical study. A similar approach can be seen in a Finnish study in progress that traced how 13-year-old school students make transitions as they reach the age of 20 (Gordon and Lahelma 2003). Specific methodological issues generated in studies such as this and mine will be discussed through the book and reviewed in the concluding chapter. In this chapter I shall briefly focus on my relationship with the women themselves.

Qualitative data that any researcher collects, and his or her interpretation of it, cannot avoid being influenced by the researcher him or herself. When a longitudinal study draws on qualitative data collected by the same researcher over an extended period of time, we need to keep it in mind that the researcher as an individual is also subject to change over time and that such changes influence the nature of data gained from the subjects and his/her interpretation of it (Saldana 2003). I have known these women since 1989 when they were 17-year-old high school students. My focus in this book is the changes they underwent in their transitions to adulthood; but readers need to know that I myself was impacted by changes over the same period.

Throughout this book, readers will see me and hear my voice, sometimes as a researcher with knowledge of academic literature and at other times as a person who carries particular baggage of the personal past and present. The researcher and the private citizen are not often separable. I do not think that these women saw clear distinctions in me either. The women were likely to have talked selectively to me, as much as they individually felt comfortable doing so and based on their perception of me. I also suspect that their perception of me, and our relationship, changed over the period of the study. I often wondered why these women were so willing to talk to me about their personal and emotional experiences. I did not think they could see any immediate or tangible benefit in this exercise.

When they shared their school routine with me over the 1989–90 school year, I was a novice PhD student and they were high school students. I was introduced to the students as 'a postgraduate student from New Zealand who wants to study how students decide on their post-school destinations'; and that students were welcome to seek assistance from me regarding their study or other matters. While the students were unsure of this vague role description in the sense that I was neither a teacher nor a student, it seemed that they came to know me as 'someone who hangs around at school and watches us in classes, but who is not a teacher'. Over the year, in particular, from six months into the fieldwork, students shared their thoughts about themselves, their personal problems and their future with me. They knew that I had been born and educated in Japan (but not in Kansai region), and that I had been in Australasia for almost seven years, as a student and a high school teacher.

During the year, I collected a large amount of data, which can be categorised in one of three ways. The first is documents prepared by schools, local education boards and professional societies (which often act as major venues for teachers' professional development). The second is observational fieldnotes. I observed the school routine every day, was assigned to a homeroom class (in the data-processing course) at Sasaki High and to two homeroom classes at Imai Technical High (in interior furnishing and machinery courses), and participated in school events and trips at both schools. I also observed the departments of guidance for life after school at each school. The third is interviews with teachers and about 100 students that I conducted in the second half of the fieldwork term. My fieldwork ended when the students graduated from high school and entered the workforce. By then I felt comfortable being at these schools: I had had lunch with students almost every day, had students explain specific regional and social dialects that were unfamiliar to me, had seen them embarrassed in classrooms, had cheered their teams at sport events, had shared their joy when they obtained jobs, and had learned about what students thought about school and how they envisaged their post-school lives. At the graduation day in March 1990, I felt that I knew the students well, and wished them the best for the new adventures that awaited them.

After that we took separate paths. I returned to complete my PhD and then take up a new job in Australia. The above study was published as a monograph entitled *School to Work Transition in Japan: An ethnographic study* (Okano 1993). Some of the students wrote letters to me, reporting on new experiences. Some even asked me to contact them when I next visited Kobe-city. When I caught up with them, I was fascinated by how the experiences of their public and private lives intertwined to affect their decisions and actions, some of which I suspected would have significant impact on their later lives. I was intrigued to learn how they subjectively understood the notion of adulthood, and located themselves in the wider social relations that they discovered. At that time I recall I had a distinct feeling that there was something new in our relationship. I could not initially pinpoint what that was; but later realised that our conversations (or interviews) assumed the 12 months that we shared at schools two years earlier. While we had moved on in our own ways and had not seen one another over the intervening two years, the fact that we were together again after that period brought something different to our relationships.

In the following years (1996, 1997, 1999, 2000, 2001) I returned to Kobe-city again. Some trips to Japan were for other projects in different parts of Japan, but on each occasion I met with at least some of the same 21 women. Other trips were made specifically for these interviews. I interviewed the same women about their recent experiences (e.g. work, relationships, families, recreation) and their views about the future. I studied personal files that I had created from previous interviews, and familiarised myself afresh before meeting each of them. Unless I was on sabbatical, these visits took place over the Australian summer, so the women came to anticipate meeting me in December–January every two years. I have enjoyed these relationships. After I started my own family, around the same time that many of these women did, we began to have something more to share with one another. Our relationship thus grew gradually into something very different from where we started at their high schools 12 years earlier. It also led me to examine their experiences in the light of on-going discussions in the West on changing patterns and notions of adulthood. I thought that the young women's stories about early adulthood would illuminate changes in contemporary Japanese society, that were seemingly driven by ordinary people getting on with their daily lives.

It is through this kind of relationship that the women talked to me for this study. I can only speculate on the motivation behind their willingness to talk to me. Initially the women might have found it an opportunity to relive, and feel nostalgic about, their carefree high school days. Some of them probably just liked talking about their recent experiences with someone who had known them for a long time, without having to hear judgemental comments. Others might have wanted to share their experiences, both happy and unhappy, with someone who was also an employee, a mother and a wife. The fact that I was not a part of their routine human relations (in the sense that I was not a co-worker, relative, in-law) might have enabled the women to talk more freely without consideration of repercussions that indiscreet utterances might have caused. They might simply have been pleased that I was interested in their daily lives, or curious about the lives of their counterparts in Australia. A few commented that my regular visits gave them a chance to reflect on their lives, in that our conversations caused them to distance themselves from uneventful yet busy daily routines.

During these subsequent visits, I collected data in three forms: interviews, observational fieldnotes, and documents. Interviews were tape-recorded with each participant's permission. I had a set of questions to ask each of them, as well as specific questions about issues raised in the previous interviews that I wanted to pursue. I interviewed most of the women individually; but some interviews were conducted as a group of close friends – some of the direct quotations of interviews in the following chapters reflect this. Group interviews have both advantages and disadvantages. All the group interviews arose from suggestions by the women who formed close friendship groups. In some cases, both group meetings and lone interviews were conducted at their suggestion. Group interviews of close friends offered me an insight into the nature of the intimate relationships that some of the women had maintained over the 12 years since they first met in the initial year of high school. Their conversation assumed a vast amount of shared experience, referring to many particular events, and of knowledge about each other (including details of family members) and their views (both shared and different). Group interviews also often led to discussion, which revealed participants' varying interpretations of an event or opposing opinions on particular issues.

Interviews were conducted in cafés, restaurants, parks and participants' homes. Some of the women proposed particular places that they liked and thought suitable for private conversations. Women with small children preferred having me visit their homes. I would show them photos of my then pre-school children, and we would share a meal. Some of the women with children wanted to meet my children, and when asked I took them with me. Our children played together during the interviews. I kept fieldnotes of our telephone conversations and interviews, recording what I observed and the major points of each interview, as well as my interpretations and issues to follow up later. Some women provided me with materials that aided their explanations, such as photos, workplace documents that they had received and created, or books that they had recently read. The majority of them sent me New Year cards, while some sent me letters and emails, reporting recent events in their lives as well as news of their friends.

After each fieldtrip in Kobe-city, which normally lasted two months, I returned with a large amount of data – many hours of taped interviews, two or three fieldnote books, photos and various documents. After each trip, I updated the profile of each woman, building on the initial 1989–90 data. Drawing on these data, and based on profiles that I had created in my initial study while they were still at high school, I developed updated profiles of each woman. I also created theme-based tables.

It was after my 1997 trip that I started thinking of how best I could present their stories and my interpretations of them. Initially I thought of presenting the stories in three chronologically ordered parts, like the British Broadcasting Corporation's '21 Up' series, which followed a group of children into adulthood as they grew up, reporting on their progress every seven years. However, while writing with this structure, I gradually began to doubt if the readers could recall my actors' trajectories of the previous periods effectively, and decided to take a somewhat compromise position. In Part I, I present the personal trajectories of eight selected women as they developed over the 12 years. In Part II, I then discuss specific themes that emerged in relation to transitions to adulthood, while drawing on these portraits and also integrating the remaining women's stories.

While striving to do justice to the stories and experiences that the women so willingly shared with me, I remain responsible for what is presented here. Their stories guide us to further understand how young adulthood is experienced and negotiated in contemporary Japan. In the next chapter we begin with the 12-year-long stories of eight of the women.

3 Portraits of selected women

This chapter presents chronological portraits of eight of the women that I have followed over the period 1989–2001. It has been a difficult task to decide which of the 21 women to include, since each of them charted trajectories to adulthood that were unique and intriguing. The selection reflects my intention to show the diversity of the women's experiences and their interpretations of them, and in so doing begins to explore the research questions of this book. The first four women, Miyuki, Kanako, Yayoi and Satoko, attended Imai Technical High school in the 1989–90 academic year and were known to one another. The remaining four women, Noshie, Sekie, Tomoe and Hatsumi, were final-year students at Sasaki High School during the same period. Some of their friends also appear and are referred to in the following portraits.

Miyuki: From cashier to display specialist

Miyuki was the youngest of a family of three girls. They lived in the suburb where her high school, Imai Tech High, was located. The family moved to the flat when Miyuki was a primary school pupil, and in 2000 she was still living there with her parents. In 1989, when I first met Miyuki, her father was driving a taxi. Her mother worked as a cleaner in a nearby shopping centre. They had been in the same jobs for many years. Her mother was poorly paid, but she enjoyed the interaction with her colleagues. I met her a few times and found her to be a polite and softly spoken, motherly woman. Miyuki's elder sister, six years her senior, married young, against her parents' advice, to a man she had met at work. Relations with her parents remained cool until after her baby was born. Miyuki's other sister, four years her senior, worked at a men's fashion store. Both sisters went to work after finishing high school.

From primary school age Miyuki wanted to become an artist or painter, since she loved drawing and excelled at it. In order to continue drawing at high school she chose the interior furnishing course at Imai Tech High. It was a pragmatic decision. Her family wanted her to find employment after high school because of the family's financial situation and her middle school teachers advised that vocational high schools offered a better job referral service for their graduates than did academic high schools. Miyuki's sister had also attended the school, and recommended it, saying that students were not required to study very hard. Miyuki liked what everyone said about the school.

At high school, where I first met her in 1989, Miyuki was talkative and friendly and mixed with a wide range of students. We caught the same suburban train, and she would chat about the latest women's magazines. Miyuki's best friend was her classmate, Natsumi, whom I also studied and who appears in later chapters. In the final year of high school Miyuki decided to apply for a cashier's position at Kobe Co-op supermarket chain. (Kobe Co-operative is a large-scale community-based supermarket chain with an extensive network of branches throughout the Kansai region. Established in 1920 by a community activist to promote the welfare of consumers, it now has 1.4 million members and employs 12,000 permanent staff members. It offers a wide range of products and services including groceries, clothing, furniture, classes for sports and cultural activities, and insurance). Her elder sister, who had previously worked there for several years, told her that the company paid well. It was also known for the high standards expected of its workers, which enabled ex-workers to easily obtain employment elsewhere. Miyuki did not intend to work there long anyway – she wanted to save up and travel overseas. Her plans after that were vague.

Shortly before Miyuki officially started her job she was required to attend a five-day training camp on an island off Kobe-city. The training for high school graduates included company philosophy, generic skills, followed by cashier's skills. She enjoyed meeting many new people there. University graduates received their initial training elsewhere. Miyuki was then assigned to a large suburban branch, where she worked as a cashier. She was cheerful and busy with learning new skills when I visited her at work one month into the job. After the novelty wore off, however, she found the job physically draining and repetitive. Within three months, one of the five new recruits at the branch had left. She became so desperate that she finally approached her immediate supervisor and advised him that she wanted to quit at the start of her second year at work. He then arranged a transfer to another branch as an 'artist' (*âtisuto*) which involved designing window displays and using lettering skills to design posters and price tags. It seemed that the supervisor was aware that Miyuki was interested in an artist position. Miyuki also suspected that he wanted to ensure that she did not leave since her early departure would have impacted on his performance evaluation.

Miyuki was happy to have work as an artist, although she soon faced a steep learning curve. As she had obtained the position without taking an examination (her supervisor had acknowledged her lettering and display skills), she felt she had to work hard to demonstrate those skills to others.

MIYUKI: When I met you in 1992, the work was really tough. One of the artists had just left. She was wonderful – very good at her work and fast – and I felt I was being compared to her. I was just a beginner artist, promoted from being a cashier. I was desperate. As the only artist I had an awful lot of work to do. I just had to keep up. So my work got a bit rough. All I was doing was managing the workload without thinking about the quality of my work – just drawing advertisements and price tags. I wanted to do my own product display, but just didn't have the time or energy. I hated the job and I hated myself for not doing a proper job.

(23 October 1997)

Although she had secured the job that she wanted, Miyuki was unhappy having to make compromises with the display tasks that she loved.

Miyuki's unhappiness at work was exacerbated by what she saw as unfair working conditions. She was disappointed when her request to take a day off to attend a pop concert was rejected on the grounds that she had already taken leave for a holiday to the USA several months before. This was particularly annoying since she had been careful not to inconvenience others by giving one month's notice so that her boss had plenty of time to arrange a casual staff member for a half day. This led her to question why workers had leave entitlements.

MIYUKI: Leave is meaningless if I can't take it when I wanted. I work to live, not vice versa … you know. Then they told me I lacked common sense! What sort of common sense is that? I don't follow his logic.

(6 February 1992)

Miyuki worked almost two hours' overtime every day but did not receive overtime pay to cover all the hours. She was frustrated with the situation but regarded it as beyond her control, as we shall see in the following chapter. She wondered why the company made employees work overtime when they could not pay them.

MIYUKI: The company wants to raise efficiency. It's all very well to be diligent, but … it's so strange. It seems to me that companies try to produce 'better' products on the backs of the workers. Who are these 'better' products for?

(6 February 1992)

Despite her complaints about working conditions, she continued working at the branch. A consolation was the people she worked with – she really liked them.

During those first years Miyuki met many people through various events organised through the workplace. It was a time of trying out new experiences. Miyuki started going out with a steady boyfriend.

MIYUKI: I met him at a *gôkon* [a party which involves two companies and both sexes]. I was the party organiser for our branch. I said to someone,

'He looks smart (*kakkoii*). What's his name?' And somebody in the other group said, 'Leave it to me. I'll tell him.' That's how it all started. Some people even found marriage partners at some of those *gôkon*. I used to talk to him on the phone everyday, and met him every weekend, so I got to know him pretty well. After that, I went out with another guy for a few months. He was tough and unique (*gottssui*) and I felt as if he lived in another world.

KO: Why did you split up?

MIYUKI: Well, he just got boring to talk to. You know, I couldn't talk about serious things. His jokes weren't funny. I couldn't talk to him like I do to Natsumi [a close girlfriend]. I now think that I went out with these guys because I felt that I had to have a boyfriend at the time. In the end I rang him and said, 'Please don't ring me any more.' That was it.

(20 November 1997)

After two years at the second branch, Miyuki was transferred again, this time to a very small branch located in a quiet middle-class residential suburb where she was required to do many administrative tasks in addition to being an 'artist'. She was assigned a part-time worker as her assistant. It was at this small branch that Miyuki learned a wide range of tasks out of necessity, and also how to work effectively with her assistant. Just as she was seeing herself managing her new position reasonably well after two years, the 1995 earthquake demolished the shop completely. Her parents' house survived. Having nowhere to work, Miyuki was asked by the company to work as a computer operator at head office. She found this job extremely boring. One of her bosses felt so sympathetic towards her that he managed to get her a transfer as an artist to another branch several months later. This was her fourth move.

Miyuki liked the new workplace, which was a large branch more like a department store than a co-op, about 20 minutes by bus from the city centre. She made display boards and signs (hand-illustrated and machine-drawn), price tags and displays. Two permanent staff and four *meito-san* (part-timers or casuals) worked as 'artists' in the supply and planning unit. Miyuki filled in as a cashier only when the place was busy.

MIYUKI: I'm lucky with this workplace. Everyone, permanents and *meito-san*, gets on excellently, like doing shopping for each other during tea break. We have a kind of *nori* [intimacy], similar to what high-school girls enjoy. Someone will say, 'Let's have a cup of tea with the cakes that I bought for us!' We do have a male manager, but he's not much use. So when he's around, we say, 'Ah, you are here today?' It's fun place to be. I want to make sure that we keep that good atmosphere.

(23 October 1997)

She was grateful for this fourth workplace since she recalled vividly the previous years when she had struggled.

Miyuki worked five days a week and normally finished at the regular time. Even when she worked overtime, she did not ask to be paid extra. Her reasons for this were different from those that she cited five years previously. She explained that it was partly because she did not want to burden the company, and partly because she feared it might negatively affect her performance assessment.

MIYUKI: If you ask for overtime pay every time, your performance assessment will go down, I think. They might think that you had to work overtime because it took too long for you to complete your tasks.

(23 October 1997)

Her comment reflects the atmosphere in the 1990s, when individual performance assessments began to be included in determining pay rises and promotions in companies.

Miyuki was perhaps happiest in her work when I saw her that year (1997). She had the kind of job that she wanted and pleasant working relationships with colleagues. In contrast to five years previously, Miyuki now considered her working conditions as extremely good. Leave was generous and the pay was good, in comparison to comparable jobs elsewhere. When a woman returned to work after a break for family responsibilities, the company acknowledged her previous work experience when determining her salary. She explained that the fact that the Co-op chain was run by a union made a difference. Although she attributed her situation to luck, Miyuki's own initiative and action deserved credit. She had maintained realistic expectations of both work and workplace. Unlike Hatsumi, whom we will meet later, she had no inferiority complex and maintained a 'going my own way' (*wagamichi o iku*) attitude. She perceived that her colleagues appreciated the skills in lettering and display that she had learned at high school. She made an effort to maintain pleasant and fun human relationships in the female-dominated workplace.

In 1997 Miyuki had no ambition to obtain a next-step promotion to 'chief', a middle-management position. Bosses would advise their subordinates to attempt the qualifying test for a group head (*shunin*), taking into account their age and performance. Having obtained a group head qualification, one could apply for the position of 'chief'.

KO: Why aren't you interested in it?
MIYUKI: It doesn't mean much in our section. In other sections it is important, especially for men, since it's one step from chief. Men usually want to climb up the ladder, don't they? But some women, say those who devote themselves to work, will say, 'We'll get that anyway when we reach 30.' Others say, 'Oh, that time again. What a nuisance! I'll study just to save face'.

(23 October 1997)

She did see ambitious women, but noted that they were often four-year university graduates who held what she considered to be more responsible positions. Most high school graduate women were cashiers, and could only aim for chief cashier. Even more ambitious, according to her observation, were her male counterparts.

MIYUKI: Well, perhaps they have the idea that their work is life-long, and that they have to support their wife and children. But there're men who don't care [laughs]. Come to think of it, a female high school graduate became a vice-manager of a branch. There are large individual differences, too.

KO: Don't you want to be like her?

MIYUKI: I do think that she is superb [*sugoi*] [laughs], but I'm looking for something else.

KO: What is it, then, that you are aiming for?

MIYUKI: When you put it like that, I feel embarrassed [laughs].

KO: You mean, you are exploring?

MIYUKI: But, you know, everyone says that … like 'I have something else to pursue' [laughs].

(23 October 1997)

I wondered what that might be.

In late 1997, seven years after leaving school, Miyuki began studying design via a junior college correspondence course. She considered this to be the most significant event in the ten years since she had left school. I recall that I was somewhat taken aback when she excitedly revealed this to me, as I had not expected it. At first, her explanation was pragmatic.

KO: You've never told me that you wanted to study at university! Why did you so suddenly start wanting to study at university?

MIYUKI: Oh well, I just wanted to see what university was like.

KO: Hm … How did you find out about this course?

MIYUKI: Natsumi first told me that there were correspondence universities. She said that she wanted to go. Then I went to a bookshop and skimmed through books on junior colleges and universities. I found a few universities that offered correspondence courses in Arts. I checked the eligibility requirements, and was surprised that I could meet them! No entrance exams, no essays and no interviews. Only mature-age students can get into these correspondence courses – as long as you're a graduate of high school and not currently attending another school, you're in!

(23 October 1997)

Miyuki thought that with her favourable working conditions (e.g. better than usual annual leave entitlements and generous pay), she could contemplate taking on a junior college distance education course. She had saved up the tuition fee. The company's generous arrangements allowed her to juggle various leave entitlements to attend the on-campus teaching in Tokyo that is a compulsory component of the course. For instance, in addition to annual leave, the company offered four six-day periods of leave per year, which she had not used extensively before. She was particularly grateful that her close colleagues were supportive of her decision to study.

After talking about her study for a while, Miyuki started reflecting her past years and readily confessed that she had changed greatly, from somebody who did not want to study to somebody who did, and that the years that had changed her were precious.

KO: So it took eight years for this change?

MIYUKI: Yes, eight years. That's a long time, isn't it? I think I'm a slow learner! [Laughs] You know what I was like at high school [laughs]. I hated studying and always tried to get out of it. I think 'normal people' encourage their children to study hard, like for entrance examinations. Not my family. They told me to graduate from high school with respectable [*hazukashikunai*] marks, and to get a job with good conditions. They told me that they had no money to let me to go to university. So if I wanted to go, I had no choice but to earn my own money.

KO: Why have you come around to wanting to go to uni?

MIYUKI: I'd wanted to for a long time – like a kind of yearning [*akogare*]. But I wasn't smart, and was told by my parents that they couldn't afford it.

KO: There're scholarships, you know.

MIYUKI: Yes ... I thought you might say that. If I had been smart, I might have thought about scholarships, but since I wasn't, it never occurred to me. Okano-san, you need steps to think about your options, right? Since I wasn't brainy, I didn't get to that step [of thinking about a scholarship]. Eight years is a long time, but I have changed my thinking gradually, and I'd like to think I hadn't wasted those years. Without them, there wouldn't be this 'me' who wants to study. So even if this challenge doesn't work out, I will feel satisfied – I did something that I had come to want over the last eight years. You know I've learned a lot over these years. My attitudes to people have changed. Of course they're not perfect, but I've come to understand more about myself. I'm a slow learner who needed these eight years, and I'm still learning!

(23 October 1997)

Those important experiences included work and personal life. Miyuki considered reading, which she had seldom done at high school, to be significant in changing her as well. Her interest in reading started when she noticed her friend, Natsumi, often reading, and borrowed some of her books – fantasy novels for young women. Later she became interested in a wider range of novels, and then in non-fiction. She started enjoying reading more when she could make sense of what she read in the light of her experience of the 'real world', which included job transfers, the earthquake, her sisters' marriages and a subsequent divorce. Miyuki said, 'I think my thinking has widened at least 20 to 30 degrees!'

Once she had enrolled at university, Miyuki told her parents the news. She and her sisters often adopted this tactic of revealing a *fait accompli* when they wanted to do something they knew their parents would oppose, such as finding a casual job and obtaining a driving licence while at high school. Her parents did not understand why Miyuki was so enthusiastic, and were concerned that her work at the Co-op might suffer from her study commitments. However, as Miyuki had paid for the course and already started it, they could not stop her.

Her elder sisters were supportive of her decision. Her second sister, four years her senior, had married and left home a few years previously, leaving only Miyuki living with the parents. Then her first sister, who had married young and left home when Miyuki was 16, got divorced and returned home for a while. It was traumatic for the family, since her husband had left her after he had an affair with a younger woman, who fell pregnant. She now supported herself and her young son by working as an insurance salesperson (a job frequently chosen by single mothers). She rented a flat near her parents' place and often visited them. Miyuki became close to her young nephew and spent a considerable time playing with him.

Miyuki planned to continue working at her present place while studying design via a junior college distance education program. She did not think that the tertiary qualification would bring a concrete benefit to her work in terms of promotion, but that did not matter to her. She planned to explore how to make use of the qualification once she had completed it. She had vague ideas of working in design.

KO: But you already work in design, don't you?
MIYUKI: Yes to a certain extent. But not everything that I do at work now is what I want. Of course, wherever you go, it will be impossible to have that.

                                                                    (23 October 1997)

Miyuki had the realistic expectation that she could not have everything that she wanted in a job, that a job came as a package containing good and bad points.

When I met her in 2000, Miyuki had been studying for two years. Besides the usual forms of correspondence study, the course required one week's on-campus study in Tokyo every year. Miyuki used her savings for her course, which she estimated cost approximately 400,000 yen per year (200,000 yen for tuition fees and the rest for materials, on-campus schooling and transport in Tokyo). She was extremely busy completing assignments. Before deadlines she would have a few sleepless nights working on her projects. She found her study to be stimulating and fulfilling, and proudly showed me many photographs of her projects. She met new people when she attended the summer on-campus sessions, including a particular mature-age student she admired. Other students and some of the lecturers seemed to inspire her. She wished to complete the course in two years, but now feared that her plan might not succeed because of her increased load at work, a point I shall turn to later.

In 2000, Miyuki had not had a steady boyfriend for several years. After ending a few relationships in her first year out at work, she preferred being with her close girlfriends, with whom she could discuss things with a freedom that had not been possible with her boyfriends. In the last two years she had been preoccupied with preparation for her university study.

MIYUKI: I don't have a boyfriend now. I tend to get passionate once I get involved in something or somebody. It is uni study that I am passionate about.

(20 November 1997)

Her full-time work and part-time university study did not seem to leave time or energy (*kokoro no yoyū*) for finding a boyfriend or for any other pursuits. Nor were her parents putting pressure on her to find a partner. In addition, as she said, her age (now 29) contributed to the difficulty in finding a boyfriend, since men tended to be looking for marriage when forming a relationship with women of her age. She thought it possible that she would not marry if her life continued as it was. She had seen her eldest sister marrying very young only to end up divorced with a small son, who was now in grade five. Her other sister had been married for five years and often complained about her marriage. These experiences made her expectations of marriage somewhat more realistic. She jokingly referred to herself as a 'parasite single' (Yamada 1999). The term, which gained media currency in the late 1990s, describes unmarried adults who live with their parents and are supported by them (e.g. in the form of meals and laundry) (Yamada 1999). Without contributing financially, 'parasite singles' can use their disposable incomes to enjoy comfortable lifestyles based on consumption. Perhaps Miyuki did not fit into this description since she regularly cooked when she returned home from work before her parents. Miyuki liked children and wanted to have them, but could not imagine raising children on her own.

MIYUKI: It's impossible to do that in Japan. It would be nice to marry, but you can't get married simply because you love someone. When I think like this I really feel like I am 30! [Laughs]

(20 December 2000)

Meanwhile, Miyuki was content with enjoying children by caring for her nephew and nieces.

In mid-2000, her tenth year at the Co-op, Miyuki was promoted to 'chief', a middle-management position, since her senior colleague was about to leave. She felt a sense of responsibility that she had not experienced before, and no longer saw herself as at the bottom of the company hierarchy (*shitappa*). Working with two permanent staff and two *meito-san* in the supply and planning unit of a large branch, Miyuki took extra care developing pleasant relationships with her colleagues, in particular the *meito-san* who were much older than she and had more extensive experience of product display. Miyuki showed me the photos of product displays that her team created for Christmas, commenting professionally on limitations and strategies. In so doing, Miyuki showed genuine respect for her colleagues' experience, their comments on her work and their contributions. While she liked the task of artist, she sometimes reflected on the earlier days when she was a cashier, and felt that it was much easier, with less responsibility.

MIYUKI: I've come a long way so I don't easily get intimidated now.
KO: Are you one of those more experienced workers?
MIYUKI: Well, one of more experienced now. But of course there are those who are more experienced than me, since some women don't leave after marriage. There are also women who have never married. Maybe I'm sort of middle rank. Maybe a bit less than middle rank. There are 18-year-old cashiers, as well as 24-year-old university graduates.
NATSUMI (MIYUKI'S CLOSE GIRLFRIEND):   But in your case, you worked your way up from cashier, so ...
MIYUKI: Well, after a lot of other things happened [laughs].
KO: Do you think you've been lucky?
MIYUKI: In a way I've been lucky. But as you remember, it was hell in the first year. I was lucky that I was kicked out from cashier's work since they thought I wasn't suited to that job. I think bad luck turned into good luck for me [laughs].

(20 December 2000)

Miyuki's main concern was that a senior permanent staff member from the section was to leave the following month. Since the company did not intend to replace her, Miyuki feared that the remaining staff would have an increased workload; that she, now the 'chief', would have to manage this; and that she would have to discharge management responsibilities such as attending meetings and negotiating with other departments. Not only did she dislike the prospect, but also she was concerned that her study might suffer as a result. She considered resigning as an option, but she was not confident of winning what she considered to be a better job. She wanted to be a display specialist. Miyuki had worked with such specialists when her company outsourced the work to an agency. Most specialists worked for an agency, and both Miyuki and her friend Natsumi believed that in such an arrangement they would not earn enough to live on.

Miyuki's priority was to complete the degree that she had started. She was prepared to give up work, should her job prevent her from achieving her goal. But she was aware that resignation was not easy; it took the senior permanent staff member six months to resign (and Miyuki was annoyed that the person had not informed her of her decision earlier). Given that she had been inconvenienced by the senior member's departure, she felt a responsibility not to do the same to her colleagues. Becoming a middle-rank manager had made her decisions more complicated, which she did not welcome. When I said farewell to her in late 2000, I wondered how Miyuki would reconcile her work demands and responsibilities with her personal goals in the coming years.

Kanako: A fisherman's wife

Kanako was the eldest of a family of six girls. In 1989, when I first met her, her family lived in a municipal housing complex near Imai Tech High where she was a student. Her father, a former Self-Defence Force soldier, worked as a security guard for a firm, and often guarded construction sites outside Kobe-city. This meant he was often away from home. Her mother worked part-time at a nearby chemist as a shop assistant. I used to see Kanako with her youngest sister, who was of pre-school age, walking around the shopping complex near the suburban station where I caught the train home. She cheerfully talked about her family.

At Imai Tech High where she studied interior furnishing, she stood out for her tall, slender and beautiful looks. She once wanted to be a television 'talent' and applied for an audition after being successful in the initial photograph and CV screening, but her mother put a stop to it. She still held a grudge against her mother years later. At school Kanako was an active member of a karate club. She was not enthusiastic about studying but respected her classmates who were. Indeed, one of her closest friends was Oriko, who was top of the class. Other than Oriko, she was close to Yoshie and Itsuko, and the four made a friendship group. (Oriko and Yoshie were also studied for this book.) At that time I could not see why the four formed such a close friendship group since they seemed to have little in common. The four had maintained their friendship until 2000.

While at high school, Kanako had a steady boyfriend, Umeo. He was in the machinery course and his classroom was next to hers. I knew Umeo well since he was one of the boys that I observed and interviewed during my 1989–90 fieldwork. Umeo was outspoken and openly defiant at school. He was suspended several times for various 'misdemeanours' during the three years of high school. I recall one incident when he returned to school with a shaved head after a one-week suspension. According to him and his friends, he had become irritated and almost punched his teacher in class. Luckily three of his friends managed to stop him. Kanako used to take Umeo home in those days. Her father was not impressed with Umeo, but the two shared an interest in judo. Umeo was an active member of the school's judo club. Teachers later told me that it was because he spent much of his after-school time in club activities that Umeo avoided getting into serious delinquency.

When deciding her post-school destination in the final year of high school, Kanako chose factory work (*ginô*) at a pearl jewellery company. She did not want a clerical position, preferring to 'do something with my hands'. She wanted to work near the *sake* (rice wine) company that Umeo hoped to work at, in the eastern part of Kobe-city. Kanako was happy when her application for the job was successful.

She received initial training and enjoyed her work at the company, sorting pearls and precious stones. She also liked her colleagues. Kanako continued going out with Umeo after work as the two had planned. Then, after three months at work, she found she was pregnant. She was only 18. After some discussion, the two decided to get married quickly in July without a wedding celebration. Kanako left her job at the pearl factory, since they would be living too far from her workplace. Her parents were not happy.

KANAKO: They reckoned I was too young but in the end they said, 'Do as you like.' I said, 'At least when I'm gone you'll have one less to feed.' They just looked at me and said, 'How could you say a thing like that!' ... My mum just accepted it cos she knew I'd get married anyway, but Dad listed the bad points about Umeo, like he was unreliable and all that ... In the end I said, 'Even if you're against it, I'm getting married anyway, so that's that.'

(13 February 1992)

Shortly after the marriage Umeo quit his first job at the *sake* brewery because of what he said were 'human relations' problems at work. He tried several different jobs, such as factory work and construction work, but none lasted long. They could not afford their own place as Umeo was not in regular employment, so they lived with Umeo's biological mother, her second husband and his mother. Umeo's father left his mother when Umeo was at primary school, leaving her to bring up their two sons by herself. While at high school, Umeo and his elder brother moved to their father's home, but Umeo later went back to his mother's since he did not get along with his step-mother.

During her pregnancy, Kanako had feelings of desperation and self-doubt about having the baby. Umeo could not hold down a job; worse still, he started having affairs with other women. Kanako, heavily pregnant by then, once paid a sudden visit to one of the women and told her off. At the age of 19, and only one year out of high school, Kanako gave a birth to a baby girl eight weeks premature. She returned to Umeo's mother's place, leaving the baby in an incubator in the hospital. For several weeks she went in every day to feed the baby with her breast milk. She was glad when she was finally able to take the baby home.

Several months later Umeo was persuaded by his elder brother and one of his uncles to join the latter's fishing boat. The brother was already working on the boat. Kanako desperately hoped that this time would be different and

Umeo would have a fresh start. When Umeo started working on the boat, he came home only at the weekend, since it was too far to travel from home to work and back every day. It was not an ideal situation, but Kanako reasoned that she needed some peace and stability for her baby. Umeo, who had previously come home drunk almost every day, was now living with his brother during the week. Kanako did not know how long Umeo would continue fishing. Umeo's mother and her second husband's mother were helpful to her and the baby, but she knew that the arrangement could not continue for ever. Once they were confident that Umeo would continue with the fishing job, the couple moved to a small rented flat near the port where the boat was anchored. By that time, the baby was nearly one year old. Shortly after this move, Kanako had a miscarriage (this baby was a boy); she blamed it on the heavy physical activity involved in moving house.

In early 1992, shortly after their move to the seaside town, I visited Kanako and her daughter. The flat was on the ground floor of a three-storey building, and had two *tatami* rooms (4.5 and 6)[1] and a small kitchen, but no bath or shower. They used a public bathhouse nearby. After I had heard Kanako's story, the three of us walked to the fishing port to meet Umeo, who was coming off his uncle's fishing boat after a day's work. On our way, we came across several of Kanako's 'acquaintances', with whom she chatted casually, introducing me as one of her high school teachers (although I was not a teacher but a PhD student doing fieldwork). The atmosphere was that of a close-knit community. From the port we all returned to their flat, and Kanako cooked a huge afternoon meal for her husband. Umeo looked tired, but said that the current job was the best to date: 'At least, I know what I'm doing.' He then explained to me the details of his work. Both smoked while I was there.

Kanako wanted to obtain paid employment to get out of the house and to supplement the family income. When asked about her main concern, she mentioned that Umeo disapproved of her going out to work.

KANAKO: I wanted to get a job but Umeo didn't like the idea ... Maybe cos my dad told him it was shameful [*mittomonai*] for a man to send his wife out to work.
KO: Really? Your father?
KANAKO: Yeah. I said to Dad, 'You can't say that! You let your wife work.' [Laughs] He said, 'Mind your own business!'
KO: I remember your mother used to work at a neighbourhood pharmacy.
KANAKO: She got sick and had to leave. But when she *was* working Dad used to go on at her about not looking after the house properly. Mum used to say, 'Well then, you should bring in more money.'

(13 February 1992)

Although the couple were in debt for things such as the fishermen's union fee, a second-hand car and the initial bond money for the flat, and Kanako felt they lived 'in poverty', they looked happy to me. Kanako seemed to be enjoying a period of relative stability. She projected herself as being happy, which puzzled some of her high school friends.

YOSHIE: I can't possibly ask her if she is happy ... because she tries to look happy and cheerful all the time. But is she really? I feel that she's enduring and persisting [*gaman*] ... I'm not even sure how long the marriage will last.

(30 January 1992)

Fumiko, another friend from high school, was more concerned with the level of debt that Kanako and her husband had accumulated over two years.

Later in the year, Umeo's father invited him to work for his boat. Umeo and his elder brother, then unmarried, switched to their father's boat. This was a happy period. Soon Kanako became pregnant again, and gave birth to their second child, a girl, in the following year. This time the baby was born full-term. Umeo's mother took leave from her work to care for Kanako and her children. The two did not use contraceptives after the second child was born, because, as Kanako said, 'We thought we'd think about it when I got pregnant again.' Shortly after the second child was born they moved again, this time to a slightly larger flat with a bath, since Kanako found it too difficult to take two small children to a public bath by herself. Around this time, Kanako started sending her first child, who was almost three, to a local childcare centre. Kanako was happy with the centre. It was run by a Buddhist temple next door, which also ran a medical clinic. The centre accepted many children from fishing families, and, according to Kanako, understood the demanding nature of their occupation and family situation. Both Umeo and his brother had been placed at the centre when they were small. Some of the longstanding carers remembered Umeo, and referred to the children as Umeo's girls.

When the second child turned one, Kanako was asked to work for her father-in-law's boat. She placed her younger daughter at the same childcare centre. This particular fishing community expected fishermen's wives to 'put in' – the boat owner for whom a man worked could also expect the wife's labour. The wife's work was unpaid – part of the package. Umeo worked for his father, so Kanako was expected work for him too, which she did without complaint. According to her, among several fishing communities (called *machi*) in the city, Umeo's community had the strictest rules. Not only was a wife expected to provide unpaid labour as necessary, but she was also not normally allowed to take up other paid employment. All the communities formed one union, so the rules of each individual community seemed only customary. Kanako delivered boxes of fish by car, made brochures for tourist fishing boats, and stood in the early morning at a ferry landing to entice customers on to fishing tours. During the diving season (*moguri no jiki* – November to May) she worked on the boat. Umeo dived for scallops, his father controlled the boat, and Kanako and her father-in-law's new wife pulled the rope to haul the diver up and attached another net before he went down again. The new wife did not always come, saying, 'I've got small children.' Kanako had children of similar ages, and regretted that she could not attend various events at the childcare centre during the busy season.

KANAKO: I felt really sorry for my girls, cos I couldn't go to things at the childcare centre, like the athletics and a festival. They told me the diving season was the most important for earning money and I couldn't skip work.

(6 November 1997)

Kanako did not like this arrangement and wanted to find part-time paid employment, but she had no choice but to continue the unpaid job for two years while Umeo worked with his father.

In late 1994 Umeo contracted hepatitis B, and was hospitalised for three months. Kanako attributed his illness to the 'fisherman's lifestyle', which included heavy drinking, smoking and tough physical labour. Umeo did not mind being in hospital; it was a break from his physically demanding routine. In the hospital he also, by chance, did some match-making. He met a classmate from his middle school days, and introduced her to one of his best friends from high school, Seikazu, who was visiting him. Umeo was proud that the two developed a romantic relationship and were now married. It was during Umeo's hospital stay that the Hanshin–Awaji earthquake occurred. Their flat was damaged, but considered habitable. They had to wait several months for the repairs to be completed, which made them feel both irritated and helpless.

Two years later, in late 1996, Umeo and Kanako had a falling-out with Umeo's father and his family. Kanako felt guilty that she had caused this situation, but did not regret that it had happened. It all started when Kanako suspected that Umeo's father's new wife was secretly misappropriating part of Umeo's wages. Kanako received Umeo's wages in cash from his uncle (Umeo's father's elder brother, who also oversaw the financial side of Umeo's father's boat) via Umeo's father's wife, and questioned the discrepancy between the money and the amount stated on the pay slip. Knowing Umeo's uncle's efficient money management skills, she suspected that Umeo's father's wife might be taking some cash out of Umeo's salary, but could not raise the issue for fear of repercussions. On separate occasions when Kanako went to the union office to pay the bills for the fish that she had purchased, she noticed many unpaid bills under the name of Umeo's father. When she mentioned this to Umeo's father via Umeo's elder brother's wife, he became furious and started accusing Kanako of telling lies.

KANAKO: I said to him, 'Why would I lie to you? I just saw a lot of unpaid bills under your name, and thought you'd want to pay them. I'm only trying to save you embarrassment.' He said, 'This can't be true. The union would have paid those bills from my wages.' I'd say his wife must've been spending his money on things for herself, like necklaces and rings. She likes buying stuff like that.

(6 November 1997)

Kanako was extremely upset at being unjustly accused of something that she did not do.

KANAKO: I explained everything to Umeo, and said, 'I can't stand them any longer. It's up to you. Work for them, or stay with me.' He chose to stay with me.

(6 November 1997)

The quarrel turned out to be more serious than Kanako had expected. Four years later, in late 2000, she and Umeo had still not seen Umeo's family, even though they lived nearby.

After leaving his father's boat, Umeo thought of quitting fishing altogether for a while. Then his uncle (his father's elder brother) invited Umeo to rejoin his boat. Kanako liked the new employer and his wife. The uncle seemed willing to intervene or offer assistance to Umeo, a member of his extended clan, whenever necessary. It was he who originally invited Umeo to join his boat and try out a fishing job when Umeo, married and expecting his first child, had been unable to hold down a steady job several years earlier. Since the uncle's two sons worked on a different boat, Umeo and another young man went out with him. Umeo dived for *shiro miru gai* (scallop shells) about 20 metres down in a suit with an emergency oxygen tank on his back. Air was pumped from the boat to the tank. For Umeo, who grew up watching his father diving, the job was familiar.

KANAKO: His uncle said to me, 'You can help out only when you have time.' He wouldn't ask me to go on a boat. And when my husband was in hospital, the uncle offered me work because he thought I needed the money. A really thoughtful and kind guy.

(6 November 1997)

Kanako appreciated that this uncle and his wife were much more considerate of Kanako and her children than Umeo's father had been – the uncle never asked her to work as a 'fisherman's wife', as was the general expectation in the community.

A disadvantage of the new arrangement was that Umeo's brother, married with two small children, found it awkward to be on friendly terms with Umeo and his family following the falling-out.

KANAKO: We think we'll make it up with Umeo's brother's family in the end. His elder brother is in a difficult position. He also works on his auntie's boat [the father's elder sister], and she took Umeo's father's side. I hope they see our side of it some day. I feel sorry for Umeo's brother, though, cos I started the fight. I know he feels upset.

(6 November 1997)

Kanako and Umeo were optimistic that time would resolve the animosity, and decided that they would get on with their lives for the present.

In 1997 Kanako, now aged 25, gave a birth to her third child, a full-term baby girl. She was in hospital for a week after the birth, so Umeo's mother came and looked after the two girls and Umeo, again taking leave from her work and leaving her husband and in-laws to look after themselves. Kanako appreciated this. Because of the acrimonious relationship with Umeo's family, the couple had not informed Umeo's father of their third baby. Nor were Kanako and Umeo told of the birth of Umeo's father's second child by his new wife, which occurred around the same time. Also, since her own mother could not help due to her health problems, Kanako's sisters offered assistance. Kanako considered herself fortunate to be offered so much help from her relatives.

Shortly after the birth, Umeo was again hospitalised for two months, this time with gallstones. This strained their already precarious financial situation.

KANAKO: Somehow we got by when Umeo was in hospital. I worked for Umeo's uncle during the day, doing this and that. Luckily one of my sisters was staying with us after her divorce. So she looked after the three girls after work, and I worked as a bar hostess at night. We got money from the fishermen's union and post office insurance. Umeo's mother paid for everything else.

(6 November 1997)

From then on Kanako took the fisherman's wife's job of managing her husband's health more seriously. Before his hospitalisation, Umeo would frequent *pachinko*[2] and mahjong parlours and other drinking places. After Kanako continuously pleaded with him, he stopped going out drinking so often. On his days off he stayed at home and played computer games with his children.

KANAKO: The girls like this, and of course it's cheaper. I'm happy about it for the time being. Sometimes he asks, 'What about my pocket money?' I say, 'What are you talking about? I don't get any. I'm letting you smoke and drink at home. So why do you need pocket money?' ... He gets drunk easily because his liver is damaged. He got hepatitis B, and then had his gallbladder out. So the doctor told us his pancreas would be damaged if he kept up an unhealthy lifestyle. So I'm careful what I cook, like trying not to let him eat fatty things.

(6 November 1997)

Umeo did have a drinking problem. He drank about one litre of *sake* every day. If he drank much more, he became irritable, bullied his children and sometimes became violent.

KO: He must enjoy being with his kids.

KANAKO: Yeah, most of the time. But when he gets drunk, he bullies the kids, a bit like a kid himself. He makes them cry.

KO: How?

KANAKO: Like, he says things like 'I don't want you any more. Get out of the house.' And he did chuck one of them out once. Even worse, he sometimes hits and kicks them, not hard of course, when they've done nothing wrong. I lose it then and stop him. He doesn't know what he's doing and can't remember. But the girls do; they say, 'Dad, you hit me last night. It hurt.'

KO: So the girls know that their father becomes violent because of alcohol.

KANAKO: Sure. So when he starts drinking, they get out of his way, cos they know he goes off at any tiny thing.

KO: Are you OK?

KANAKO: He often hits me. Look, there and there [showing KO several bruised spots on her body].

KO: Does he say sorry for his actions?

KANAKO: No way. He says, 'It's impossible for me to do something like that to someone I love.' What can I do when he says that? So I just try not to let him drink too much.

(6 November 1997)

So Kanako stayed at home as much as she could, because in her absence he tended to drink much more.

While keeping a close eye on her husband's drinking and diet, she managed to care for the three girls. When I was visiting them, as soon as her first child came home from school, Kanako opened her communication book (*renraku-chô*, a book used for parent–teacher communication which parents read and sign every day) and checked what she needed to do for the following day (e.g. homework to complete or extra things to take). She then supervised the homework, which her daughter had to finish before she was allowed to visit her friend. Kanako made bags for the girls to take to school and childcare. Umeo had no hesitation in saying that Kanako was a good mother.

UMEO: We're always arguing ... (pointing at Kanako – who was preparing a snack for the children – and talking to me so that she could not hear him). Don't you reckon Kanako's a fully fledged mother now?

KO: Yes. A very strong one, too. I've been impressed.

UMEO: That old saying 'A woman may be weak but a mother is strong' is true, I think.

(6 November 1997)

Indeed, Kanako was a devoted mother, although she denied it when I mentioned it. She was strict with her children about greetings and manners ('Don't eat while you're walking around the house') and in not letting them eat sweets. She created photo albums and sewed school bags for them.

As we saw, Kanako continued to harbour her desire to take up paid employment. Umeo's hospitalisation gave Kanako an opportunity to take up paid employment on a casual basis to support her family. She did this part-time for a few months. She carried fresh shrimp (*ebi*) to a water tank at night, sorted dead ones from live ones, arranged them for display and sold them during the day. She also took up a hostessing job at a nearby bar at night. Kanako enjoyed bar-hostessing.

KANAKO: Sure, I like to earn money doing the kind of work I like. I like hospitality work [*sekkyakugyô*], talking to different people and listening to their stories. But a fisherman's wife's work is different. I have to help with my husband's work, manage his health and look after him. The men don't do a thing when they come home. When I see other fathers who help out with housework and look after their kids, I feel jealous. I want him to take the kids to a park sometimes. He never does that.

(6 November 1997)

Once Umeo returned to work, Kanako gave up paid employment and stayed home with the youngest child, who turned three in 2000. While wanting to work part-time for cash, she did not think it would cover the cost of childcare.

In early 2000 Kanako and Umeo bought a newly built flat, located between a Japan Railway (JR) station and the port where Umeo's uncle's boat was kept. They borrowed the total amount. Buying the flat was Kanako's idea. Fishermen in the port are often given a house by their parents, a practice called 'a division of a new house' (*shintaku-wake*). The couple did not receive anything. When Umeo's elder brother bought a flat several years before the falling-out, he invited them to buy into the same building, but Kanako and Umeo had no savings. Interest rates were high. Then the 1995 earthquake occurred, which not only damaged their rented flat and inconvenienced them but also brought unexpected benefits.

It was the special housing loan system for earthquake victims that prompted Kanako to consider buying the flat. She thought if they did not buy it using the system, it would cost them more in the future. According to Kanako, the *shinsai fukkô* (literally, recovery from the earthquake damage) system allowed victims of the 1995 earthquake to borrow the entire amount at the low interest rate of 0.3 per cent until just before Kanako bought the flat. Umeo was not supportive at the beginning, but on seeing a display room he changed his mind and decided on the spot. They were first told that a deposit was not required. But since their previous year's income was low, they had to pay 1.3 million yen as a deposit from their savings, and another 1.3 million yen for miscellaneous costs.

KANAKO: We were in trouble. Then the sales person mentioned that our union might help, and rang them for us. I had no idea the union would do that for us. It was great.

(21 December 2000)

Armed with the loan from the union, they were able to use the special scheme effectively.

The flat was a 3LDK (three bedrooms, one lounge–dining room and a kitchen). They used one room as a family bedroom. It had a double bed and a triple bunk-bed (but when I visited, Ayane, the youngest, was sleeping with her parents). There was a room for the children, and a living-room. The children's room had two desks, Hello Kitty and Winnie the Pooh curtains, and lots of soft toys. When their friends came, they played there. The living-room had a television and a VCR. The new flat was Kanako and Umeo's fourth move since their marriage: first Umeo's mother's place, then a small one-bedroom flat without a bath (that I visited in 1992), then their previous flat with a bathroom (that I visited in 1997), and finally their own flat.

Umeo, according to Kanako, had settled down since moving to the new flat. For example, he stopped going out at night. He only went out drinking once every two or three months, and to *pachinko* once a month. Umeo himself felt that he had settled down (*ochitsuita*). He said that without Kanako this would have been impossible. He was aware that he spent much more time at home now, and explained that this was because he would feel exhausted (*shindoi*) if he went out drinking (*nomi aruku*), because of his age. He did not find it fun any more.

UMEO: When I was young, like 20, I could drink all night and still go to work. Not any more. Anyway, I like having fun with the girls at home.

(21 December 2000)

This change in Umeo made Kanako happy. That said, they both drank and smoked a great deal. Between them they normally emptied a 1.8 litre bottle of *sake* over two nights. Umeo was advised by his doctor to avoid alcohol, but he could not stop enjoying his drink.

KANAKO: We know he shouldn't [be drinking too much]. But I can't stop him. He says that he doesn't want to live long, just long enough to see the girls married.

(21 December 2000)

Kanako understood Umeo's needs well, and seemed to control his diet and drinking in ways that were manageable to him.

Kanako had maintained a healthy relationship with her own family. In 2000 her parents still lived in the same municipal housing complex, which had now almost become an empty nest. Out of six girls in the family, five were married, while the youngest attended a local high school. Except for a sister who lived in Okinawa, all resided in Kobe-city or nearby. One sister was divorced, after Kanako persuaded her to leave a violent husband. Her father, still in his 50s, had left his job as a security guard and now drove a taxi. While he had been against her marriage initially, Kanako thought that he had changed his mind now that he was besotted with his grandchildren. Her mother, still in her mid 50s, suffered from various health problems. She had had an operation, was deaf in one ear, and had increasingly weak eyesight. Kanako felt sorry for her mother, who was lonely now that she had no small children. The family remained close-knit. Kanako's sisters often visited her, and took her children out. In 2000 the whole family, with their partners, had gone to watch the youngest sister's final athletic meeting at high school to celebrate the 'last' school event for the family.

Kanako's relationship with Umeo's biological mother had been excellent. As we saw earlier, although she was living with her second husband and his elderly mother, she invited the newlyweds to live with them, an arrangement that lasted over one year. Both the mother and her elderly mother-in-law looked after Kanako after the premature birth of her first baby. Kanako appreciated this since the couple had little income from Umeo's erratic employment, and was grateful for the sense of stability it gave to mother and baby. When Kanako had her second and third children, Umeo's mother again took leave from her work in order to help her. When Umeo was hospitalised, she contributed her own money to Kanako and her children. Kanako looked on her as a mother.

Kanako and Umeo had no hesitation in saying that their marriage was not perfect, but added that it was OK for the time being. Kanako thought that frank communication helped.

KANAKO: When we argue I say, 'I can't put up with you any more. I'm leaving and taking the girls with me.' Then he says, 'You're lucky. You can solve the problem by leaving me, but I can't, because you fought with my dad. I don't have contact with him and have no one else. I want to bring up my girls.' When he says that, I can't leave him, because I don't think that he can look after the girls ... We say what we think on the spot. We yell, hit each other and break things by throwing them around. But I think we're OK ... saying what we think lets us let off steam.

(6 November 1997)

Talking about recent marriage break-ups of people that they knew (e.g. Yayoi and Fumiko, Kanako's younger sister), Umeo was philosophical about his own marriage.

UMEO: We argue a lot, and talk about divorce a lot. Somehow we're still together ... maybe that's our destiny [*kusare-en*].

KANAKO: Yeah, we talk about divorce nearly every day.

(6 November 1997)

Kanako explained that her journey with Umeo had been challenging, marked as it was by unemployment, poverty, his affairs, drinking and illnesses, and what she described as his 'all over the place' (*mechakucha*) character. However, she thought that Umeo had adjusted reasonably well to family life now.

KANAKO: I think he changed after our second child came along. When I found out I was pregnant with our third baby, I gave him a few conditions for going ahead with the pregnancy. He had to spend more time with the kids, rather than spending all day at *pachinko*. I told him straight, 'If you don't play with the girls now, do you know what will happen to you later? In no time at all, the girls won't want to play with their dad. If you haven't got a good relationship with them now when they want you, they won't want to know you when they're older.'

KO: That's rather severe.

KANAKO: I told him to look at my dad, who gets home from work and sits alone drinking beer, with no one to talk to. We girls didn't like him much ... he was always away. I told Umeo, 'You'll end up like him.'

(21 December 2000)

In 1999, Umeo started judo again. Their first and second daughters had been learning judo, and this remained a shared interest in the family. Kanako's father was also a judo player. Umeo played judo on Sunday mornings, and recently had been asked to act as an instructor for the children's club. This was a pleasant surprise for Umeo, who now trained even harder in order to perform the role to his satisfaction. Kanako was pleased to see that Umeo had developed a healthier weekend routine.

Umeo seemed happy with the stable family life that he had never had himself. He also expressed his attachment to his girls.

UMEO: I hate to think of the future when my girls marry and eventually leave home ... I don't want them to marry fishermen; that life's too hard ... In fact now could be the happiest days of my life – having small children in a lively and noisy household.

(6 November 1997)

In late 2000, Kanako was also content with her humble life. While walking me to the JR station with the youngest daughter on a windy winter's day, she said, 'I'm the happiest since we got married.' But then, over the past 12 years she had always been amazingly optimistic and positive about life and what lay ahead, even when others, like myself, thought how demanding her life could be. A previous comment came to my mind.

KO: You do have such a demanding life [*taihen sô ne*].
KANAKO: Not really, I think I somehow live to please myself. [*Sô demo nai. Kekkô dôrakuni ikinuiteru kotobakari.*]

(6 November 1997)

Kanako then gave me her usual bright smile.

Yayoi: 'I didn't think it would be so hard to get a divorce'

Yayoi was 17 when I first met her at Imai Tech High in 1989. She was living with her parents, an elder sister and a younger brother in a *shitamachi* area of Kobe-city. Her father was a public servant at a local post office. This was his second job. When he first moved to Kobe-city from the country with a middle school education, he worked in a tailor's shop. Her mother stayed at home, doing sewing outwork (*naishoku*). Her elder sister had finished high school and worked at a local post office, while her younger brother was still in middle school. Since she was small, Yayoi had wanted to become a hairdresser. At the end of her compulsory schooling, she still wanted to be a hairdresser but was persuaded by her mother to abandon this dream. Her parents, neither with high school education, wanted their daughter to proceed to a senior high school. Yayoi wanted to 'do something with her hands', and chose an interior furnishing course.

At Imai Tech High, Yayoi was the secretary of the school's Student Council. Her best friend Fumiko was the president of the Council, the first female president in the male-dominated school. Yayoi and Fumiko were outgoing and were seen by others in their interior furnishing class as 'serious types'. Boys took them seriously in the sense that none dared tease them. Yayoi had a steady boyfriend, a graduate of the same school. When deciding on her post-school destination, against the advice of her mother and her teachers she chose a sales position since she liked relating to people. Her mother wanted her to obtain a clerical job, which required a high school diploma (unlike a sales position), as she saw this as more respectable than a sales position. Her teachers suggested a technical drawing position, saying that she should capitalise on skills that she had acquired at school.

Yayoi was delighted to obtain her first job preference, seeing herself as a glamorous sales person in a modern, prosperous, electrical goods department store (which, incidentally, went bankrupt in the late 1990s because of the recession). She enjoyed meeting new people during the initial one-month full-time training, but her dream was shattered when she was assigned to clerical work in a computer repair workshop located far from the main building. Encouraged by her colleagues and bosses she stayed on, but was happy to leave when she married at 19. Yayoi had no hesitation in leaving her job, as she thought that her husband's work was for life while hers was not. This turned out to be an ironic position to take.

In the first year out of school, Yayoi experienced what her high school friends described as *shakai-jin debut* (turning from a studious student to a playful woman), in which she underwent a complete change driven by consumerism and triggered by a new group of 'friends' at work. Yayoi had been a simple and studious student while at the male-dominated technical high school, and had gone out with a student one year her senior, whom everybody assumed she would marry. During her orientation at the large electronics chain-store, Yayoi encountered what she described as 'glamorous' (*hanayakana*) girls and 'new ways of entertainment', and started enjoying the kind of after-work activities that they participated in as a group, such as dressing up and socialising with young men at restaurants and night clubs until late at night. The whole experience was 'refreshing'.

YAYOI: Fumiko says I had a *shakai-jin debut*. It's funny to say that I blossomed and went off the rails [*furyô*] after becoming a *shakai-jin* ... usually it's the other way around. You enjoy being a bit of a delinquent at school and then straighten up once you're a *shakai-jin*. But I didn't get that chance. My boyfriend at the time was always with me when we went out, and he didn't like me dressing up.

(31 January 1992)

She had never had such a good time, and realised what she had missed out on until then. Her parents were not happy but saw it as a transient stage.

But her boyfriend of two years pleaded with her to return to what she used to be. He was a former president of the Student Council of Imai Tech, and according to Yayoi and Fumiko (her best friend), a studious and 'conservative' man who valued a peaceful and 'ordinary' life. Although Fumiko and his best friend attempted to reconcile Yayoi and her boyfriend, Yayoi was adamant that the relationship was over. Fumiko claimed, 'He was a nice guy, the type of man who would make a good husband, you know. But Yayoi wanted something else then. I tried my best to save it, but I could only do so much.'

Yayoi met Zen, her new boyfriend, at work when he delivered goods to her workplace; he was one of her 'new friends'. He was eight years older than she was. Yayoi's proposed marriage to a delivery-man met with opposition from her family, who saw him as unreliable. Zen returned from Kobe-city to his home city several months prior to the wedding, having obtained a transfer to his company's branch there. However, he quit his job and was unemployed at the time of the marriage, which the two meticulously covered up in order to create a 'respectable' appearance. Even her family did not know that the man was unemployed. The two organised what they considered was an expensive wedding in a wedding parlour, and went overseas for their honeymoon. Yayoi spent all her savings, one million yen, on hiring wedding outfits (a Japanese wedding kimono, a white wedding dress and an evening dress). She was proud of the wedding and showed me the video and photos. Since Zen was the firstborn son, Yayoi was prepared to care for his parents in their old age but was worried about his younger sister, who was then having an affair with a married sushi chef whom she brought to the wedding.

After the wedding Yayoi moved to the provincial city (three hours by train from Kobe-city) where Zen and his parents lived, and moved into a rented flat. At that time, Yayoi thought she was in love, which she believed would overcome all their problems. But as we will see later, her retrospective account in 2000 revealed more complexity in her decision-making: she later suspected that it was her attempt to escape from her own family that was most influencing her at the time. Yayoi initially looked for a job as a diversion from being a full-time housewife and landed a part-time job, but the situation changed when Zen proved unable to hold down a job for long. She found herself having to support them both: in her words, a hand-to-mouth existence. She even declined an offer of a permanent position in favour of a casual job at the company where her husband worked, because he pleaded with her to work there. Yayoi then realised that he had problems with managing human relationships at work. She was so desperate for Zen to find stable employment that she was prepared to forgo a permanent position for herself.

When I visited the newlyweds in the snow-covered provincial city in early 1992, Yayoi quietly confessed that the situation was very demanding: managing in-laws whom she disliked, her husband's unstable employment, and their financial constraints. However, she projected herself as content with the situation both to her own family and to close friends. She had financial problems, but could not seek help from her parents because, she said, her pride did not allow her to do so. At that time, she was relieved that Zen had finally settled into a job; he had been working at the same place for a month, having tried several jobs at which he failed to last long. When I said farewell to Yayoi at the snow-covered railway station, she told me that she liked sharing with me her immediate problems, which she could not reveal to her family and friends (because of her 'pride'). I wished her the best. Two years later I received a letter from her, which plainly informed me that she had returned to her parents' home 'due to various reasons which I need to explain to you the next time I see you'. When I met her in 1996 and 1997, Yayoi had a long story to tell me.

Zen had not continued in the job that Yayoi hoped would last, and remained intermittently unemployed. Yayoi supported the household through casual employment.

YAYOI: He'd work somewhere for a while, and then refuse to stay. If you saw this in a young child, you'd say it was 'stranger anxiety' [*hitomishiri*]. He couldn't manage relationships with his superiors and subordinates. You know, human relationships take time. When you go into a new workplace, you have to start all over again. But he's impatient. I also think he had a sense of assumed dependence [*amae*] about returning to his home town. After all, his parents did give him financial support when he returned.

(15 October 1996)

Amae was a term that Yayoi often used to describe her husband.

YAYOI: I now think working at the same company as my husband was a bad thing. When I was there, he depended on me, like thinking that I would somehow sort out everything [*nantoka naru*]. When I was working, he counted on my income. After he quit, I continued at the same place. I felt so miserable.

(15 October 1996)

Yayoi also began to notice Zen's spending habits; he spent what she considered to be an excessive amount of money on his recreation (*pachinko* pinball, drinking, etc.)

YAYOI: Sure, everyone prefers playing to working. I'm the same. It was OK to splurge on recreation before, cos we both worked full-time. But I didn't realise that his habit was this serious. Once you get married, you have to manage your own life. Like, first you have to put aside your living expenses, and if you still have some money left, you can use it for fun. But a man who's got into the habit of playing hard can't stop this habit even if he is married and the situation has changed. At first I thought being out of work was the cause of the problem. He would hang around the house, and if I couldn't give him any more money he would go and ask his parents.

(15 October 1996)

Then a friend of his father offered both Zen and Yayoi jobs. Zen insisted that Yayoi worked with him there, and she agreed. She was prepared to do anything to get him back into employment. He stayed in this job longer than he had in previous jobs. For a while life was peaceful. Yayoi savoured a temporary stability in her married life.

It all changed when Yayoi discovered that her husband had been embezzling the company's money. She had noticed 'strange' telephone calls from clients (demanding money that was supposed to have been paid) over the preceding months, but did not associate this with the money disappearing. Once she suspected Zen, she challenged him and begged him to stop. By this time, the sum had climbed to over 500,000 yen. Meanwhile she felt that she had to cover it up before the company president found out. She explained everything to her husband's parents and asked them to lend him the money, but they did not believe her story and started accusing her of trying to get money from them for her own use.

Thus began Yayoi's lone attempts to earn extra money so that she could return the missing money to the company before anybody noticed it. In desperation, she approached the owner of a local night bar, which she used to frequent, and asked her to lend her 500,000 yen with the promise that she would work there until she repaid it. This was based on what she called 'women's trust'. It was a big ask, she knew. The owner was reluctant initially, but the manager (*mama-san*) volunteered to be a guarantor (*hoshônin*) for Yayoi. She was sympathetic to her plight, having herself returned to her parents' home with her child after her marriage broke down.

YAYOI: She said, 'I won't ask you why you need the money. But I'll offer myself as a guarantor since I know how desperate you are.' Then she approached her boss [the owner] for me. The big *mama-san* [the boss] was not impressed, but in the end she gave in. She herself had gone to Kobe-city to work and returned alone with two children.

KO: You were lucky.

YAYOI: Yeah. Even now I think that. It was just a verbal agreement, lending 500,000 yen to a total stranger … I could have run away with the money, you know … Anyway, so I used the money to cover it up.

(6 November 1997)

Soon Zen's parents discovered that Yayoi was working at the bar, which they considered disgraceful (*mittomonai*), and lent the money so that Yayoi could repay the borrowed sum to the bar. This enabled her to stop working at the bar, but only for a short time. Zen started appropriating the company money again, and Yayoi returned to hostessing at the bar, secretly.

YAYOI: I slept only two hours a day, working in the office during the day and hostessing at the bar at night. But the amount of missing money was getting bigger. I was always exhausted, but I didn't give up. But then he started stealing money [for his recreation] from our bank account, which I controlled. He got an extra ATM card by taking my card while I was asleep, and got the bank to make another one by showing his ID as my husband. Because he returned my card immediately, I did not know that he had another card. How smart was that!

KO: Did you talk to him about it?

YAYOI: Of course I did. Every day was like a war. We argued a lot, but he didn't change.

(15 October 1996)

Around this troubled time, Yayoi became pregnant. This made her give serious thought to the future of the marriage.

YAYOI: Then I found out I was pregnant. I knew I was in real trouble. I had to think hard about what to do.

KO: You didn't tell your husband?

YAYOI: No. I was still thinking what to do. I had a miscarriage anyway, maybe because I was so exhausted. But this [the miscarriage] made me decide that I should go home to my parents. Because the baby floated away [*ryûzan*, Japanese expression for a miscarriage], I no longer had a reason to hesitate. If I hadn't lost the baby, I'd have thought harder. I might have tried to straighten him out, using my pregnancy as a weapon, for example.

(15 October 1996)

At that point, Yayoi decided to tell the company president everything. By then her body could no longer take long hours of working double shifts, and the amount of money that she had to cover was increasing rapidly.

YAYOI: Would you believe, the president and the book-keeping people knew what was happening, I mean … [silence] … I'd been trying to cover up the money that Zen had stolen. But they didn't raise the issue because I was so desperate to keep up appearances. I said to the president, 'I can't repay the money this month. I am sorry.' The president said, 'This is not your problem, it is your husband's problem. You have done your share. It is not right that you follow it up simply because you are married. Why don't you go home [to your parents in Kobe] until things settle down? I will talk to his parents.' Then he took me to Zen's parents' house and told them everything.

(15 October 1996)

Zen's parents refused to believe the story but, not wanting to make matters worse, said that they would pay the outstanding money. The president explained that this was less about the money than about their son. Yayoi was grateful for her employer's initiative. Then the parents said, 'This is a family problem. We don't want you to interfere in family matters. We will pay you the money that is missing.'

YAYOI: On the way back, the president said to me, 'It's not working, I'm telling you, if that's the parents' attitude towards their son. I didn't come all the way here to ask them to repay me the missing money. That wasn't my purpose. I'm sad that they didn't understand why I came with you. They are not going to understand what you've been doing for your husband. I tell you, honestly, that you'd better go home now.' Then I packed my belongings and went home.

(15 October 1996)

That night Yayoi finally left Zen and returned to her parents without saying anything to him. It was early spring 1994. She had been married almost two and a half years.

In retrospect, she regretted having been unable to comprehend the situation during the two and a half years. She knew that she could no longer endure her husband's emotional (and financial) dependence on her, and his inability to change the spending habits that had led to stealing money to support those habits. Lack of support from Zen's family meant that Yayoi had assumed all the responsibility for Zen.

KO: Why do you think that you put up with the situation for so long? Did you love him so much?

YAYOI: Mm ... I don't think so. It was pride. I left home to marry him against my parents' wishes. I said that I was leaving Kobe-city in front of everybody after the wedding party. How could I admit defeat to everyone? I couldn't bring myself to go home. That's why I struggled on for a year and a half. Maybe I thought I was in love at the beginning.

(15 October 1996)

Yayoi's parents were shocked but supportive.

YAYOI: I rang my mum and said that I was thinking of coming home after tidying up the place. Without asking further, she said, 'Leave there right now. If you don't have any money, catch a taxi. We'll pay when you get here. If you don't leave now, you never will.' But I had the money that the company president had given me as a farewell present that day.

(19 December 2000)

Recollecting what happened that day, Yayoi said that her mother's advice was wise. Had she not followed it, she might have stayed there longer and been persuaded by Zen, as had often happened previously.

Yayoi's sudden return to her parents' home was unexpected. She had not displayed any sign of a troubled marriage. Her parents had interpreted no news as good news. When she explained, her father nearly fainted. Her mother said nothing, except to ask her if she intended to return to Zen. Yayoi's answer was firmly negative. From then on, her parents gave her what Yayoi considered to be absolute support.

The divorce procedure turned out to be what Yayoi described as an absolute nightmare. She had not realised how difficult it was to gain a divorce. A few days after Yayoi returned to her parents' house in Kobe-city, Zen, his parents and the couple who had acted as go-betweens for their wedding came to see her.

YAYOI: All five were desperate to get me back. I guess they wanted to save face. Dad said, 'My daughter doesn't want to go. Having heard her story, I support her decision. We would like to have a divorce. This marriage is over.' The go-betweens had no idea why I left him ... Obviously, his parents hadn't explained to them. They begged me to return. The go-betweens thought that I, a city girl, couldn't adjust to country life, and that I should have visited my parents more often, but of course we didn't have the money to do that. Then they asked me to return after having a 'rest' time with my parents. My mum got angry. She said, 'It seems that you two don't know anything. We have nothing to say, but want a divorce. We don't say why, please ask Zen's parents.' So then they all left.

(15 October 1996)

During the meeting, Yayoi managed to keep silent as strictly instructed by her father, who said, 'You might say something unnecessary, and complicate the meeting.'

Shortly after this visit, Zen rang Yayoi and pleaded with her to return, but she was firm in her refusal. Then Zen came to meet her by himself. Yayoi's mother was concerned at her meeting him, but Yayoi assured her that it would be all right, since it was in a café and during the day.

YAYOI: He reckoned he'd started working. We talked. I said that I couldn't trust him any more, no matter how much he said that he would make an effort [*ganbaru*]. I'd persevered enough, and given him heaps of chances. Then he said, 'This time is different, I will renew myself and *ganbaru*.' I then lost my temper. 'What are you talking about now? I've heard you say that so many times. How can I trust what you say? I was deceived [*damasareta*]!' Then he said, 'OK. I've nothing more to say'; then he left. We didn't hear from them for a long time.

(15 October 1996)

Yayoi and her parents were eager to finalise the divorce quickly, and wanted Zen to give his stamp of approval to the divorce application. Her parents travelled a long distance to visit Zen but could not meet him. Zen's parents told them that their son had not decided, and that parents should not inter-vene because it was a matter for the couple. This response angered Yayoi's parents, who immediately visited the go-betweens. The go-betweens, hearing the whole story for the first time, were sympathetic, saying, 'We have chil-dren too.' Yayoi's parents and the go-betweens then visited Zen's parents together.

Zen's parents were taken aback by this visit, and politely requested the four to leave. They returned to the go-betweens' house, and decided that the go-betweens would discuss the matter with Zen's parents when they had calmed down. However, Yayoi's parents did not hear from them for a few weeks. When they finally contacted the go-betweens, they learned that Zen's parents were still reluctant.

YAYOI: Then two months passed. I decided that I should go and get his signature. As Zen's parents said, this was a problem between us two. When I said this, my parents must have felt sorry for me and said,

'Don't worry, we will get it sorted out.' I thought that I was still a legal member of his family on the family registration system [*koseki*], which in theory allowed me to do things that others couldn't do, like entering their house without permission. Zen's parents were legally my parents. Still being married to him, I could do anything. I just couldn't forgive myself for making my parents feel so miserable and powerless. Until then I had a slight temptation to return to Zen, like when he came to see me. The sight of my parents at that time drove that away. I felt so sorry that I had caused so much grief for my parents, and unless I did something, this would continue.

(15 October 1996)

Yayoi and her father again travelled to Zen's parents' house. When Yayoi entered the house, Zen's grandmother shouted, 'Don't enter a stranger's house!' to which Yayoi responded, 'I'm not a stranger. I'm legally a member of this household!' She talked to Zen, and finally got him to sign the divorce application form. Although Zen was told by his grandmother not to sign in the absence of his parents, he was not deterred. For Yayoi, it was the first time she had seen him rebel against his parents.

Yayoi and her parents were glad when the divorce was finally settled in June, three months after she had left her husband. Yayoi cherished the tranquillity of 'ordinary life' at her parents' home. When she returned there, her elder sister was also staying, with her newborn baby. Yayoi helped to look after mother and baby for several months. Living with her parents and a younger brother gave her a sense of security and stability that she had not experienced with Zen. She was comfortable. She now had to put her life back together and find a job.

When her sister and her baby left, she worked as a casual waitress at a nearby coffee shop for several months. It was a revealing experience to her.

YAYOI: At first I felt inferior [*hikeme*]. I was young but already divorced, 21 going on 22. The coffee shop was a great place to work. It did me a lot of good. All the workers were university students working casually, the same age as me. I felt *hikeme* at first, and ended up very envious. People my age were thinking of dream jobs, like becoming a school teacher or kindergarten teacher. I was with these people just under a year. I was at first out of place but got used to them gradually, and we started going out together sometimes. They were all very nice to me. Being with them, I got to feel relaxed [*ki ga rakuni nattekita*], there was no point in thinking about the past [*kuyokuyo kangaeru*]. You know, these people were looking ahead and following their dreams, like 'I want to do this or that in the future.' They were so different, and yet the same age as me.

(15 October 1996)

Yayoi was also surprised to see that the university students had no interest in marriage, and attributed that to the fact that they were enjoying themselves now and planning for their own future. They had a significant influence on her.

While Yayoi was working as a casual waitress, her mother's younger brother found a job for her through his social network at a company that designed and constructed arcades. She did not think that she could decline this offer given the economic circumstances. In late 1994, she took the job on a casual basis with the hope that it would become a permanent position if her performance was satisfactory. She later obtained a permanent full-time position.

YAYOI:　My uncle said, 'You'd better settle into somewhere. After all, casual waitressing is just that.' I wasn't keen since I was enjoying the job at the coffee shop so much. But I thought about the future (like super-annuation), and decided that I had no choice but to grab this job. We had a recession, and there weren't many jobs, even for new graduates, and almost none for others who had had previous jobs [*chûto saiyô*]. I thought I should take this while I could still be in demand. I've been there for almost two years now.

(15 October 1996)

She was first employed in a clerical position at the company. However, when her seniors discovered at the first briefing that Yayoi understood technical drawing and arcade plans (which she had learned at Imai Tech High) and knew how to use Windows 95 (which had just gone on the market), they decided to place her in the design department instead. She started working there doing miscellaneous tasks, but later received on-the-job training.

Since the divorce, Yayoi had gone out with three men. Her relationships with the first two did not last long, because, she said, the men started talking about marriage. Yayoi neither desired nor intended to remarry in the future. She thought that she had experienced more than enough troubles in enduring her ex-husband's improvidence, and especially in getting him and his family to agree to a divorce.

YAYOI:　It's been almost four years since I got a divorce. I will never marry again. My marriage was bad enough, but getting a divorce was even more difficult. A married relationship is so different from an unmarried one. Once you are officially married on the family registration, it's no longer just a matter of your personal relationships. Many on-lookers [*gaiya*] also get involved. The relationship becomes not only the couple's but every-one's. I never want to get dragged into that complication. I've had enough.

(6 November 1997)

Yayoi was disappointed that those men were reluctant to have a relationship without considering marriage.

Then she met Masa, who could offer the kind of relationship she wanted – one without the prospect of marriage. Masa was her boss at work. He was married with two teenage children. He was kind to her from the outset. For example, when Yayoi and her family were living in a tent after the Hanshin earthquake destroyed their house, he invited her and her mother to have a bath at his house (30 minutes' train ride away). When Yayoi's family planned a new house, he helped them enormously. Her parents respected him, but were not aware that their daughter was in a relationship with this married man. Yayoi enjoyed the relationship.

YAYOI: I think our relationship has lasted this long because he is married with children. He has no intention of leaving his family, and I don't want him to. In this relationship, there's no prospect of marriage, which is great. The men that I went out with all started talking about marriage in a subtle way after a few months. He never does that.

KO: Is his wife aware of this?

YAYOI: I don't think so. But even if she is, I don't think that she would mind as long as her family is not affected. I think his wife must be reasonably happy. They can live on his income, she goes to culture centres during the day, and devotes herself to looking after the kids. I think that married women can have a comfortable lifestyle as long as they can live on the husband's income. She can work part-time if she wants her own money. Look at me! I have to work to survive.

(6 November 1997)

Yayoi was philosophical about marriage as an institution, claiming that marriage makes a relationship between two individuals into something else.

The 1995 earthquake had significant consequences for Yayoi's immediate family. The house where she had been living with her parents and her younger brother, was flattened. Fortunately, no one was injured. Her father feared that if he did not stay on the site the land might be claimed, which Yayoi considered was bordering on paranoia. Consequently her father and brother continued to camp on the house site. Yayoi and her mother stayed with relatives for a while until her father set up a proper camp. It was during this time that Masa, her boss, occasionally invited her and her mother to his home to bathe, which contributed to the development of their relationship. In the end, her father and her younger brother, who had just started work after finishing high school, took out a two-generation housing loan in the special scheme for earthquake victims (the same one that Kanako used) in order to have a new house built on the small plot of land. Yayoi's boss assisted her family in many ways, using his network to arrange builders and plumbers, who were in demand during the post-earthquake reconstruction.

Another consequence of the earthquake was Yayoi's sister's marriage break-up, which subsequently affected the family. Her sister's daughter was two by then. Their flat was destroyed, which forced them to relocate. Yayoi was not impressed with the husband, describing him as utterly hopeless. Within a year, her sister left the marriage, and started to live in a small rented flat with her daughter near Yayoi's parents' place, so that her mother could help her out. Yayoi's sister was a high school graduate public servant and managed to support her daughter financially. Yayoi's family became increasingly intimate. Often the whole family, including Yayoi's sister and her daughter, ate dinner together, and the young niece often had a bath and stayed overnight. This was partly because her sister could only afford to rent a small flat and the young girl preferred being at her grandparents' house.

This situation prompted Yayoi to consider moving out of her parents' house in order to make room for her elder sister and niece. She thought it made more sense for them to live with her parents, given that her sister worked full-time and had a child. Yayoi investigated the possibilities. She decided to buy a newly built flat not far from her parents' house by making use of the special housing loan scheme for earthquake victims. When I met Yayoi in late 1997, she was in the process of finalising her purchase.

Yayoi liked working at the arcade company, first because her colleagues had helped her family extensively when the family lost their house; she still remembered this fondly. After joining the design department, she had received on-the-job training. This process was accelerated shortly after the earthquake, when the company became busy with the post-earthquake construction boom. This was excellent timing for her career development. First, she learned to modify arcade plans in response to clients' requests. Then she gradually learned to design arcades herself, first as an assistant to the designer and by 2000 on her own. Yayoi's job involved much physical activity. When a client put in an order, she visited the site and measured it by climbing on to the roof or on to the arcade. She then designed an arcade incorporating the clients' needs and desires, and provided them with a cost estimate. She visited government offices to obtain approvals, and was basically responsible for her project until it was taken over by the construction department of the company.

YAYOI: I can't say, 'I can't climb on to the roof because I'm a woman,' can I? The clients would say, 'Forget it!'
KO: You aren't scared?
YAYOI: I'd be lying if I said I wasn't scared. At the beginning I didn't want to. I used to get men to go up and take photos. But when I started drawing up plans I found so many things that weren't clear. Photos aren't enough, you know. I didn't like that. So in the end I decided to go up myself, but only in the last two years or so.
KO: Do you enjoy the job, I mean your work content?
YAYOI: Well … rather than say I enjoy it … It took me a long time to really start understanding what to do. I've been in the company over six years, but it's only in the last two years that I've been able to answer clients' questions. Before then I couldn't answer a thing. Sometimes I didn't even understand what they were asking!

(19 December 2000)

In 2000, four workers did the same job as Yayoi, including two men, both graduates of a design course at a prefectural technical high school. One of the four workers was a new female recruit who had just graduated from Kobe University. So far, Yayoi had managed human relations at work well.

KO: How are you getting along with this new woman?

YAYOI: OK, I think. She is a university graduate, right? She's obviously studied much more at school. Even if I've been working on the site for this long, she's got much more basic knowledge. I know it. She seems to think I'm experienced with arcades and construction sites. I'm also older than her, so she doesn't say much [make unreasonable demands]. We don't have the kind of problems that female workers often have. We respect each other. But I do have a problem with an older female clerical worker in the office.

(19 December 2000)

Yayoi disliked the woman, who often preached to her and younger female workers by talking of what things were like in her day: 'When I was your age, I was married with children and working full-time.' She also complained about her own family, which included demanding in-laws. Yayoi was initially annoyed with her, but now did not mind it, thinking that the woman was under pressure and could relieve it by talking to her colleagues like that.

Having worked at the arcade company for six years, Yayoi saw her work very differently from a few years ago. She was happy with her colleagues and seniors, and considered herself fortunate to be given opportunities to develop her skills. The work also acted as a welcome diversion from the emotional and physical traumas resulting from her marriage breakdown.

YAYOI: I feel that I've changed my attitudes towards my job and the company. Maybe because of my age. Before I was at the bottom of the hierarchy [*shitappa*] and young, and didn't think about how the whole company was going and how it affected me. Now I understand the company's financial situation more, and also what individuals can do for the company's performance. After all, I've got a big loan and I need a job. You know, I travel a lot these days. I've just got back from a two-day trip to Nagasaki to see a client.

(19 December 2000)

Now that the initial post-earthquake reconstruction of Kobe-city was almost complete, she was encouraged to get orders from elsewhere.

Yayoi was enjoying living in the flat that she had purchased a few years earlier. After five years, she still maintained a relationship with Masa, her married boss, who often visited her flat. She did not want marriage but wished for children. Her parents talked about her having children, emphasising that her biological clock was ticking. Yayoi discussed this with her boyfriend. He was willing to recognise paternity but had no intention to marry her. She liked this since she did not want marriage. However, she was hesitant about having children on her own.

KO: Why?

YAYOI: I feel hesitant about becoming a parent.

KO: You don't like the idea?

YAYOI: No, it's not that I would dislike being a parent. When I was young, I wanted to get married early and have kids. But these days I think about things more seriously. I look at my sister, who's divorced, works full-time and has a young kid, and I reckon that you really have to work in order to support a family and earn a reasonable income. So your work rules your life. Although my parents would look after my child like they did for my sister, is it really a good thing? I'm not sure how I would cope with that situation. My ideal is to be a housewife. I've told you before.

KO: Do you still feel that way?

YAYOI: Of course. I've always had this ideal but failed in getting there so young!

KO: You could try once more.

YAYOI: But the reality is different. Maybe you may think I'm contradicting myself. Although I want to be a housewife, now that I'm used to working life … I mean it's my routine … I'm not sure I can cope with being home all day. In any case, it would have been much better to get married and have kids young when I didn't think too much about these things. Now I think too much.

(19 December 2000)

When asked to envision herself in another five years, her focus was on her work and herself as an individual, rather than on her relationships.

YAYOI: Well, I actually enjoy my work because I now understand much more about it. But the work is still hard. So I have a feeling that by 35 I will reach my limit. I will be going downhill – both intellectually and physically. I don't know if I will be able to climb up on the roof, walk over cables and so on, you know. That's my main concern. So before then I want to study something. I've never thought of this before. At school I always thought of playing up.

(19 December 2000)

Yayoi was content with what she had at the age of 29 when I saw her in late 2000. Her appreciation of what constitutes happiness seemed to have changed over the years. When we departed in the cold late evening she said to me,

YAYOI: I am happy now. My job's secure, and my work ability has been acknowledged to a degree. I have a boyfriend that I like. I have no pressure to marry. I have a good relationship with my family. I am happy that I can honestly say I'm happy.

Satoko: 'I'm the breadwinner, and it's hard'

Satoko was the only child of a single-mother household that also included her maternal grandparents. Since her mother had always worked long hours in a full-time job to support the family of four, Satoko said that she was brought up by her grandmother. 'I don't remember sleeping in Mum's futon; I always slept in my grandma's.' Satoko recalled her mother working in various jobs, including as a shop assistant at a railway station kiosk.

Satoko's mother rented two sets of rooms in a *bunka jûtaku* (old-style flats), since one set had only one four-*tatami* room and a kitchen. Then they moved to a house next to the *bunka jûtaku* building, and rented an upstairs set only (one room of two *tatami*, and another of four-*tatami* size). They shared an entrance with the people who lived downstairs. They lived in this arrangement, known as *magari*, until the family moved to their present flat shortly after Satoko went to Imai Tech High. When Satoko was of kindergarten age, her mother obtained a casual job through a friend as a kitchen assistant at Kobe University Hospital, and had been there over twenty years. She worked hard to gain a qualification as a cook so that she could get a permanent position there. Satoko remembered her mother studying late at night at the end of a long working day. Her mother was a middle school graduate (i.e. with compulsory education only), so her colleagues were surprised when she beat them in the examination to qualify as a cook. Her grandmother died shortly before Satoko graduated from high school.

After completing compulsory education at a middle school known locally as a 'tough' school, Satoko studied interior furnishing at Imai Tech High, where I first met her. While at high school Satoko was a loner, not belonging to a particular friendship group. It was not that she was excluded; if a group project had to be done, she easily teamed up with someone. For the graduation project it was Kanako. Perhaps it was because of her relative isolation that she tried to get close to me when I spent a year in her class. She would sit next to me on a school excursion, and looked for me at the school canteen. She was also close to many teachers, and seemed to like having 'big brother' figures around her. Satoko's enthusiasm at the time was for baseball. She used to play it every Sunday, and talked about it all the time, which, according to some girls, put them off her. Other girls considered Satoko to be somewhat 'odd' (*kawatta hito*). She was somehow less 'feminine' than her female classmates, in terms of speech and mannerisms.

When deciding her post-school destination, Satoko's first preference was the public service, like her mother who worked in a public hospital. However, she failed the public service examination, and went to second-round offers of jobs in the private sector. Teachers recommended her for a technical drawing position at Matsushita Electronic, saying that she was lucky to find such a position in the second-round offers. She sat a selection test and was excited to obtain the position. The job involved designing electronic wiring boards according to client specifications. She found the work satisfactory, and being close to home was convenient.

Satoko married Moto, three years her senior, in 1993 when she was 21. She had met him at work four years earlier. The relationship started when Moto asked Satoko to move his orders to the head of the queue so that they could be completed on time. In return he offered to buy her dinner. Gradually they became close, and married without a wedding party or a honeymoon. The two had a long truck trip in the countryside just before their marriage, as a substitute honeymoon, which Satoko greatly enjoyed and talked about in detail. They started living in a rented flat near his parents' place in a suburb of Kobe-city. His aunt lived in a flat next door.

Moto resigned from his job due to human relationship problems at work shortly after the marriage, and started working as a self-employed truck driver. Satoko took a loan to buy him a 4-tonne truck. Working for a large company made it relatively easy for her to get a loan. As with any self-employed work, his income was always unstable.

SATOKO: He's got a one-year contract with a company right now. He's reliable, so he should be able to get the contract renewed for another year. Still, I can't stop working because we don't know what'll happen to his job.
(20 November 1997)

Moto's precarious position meant that Satoko became the breadwinner with her regular income from Matsushita.

A year later, in mid-1994, Satoko gave birth to a boy. She was 22. She took three months' maternity leave and returned to work on 'child-rearing work hours' (starting late and finishing early) until her son's first birthday. Combining work with childcare was demanding, but living close to her workplace made the situation manageable. Then the Hanshin earthquake hit. Satoko's flat was damaged but remained habitable. Her work continued as usual for another year, until the company decided to move Satoko's department to a city near to its headquarters. This was shortly before she had her second child at the age of 24. She took eight months' family leave. When she returned to work, commuting turned out to be a nightmare. She left home at 8 a.m., drove to a childcare centre near a railway station, and took a train for one hour, in order to arrive at work at ten in the morning. She was using flexi-time, working from 10 a.m. to 6.30 p.m., to accommodate dropping her children in the mornings.

The situation became more difficult for her when she was 'dropped' (her expression) from a technical drawing position to another job a few months before I met her in late 1997. The designer's position had been satisfactory in that she only had to complete an assigned number of drawings by a set time according to the expected work quota (about 10 to 15 drawings). She could therefore predict the amount of work and make plans accordingly. Now her job involved receiving orders from clients, and passing these orders to various branches of the company. Since the number and complexity of the incoming orders were unpredictable, she never knew when she would finish work for the day, which made life difficult for her.

SATOKO: I've been asking for a transfer to Kobe-city branch, but no luck so far. I just don't understand why they gave me this job so far away from home. I've got two small children. The work is demanding, but there's no use in complaining to the company, so what can I do? I've got a loan to pay off. Who knows what'll happen with my husband's job as well? Even if I quit, I mightn't get a better job.

(20 November 1997)

Thus, although she was dissatisfied with her job, she had no choice but to stay in order to be the main breadwinner for her family.

Working full-time at an office far away, being responsible for looking after her two boys and having a husband who worked irregular hours made Satoko's daily existence extremely stressful. She had lost 5 kilograms since leaving school.

SATOKO: My life's too demanding [*shindoi*]. I don't know how I keep going. I get fevers, but I still have to go to work. I feel guilty when I go home early because I feel rotten. I seem to have a cold all year [*mannen kaze*]. There's no way I want any more kids.

(20 November 1997)

Satoko received support from her husband's family, without which she would not have managed. She could not depend on her mother's help, since she was still working full-time to support her own father, who was in a nursing home.

SATOKO: I wake the boys up at seven o'clock, when my husband leaves for work. After breakfast, we leave home around eight and I drive maybe half an hour to the childcare centre near a JR station, and catch the train to work. This was the only childcare centre which took kids under one year old and which was near a JR station. I leave the car in a rented car park, sit on the train for an hour, and get to work just before ten. My husband comes home around seven at night. I don't get home till about ten. So my husband's aunt, who lives behind our flat, picks up the boys from childcare, and takes them to my parents-in-law, who also live here. Auntie doesn't work cos she's got health problems, but my parents-in-law work until 4.30. The kids are fed and bathed by their grandparents, before my husband comes home.

(20 November 1997)

It was because of this 'tight' schedule that I asked her to talk to me on the train on her way home from work.

In 1997, Satoko's future concern was how to manage the family once her elder child started school in two years' time. The best possible plan for her was for the family to move into her own mother's flat, which was much more spacious than their rented flat, and which her mother was paying off. In three years' time her mother was due to retire. Then, Satoko reasoned, her mother would be able to take the boys to and from school. But she was also concerned about how her husband's parents would respond to this, given that he was the eldest son of the family.

In late 2000, Satoko was still unhappy with her workplace, in terms of both job content and human relationships, but had continued at Matsushita. It was her tenth year there. Then her department moved again, this time to a location even further from her home. According to Satoko, the move was intended to save production costs in the midst of the recession. It now took her another 20 minutes to commute. Her job content changed again – she returned to designing electrical wiring boards. She liked this work better, but still wondered why she had been given so many different assignments over the years. Her relationships with colleagues had not been pleasant, but were bearable. Satoko did not have friends among the other permanent staff. Instead, she went out for lunch with agency workers. She did not have the sense of 'belonging' that she would have liked, but was committed to the company. This commitment seemed to have been reinforced by the recession.

SATOKO: There're female workers, but most of them quit when they have kids.
KO: I guess you are going to continue working?
SATOKO: I guess so, now that I've come this far. My mum told me to work for at least 25 years cos it makes a difference to your superannuation.
KO: You've been working there for ten years. Your income must have gone up?
SATOKO: Not that much.
KO: But you have a permanent job at a large company.
SATOKO: Yeah but these days even banks go bankrupt. Look what happened to Sogo department stores. You know, about half a year ago, people were talking about closing down our department!

(26 December 2000)

With the recession, employees were required to undertake extra work and Satoko had to work more hours of overtime.

Satoko's husband had acquired another vehicle, fitted with a crane. He now employed one of his cousins as a casual worker, and was contracted to a company annually. Satoko was unsure of her husband's business prospects, in particular how he managed his employee.

SATOKO: I think he's the wrong type to be a boss. He'd be better off as an employee. He's just not sensitive enough. No wonder his cousin complains. So I reckon it'll be even harder to employ people who are not family [*chi no haitte inai hito*]. That's why I'm not sure if he'll be in business in five years' time.

Satoko had developed excellent relations with her husband's parents. When she raised her wish to move into her mother's flat when her eldest son started school, her mother-in-law was very supportive. Although Satoko's husband was their first son, and his younger brother lived far away, near Tokyo, the mother said that the younger son would eventually return to Kobe-city to care for them in their old age, since his wife's family also lived in Kobe-city. The mother was happy that Satoko's husband would move in with Satoko's mother and care for her when the time came. It was an unexpectedly encouraging response for Satoko. She suspected that her mother-in-law's response derived from her traumatic experiences with her own mother-in-law, which might have made her determined to avoid a similar situation for her daughter-in-law.

Satoko's 1997 plan for the future was to eventuate in March 2001, just before her eldest son started school. The whole family would move into her mother's more spacious flat. Satoko said, 'Mum will take the older one to school and pick him up in the afternoon so that he will not become a *kagikko* [latchkey child].' Satoko would continue to drop the younger son at a childcare centre, and her mother would also pick him up later. However, Satoko's worries continued.

SATOKO: I've no idea what I'll do in the school holidays. It'll be too much for my mum to look after him all day for a month. That's why a childcare centre is great.
KO: What would you like to be in five years, say, when you're 35?
SATOKO: Not so many changes, I hope. We'll be living in Mum's flat, but I'll still be working until eight or ten at night. I suppose I'll still be slaving away, complaining with no one to listen to me. Just like now [laughs].
KO: You may be working closer to home by then if your request is successful.
SATOKO: No use counting on that. No one will have me.

(26 December 2000)

Perhaps it was Satoko's nature to worry about the future and complain about immediate dissatisfactions. It was also in her nature to effectively manage what seem to an outsider to be extremely demanding daily routines she faced.

Noshie: Between two worlds

Noshie was a third-generation Korean. Her paternal grandmother came to Japan at the age of three, and had lost the Korean language when she met her Korean-speaking mother-in-law. Before she left Korea, Noshie's grandmother had been strictly instructed not to use the Korean language in Japan. Noshie's father was born in Japan and received Japanese schooling. Noshie's mother died when she was two years old. Her father remarried, and he and his wife lived with his parents for a while, but because of problems between the new wife and his parents, the two moved out, leaving Noshie to be brought up by her grandparents in *shitamachi* Sakura-ward. Growing up in an area inhabited by many Koreans, it was only when she was in grade five that Noshie realised that she was different from 'Japanese' and was a Korean. When she was in the second year of high school, she moved to her father's new family in the city centre following conflict with her grandfather.

Noshie got along well with her younger step-sister, but not with her step-mother, a fact that she often shared with her friends at high school in 1989–90.

While studying commerce at Sasaki High, Noshie was a cheerful, outgoing and sociable girl. She had a wide range of friends, and was able to move from one group of students to another with ease. I recall being impressed with the way she could converse equally well with a group of studious girls and then with the group known for delinquent behaviour. She talked openly about her Korean background with her friends, both Korean and Japanese. Some teachers, however, considered her to be loud and disruptive, and did not think highly of her. Noshie wanted what she considered to be a 'proper' clerical job, but failed in an employment examination. Her teachers urged Noshie to attempt second-round offers but she remained reluctant, which puzzled the teachers.

Noshie was one of the small number of Sasaki High graduates who had no job lined up by the time of the graduation ceremony in February 1990. Her original plan was to find a permanent clerical position while working casually. Her father, however, insisted that one's first job was very important and meant a clean start in adult life, and arranged a job through his friend. It was a checkout position at a new branch of a chain restaurant located one hour by train from her home. Although reluctant initially, she was persuaded to take up the job with a verbal promise that she could move within three months to a clerical position at the headquarters of the chain in the city centre.

For a while after the restaurant opened, the place was so busy that she worked from 10 a.m. to 10 p.m. with only a five-minute lunch break. She developed blisters on her feet.

NOSHIE: I thought of quitting, but my dad told me to stay at least a month. But because I was so exhausted, I took a day off in protest. They said, 'We are to blame to a degree by making you work without a break.' But I know I was wrong not to even ring them. So I went back to work.

(26 January 1992)

Meanwhile, three permanent workers at the restaurant resigned one by one. One girl became afflicted with a kind of mental illness where she lost her sense of taste due to the monotonous nature of the work. Another woman found it intolerable to have nothing to do at the cash register when there were no customers to serve, and resigned after two months.

NOSHIE: I didn't find the work interesting, but I thought that I would eventually be doing clerical work at the main office ... But nothing happened after four months and I started to get worried. I talked to a branch manager, who contacted the head office and then told me, 'Your desk is waiting for you.' But still nothing happened ... In the end, Dad complained to the company, and I got a transfer.

(26 January 1992)

The clerical job that she had long wanted differed from her expectations. Noshie did not like the new office. It was in a department of the head office that included numerous small companies (restaurants, hotels, shops, etc.). In the same office she worked alongside 20 workers, only five of whom were clerical workers, the rest being senior management staff whom she described as *erai-san* (literally, Mr Clever). Having joined the office at an unusual time (normally new recruits join in April), Noshie felt awkward. She believed that what she had learned at school, such as word processing and book-keeping, were useful for her new job, but after a year in the position she started feeling that she was not suited to it.

NOSHIE: I know that I wanted this job so much. But to tell the truth, I don't like some tasks. When I am asked to do detailed profit calculations and so on, I feel stressed out. But I do like some things. I was in charge of making ads for display and for direct mail, such as 'Our spaghetti is nice'. When I first saw an advertisement that I had created at a branch restaurant, I felt, 'Wow!' I can't explain the feeling well. When return envelopes came to the office containing my word-processing work, I felt good. It's strange, because when my boss said that my work was good I didn't feel this, but when I saw with my own eyes my work being used ... you know, I got motivated [*yaruki ga detekita*]. If I only had to do this sort of work, it would be great. But the reality is different, of course.

(26 January 1992)

Noshie thus experienced some joy in her seemingly mundane clerical job.

Noshie was unhappy with working conditions initially. Her pay was lower than her contemporaries', which she attributed to the fact that she had entered the company without a 'proper' (*chanto shita*) examination. She worked from 9.00 to 5.30 p.m. five days a week. The work was not demanding. And the company adopted a policy of 'no overtime work'. This meant that usually she could go home at 5.50 p.m. But at other times, no matter how much overtime she did, she would not get paid for it at all. Given that she was dissatisfied with both the work content and conditions, she was thinking of resigning.

In 1992 Noshie earned about 100,000 yen per month. She deposited half of her salary into an untouchable term account, as instructed by her father. When Noshie first lived with her step-family, her father suggested that she not contribute to the household budget but instead save for her own marriage. She used the remaining 50,000 yen for herself, including transport and lunch expenses. She felt that she received monthly pocket money of 50,000 yen, rather than an income. In that sense, Noshie did not think that receiving a regular income gave her a sense of adulthood. In her second year of work she decided to leave her father's family for more independence. Around this time her grandmother suffered a mental breakdown – which Noshie attributed to her grandfather's difficult nature – and left her husband to live alone. The family felt that someone needed to live with the elderly woman since she had suffered from heart problems. Noshie volunteered to live with her, and liked this arrangement since she had always loved her like her own mother. Her father contributed financially, but Noshie felt responsible for her grandmother. It was partly for this reason that she was hesitant about leaving her job.

Noshie considered herself lucky, at least in terms of her work environment. She never faced bullying at work, in contrast to some of her friends' experiences. She made many mistakes, but bosses and seniors said, 'That's OK. Persevere and try harder [*gambatte*].' But she did feel uncomfortable working with female university graduates on a daily basis. This was her first direct continuous personal contact with such people. She had in the past had casual and one-off encounters with such graduates and their aspirations, but she was now *required* to maintain pleasant daily contact with them. Noshie saw these unfamiliar women as coming from 'proper' families and living on the other side of town, and almost automatically associated them with their families' wealth, fathers' occupations and places of residence. When referring to these women, she used expressions such as *sodachi ga chigau* (literally, having a different upbringing) and *ojôsan* (proper unmarried ladies), and differentiated herself from them by referring to herself as being 'born and bread in *shitamachi*'. She found it demanding to maintain a routine conversation with these women, because of what she described as different past experiences. She did manage to keep pleasant relationships with them but did not feel comfortable being with them continuously. While curious of, and friendly with, these female graduates, Noshie felt distant from them. At this point I was curious to ask if she had felt the same about me when I was at her school two years previously. She responded, 'Well, I didn't have to be with you all the time, even though you were hanging around school all day, when I was getting to know you.'

Noshie knew that the company was aware of her Korean background when they accepted her. Her father's friend who introduced her to the company telephoned shortly before she started work and said, 'This company doesn't care about your Korean nationality. So don't worry.' No one mentioned Noshie's Korean background, despite the fact that the company had not previously employed Koreans. Noshie used her Japanese name, as she had long done; and suspected that her colleagues were unaware of her nationality. It was not that she wanted to cover her identity, but saw no reason to bring up the issue. It was later in the year that Noshie learned by accident from a workmate that some of her colleagues knew of her *zainichi* background.

NOSHIE: One day we were having lunch together and talked about the upcoming election. I said, 'Since my family is Korean we don't receive notification to vote.' My colleague said, 'Oh, I thought that you were concerned about other staff knowing of your Korean background.' I said, 'Really?' She went on, 'I thought that you were concerned about it, so I haven't mentioned it.' I said, 'No, not at all, I'm not bothered.' And we laughed. There are people who don't like Koreans, but I can usually tell after talking to them for a while. I don't talk about my background to those people ... there's no need to aggravate the situation, is there? You see, I grew up in an area where there were lots of Koreans. I haven't had any bullying personally, including here at work. That aspect of this company is great. I know a Sasaki High friend who quit her job because of bullying. She didn't get anti-Korean remarks directly, but one of her colleagues, not knowing her Korean background, said negative things about Koreans. They didn't mean to hurt her, but she felt so uncomfortable that she eventually left. Wait, come to think of it, I had a similar experience at the restaurant.

KO: What did they say?

NOSHIE: Well, I casually said, 'Although I now live in A-town, I used to live in B-ku.' Then one of them said, 'B-ku? That must be annoying [*urusai*].' I was wondering what she meant by 'annoying'. Then she said, 'Because there are many Koreans there.' I couldn't say anything and kept quiet.

(26 January 1992)

Although everyone at work knew about her *zainichi* background, Noshie never considered adopting her Korean name. She showed me a photograph of the Adult Day ceremony organised by the Kobe municipal council. She wore a colourful *chogori* ethnic costume. The photo included several of her Korean friends in *chogori*, Orie, another Korean woman in this study, in kimono, and Japanese friends in kimono.

When I met her early in 1992 she did not have a steady boyfriend, and had no plans to marry in the near future. While she and her family considered it ideal for her to marry a fellow *zainichi*, she knew this would be difficult since young people did not identify themselves as *zainichi* until they became close. She understood the reason why some Koreans chose an arranged marriage.

NOSHIE: I've been told that the most important thing about marriage is that you can get along with your partner's family ... Otherwise, even if you love him, you wouldn't be happy. You know some people elope because they couldn't get their family's approval?

SEKIE: It's romantic, isn't it?

NOSHIE: Well, I know some people who were happy after eloping. But if you want to get along with your partner's relatives, I think you need to make an effort.

(26 January 1992)

Noshie had seen many marriage breakdowns while living with her grandparents, and seemed willing to listen to comments from her relatives.

Noshie had settled into a stable routine when the 1995 earthquake occurred. She was living with her paternal grandmother on the third floor of a council housing complex. The damage to the flat was considerable; it was later classified as 'half-destroyed' [*hankai*]. Plates and bowls came down and were broken, but the flat itself was habitable. She was scared to see surrounding houses burnt down to the ground. Initially Noshie and her grandmother went to a refuge (a nearby school), but did not stay there long.

NOSHIE: So many kids were running around there. My grandma had bad legs, so we were afraid that these kids would bump into her. Grandma said that she couldn't sleep and wanted to go home. Neighbours said, 'What will you do if there's another earthquake? Stay here.' But Grandma said, 'If the apartment block falls, this refuge will fall, too. There's not much difference.' She was stubborn. So we were there only one day and went home. As soon as we got home from the refuge, she told me to fill up the bath. I said, 'What are you talking about?' Anyway, to please her I did that and filled up lots of containers. It saved a lot of work later, since the water was cut off soon after that. It was hard work to carry buckets of water upstairs, even to the third floor. Can you imagine carrying those buckets to the fifteenth floor? The lifts weren't working. I thought I should listen more to old people then.

(22 November 1997)

Noshie did not go to work for a week. The company building was intact but all the surrounding buildings were ruined. The company asked only those whose homes had not been significantly damaged in the quake to return to work, since the offices needed to be cleaned up. Noshie had to walk there. Since it took so long to get there, she thought about buying a small motorbike. She was glad to return to work since staying at home all day was boring.

Later in the same year Noshie was transferred to the private secretaries' room (*hisho-ka*) at the company. This resulted from a series of events following the earthquake. In the disaster a private secretary lost her rented apartment – it was completely destroyed. Her mother, in a provincial prefecture, insisted that her daughter return home. There was a problem in replacing her, however, as few women wanted the position. Several girls were transferred into the job, but none lasted long, saying that senior secretary in the office was too difficult to work with.

NOSHIE: So it was my turn to give it a go, since I wasn't allowed to refuse the transfer. When I started talking with her, I found she wasn't too bad. I mean, she was strong-minded and strict [*kitsui hito*] and sometimes scary, as I'd heard from others, but that was only when she was talking about work. Anyway, she is really good at her work, and has high standards that she wants me to have. She is strict and fierce, but only when she has to be, in order to get the work done. The more I got to know her, the better I got along with her.

KO: But then you've always been good at getting along with different people.

ORIE: Among us she is the best at that [laughs]. People find her very easy to get along with.

SEKIE: Noshie doesn't make enemies.

NOSHIE: So we get along very well in the office.

(22 November 1997)

Basically, her job involved working directly for the company president and other senior managers, doing clerical work as instructed and miscellaneous tasks (*zatsuyô*) such as making tea and cleaning rooms. Compared with her previous position, she had less of a workload. She could even make personal telephone calls, and do her own personal business, when not busy. She did not have to work overtime either. She also found unexpected practical value in the seemingly boring job.

NOSHIE: My senior is a 36-year-old woman. She used to be private secretary to the president of XYZ Bank, and is very proper, effective and efficient [*kicchiri*]. She's been teaching me things like manners. I see it as 'training for a bride' [*hanayome shugyô*]. As you know, private secretaries have usually taken a special course at a *senmongakkô* [post-secondary vocational education institution] or junior college, and have got qualifications in deportment. I've got nothing like that. She's taught me from square one, like how to serve tea. She teaches me very properly – even flower-arranging. I'm grateful.

(22 November 1997)

The senior also encouraged her to take up *naraigoto* (lessons in skills and/or self-cultivation): 'Women of your age should be cultivating yourselves by taking up more *naraigoto*.' It seemed that the senior woman treated Noshie like a younger sister, and was willing to train her both for work and for private life. Noshie, rather than considering this offer paternalistic or autocratic, or an imposition of middle-class values, accepted it gratefully and treated it as a great learning opportunity. Noshie confided in her about her personal life, for instance about being *zainichi* and her relationship with a Japanese man. The senior woman seemed to have had a significant impact on her perspective, as we will see later.

When I met her in 1997 Noshie presented herself as 'settled'. She wore simple but elegantly cut clothes with no make-up. She did not hesitate to say that she was content with her work and her colleagues. She was also engaged to her Japanese boyfriend, Oki, whom she had known for five years. Oki grew up in a family of three boys also in *shitamachi* Sakura-ward, and was Noshie's classmate at the local middle school. He studied civil engineering at university after spending a year in full-time preparation for the entrance examinations. In mid-1992, the two met at a wedding party of a mutual friend. Since graduation, Oki had been working for a small construction company as a site manager. His parents' house was demolished in the earthquake, and the family moved to a newly built house in a north-western suburb of Kobe-city. As Noshie had expected, Oki's family was not happy with their son's marriage to a Korean girl, but they eventually agreed to it. In particular, Noshie was disappointed that his family, despite having known about her Korean background from the early period of their relationship, had not brought this up earlier. Her Korean background did not matter to them as long as she was just a girlfriend of their son, but the possibility of marriage raised grave concerns. The case demonstrates how what other women in the study called 'complexities' arise when a marriage is proposed. In any case, Noshie remained optimistic about her marriage, and wanted to think that reconciliation had been achieved.

Noshie's family were not as strict in their expectations about 'Korean marriage' as were some of her friends. Her paternal grandmother, according to her, was very 'enlightened' (*hiraketriru*) in that she considered one's nationality irrelevant; but her grandfather was strict. Many of Noshie's uncles had married Japanese. Noshie suspected that she received more pressure to marry a Korean man because of her gender.

NOSHIE: Because I'm a woman, they were more eager to get me to marry a
        Korean man. They think that Korean women married to Japanese men
        face a hard time.

(22 November 1997)

As experienced by many *zainichi* women, Noshie was forced to attend one meeting as a prelude to a potential arranged marriage in order to diffuse relatives' constant pressure. She already had a steady Japanese boyfriend, Oki, and felt guilty about attending the meeting without any possible intention to marry the man, but just to please her relatives. Noshie was aware that her relatives would prefer her to marry a Korean man, and that such a meeting was one of the few ways to meet eligible Korean men.

Noshie was worried that she did not possess the knowledge and skills in 'Japanese customs' to marry a Japanese man. She revealed her concern to her senior colleague at work and was encouraged by her replay – that there was diversity within so-called 'Japanese customs' and 'Korean customs', depending on regions and families, and on marrying she would therefore need to learn new customs anyway.

ORIE (A *ZAINICHI* GIRL):   For example, the Korean *hôji* [annual Buddhist ser-
        vice for deceased relatives] is very different from the Japanese one. My
        brother's Japanese fiancée was invited to attend a *hôji* to see what it was
        like. She was overwhelmed and said, 'I can't possibly do that.' But she
        has been making an effort to understand this, it seems.
NOSHIE: I talked about the Korean *hôji* to my senior. She said that *hôji* is
        different in different parts of Japan, and in different schools of Bud-
        dhism, and that whoever a woman marries she has to learn the custom

of the husband's family. She encouraged me, saying 'You will manage
OK.' You see, I was very worried about the Japanese customs. I didn't
know them and thought I had to learn a whole new set of customs.

ORIE: Yes. I don't know how to make the New Year dishes [*osechi ryôri*]. If I
marry a Japanese man, I will have to do it and it will be the first time!

KO: But there are so many Japanese young women who have never made
osechi ryôri [laughs].

NOSHIE: That's exactly what I hadn't understood before. My senior said,
'Don't worry about the Japanese customs, since many Japanese don't
know them. That's why there are so many books on New Year food and
ready-made dishes on the market.'

(22 November 1997)

Noshie was also aware that the customs themselves were changing. When
she was small, the *hôji* and other customs were very lavish and everyone was
expected to contribute enormously. In recent years many of these events had
been simplified. She noted that fewer people came to their families' *hôji*, that
the events were on a much smaller scale, and that ready-made dishes could
be offered, rather than expecting all female relatives to start preparing the
food two days in advance. From this year, Noshie's family started visiting
surviving relatives in Korea instead of holding *hôji*.

Noshie was deeply moved by her recent visit to Korea. She had visited
Korea before, but this time was different. Noshie, her father, her paternal
grandmother and two cousins visited the grandmother's siblings, nieces and
nephews. They were hosted extremely well. Noshie noted, in particular, that
her grandmother and all elderly people received much more respect than in
Japan; and felt that she should emulate this. Her grandmother and one of
her cousins acted as an interpreter, since Noshie had little knowledge of the
language. Her father could communicate in a basic way, having informally
taken up the language when he was over 30. Her cousin had studied the
language formally, and impressed Noshie. For the first time in her life, she
contemplated learning Korean.

Noshie married Oki in mid-1998, and they went to Central America for
their honeymoon. She soon fell pregnant – it was a honeymoon baby. She
resigned from her position when she was five months pregnant. It was not an
easy decision. The company did not require women to resign after giving
birth, and had a system of maternity and child-rearing leave. Given that
Japan was undergoing a recession, Noshie was fully aware of the difficulties
in finding comparable employment.

NOSHIE: I thought about it a lot. Should I persevere [*gambaru*] by using
maternity leave? It would be awkward for a private secretary to be
heavily pregnant, since the work (serving tea, making copies for the
company president and his guests) is so conspicuous. In the end I decided to leave at that point because I was afraid that colleagues would

have to cover for my absences. I didn't want to cause any inconvenience [*meiwaku o kakeru*] to my colleagues.

(30 October 1999)

Thus she quit a job that she liked, and prepared for motherhood.

When I met Noshie in late 2000, the couple had been living for almost two years in a small, prefabricated house owned by Oki's parents in *shitamachi* Sakura-ward. Noshie's in-laws had lost their house (it was burned to the ground) at the time of the earthquake. Her husband's uncle lived in a hastily built prefabricated house on the site while waiting for his own flat to be built. When he moved out of the house, it became available but needed to be renovated. So after marrying, the couple lived with Oki's parents for two months while the renovation took place. Their decision to move into this prefabricated house was mainly based on financial grounds, as they did not think that they could afford rent.

Noshie was happy to have a daughter. She confessed that she suffered from post-natal blues (*ikuji noirôze*) to a degree, which she attributed to the fact that her daily routine was completely disrupted by the baby.

NOSHIE: My world-view has changed since I had a baby. Yes, I felt grown up [*otona*]. When I first saw the family medical record [*hokensho*] which lists the names of father, mother and child, I felt, 'Wow, we are a family!' I am happy, I don't get tired of looking after my baby all day. I'm often told that a child is a baby only for a short time, but it doesn't seem like that to me [*pin to konai*]. But I want enjoy this period fully.

(30 October 1999)

Noshie's husband was regularly transferred to various construction sites and his weekday absence made the task of bringing up the baby extremely demanding. In the year the baby was born, he was assigned to distant jobs, and came home only at weekends, so that during the week Noshie had to manage on her own. She appreciated the support she received from her grandmother, who lived nearby. Her husband's parents looked after the baby on Fridays, feeling somewhat responsible for the demanding time that Noshie suffered due to their son's absence. Noshie looked forward to Oki's transfer back to Kobe-city the following year, but was unhappy that in the future he could be transferred to distant jobs again on a regular basis. It was the nature of his job.

NOSHIE: So he's thinking seriously of leaving the company if that happens again. He misses seeing our daughter grow. I need him now. I asked him not to do this while she is small. You know, he has changed so much since our baby came. I thought I knew him well, but I've discovered new things about him. I didn't expect that he would be such a good father and so reliable [*tanomoshii*].

(26 December 2000)

In 2000 she seemed to be enjoying motherhood.

KO: What's your daily routine?

NOSHIE: Well, in the morning, my daughter plays at home while I do the housework. I normally let her play in front of our house so that she can run around outside. After having lunch at home, she has a nap. Then we often go to a park. I chat with other mothers at the park. Sometimes my close friends come to our house with their children. Actually, I have a good friend who has a child the same age as my girl. We sometimes go to playgrounds and a play centre where she can play with different kinds of toys. In the children's hall run by the municipal council there's a kids' club that you can join for free. They organise things like a Christmas party. I've become close to some of the mothers there. One of them is an ex-kindergarten teacher, from whom I've learned a lot about children.

KO: Are there maternal health nurses in that building, too?

NOSHIE: Yes, they're on the second floor, and they teach us various things.

(26 December 2000)

Noshie was disappointed that she could no longer go out with friends, but developed different ways of socialising. Often she would visit friends with the baby, or they came to her house with their children. They often went to playgroups together.

Noshie's relationship with her in-laws looked peaceful, at least outwardly. After all, they had been generous in letting the couple live in the house on their land rent-free. While the arrangement enabled the couple to save, Noshie felt that they had been accumulating a sense of debt (*kari*), which she disliked. Besides, since her husband was the eldest of three sons, her in-laws were convinced that the couple would live with them in the near future, and that the current arrangement (of the couple and their child living in an uncomfortable prefabricated house) was temporary. It must be said that prior to her marriage Noshie had accepted that she was marrying the eldest son of the family and would care for his aged parents. This had not changed. She was willing to care for them when they were so old that they needed help, but did not wish to live with them now.

NOSHIE: I want to move out of the house. My in-laws want us to live with them. So they see the current arrangement as temporary and we will soon join them. I think they are convinced that will happen. That's why they don't charge us rent. I've thought about it a lot, and think we'd better move out of the house. I think we should tell them we've been saving as much as we can while not paying rent, and that we've been looking for a house. Otherwise, they will stay convinced that we will move in with them soon. I've accepted what they've said so far, but I'm reluctant to live with them right now.

(26 December 2000)

She became firm about this, having observed her in-laws firsthand while living with them for two months. Noshie considered that the in-laws had excessively intervened in the couple's affairs, such as by insisting that she purchase various items for the baby. She thought that her father-in-law was too self-centred (*wagamama*), and felt sorry for her mother-in-law, who tried to please him all the time.

In late 2000 Noshie was generally happy, despite the on-going problems mentioned above. She was optimistic about the future. She wanted to have another baby soon so that she could return to the workforce.

NOSHIE: I want to have another child, hopefully next year. We want a boy – well, my husband's parents are keen to have a boy. So I've been reading books on how to conceive a boy! But I don't know if it will work.

(26 December 2000)

Sekie: 'It was worth the hardship to become a nurse in the end'

Sekie was born and grew up in *shitamachi* Sakura-ward, and went to local schools before studying commerce at Sasaki High. She lived with her parents and a younger sister. As a high school student, she had long plaits and wore large glasses, and was friendly and articulate. I recall that she stood out from her peers at Sasaki High because she had a clear vision about her post-school destination – nursing training – an option considered by many of her classmates to be an unattractive job option which was seen to be extremely demanding both physically and mentally. When Sekie was at primary school, she had wanted to become a model, since she saw it as one of the few jobs where her height would be an advantage.

Her wish to become a nurse came later. She thought that she was influenced by her aunt commenting on her gratitude for the nursing she had received during a stay in hospital. Sekie saw firsthand how competent and 'cool' (*kakko-ii*) a nurse could be.

SEKIE: I was amazed how efficient but kind and thoughtful the nurse was to us when my uncle died in hospital. I thought, 'Wow, ordinary people can't do that.' But when I talked about nursing with my friends, I started thinking it might suit me. I'm not put off by the sight of blood, like many girls are. I'm quite organised. I like helping other people, you know. I think nurses are quite cool. Besides, what other kind of job would I get? I didn't want to be an office worker like my mum. She thought nursing was a great job. My dad wasn't interested – I mean, he was always tired after work and I hardly talked to him those days.

(13 October 1989)

She chose to apply to Kawa Surgical Clinic to train as a nurse because one of her friends' elder sisters had worked there and recommended it. Sekie had such confidence in this clinic that she did not bother investigating other clinics that might have offered better conditions, which she later came to regret. She asked the school to request a recruitment form from Kawa Surgical Clinic. Sekie was accepted by the clinic, which then required her to sit entrance examinations for a private nursing college and a municipal nursing college after her graduation from high school. She passed both examinations and opted for the municipal college.

Sekie started working as a trainee assistant nurse (*kango minarai*) at the clinic one week prior to the commencement of college. She soon discovered how tough the job was. She was a live-in trainee in the morning and in the evening, and studied at the nursing college in the afternoon. She was to be paid the basic monthly salary of 90,000 yen by the clinic, which was also to pay her monthly school fee of 20,000 yen.

SEKIE: We were supposed to start at 8 a.m. to prepare for the day before the qualified nurses started at nine. But we just couldn't get through the work. So we'd start at seven, work until midday, grab a quick lunch in ten minutes, then catch a bus to the nursing college. The classes went from 1.30 to 4.30. Then we'd go back to the clinic by bus, have dinner, and start the evening shift at 5.30. Patient consultations finished at 7.30, but we worked until eight and sometimes until midnight – there were so much work to be done. Soon one of the new recruits left, and moved to another clinic. She was from the country, and perhaps found the place too harsh.

(26 January 1992)

About one month later, the father of one of the girls complained to the clinic about the dormitory, saying it differed from what was represented on the recruitment card. The dormitory lacked sufficient space because the clinic had taken in eight girls that year, more than normal. As a result, Sekie was asked to commute since her home was closest to the clinic. The assistant nurse trainees were accommodated in an ordinary house of eight rooms, and three girls slept in a six-*tatami* room. Sekie described the situation as 'horrible', in that a new girl could not even enter her room without going through her senior's room.

SEKIE: The clinic wants us to live close by so it can count on us in an emergency. It costs too much to get qualified nurses. A qualified nurse's rate is three times as much as ours.

(26 January 1992)

Sekie thus came to develop her own understanding of how the system of apprentice assistant nurses worked. Thanks to the indignant father, the clinic rented flats for new recruits in May, and Sekie was one of the trainees asked to move there.

The work was exhausting for new trainees. Although they were supposed to work five days a week, it was really six days, since on Saturdays they still worked in the morning and went to school in the afternoon. On Sundays they took turns, and those on Sunday duty received one day off in the week; but since they still attended school in the afternoon they had no break at all during that week. Furthermore, from June, new trainees were put on a night shift, which aggravated the situation. A trainee on night shift worked in the morning, went to school in the afternoon, worked in the evening and stayed at the clinic overnight (visiting patients, doing paperwork and attending to the ambulance). She worked the next morning, went to school, and could finally rest that night. This meant about 48 hours without rest. Again, the concerned father complained.

SEKIE: It was so demanding [*tsurai*], and I wanted to give up. But this father really saved us! Because of him the arrangement was changed a bit. Would you believe, one of us collapsed at school because of exhaustion. In normal classes we could just sit and even sleep. But if there was a practical session, those who had night shift would be on their feet for two days! We were just too tired. The college knew how tough the clinic was on trainees, but did nothing about it.

KO: Why?

SEKIE: Because the college was supported by a doctors' association. Of course, the doctors at our clinic were also members. So the nursing teachers, who were employees of the college, couldn't ask the clinic to make life easier for us girls. They pretended not to notice our problems. But when somebody collapsed during a practical, it was a different matter. Suddenly we no longer had to work in the morning after a night shift. I think that would have been in August.

(26 January 1992)

After this change, Sekie continued her demanding routine, questioning if she had made a wise decision in taking on nursing. She also lamented that she could not keep up with her school friends. She was disappointed with nursing as an occupation at the clinic, since she considered that nurses there were under such time pressure that they no longer displayed what she had idealised as 'kind-heartedness' to their patients. Sekie feared that she was becoming like them. But she did meet nurses who she considered 'real nurses' at a teaching hospital where she did practice sessions.

Although her work restricted her social life, Sekie did have a relationship. She went out with a visiting doctor for a while. When he proposed marriage, she dropped him. She thought that she was too young at 20, that she had not finished her training, and, most importantly, that the liaison would cause considerable discomfort to her mother, who would feel out of place meeting the man's relatives.

SEKIE: If he'd been a self-made rich man, it would have been OK. Family status, in particular the known family lineage, was a problem. His father was a university professor, and his mother was a daughter of the president of a large company. All his relatives lived in a different world from us. I didn't know if I could handle it.

NOSHIE (SEKIE'S CLOSE FRIEND): I agree. If I had been you, I would have thought the same. If he were just rich, it would have been different. In this case, his world is just too different from ours.

SEKIE: I might have handled it OK, but I would have felt sorry for my mum.

KO: But you two liked each other, didn't you?

SEKIE: Very much.

KO: Did you talk to your mum about this?

SEKIE: Oh, I said hypothetically, 'If I married a rich man, would it bother you?' She said, 'Of course it would. I can't associate with people like that.'

(26 January 1992)

Sekie clearly distinguished marriage from a romantic relationship, and understood that romantic love alone was insufficient for a good marriage. For her, an appropriate marriage required parental approval on both sides and equivalent social status. She also saw a distinction between social status and wealth; it was the former that was significant.

When I met Sekie in January 1992, she had persevered at her workplace for 21 months. She was positive about her career, and displayed confidence in her work. She explained to me that it was only recently that she had started feeling better about her career. She also felt a sense of personal growth. It happened when she experienced a moment of 'enlightenment' at work, which gave her the motivation to struggle on in the face of difficulties.

SEKIE: Yes, I do feel somehow that I've grown recently. You know that I hated the job and wanted to leave many times. That was until the final practical placement last December. During that placement at a teaching hospital, something happened to me – nothing special, but important for me. When I was taking care of a patient with shoulder paralysis, an idea of supporting her without hurting her occurred to me, and I suggested this to my supervising nurse, since we were required to report everything to her. She said to me, 'It's an excellent idea. You have been observant and very thoughtful.' I thought, 'This is nursing, noticing the needs of a patient that ordinary people don't, and helping accordingly.' Then, I started to feel good about myself and my job. I started thinking that I had complained too much about my work without making an effort to understand it. Then I started feeling a sense of growth – I mean that I was becoming an adult.

(26 January 1992)

Sekie was nearing the end of her training as an assistant nurse (*jun-kangofu*). She was preparing for the end-of-term examinations. If she passed, she would graduate from the college and be eligible for the qualifying examination. She knew that she had to work at the clinic for a year after she qualified as an assistant nurse. This is a system called 'service for gratitude' (*orei hôkô*). Although not legally binding, it means that after qualifying, a trainee is expected to work for one year for the clinic that has paid for her training. Otherwise, she has to repay the fees. Sekie questioned the fairness of the system, and told me that her lecturers at the college considered the system illegal. But no one so far had challenged the system, because, as Sekie reasoned, nurses feared that their employment prospects would be affected since their employers all supported the system.

It was around that time that Sekie contemplated her long-term career plan post the 'service for gratitude' period. She thought of studying further and upgrading her qualification to nurse (*sei-kangofu*).

SEKIE: I think I know my work much better now. I do have a wish to learn more about it, but I'd have to go to a higher school. You see, an assistant nurse is not a real nurse. At small private clinics like ours you see many assistant nurses, but large hospitals no longer employ them, because we've only learned the basics. In order to learn real nursing, you have to study further. At one teaching hospital, a supervising nurse asked us trainees if we were planning to get a higher qualification. I said that I hadn't decided. She said, 'You must. There's a large gap in the level of professionalism between doctors and nurses because of the system of assistant nurses. Nurses must gain more professional qualifications.' There's been talk about abolishing the assistant nurses in the public system. But it continues because the doctors' association has so much power. Doctors in private practice like at our clinic want to have assistant nurses because they are much cheaper. They can also have trainees like us, who do all kinds of things around clinics even more cheaply! I used to envy the girls who worked at small clinics without hospital facilities. They had no night shifts, no evening work, and sometimes earned more than I did. But I later realised that I had learned a much wider range of skills at our clinic, which was not a bad thing.

(26 January 1992)

After 21 months in the job, Sekie started accepting her nursing career, and waited for the certification examination.

After qualifying as an assistant nurse in March 1992, Sekie did one year of 'service for gratitude' at the clinic. Since she disliked the clinic, she had no intention of staying there beyond the required time. During 1993 she found a position at a small general practice clinic in a wealthy inner-city area through an employment magazine. Actually she had regularly passed the clinic on her way to nursing school, and had thought that it would be a pleasant place to work. She applied for the position and succeeded over nine other applicants.

The clinic was staffed by a doctor (the owner), two nurses (a qualified nurse and Sekie), an acupuncturist (*hari no sensei*) and two receptionists. Sekie worked four days (9 a.m. to 7 p.m., with an afternoon break from 1.00 to 4.00), and half a day on Saturday. It offered a regular lifestyle and no overtime work, and the work relationships were pleasant. The doctor was a 52-year-old Japan-born Chinese, who had gone to Kobe ethnic Chinese School and then to a Japanese university. Sekie described him as 'very energetic, both emotionally and physically'. Clients included many Japan-born Chinese from afar, as well as local residents. Many foreign residents were clients, since the doctor spoke English as well as Chinese. Sekie earned much more than she'd dreamt of, and was content with the work and her colleagues. This made up for the hardship of the previous three years.

Sekie soon settled into the new job and the daily routine. She went out with several men and had fun, and resumed the active social life that she had been used to at school. Then the Hanshin–Awaji earthquake struck.

SEKIE: At the time, I didn't know what was happening. As soon as I went outside, I knew it was an earthquake. Everybody was heading for the refuge [*hinansho*], a school gym in our neighbourhood. After we got there, many more people arrived. It was packed and we had to sleep crammed in together. A nasty cold started spreading. We'd thought that our house would have been destroyed, since people at the refuge said hardly any houses were left standing in our area, but I went to have a look anyway. It was still there! There were no tiles on the roof, but it was habitable, so we went back home. Then a fire started in the area. It was so quiet – I mean no cars and no people – that you could hear the sound of houses burning. The fire reached our next-door neighbour. By then we had packed what we could and were ready to go. Then suddenly the wind changed direction. Our house wasn't touched. It was lucky, I suppose ... but I'm not sure. We repaired the house and went on living there. We must have been at the refuge for only two days. It was weird living in our old house. There were so few houses around. The others had collapsed or been burned down and the people had gone to temporary accommodation. I was scared walking in the evening. So dark and no people. There was a rumour that Vietnamese people were stealing things. The water was off for a month. The power was put back on before the water was. The gas was much later. We went to a public bathhouse.

(22 November 1997)

After the earthquake Sekie did not think about her work for a while. She suspected that the clinic would be too damaged for normal business. She was wrong. Although shitamachi Sakura-ward, where Sekie lived, received the heaviest damage for the reasons that I mentioned in Chapter 2, the clinic was in Matsu-ward and it was providing services to an increasing number of injured patients arriving from afar.

SEKIE: I couldn't think of my work at the time. Virtually all the buildings
had collapsed as far as I could see from home. I just didn't have time or
energy to spare [*yoyū*], and didn't contact the clinic for a while. There
were no public phones either. But my *sensei* [the doctor] knew that my
area was the most damaged and told me to take as much time off as I
liked. The clinic wasn't damaged, and he was managing on his own. But
injured people were coming in all the time, so I went back a week after
the earthquake. I cycled to work since there were no trains. I saw lines of
people walking to work in the morning – a spooky sight!

(22 November 1997)

Thus Sekie's life returned to some kind of routine: working during the day
and managing a difficult home front. She considered that her family was
lucky compared with many people in her neighbourhood. Later, Sekie's family
decided to have the damaged house demolished and build a new house on
the site. It was a difficult decision since the house had been built by Sekie's
maternal grandfather before her mother was born. Sekie recalled an old
proverb: 'A builder's own house is strong.' But the family considered it the
opportunity of a lifetime to capitalise on the special loan provided for
earthquake victims. The interest was 0.3 per cent fixed for the entire loan
period. The family lived in a rented flat for three months while the house was
being built.

In early 1997, shortly before I met her again, Sekie became the only nurse
at the small clinic. The other more experienced nurse resigned in order to
pursue a freelance DJ career at a local radio station. Instead of employing
another nurse, the doctor offered Sekie more hours with a salary increase of
50,000 yen, bringing her pay to 230,000–240,000 yen a month after tax.
Sekie reasoned that the clinic saved a lot since a fully qualified nurse's salary
was substantially higher than hers. Sekie found it a comfortable arrangement
as there was not too much work, she was unsupervised, and when there were
no patients she could do whatever she liked, for example read magazines. At
this point she liked the job; it also gave her sufficient money and free time.

Around this time, Sekie started to have second thoughts about pursuing a
higher qualification (nurse or senior nurse, *seikan* or *kôkan*), although she
had been keen on the idea a few years earlier. She feared that the system of
assistant nurses might be abolished in the near future, but at the same time
took the realistic view that many private clinic doctors would oppose such a
move since they benefited from employing inexpensive assistant nurses.
While theatre nursing in large hospitals required fully qualified nurses and
senior nurses, Sekie decided that there were tasks at small clinics that did not
need such high qualifications. Perhaps she was enjoying herself so much after
the strenuous two years as a trainee that she just wanted to have fun. She
took tennis lessons, went out with friends often, and travelled overseas.

In late 1997, when I met her one Saturday afternoon after she had finished
work at the clinic, she was a happy 26-year-old woman with a career. She

looked fashionable in jeans and a black shirt and cardigan, with light make-up that suited her. She was wearing comfortable shoes that suited her work and seemed to have acquired her own style of presentation. She was natural and unpretentious. After having lunch at a restaurant she frequented, we met up with Orie and Noshie. She was a good listener and spoke slowly, a trait that had not changed since her high school days.

According to her friends, Sekie was attractive to young men. She liked her romantic relationships to be for 'play' (*asobi*) and went out with different boyfriends almost every six months, which was difficult for her friends to keep track of.

NOSHIE: One day she introduced me to her boyfriend. He wasn't like the one that she'd been talking about. Then I found out that this man was the *new* boyfriend! That was embarrassing.

(22 November 1997)

When I met Sekie in late 1997, she had been seeing her latest boyfriend once a week for the last six months but did not think it would result in marriage. She described him as 'somebody whom I go out and play with'.

SEKIE: Look, I just can't get serious about a relationship.
KO: How many steady boyfriends have you had so far?
NOSHIE: Hum … I think she's had one or two new boyfriends every year.
KO: That would make a large number over the last eight years! [Noshie, Sekie and Orie laugh]
NOSHIE: When she's involved she's serious about the relationship, and says, 'This time it's different.'
KO: You mean you get tired of the man easily, or a new man appears?
SEKIE: [Laughs] I wonder what it is about me. I just want him to keep a certain distance from me. I know this seems selfish. It's OK when I'm going after him. But when he chases me, I feel that way. When the man gets too serious about the relationship, I just become hesitant.
NOSHIE: Yeah, that's the way it is with you, Sekie, from what I've seen.
ORIE: That's terrible!

(22 November 1997)

Her parents had been urging her to marry for the past two years, but she had taken their concerns lightly. They were aware that she had a steady boy-friend, and wanted her to introduce him to them. But Sekie saw no point in doing so if she had no intention of marrying him. When she saw her friends married young with children, she thought that they were happy but was aware of the restrictions imposed on them. She knew that she was not ready for that. She wanted to enjoy herself for longer.

In mid-1998, several months after I had seen Sekie, I was surprised to receive a letter and a beautiful photo of her wedding. She had married the boyfriend mentioned above, and they had gone overseas for their honeymoon. The event surprised her friends as well, who had long considered Sekie to be a cautious type, who would not decide to marry after only seven months of courting. Ikuo, her husband, was born and bred in Sakura-ward like Sekie, and had worked in different jobs before they met. At the time of their marriage, he was a manager of a pizza chain restaurant, a job for which he had little enthusiasm.

In late 1999 when I met her again, Ikuo was driving a small van for a delivery company, and doing a night course in electrical wiring at a local vocational school (*shokugyô gakkô*). Sekie's father worked in the field, which Sekie suspected might have guided her husband's decision, since Ikuo had no definite desire for a particular occupation; perhaps he was content to get advice from his father-in-law. Sekie's father was happy with Ikuo's decision.

KO: Why did he suddenly become so serious [*majime*]?

SEKIE: Marriage, I think. Even if he'd stayed in that job [manager of a pizza chain restaurant], the prospects weren't good. He must have decided he should have a proper job [*chantoshita shigoto*]. A proper job needs a qualification, you know. Now he studies a lot, so I have free time to myself every day. Also, he doesn't like the fact that I earn more than him. He seems to want to arrange things so that I don't have to work. But I want to work. Working is more enjoyable than just staying at home. I get bored on Thursdays on my day off. Today is great since I can talk to you.

KO: What has changed most since you got married?

SEKIE: Well ... I'm settled emotionally and psychologically. My daily routine hasn't changed, though, since I'm still working full-time. My parents' home is nearby. But just I feel settled [*ochitsuita*].

(9 December 1999)

One year later, her husband finished his course and started working for an internet cabling company. While there were many jobs in his field, the salary was lower than expected. Every day he left home at seven in the morning with his lunch, which Sekie made by getting up at half past six. He came home after eight at night. She left home at half past seven in the morning and was home by seven in the evening. Because of this, Sekie ended up doing most of the housework, which she felt she had no choice about, given the circumstances. Also, she and Ikuo had time off on different days of the week, so she had time alone to do what she liked, and took guitar and golfing lessons and went swimming weekly. Both took English conversation lessons together.

After their marriage, the couple bought a new house near Sekie's parents, using the special loan for earthquake victims.

SEKIE: I was moving out of my parents' house once I was married anyway. I worked out that the loan repayment would be less than rent for a flat, which would be over 100,000 yen, as well as a body corporate fee [*kyôsaihi*] and car park (20,000–30,000 yen). Many people buy flats in high-rise buildings, but I didn't think highly of that. After the earthquake so many new flats were built, but you don't know the quality of the building; I felt they were not well built. Besides, when you come to sell it, you mightn't get what you paid for it. But a detached house will keep its value because of the land. Behind the new house we bought, my younger sister and her husband also bought a detached house. It was so easy to get a loan because of the earthquake; you didn't even need a deposit, and the interest rate was fixed at 0.3 per cent. We got a 35-year loan. I hear that the government is now thinking of extending the period that this loan is available. Many of our friends bought houses or flats using this special loan.

(9 December 1999)

Sekie seemed to be well informed and capable in financial matters. She preferred a detached house on a block of land to a flat because the land would have higher capital gain, and she decided to pay their housing loan monthly rather than with their biannual bonuses, although the latter is very common among young people.

SEKIE: We pay the loan monthly, not by bonuses. Counting on bonuses is bad, you know. You would be in trouble if your bonus was less than expected or, worse still, you might not even get a bonus if your company isn't doing well. I hear stories of people repaying loans by using their savings! If you pay monthly, you know what to expect. If you get a bonus, then you can repay more.

(9 December 1999)

Sekie's own family was close-knit. Her parents, her sister and Sekie lived near one another and often shared meals. Her sister had married a Japanese-American from Hawaii six months after Sekie's wedding. Since he had no relatives in Japan, Sekie's family welcomed him like a real family member. Her sister and her husband purchased a new house right behind Sekie's new house. Later, Sekie and her mother decided to swap houses (although not on the official documents). Sekie and her husband now lived in her parents' house.

SEKIE: It's more convenient for my pregnant sister – coming home late from work. My mum will help her with the baby. Also, our own house was bigger, and so better for a family with a child. Anyway, we won't be having kids in the next ten years, and in that time we want to repay as much of the loan as possible.

(7 December 1999)

It appeared that Sekie's family was matrilineal. Her own parents were in a similar position. Her father married into her mother's family and lived in the in-laws' house. Sekie's husband had a distant relationship with his own parents, even though they lived in the same inner-city suburb.

Sekie was happy with this living arrangement for the time being. Her sister was very grateful to her for being able to live behind their parents' place, particularly after the birth of her baby. Both Sekie and Ikuo often dropped in on their way home from work for a family dinner, which her mother cooked. Seeing her baby niece had an unexpected impact on her. Several of her school friends also had babies that year, including Noshie. She began to think of starting a family in the next five years or so, while Ikuo was keener to start sooner. Sekie contemplated how she could have both: a baby and her nursing career.

SEKIE: I want to continue working at the clinic for a few more years. It's been comfortable and the pay has been good. I don't think of having kids before 33. The clinic doesn't have maternity leave. I think financial stability [*okane no yutori*] is important for relations within a family and a marriage. In ten years, my husband's work will be stable. Then I can perhaps get a job in a large hospital before having children. A large hospital would offer maternity and child-rearing leave, and would have its own childcare centre, free for staff.

(26 December 2000)

Sekie seemed to be well informed about what was involved in bringing up children. She saw this firsthand almost every day with her baby niece. Sekie and Ikuo often looked after the baby so that her sister and her husband could go out. When I had lunch in a private room in a noodle restaurant with Sekie, Noshie and her daughter, Sekie was adept at looking after the one-year-old child when she started to grizzle. Sekie had a clear idea what she wanted over the next few years: a child, maternity leave and the opportunity to return to nursing after that.

Tomoe: 'The Korean bank was comfortable, but agency work suits me better at the moment'

Tomoe is a third-generation Korean. She was born and grew up in Sakura-ward, where a large number of ethnic Koreans lived. She had three sisters and one elder brother, but her brother had left home to go to a university in another city when Tomoe was at primary school. Her father was a second-generation Japan-born Korean, and Tomoe and her sisters had no contact with his relatives for reasons that she did not know. She suspected that complications had occurred in the past. Her maternal grandfather had come from Korea and married a Japanese woman. Both grandparents were dead. Other than her maternal grandfather's nephews and cousins in South Korea, Tomoe's mother's living relatives were all Japanese. Tomoe went to neighbourhood primary and middle schools with many Koreans. She dreamed of becoming a hairdresser while at primary school, but clearly remembered her mother's negative view of this. She chose a data-processing course since she knew that she needed to take a vocational course that would help her obtain a job after high school. Tomoe liked Sasaki High's data-processing course, which had an entry system that gave weight to applicants' middle school achievements rather than just one examination. Being surrounded by many Koreans in her earlier school years, Tomoe was only reminded that she was different from her Japanese peers when she started high school. Then she began to feel that her daily life was somewhat 'different' from that of her friends.

At Sasaki High Tomoe studied data processing (*jôhô shori*) and was part of a friendship group of four (with Moko, Mutsuko and Norimi). Those girls were all Japanese and aware of Tomoe's Korean background. At school I often used to see the four together during breaks, at lunch time and going home. The group shared many outside-school activities as well, and seemed to know one another's daily lives in detail. I noticed at the time that that was why, when conversing, they finished each other's sentences so easily. They sometimes talked about Tomoe's Korean background as well. Tomoe was open about her ethnicity and what it involved to those girls, and later to me, but did not publicly announce it to others. Other classmates seemed aware of it, however. There were two other Korean girls in her class, but Tomoe was not particularly close to them. She respected Ayako, who was an active member of the school's Korean Cultural Study Club (*Chôbunken*, an after-school club where ethnic Koreans learned the Korean language, culture and history, and about human rights issues), but she did not like Kai, who, Tomoe claimed, pretended to be a proper middle-class girl (*ojôsan*) when she was not. Another characteristic that struck me at the time was the extent to which Tomoe was concerned with her appearance. She often advised her friends, and me, on hairstyles and clothes in great detail. Academically, she was a conscientious student and achieved reasonable marks.

While I was at Sasaki High in 1989, Tomoe's parents separated, and the mother and girls moved out of the house where they had long lived. The father stayed on in the old house. The house was not theirs but the land was leased to Tomoe's maternal grandparents (*shakuchi-ken*). I recall a day around this time when Tomoe was very upset. She explained that they were having difficulty in finding a flat to rent since some landlords did not want 'foreigners'. The three friends were furious on hearing this news.

Her father, according to Tomoe, was a member of the Association of North Korean Residents of Japan (Chongryun), which supported the Pyongyang regime and its ideology. He was fluent in the language, which he conscientiously studied, and hoped that his children would follow in his footsteps. After separation the girls only occasionally visited him. Her mother did paid work at home. One of her elder sisters, aged 27, worked at a shoe factory, having left her first job as a make-up consultant at a local pharmacy. Another sister, aged 22, was a clerical worker at a pharmacy wholesaler, but wanted to take up agency work. Her younger sister was 14 years old. Tomoe's elder brother's relationship with his family became distant after he left home to go to university in another city. To everyone's surprise, he became a committed member of the youth division of the Association of South Korean Residents (Mindan) on the university campus. Devoting much time and energy to the cause of Mindan's youth division and not focusing on his studies, he took eight years (the maximum time allowed for graduation in most Japanese universities) to complete his degree, which led to his family nickname of 'money-eating insect' (*kanekuimushi*).

When deciding on her post-school destination, Tomoe opted for a clerical position at an ethnic Korean bank. Her mother was not pleased since she wanted Tomoe to pursue programming, which would utilise what she had learned at school, but Tomoe was not confident of her skills. Her homeroom teacher also advised her to opt for a programming position, but, after learning of Tomoe's wish for a clerical position, suggested a mainstream Japanese company, as it would offer better conditions, wages and benefits than those available at a Korean company. Tomoe's decision was based on two reasons. She panicked somewhat on realising that Koreans had limited employment opportunities, despite the school's earlier advice to the contrary. Furthermore, she also thought that a Korean bank would offer a more comfortable working environment, given that all employees would be Japan-born Koreans like herself. Her father, as a member of the North Korean organisation Chongryun, enthusiastically supported her decision, although I felt this was somewhat strange at the time since the bank was owned and run by South Korean residents in Japan. Her elder brother and his wife, both active members of the South Korean organisation Mindan, were impressed with her decision. Tomoe explained that it was not unusual for a family to have members in both the North Korean and the South Korean associations. (I noted then that several Korean students at Sakaki High had similar family relationships with the two associations.)

Tomoe sat an examination for the bank and was successful. Tomoe started full-time training one month prior to the official commencement of work on 1 April that year. The training program was systematic and included information about the company and generic skills such as greeting and telephone manners. On the last day of training, she was given the bank's training handbook and had an interview with senior managers. One of the 35 new recruits left during the training. For the training period she was paid 700,000 yen, slightly less than her monthly salary. On 1 April the company staged a formal entrance ceremony and announced the new recruits' placements on the following day. Tomoe was glad to learn that she was to go to the head office, but on her arrival a manager took her to his local branch instead. She described her first day at work.

TOMOE: People were so busy that they didn't have much time for me [*kamatte moraenakatta*]. I was made to sit at a desk in the corner, and only said

'Welcome' [*irasshaimase*] when customers arrived, and 'Thank you for coming' [*arigaoô gozaimashita*] when they left. I was not allowed to touch the money. Not having much to do, I was absent-minded [*pô to shiteita*]. I felt I was the only one who had little to do [*hima*] since everybody seemed too busy to spend time with me. But on the second and third day, they started teaching me various tasks. I was happy about that.

(1 February 1992)

Tomoe found the early start to the day demanding, but she gradually settled into the routine.

For Tomoe, the most difficult aspect of working life was the lack of free time to socialise with friends. The bank offered an annual leave entitlement but very few staff seemed to use it. In her first year, she was given six days in addition to a one-week summer holiday and a three-day New Year break. Since her senior colleagues did not take recreation leave, Tomoe found it difficult to apply for leave, being junior and new.

TOMOE: Although we are theoretically allowed to take leave for whatever reason, we can't. Nobody takes that much time off. You just don't feel right about applying for it. I haven't heard of anyone taking leave to go on a trip. If you want to travel, you leave Friday evening and return Monday afternoon [start work late on Monday].

(1 February 1992)

Not only could she not take leave, but also the irregular nature of her work made it impossible to make plans to meet friends.

TOMOE: If there's a discrepancy in the cash, we look everywhere for records, even in the rubbish bin, until we solve it. Sometimes this can take until ten or eleven at night! I've no idea when I'll finish work every day, so how can I make a date with friends. Of course, we aren't paid for that kind of overtime work, since the cash and the transaction records are supposed to match. I mean, if not, it's our fault! But then we sometimes apply for overtime pay by writing other reasons like 'sorting out accounts'! [Laughs]

(1 February 1992)

Tomoe was disgruntled at having to do so much unpaid overtime. She was becoming increasingly unhappy at work.

Another unexpected aspect of her work was what she considered were excessive requirements on the part of the bank. In the first two years, all female workers were required to undertake monthly training, and at the beginning of the following month's session they were tested on what they had learned the previous month. In addition, the bank ran proficiency examinations (both written and practical) twice a year, and awarded grades based on results. Tomoe was unsure if her marks affected her salary, and found the testing stressful. While she understood, and appreciated to a degree, the bank's underlying intention (i.e. increasing the clerical skills of workers and maintaining a high standard), she hated the system because, she said, the certificate issued by the bank was not recognised elsewhere. She considered the system 'unfair' as the test did not measure clerical capacity accurately, and because everybody, regardless of length of service and experience, sat the same test. In the end she approached her immediate boss about this, something few new recruits had the courage to do. In the following interviews with Tomoe, some of her best friends from high school were present.

TOMOE: People with ten years' experience and new recruits are sitting the same test. Can you believe it? It's stupid! That's not all. The test is next month, so the senior staff have organised a study session after work every day, like for reviewing past questions. It's agony! I hate it. I don't like the test, but not only that, the content of work, and getting on with the other people. Small things pile up and I've started feeling that everything is wrong, you know. So I said to my boss [*buchô*], 'I don't like the way you do things and I cannot go along with it.'

MUTSUKO: I remember that bit well [laughs]. Tomoe was so depressed.

(1 February 1992)

Tomoe's boss explained to her that the examination was the company's policy and that employees were required to follow it. He went on to suggest that she resign from the job if she was not willing to accept this. As a result, Tomoe resolved to leave the bank.

However, the resignation process was more complicated than Tomoe had imagined. When I met her in February 1992 she was still working for the bank. She had submitted an official letter of resignation, which her immediate boss had approved. It then had to be approved by managers [*buchô*] of other departments and other senior executives. She realised that her request was being discussed. Tomoe's immediate plan after resigning was to work casually [*arubaito*] at a hair salon that a friend owned. The friend promised to teach her skills, which Tomoe thought would be an opportunity to see whether she was suited to the work. Her mother was unhappy with this plan, and urged her to look for a 'better' job.

On a positive note, Tomoe was genuinely pleased that through her job at the bank she had been able to make friends with many Korean people of her own age. It provided her with an all-*zainichi* environment for the first time in her life. All of her colleagues and bosses were South Korean *zainichi* who, Tomoe said, understood her situation. The bank organised sight-seeing trips to South Korea, as well as other cultural activities like Korean dancing. Tomoe liked that aspect of the workplace, but disliked the employment practice that treated female workers as temporary staff with an employment period of, at most, three years. This, she claimed, was typical of Korean firms and worse than the treatment of women employees in Japanese companies.

Following encouragement from her colleagues, she joined the youth club of Mindan (the Association of South Korean Residents of Japan) and made many more *zainichi* friends. Tomoe felt that working at the bank heightened her sense of being a Japan-born Korean. She took it for granted that she would wear an ethnic costume, the *chogori*, on the Adult Day ceremony organised by Kobe municipal council, along with her friends from the bank. She proudly explained that she had had a tailor make her costume, with a matching bag and hair decoration made of the same fabric. She also showed me a photo of her high school friendship group of four taken on that day – Tomoe in *chogori* surrounded by her three friends Mutsuko, Norimi and Moko in kimono. In addition to the municipal ceremony, she attended the Adult Day party organised by Mindan. Her network was becoming more and more Korean-dominated, although she had hardly had any *zainichi* friends at high school. Tomoe still maintained close contact with her close non-*zainichi* friends. Her three high school friends felt slightly sad that Tomoe was called by her Korean name by her new-found Korean friends ('It's as if our Tomoe had become a person from somewhere else' [*mukô no hito*]), but at the same time they were happy for her. They asked her if she wanted them to call her by her Korean name, but she said no. To her three Japanese friends, Tomoe remained Tomoe.

In early 1992, Tomoe was contributing about half of her salary (45,000 yen) to the household (her mother, two elder sisters and one younger sister, who was still at high school). Two elder sisters contributed 50,000 yen each. She saved 20,000 yen, and spent the rest on herself. Since she normally spent 10,000 yen at her friend's hair salon, not much was left every month. Tomoe's enthusiastic interest in hairstyles had not diminished after high school. She had recently had a 'straight perm', but did not like it, and had had it reversed. She also offered me a detailed analysis of, and advice on, my short hair.

The household budget was tight since the rent had recently gone up by 3,000 yen. Tomoe's second sister was planning to leave her present job once she had received her summer bonus. The eldest sister worked casually (*arubaito*) or as an agency worker, whenever it suited her. When Tomoe's mother first moved into the flat with her four daughters, she did housework in the morning, left for her insurance sales job in the afternoon, and then went to her second paid job in the evening. Several years later, she rented a small house in the city for herself and took up the kind of paid job that she could do 'at home' in a more relaxed environment, or occasionally with her friends. This house was in the same area as her former house, and many of her old friends lived nearby. She must have missed the familiar community. Gradually, Tomoe's mother stopped coming to visit the flat. This meant that the four daughters shared the housework.

Tomoe eventually resigned from the bank in her third year there, several months after I first heard her complaints. After quitting the bank, she worked casually at a local bakery while receiving unemployment benefit from the Public Employment Security Office. Then her elder sister found an agency job (*haken*) at a mobile phone company, telling Tomoe that agency wages were much better than casual wages. Tomoe had an interview and got the job. She was initially on a three-month contract, but the contract was renewed every six months for almost three years, until mid-1997. In the end she was the longest-serving *haken* worker in the company.

During those three years of relative stability (1994–97), two major events affected her. One was her father's death due to illness. After his death, his estranged wife, Tomoe's mother, returned to her parents' house where her husband had been living alone. The other event was the Hanshin–Awaji earthquake, which hit the region in January 1995.

TOMOE: Mum's house was completely destroyed. We four sisters were living in a rented flat at the time. Our place was almost destroyed and our neighbour's was burnt down. Our landlord told us to wait until he had cleared the place up, so we moved out. The five of us, my mum and my four sisters, went first to our uncle's place in another suburb for about two months. Another family was also sheltering there – there were 15 of us together. Imagine that! [Laughs] Then we moved back to our old flat and Mum joined us. I think it was March when the five of us started a new life there. Gas was put back on at the end of May. We only had one small gas stove for cooking. We boiled the bath water on it. Fortunately a public bath was nearby, but it closed about nine at night. So often I couldn't make it. Every night we used to boil water on the stove and we shampooed each other's hair [laughs]. You wouldn't believe how we managed! [Laughs]

(14 November 1997)

Tomoe sounded almost nostalgic recalling the details of how the family managed in such primitive conditions.

Since settling back into the flat after the earthquake, the five women had lived together, just like in past years when Tomoe was a high school student. But her mother's position in the family had changed.

TOMOE: Mum is like a dependent flatmate [*isôrô*]. Her only job is the washing. When she feels like it, she does the cooking. Our shared residence [*kyôdô seikatsu*] is going well. Everyone puts into the kitty and we use the money to pay our expenses. When I left work, I volunteered to cook dinner for everyone, and waited until midnight, but nobody came home. These days my eldest sister often stays away overnight.

(14 November 1997)

The rent of the flat was over 100,000 yen. Tomoe now contributed 60,000 to the household. She was pleased to be close to her family, especially her sisters.

They borrowed each other's clothes, and could talk about intimate matters openly. Their boyfriends often visited and stayed for meals. Tomoe contrasted this with her relationship with her brother.

Tomoe's brother (the eldest sibling) married a Japan-born Korean woman a few months after the earthquake. They had met at university in the youth division of the Association of South Korean Residents of Japan, learned the language together, and been very active in the Association. They organised a very 'Korean' wedding with their close friends, and all the family members turned up in ethnic costume. The wife had grown up in the Korean-concentrated area of Osaka city, and maintained many 'Korean' customs. Tomoe's mother was extremely glad that her son had found a Korean wife. Tomoe and her sisters could not believe how lucky he was. In 1997, the couple had a one-year-old son, who, according to Tomoe, was being brought up as 'ethnic Korean'. For example, the young boy was not given a Japanese name. Tomoe's family had been urging the couple to give the boy a Japanese name as well, but the couple were determined.

KO: Why is it that your brother is so different from the rest of the family? He seems to have a different sense of ethnic identity [*minzoku ishiki*].

TOMOE: Really? Maybe because my brother had a defining encounter in meeting his wife. I used to think that I'd definitely marry a South Korean, but in reality it is difficult. You can't find one.

KO: Why don't you go regularly to Mindan?

TOMOE: Well, I just don't feel comfortable there but can't explain why. But I did go to the Adult Day ceremony.

MOKO: Didn't you go there sometimes?

NORIMI: I remember you saying that you might learn the Korean language when you were at high school. It was because your sister was going to, or something.

MUTSUKO: Yes, I remember too.

TOMOE: My sister went. But I didn't.

KO: But your father was a Korean-language teacher, so you could have learned from him.

TOMOE: He had the North Korean ideology [*shisô*]. So it's a bit complicated [*yayakoshiii*]. You know, even my brother can read and speak Korean. I think that he started learning the language after he went to Mindan.

ALL: Wow! [*Sugoi!*]

TOMOE: We sisters are no good at it. We can only understand words for food or a few other words here and there.

KO: Doesn't your brother influence you in that respect?

TOMOE: Not really. His life has been quite separate. After high school he left home and went to university. He lived by himself and got involved in the Association [Mindan], and has changed. We haven't lived with him for more than ten years. When he left I was a primary school kid.

(14 November 1997)

Tomoe's brother, being the family heir, hosted various Korean customary events at his home after he married. The girls and their mother travelled to attend events such as funeral anniversaries.

The legacy of the earthquake was in the family's mind. Tomoe's brother, sisters and relatives tried to persuade her mother to sell the leasehold of the land where their old house had once stood. After the old house had burnt down, the land remained vacant. The right to use the land permanently had been purchased by her mother's father, and now belonged to her. The house itself did not belong to them, because of some complicated contracts that were drawn up during the pre-war years. There were many similar arrangements in Kobe-city that people long took for granted, but after the earthquake devastation, problems such as Tomoe's mother's case surfaced. It was a small piece of land of 12 *tsubo* (one *tsubo* is equal to 3.3 square metres). One of the neighbours had recently approached Tomoe's mother and shown an interest in purchasing the leasehold in order to build a larger house. Everyone thought this was heaven-sent, since the family, according to Tomoe, could not afford to build a new house. However, Tomoe's mother refused the offer, saying that the same people had bullied her a long time ago. All the relatives had been urging her to sell, saying, 'Who else would want to buy the land in such an inconvenient place?'

TOMOE: The problem is that the leasehold [*shakuchi-ken*] will expire if the land is left without buildings for a certain period. That's why she should build a house, or sell it soon, while the neighbour wants it and we'd get a better price, right? But she doesn't understand this.

(14 November 1997)

The family's attempts to persuade the mother continued. The matter was urgent. More than two years after the earthquake, the family had to move out of their flat again, while the entire building was rebuilt. The landlord had decided to take advantage of the local government's offer to pay half of the building cost. During this time, the owner was expected to ensure that the tenants were given an equivalent flat elsewhere. The current flat was a 3DK (three bedrooms, one dining room and one kitchen). Tomoe and her sisters wanted an extra room for their mother.

Meanwhile, Tomoe quit the company where she had been an agency worker for three years. She could no longer get along with the division manager (*kachô*).

TOMOE: After I left the mobile phone company, I was offered several jobs, but I didn't take any of them. I wanted a long-term contract. But at that point it wasn't worthwhile, because we'd planned a trip to Los Angeles. Anyway, I wasn't all that well in October and November. So I decided to wait until my return from the trip and, then visit PESO [Public Employment Security Office] again.

(14 November 1997)

On her return from the trip, Tomoe found a short-term contract job. Then she landed a long-term contract (i.e. three or six months renewable). It was a clerical position at a life insurance company, where she was required to learn Windows Excel at a company-sponsored workshop. Tomoe was not confident in using the program after only one workshop, so she began to think about her next move.

Tomoe liked the flexibility that *haken* work offered her. She could decline a job if she did not like it; the work was normally on short-term contract but was often renewable; and agency work offered a monthly take-home salary substantially higher than that of permanent workers. She also recognised the disadvantages of agency work compared to permanent work. The pay could fluctuate greatly and there were no biannual bonuses, but agencies offered medical, unemployment insurances and pension plans. Tomoe initially took up these offers, but later realised it was extremely difficult to receive the benefits when she wanted them. She concluded that it was not worthwhile taking out insurance in her present circumstances.

When I met her in late 1997 Tomoe had a boyfriend with whom she had gone out for almost ten months. She met him at her girlfriend's party – he was one of her friend's colleagues. The two had recently been to the west coast of the US with a group of friends. They saw each other frequently. Tomoe, now 26 years old, was keen to get married and was wondering if her boyfriend would offer what she wanted in a marriage.

TOMOE: I would like to marry. I am more suited to being a housewife than working outside.
MUTSUKO: Yes, we all know that you're the one who wants to get married the most!
TOMOE: I dream of a life where I wait for him to come home from work. I also want kids. But many people have said to me that the reality of marriage is different, and that I have too many expectations. My present boyfriend? I'm starting to feel that he is not the marrying kind. He is 29, a good age for me, but he doesn't seem to have the maturity [*jikaku ga nai*].
(14 November 1997)

Tomoe was very cautious and rational about marriage. She identified various aspects of her boyfriend that she was concerned about, and discussed them with her close friends so that she could get feedback. Her concerns centred on what she considered his lack of leadership in their relationship, his indecisiveness and his inability to communicate his feelings. She wanted him to be more outgoing and 'energetic'. Her friends did not necessarily agree with all of her comments.

TOMOE: I like a manly man, who says 'Follow me' and takes the lead. I want to follow him. But that's assuming that we think alike on some things. I like a high-handed [*gôin*] person. My boyfriend is not. He always asks me, 'What shall we do?' and he can't make up his mind [*yûjûfudan*].

MOKO: It's not fair to call that indecisive!

TOMOE: Although he is already 29, he's got no savings, and isn't thinking about his long-term future. Also, when we're going out, he doesn't know where we're going or how to get there. I don't like a man like that.

NORIMI: I would be put off by a man like that.

TOMOE: No, well, I get more and more disappointed with him when I see him not being able to remember how to get to places.

MUTSUKO: Just get him to write down the address.

TOMOE: He doesn't have any go [*haki ga nai*]. Like he's not willing to go out of his way to please someone. He is just too honest with himself. He could pretend to be happy if that makes me happy. He lacks that kind of sensitivity [*yasashisa*].

MUTSUKO: I must agree that he is not all that sociable.

TOMOE: Yeah, he's shy with people he hasn't met before. He talks well with somebody that he knows well. The beginning of our relationship is a good example. He rang me initially because his friends gave him my telephone number. He still hasn't asked me to go steady. I'm not happy.

(14 November 1997)

Tomoe wanted him to be more interested in what she did, such as noticing what she wore, and to express his emotions more. She had asked him to make an effort to do so, and although her friends acknowledged that he had tried to accommodate her, she was still not satisfied.

TOMOE: I don't like nagging him to change this and that, because it makes me feel self-centred and demanding. He doesn't ask me to do anything. He's never been in an environment where somebody did a lot of things for him, so everything that I do for him is new and nice. He looks happy because I do things for him, but doesn't say he's happy. Don't you reckon you'd say something if you were happy?

(14 November 1997)

Despite her eagerness to marry, Tomoe did not want to continue the relationship if he had no intention to marry her, or if he was unsuitable as a marriage partner. She was in a dilemma, asking herself if she should continue the relationship. He did not seem interested in marrying anyone. To make things worse, his colleagues and friends kept asking her when they were getting married. While Tomoe concluded that he would not make a 'good husband', she was finding it difficult to leave him, both emotionally and socially. That frustrated her.

TOMOE: But I haven't been able to make myself leave him. I'm used to being with him all the time and I'm scared of losing his friendship group, which I enjoy so much. I'm scared about how I'm going to spend the time alone.

(14 November 1997)

Indeed, she loved being with him. Late that night, when the five of us parted at a JR station after the chat and interview, Tomoe rang her boyfriend on his mobile phone; he was out partying, and she wanted to join him. Seeing this, Norimi smiled at me and said, 'Here she goes again. I'd rather go home and spend the remaining hours of the day by myself.' As she disappeared into the crowds on the street, Tomoe said to me, 'I'll let you know what I decide. Wish me luck!' She was already excited about seeing her boyfriend again.

Tomoe continued working at different casual jobs after returning from the USA trip in late 1997, and then secured a permanent clerical job through the Public Employment Security Office (PESO) the following year. She considered herself lucky, since the job market at the time was poor. Her elder sister had found it when job hunting at the PESO, but noting that she was too old for the position, which stipulated that applicants should be no more than 27 years old, she recommended it to Tomoe. Tomoe sent off her CV and hoped to get an interview, but to her disappointment the job had already been given to someone else. One week later, however, she received a call from PESO asking her if she was still interested, as the worker had left within a week. She thus started working at a wholesale shoe company close to her flat. It took her only eight minutes to get there by bike, which enabled her to save the bus fare that she received from the company.

When I met her again in late 2000 Tomoe was happy with this permanent job, which she had held for over two years. She had opted for agency or casual work after quitting her first job in 1992, because of the flexibility of short-term work; but now preferred a permanent position. She was more realistic about the job market now. The job might not be ideal but it was enough for her present needs. Her view on agency/casual work versus permanent work was determined by her personal circumstances, such as her earlier desire to travel overseas and have an active social live, and now her wish for a stable working life in the face of upcoming changes.

When I met her with her three friends in late 2000, Tomoe was in the midst of preparing for her wedding, just over a month away. She had accepted a proposal from the boyfriend about whom she had spoken in 1997. She was excited about the marriage, while sharing her anxiety about her partner with her friends. But at the same time she seemed to have worked hard to overcome her anxieties by taking pragmatic initiatives.

Her fiancé, Hajime, three years her senior, had grown up in Sakura-ward, where Tomoe lived. He worked for a subsidiary of a large metropolitan gas company maintaining commercial air conditioners and heaters. Hajime still lived with his mother, who had divorced when he was very young. He had been living like this for ten years, while his married elder sister and an unmarried elder brother lived elsewhere. His mother worked full-time, and Tomoe described her as a woman from the country who took good care of everything and had old-fashioned ways; for example, she did not use a microwave. Tomoe liked Hajime's mother, and felt irritated when Hajime was not sensitive or kind to her. He never took his mother to a restaurant, or gave her presents on her birthday and Mother's Day. Tomoe's biggest concern with Hajime was his inability to manage his money, which she considered to be a sign of his immaturity.

TOMOE: When he proposed to me I said, 'I can't think about it now since you're so unreliable [*tayorinai* and *shikkari shiteinai*].'

KO: [Surprised] Did you say that to him?

TOMOE: Yeah. There was no way I was going to marry him like he was. He had no idea about how to manage money [*kinsen kankaku ga nai*].

KO: You mean, he has no savings?

TOMOE: Exactly. I said to him, 'You've got nothing in the bank; you don't pay your mum board; impossible.' Then a week later he proposed to me again. I said, 'What's changed since last week?' Then he kept saying he would try hard [*ganbaru*].

KO: And? Has he changed?

TOMOE: Of course not. [Laughs] That's why we had another quarrel the other day.

KO: When you say he is not reliable [*tayorinai*], do you only mean he doesn't have any savings?

TOMOE: Well, not just that. How can I say … you know. He isn't like an adult. He is like a child emotionally [*kankaku*].

KO: For example?

TOMOE: OK, for example, he doesn't pay his mum board. It's like his mum works full-time and supports him.

KO: What is he using his money for, then?

TOMOE: That's what I don't know. Not that he buys a lot of clothes. He says, 'I spend all my money on our dates,' but I don't think so. He's hopeless with money, he doesn't even know how much rent we're going to pay.

(12 December 2000)

After agreeing to marry him, Tomoe took the management of his money into her own hands in order to have the kind of wedding that she had always wanted. She was knowledgeable (at least more so than her fiancé) and pragmatic.

TOMOE: I've been saving through a financial planning scheme [*zaikei*]. When we decided to get married in May I had only one million yen saved. Since then I've increased the monthly payments and added bonus payments to this scheme so that each of us can save two million yen for the wedding. He only had 20 or 30,000 saved up. He said that he would give me 150,000 yen from his monthly salary and 350,000 yen from his summer and winter bonuses. Since we had eight months to save before the wedding, I calculated that we'd save four million yen. But in November he gave me only 70,000 yen (instead of 150,000), saying he received less than expected because of reduced overtime work!

KO: So did he give the cash to you?

TOMOE: Yes, what do you expect? He can't save himself. That's why I put his money into my bank account set up for this special purpose.

MUTSUKO: Wow!! You've got good financial sense.

TOMOE: Then I wrote down how much he gave me each month.

KO: He really trusts you, doesn't he?

TOMOE: He got 500,000 yen for his summer bonus, used 150,000 yen for his car loan, and gave the rest to me. For his winter bonus he got 560,000 yen, but still only gave me 350,000 yen. He took the extra for his pocket money, instead of giving it to me to make up for the November payment. That was why I got irritated, you know. He doesn't manage his money well.

(11 December 2000)

Her friends were impressed with the ways in which Tomoe implemented her saving plan for the wedding.

Tomoe's family was supportive of her marriage to Hajime, a Japanese man. Her sisters had got to know him very well as he often came to their flat. Her elder brother, who had a distant relationship with his sisters but was called upon for consultation, was also supportive of the marriage. But he gave a talk to both Tomoe and Hajime about what his sister's marriage to a Japanese man would involve.

TOMOE: My brother asked Hajime to respect my nationality and my personal integrity [*jinkaku*], since having Korean nationality [*kokuseki mondai*] can lead to problems like discrimination. I mean, even after I marry, my *zainichi*-Korean background will not change, so my brother asked him to please understand this for my sake. I liked him for saying that for me. We will register our marriage at the Ward Office [*kuyakusho*], but my family registration [*seki*] will remain South Korean. When we have a child, its name will be entered as one of ours, maybe my husband's.

MUTSUKO: What about your family name?

TOMOE: I will take up his Japanese name, Toyama. I mean my Japanese name [*tsûshômei*] will be Toyama, but my real name will be the same. In South Korea women don't change their family names after marriage.

(11 December 2000)

Tomoe was moved by the actions of her brother and felt much closer to him than before. She considered that her brother, now a father of two sons, had become more caring of his birth family.

Tomoe, her mother and three sisters remained very close. One notable recent change was that her younger sister had fallen pregnant, later married her Japanese boyfriend, and had left the flat. She had recently given birth and come back to live with and be cared for by her natal family for a period following the birth (a traditional practice in Japan). Every day her husband dropped in to join them for dinner. Tomoe was excited to have a baby in the flat.

TOMOE: My sister has been with us for one month now and should be going home. But she says 'I can't manage this [baby] by myself.' You see, we all take turns looking after the baby. Like my mum does it until three in the morning, and then somebody else takes over. I look after the baby when I get home. It's great for the new mother. She reckons, 'It's so comfortable here that I can't go home.'

MOKO: Why don't you all move to a large place and live as an extended family? (Laughs)

MUTSUKO: Whose child is this?

TOMOE: Yeah, sometimes we really wonder whose baby it is. Other than breast milk, anyone can feed a baby.

(11 December 2000)

Seeing the baby, Hajime was keen to have one of his own. Tomoe wanted to have three children in the future, but only after they had established what she called financial stability. She believed that financial stability was important for a relationship.

The wedding plans were underway. Tomoe was to wear a white wedding dress, a colourful *chogori* (not a wedding one) and a Western evening dress. She had a *chogori* boutique tailor her dress. Hajime suggested that she wear only two costumes by excluding the evening dress, since he did not see any point on spending money on another dress.

TOMOE: But then I thought, his family and relatives are Japanese. If I wear *chogori* at the end of the wedding party, I will be saying farewell to the guests in *chogori*. I thought maybe they wouldn't like that.

KO: Why?

TOMOE: You know how you take a formal photo at the end. Lots of snap-shots as well. So I thought it wouldn't be right. I don't want to make them feel uncomfortable. I really wanted to wear *chogori* for my wedding. So I think that this is the best compromise. I'm not going to give up three dresses.

KO: Do many *zainichi* women wear *chogori* at their weddings?

TOMOE: Don't know. My younger sister didn't. But I worked in a South Korean bank [*Kankoku-kei*] and have many Korean [*Kankoku-kei*] friends. And I wore *chogori* at the Adult Day ceremony. I gave you that photo, didn't I? Perhaps I feel the strongest about this of all us sisters.

(11 December 2000)

With the wedding looming, Tomoe had already rented a flat near her mother's flat. She envisaged that she would often drop into her mother's flat with Hajime for dinner. She wanted to stay in her permanent full-time job as a clerical worker at the shoe warehouse for at least another two years, so that she could obtain a retirement benefit. Although she did not expect the amount to be large, it was important for her in planning the next stage of her life course: staying at home with children. When we parted in December 2000, one month prior to her wedding, Tomoe was looking forward to the future and was genuinely happy with what she had achieved.

Hatsumi: 'I've lost the custody of my daughter'

Hatsumi was born and grew up in *shitamachi* Sakura-ward, and went to local primary and middle schools. When I first met her in 1989 she was living with her parents, an elder sister and a younger sister in an old rented house. Her father did manual work at a delivery company, her mother was a factory worker at a local shoe factory, and her 20-year-old sister was a clerical worker at another shoe factory. Hatsumi opted for the commerce course at Sasaki High, since her parents had told her that they could not afford to send her to post-secondary education and that she would enter the workforce after high school.

She was polite and spoke well, being able to adjust to the speech patterns and manners of a given context. Among hundreds of high school students that I met in that year, Hatsumi was the most skilled user of honorific. She was an active member of the school's broadcasting club and served as an announcer for several school events. It was perhaps through her speech patterns, certain mannerisms and academic marks that she projected herself as middle class. She was highly regarded by her teachers, perhaps because she was conscientious in her academic work and co-operative in class. She was humble when talking about her capabilities (her announcer's skills, academic work etc.), perhaps because she set a high standard for herself and was something of a perfectionist. Some girls considered her to be a snob, but given that she was involved in the school broadcasting club and was reserved in temperament, she was generally excused. She was selected by her English language teacher to enter a local English speech contest, and I was asked to help her prepare for it.

At that time, Hatsumi, along with some of her female peers, held two distinctive aspirations, one long-term and the other short-term, that she hoped would assist her to achieve the more important long-term goal. Her passion was to go to a post-secondary specialist school to eventually become an announcer in radio, shopping centres and bridal halls. This interest was first triggered when she was on a broadcasting committee at primary school. She joined the broadcasting clubs in both middle and high schools.

HATSUMI: I know that such jobs are hard to come by, and you have to have proper training in advance. So it's better to get a stable, permanent, full-time job such as clerical work now, save money for the training school, and then find an announcer's job while holding down the first job. After

all, these announcing jobs are mostly casual. Realistically, I don't think
you can make a living that way.

(14 October 1989)

Hatsumi therefore chose a clerical position so that she could utilise what she
had learned in the commerce course at school, and looked for companies
that she considered to be of a good size, located in the city centre, and preferably in the retail industry. She sat an examination and obtained a clerical
position at a large pharmacy chain. She was overjoyed and looked forward
to the beginning of her working life.

It did not, however, turn out to be what she had expected. After receiving
the usual systematic training for new recruits, the company announced their
placements. To her disappointment, she was assigned to the company union
office.

HATSUMI: The biggest shock was when I was assigned to the union at head
office at the end of training. I had expected to be a retail clerical worker
at a shop. The union office was small and had only middle-aged men.
One of my seniors yelled at me when I made mistakes, which made me
cry in the toilet. For the first few months, I really wanted to become a
high school student again. When I saw young people in school uniform,
I felt so envious. When I saw students in Sasaki High uniform, I felt I
wanted to return to the school.

(9 January 1992)

While she gradually learned to accept her lot, she was overwhelmed by the
demanding nature of the work.

Hatsumi soon realised that her working conditions were better than those
of many of her high school friends. Her office encouraged her to take full
annual leave for example, since the union worked hard for workers' leave
entitlements, as well as such entitlements as due payment for overtime work
and the re-employment scheme for women returning from family leave.
However, Hatsumi still felt uncomfortable about exercising her entitlements
since she feared that she would not be able to keep up with her work. She
had taken only three days of leave so far (over 21 months) – two half-days
for two funerals, one day for an exam at an English conversation course, and
the other day for some other reason she has since forgotten.

Hatsumi worked about 30 hours overtime per month in the first year,
more than the upper limit of 20 hours prescribed by the Labour Law. She
was instructed to fill in 20 hours' overtime and the remaining time in the
section called 'other allowance', and was paid for the hours that she worked,
at least initially. But she gradually started to feel that she did not deserve
such overtime payments, and decided to apply for fewer hours than she
actually worked. Hatsumi somehow believed that she was not keeping up
with work through her own inability (rather than an excessive workload for

the number of staff), and that she had to make up for her inadequacy by working extra hours.

Hatsumi was stressed and annoyed because she thought she was making too many errors in her job, and because she felt that her work excessively dominated her life. She seriously considered resignation, and consulted with her friends, family and close colleagues. She also expressed her wish to resign to her immediate boss at a six-monthly performance appraisal meeting. When she explained that she could not perform well and had lost confidence, the boss said, 'That is not a reason for resignation. Everybody lacks confidence in performing some tasks. Please persist [*gambatte*]' (9 January 1992). She was not persuaded by her boss's comment, and still considered resignation as an option. What stopped her from proceeding was that she did not know what sort of work she would otherwise do.

On the plus side, the income generated by her first permanent job gave her a positive feeling about herself. She lived with her parents and a younger sister who was still at school. Hatsumi contributed part of her monthly salary (30,000 yen) to the family budget, which was tight since her father was not well. She also gave pocket money to her parents from her biannual bonuses. Her parents appreciated her contribution, which made her feel like an adult.

Although her monetary contribution to her family was important for her, it alone was not sufficient to make her happy. She wanted to improve the situation by becoming what she considered to be more 'independent'. Hatsumi saw herself as unreliable (*tayorinai*), and was not happy with herself at work. She also thought that people around her thought that she was unreliable. She decided that the experience of an overseas working holiday would give her more self-confidence; and started taking English conversation classes to prepare herself for it.

When I parted with her in early 1992, Hatsumi was anxious about her future. She was not happy, both with her work and in her family situation, and genuinely wished for change. But she also seemed to perceive obstacles that were almost beyond her control. Without viable alternatives that she could see, Hatsumi stayed on in her first job.

When I met her again in late 1997, many significant events had transformed her life from that of a single office woman. She had married, had a baby daughter, had been divorced and had lost the custody of her daughter. She explained the series of events of the previous five years. In the fourth year of her first job, she met an ex-classmate from middle school at a party. Akira was a chef in a Japanese restaurant. The two went out together, and Hatsumi soon found herself pregnant. She thought she was too young to have a baby and wanted a termination. Akira, however, pleaded with her to keep the baby. She contemplated options, but could not decide what to do and often cried. Her father opposed the marriage, and told her that a young chef would be tempted to play around and that she should find a 'salaryman' – an ordinary employee – as a marriage partner.

HATSUMI: I was thinking, since everybody would marry sooner or later, and I was fortunate to become pregnant, it was time to get married. My friends said that many women had difficulty in getting pregnant and that I was lucky. We were both over 20 years old. I had some savings, and thought that we would be able to survive as long as I continued working.

KO: You were also in love, weren't you?

HATSUMI: I must have been. But if you ask me what I loved about him now, I can't answer. At that time, I was eager to have a boyfriend, and I now wonder if I was in love with being in love, rather than in love with what he was.

(24 October 1997)

Hatsumi also admitted that she was emotional in finally deciding to marry.

HATSUMI: My father said, 'If you have an abortion, you must not go out with him any more.' I was annoyed with him for saying this and responded, 'If you say that, I will go ahead and have the baby.' I just didn't want my parents to interfere in this.

(24 October 1997)

In the end, Hatsumi married Akira at the age of 21, within three months of meeting him. The couple moved into a modern flat near Akira's mother, who lived with her unmarried elder sister and their mother. Hatsumi notified her employer of her intention to resign but continued to work up to one month before the baby was due. In retrospect, she considered that the marriage was all right until their baby arrived. Working full-time, she did not feel that her lifestyle changed drastically. One of her high school classmates, Sayaka, recalled that when she met Hatsumi she looked happy in a maternity dress that her mother-in-law had made for her.

Hatsumi confessed that she experienced what she described as 'marriage blues' and cried over small things, because she could not get her way all the time. She did not have the time to taste the happiness of being newly wed. She was busy at work, handing her job over to a new employee and feeling guilty towards the company for her sudden resignation. Akira did not understand why Hatsumi, whom he saw as only a junior clerical worker, had to work long hours, and he became irritated. Once he locked her out when she came home late. She wanted to have fun but was told not to because she was a mother-to-be. Worse still, she started feeling physical discomfort from her growing belly. Hatsumi hoped that this anxiety would be temporary and the arrival of baby would solve the problem.

Hatsumi noticed Akira's family's relative wealth and what she considered to be the 'difference' in lifestyle.

HATSUMI: Since Akira's family was reasonably rich, their sense of money [*kinsen kankaku*] was different from mine. You see, my family was poor.

Akira's mother's family must have had money because she went to high school. Women in their mid-50s who went to high school are from rich families. I hear that her parents worked hard to save.

(24 October 1997)

Akira's mother was a travelling fish seller on a small utility truck (*gyôshô*). Her sister was a qualified cook at a government school. Akira's younger brother studied medicine, and was the pride of the whole family. Hatsumi was overwhelmed when Akira bought her two engagement rings with different settings of diamonds. This was despite the fact that she told the family that she wanted only one, and that the setting was too large. His family preferred to eat only a particular cut of meat. His grandmother gave the couple one million yen as a wedding present. Akira's aunt (who lived with his mother) had an external saleswoman from the Sogo Department Store bring a selection of fur coats to her home before deciding to buy one.

HATSUMI: I'd never met people like that. They always buy expensive good-quality things. Not cheap stuff. I always compromise because something is beyond my means. I'm happy to receive presents from them, but when I was told to behave like them, I couldn't.

KO: So you didn't find it comfortable?

HATSUMI: No, not at all. And they sometimes said things like 'That family has no money.' I wanted them to stop describing people in those terms in front of me. A person's value is not determined by how much money they have.

(24 October 1997)

She had hoped that her baby would ease the discomfort that she had been experiencing with her husband's family.

Hatsumi had a difficult birth, and declined Akira's wish to be with her at the birth. Both families celebrated the arrival of the baby, Maki. Both Akira and the in-laws were overjoyed. Everything looked perfect for a while. However, the arrival of the baby was not to be a solution to Hatsumi's unhappiness. She suffered what she called the 'baby blues'.

HATSUMI: My baby and I stayed at my parents' house for one month after leaving the hospital. I was at a loss – I didn't know why the baby kept crying. When I went out to buy groceries with the baby in her pram, she would start crying on the way. I felt others watching, and returned home without buying anything. I couldn't even go shopping. Then around six months, she cried for no reason at night. After the earthquake, she often cried, recalling the shake.

KO: What about your husband, Akira?

HATSUMI: He wanted to help me with the baby, but I didn't want him to.

KO: Why not?

HATSUMI: I don't know. At the beginning, I had post-natal depression and couldn't do anything by myself, so I asked him to be with me.

(24 October 1997)

Once Hatsumi got over her initial depression, she did not want her husband to be involved with the housework. She became more and more irritated at what she considered her inability to manage a household.

HATSUMI: I did my best in cooking the dinner, cleaning the house and doing the laundry. I was hopeless at cooking, and since Akira was an expert cook, I tried to make my own sauces rather than using ready-made sauce mix. I did try hard at cooking. But I was hopeless at keeping the house tidy and attractive. My in-laws later told me jokingly, 'Why do you want go out to work when you can't even manage your housework?'

(24 October 1997)

Hatsumi perceived her husband as good at housework. He complained about Hatsumi's poor housework skills.

HATSUMI: Well, because I was so hopeless at housework, he couldn't but help me. But after helping me, he told other people about it as if he had done something wonderful. If he was going to do that, I didn't want him to help me. I explained this to him many times, but he didn't understand me. He was very particular about money, and said that we should be able to live on 60,000 yen per month. Well, at that time I didn't know how to manage money. I just spent it as things came up.

(24 October 1997)

Hatsumi was losing self-confidence. This was not the first time. After two years at her first job she had complained of losing confidence in her ability to do office work. After marriage, she lamented her lack of household and baby-care skills. She felt that her in-laws were constantly watching her. However hard she tried, she did not think she was making any improvement. Her husband did not like her buying CDs, which was one of her few consolations at the time. She was frustrated that her baby determined when she went out and where. None of her friends had babies. She was often told to defer something that she wanted to do 'because you are a mother'. She deplored this, saying, 'This was not what I had expected.' Her friends did not appreciate her problems, saying, 'Why aren't you happy being with your beautiful baby?' She became increasingly annoyed and irritated by small comments that her in-laws made about her and the baby.

HATSUMI: My self-esteem went down after marriage. I had the marriage blues. I was poor at keeping the house tidy, and at managing money [*yarikuri*].

KO: Did he say that?

HATSUMI: Yes, but also, I thought that he was always eager to help because I was slow. That made me feel even worse. I was not relaxed [*ôraka*] about my child. I easily got angry at her. I fought with the child, saying, 'I am not going to talk to you any more.' Do you think a normal mother would do that?

(24 October 1997)

During the following months, when Hatsumi was weighed down by her negative feelings about housework, her baby and her in-laws, her father died of cancer. Losing the household head, her mother and the family felt vulnerable. This made Hatsumi even more miserable.

Within a month of her father's death, the earthquake occurred. Hatsumi's flat and her husband's family's house were both safe. Her mother's rented house was destroyed. Her married elder sister, who was pregnant, also lost her home.

HATSUMI: I didn't want my sister to live in a local school gym – she was pregnant. So we invited them to stay with us. My mum, my younger sister, my elder sister and her husband all moved into our flat. It was a difficult time for all of us in such a crowded place, but it couldn't be helped. We had just had a once in a lifetime natural disaster, right? But my husband's parents got jealous and said that my husband had married into my family! So insensitive. I hated that.

(24 October 1997)

Hatsumi lost respect for her husband and his family. Her feelings towards them worsened. Her own family left Hatsumi's flat after a few months. Her mother and her younger sister went to live in one of the rent-free housing units that the Kobe-city government set up for earthquake victims (*kasetsu*).

Hatsumi started a part-time job in search of a diversion from her increasingly intolerable frustration. She was staying at home with a one-year-old child, and felt constantly watched by her in-laws, who lived nearby. Around the same time, her husband started driving a long-distance truck at night, since the job market for chefs was poor and the other job was better paid. As a result, she hardly saw him, which affected the relationship. On weekends he stayed at home watching television rather than taking her out. Hatsumi was bored. She was so frustrated that she just wanted a place that she could escape to. She reasoned that if she had a paid job outside the home, her husband would help her if she could not keep up with the housework.

Hatsumi's in-laws criticised her for taking up paid work and leaving her young child in a childcare centre. They said, 'Can't you manage on your husband's salary? Why not?' She did not mind leaving her child in a childcare centre, since she had been placed in one as an infant. She reasoned that the child would make friends in the same age group and get used to a group-oriented life.

HATSUMI: I felt that the childcare centre was much better at toilet training than me. I wasn't good at that. And that made me feel that my daughter was all right without me.

(24 October 1997)

Hatsumi found solace in a mundane clerical job at one of the many post-earthquake construction sites. She made friends and was happy at work.

One day she went to see a movie with a male colleague, who Hatsumi felt was sympathetic about her plight. In retrospect, Hatsumi realised that this was a 'reckless act' on her part, because the incident became a trigger for the marriage break-up. They were not sexually involved. When Akira, Hatsumi's husband, found out, he was furious. The two had heated arguments. At the end, Akira hit Hatsumi and pushed her out of their flat. Seeking to avoid further possible violent confrontation, Akira arranged for his mother to take their daughter, Maki, and for Hatsumi's mother to take Hatsumi to her home. When Hatsumi returned to their flat the next day, Akira told her that he would seek formal mediation if she wanted a divorce. This came as a shock. It made Hatsumi see that it would be intolerable to live with him for the rest of her life, and she returned to her mother's house to think it through. At that point she decided to leave her child at Akira's mother's house while she sorted herself out, a decision that she would later regret enormously.

In the following month, Hatsumi continued to work at the construction site office, while living with her mother and younger sister in a one-room rent-free housing unit for earthquake victims (*kasetsu*). Her husband's family was furious, called her 'a failed mother' (*hahaoya shikkaku*) and told her not to visit her child for one month. This hurt her.

HATSUMI: My husband's family created an atmosphere where I couldn't visit my daughter at their place. I became emotional when I heard my daughter crying in the background when my husband happened to telephone the flat while I was there to pick up my things. But I wasn't in a state where I could rationally think of my child. I was more concerned with what would happen to my marriage. Was I going to be persuaded to go back to him? Of course I wanted to get out of it. I think that people around us blamed me. After all, I was the one who did such a reckless [*kar-uhazumi*] thing and left them. I was still thinking that if he pleaded with me to go back to the marriage, I might be talked into it. So I didn't think of what was going to happen to my child.

(24 October 1997)

When Akira brought a divorce application form to Hatsumi at her mother's place, he had named himself as the child's custodian, and asked Hatsumi to agree to it. At that point she was tired of everything of the situation, and just wanted to be out of the marriage.

HATSUMI: I couldn't stand the thought that as long as I was married to him he was going to chase me like that. I just wanted to run away from it.

(24 October 1997)

She signed the form, thinking that she would handle the issue of child custody later on. This was to be her biggest mistake and one that she would deeply regret later.

One week after the divorce application form was lodged, Akira visited Hatsumi at her mother's home and said, 'Are you happy with the current arrangement? Let's meet together and think about our child's future.' Hatsumi, her mother, Akira and his mother met in the latter's house. Hatsumi had not seen her daughter for over a month. Seeing Hatsumi, her daughter cried and would not come near her. She was just over two years old, but she was not able to speak much.

HATSUMI: I was stunned and speechless. When Akira saw this, he said to me, 'Look at what you've done to your own daughter.' Hearing this, I thought I couldn't live with somebody like that. I would have felt differently if he had said, 'Once we start living together again you will be all right.' Then I decided that I had no choice but to go to court.

(24 October 1997)

She realised then that she really wanted her daughter back.

Hatsumi went to the legal aid service (*muryô hôritsu sôdansho*). She was told that it would be extremely difficult to change the custodianship so soon after the divorce application was submitted, when the situation had not changed substantially. If the situation had changed drastically since the application was submitted, she would have a chance. She was still living in the one-room emergency housing unit (*kasetsu*) with her mother and her younger sister, and had no full-time job. Akira, in contrast, lived in a modern flat and had a regular income, and his mother could act as a carer. Hatsumi became pessimistic and withdrew her application.

KO: Well, if you get a flat in the municipal housing complex and several years pass, could you consider applying for custody?

HATSUMI: I don't know. Even if I get legal custody, I won't have seen her for so long. I hear that Akira's family was saying horrible things about me, like 'Your mother abandoned you and just left.' [Tears] I know this because a friend of mine overheard this when she took a photo of my daughter for me at a local festival. She was told by Akira's mother not to stir up trouble since he was to remarry soon.

(24 October 1997)

When I met Hatsumi in late 1997, she had not seen her daughter for over a year. Since Maki had moved to another childcare centre, Hatsumi no longer heard reports on her growth from teachers at the old centre. She was convinced that the new centre (a private one) would not let her meet her daughter. On my suggestion that she see a lawyer from the legal aid service, she expressed concern about the cost.

HATSUMI: Besides, I haven't seen her for such a long time. Of course I want to see her, but I don't want to confuse her, either. So far, she hasn't had an easy childhood. I know how hard it was for her to experience her parents' separation, and I just want to leave her in peace. I really don't know what I should do now. I don't think Akira's family will let me see my daughter, saying that I was to blame.
KO: Time may heal their feelings.
HATSUMI: I don't think so.

(24 October 1997)

She remained extremely pessimistic about her chance of regaining custody of her daughter.

Hatsumi regretted that she had not been as assertive towards her husband and his family as she had wanted to be. Indeed, she often mentioned that she 'was talked into accepting it' (*umaku marume komareta*).

HATSUMI: There were differences in the way that we two went about things. I mentioned things that I didn't like about him. But he was good at talking [*kuchi ga tassha*], and I can't express myself well. So I was always persuaded into doing what he liked [*umaku marume komareta*]. After we separated, he once came with my daughter to my mother's place, and yelled at me so that the neighbourhood could hear. Maki was frightened by his loud voice. Why did he bring her? To make such an innocent child see our ugly relationship? I hated it; why did I have to be harassed even after divorce? You know, I really wanted to have more time to think about our future – a month's separation was not enough. If I'd had more time, been able to set up a five-year savings plan and find a suitable place to live, I might not have lost my daughter. I asked him to give me more time, but he said that one month was long enough to think it over. He gave me only two options: returning to him then, or immediate divorce. I was not strong enough, and was talked into accepting his options.

(24 October 1997)

Hatsumi found a permanent full-time position in late 1996, five months after the divorce was officially finalised through mediation (*chôtei*). This offered her some stability in her life after the trauma of divorce and separation from her child. She considered herself fortunate, given the depressed employment market. Desperate to find a permanent job, she had sought assistance at the Public Employment Security Office, and an officer had suggested a position that he thought was suitable for a graduate of a commerce high school. It was a clerical position at the office of the prefectural association of *shakaihoken rômushi* (social insurance professionals), which had a staff of five. Initially she had had no idea what a social insurance professional did, but explained to me that he or she managed employment insurance and payrolls for small and medium-sized companies – something that a personnel department would do in a large company. The association had approximately 850 registered members. Over 500 of them ran their own business. When employing her, the association acknowledged her previous work experience.

HATSUMI: They recognised my experience gained with my first employer – three years and ten months – when deciding my pay. I guess that my age counted too. The recruitment card said the monthly salary was 140,000 to 160,000 yen. I got 160,000 yen per month. My pay was much better than for new high school graduates without experience.

(24 October 1997)

Hatsumi found the job 'secure' in that the office would not go bankrupt (unlike many small companies that got into trouble around that time), but the salary was not generous. She did not have much in common with her colleagues – grey-haired middle-aged men – but the office atmosphere was tolerable. The job did not involve any overtime, and she finished work at 5 p.m., which she liked. Hatsumi was not enthusiastic about the work content or workplace, and ultimately wanted to change jobs, but for the time being she persisted since she needed the money to meet basic needs.

In late 1997, Hatsumi had been living with her 56-year-old mother and a younger sister in a rent-free temporary unit for earthquake victims (*kasetsu*). Her mother continued working in a small shoe factory, complaining that the work was demanding for older people like herself. She had had an operation for cancer 15 years previously. Hatsumi's younger sister was unemployed, having left her first job, which her high school had introduced her to. Hatsumi was thus the household breadwinner. She was expected to be a stable income-earner. Facing this family situation, permanent employment now had a different meaning for her. She cherished a relatively uneventful and quiet life, and felt grateful to have a caring family. In return, she wanted to care for her mother in her old age. However, her self-confidence diminished further when she saw that her blood relatives no longer thought highly of her judgement.

HATSUMI: I'm just an ordinary person who has no ability; no, in fact, less than an ordinary person. What I say no longer counts much, I feel. Before, they used to consult with me, and sometimes accepted my suggestions. I could also take the lead. After the divorce, I'm not taken seriously, even by my family members, in particular my younger sister.

(24 October 1997)

Hatsumi found consolation and relief in still seeing the man the liaison with whom had triggered her divorce and the loss of custody of her daughter. She realised, also, that this was unacceptable in the society (*seken*), and felt guilty about it.

HATSUMI: I think I must be cunning [*zurui*]. I still see that man. I liked him because he treated me as equal, tried to understand me, and was sympathetic to me. No one knows that I am still seeing him because people would be shocked. 'Ah that man, the cause of the divorce!' To him I can say, 'I don't think so.' But I couldn't say that to my ex-husband. I was always talked into accepting what he said. Strange, I don't know why.

(24 October 1997)

Hatsumi sometimes burst into tears, particularly at night, and was considering seeking counselling.

While she acknowledged that she had little time and energy (*yoyū*) to contemplate her long-term future, she knew what she wanted in the coming few years. First, she wanted to move out of the temporary accommodation for earthquake victims to a permanent residence. The family was on the waiting list for a place in a municipal housing complex. She did not want marriage.

HATSUMI: I don't want to marry again. I don't want to make the same mistakes. I'm scared. I want to get a qualification but don't know what.

(24 October 1997)

She said that she would consider remarrying only if the marriage enabled her to accept her daughter into the family. She also considered herself too immature to marry a man with his own children. Hatsumi also wanted to find a long-term 'career', but was unsure what that was. She thought of being a nurse, a social insurance professional, a childcare worker, a dental nurse and a carer for the aged, but nothing appealed to her; or she did not think that they were within her reach. When we parted in late 1997, Hatsumi said that she would explore her options. It seemed that her fear of uncertainty and/or her lack of self-confidence made it difficult for her to turn her wishes into concrete plans.

When I met Hatsumi in late 2000, she seemed more settled in many ways, and slightly happier, than in 1997. She wore simple and elegant clothes with a smart conventional black coat. Her dyed brown hair and light make-up created a somewhat softer impression. She had moved out of the temporary unit to a flat in a municipal housing complex. Her elder sister lived nearby with her husband and their two children. Her younger sister had married two years before, and lived in the same housing complex as Hatsumi. Hatsumi, her mother and two sisters remained close. Hatsumi wanted to live alone as she continued to feel insignificant in the flat but had to be sensitive to her mother's needs. She was resigned to the current arrangement as it saved money.

Hatsumi had not seen her daughter for over four and a half years. Maki was to turn six soon, and to start school in a few months. She had spoken to her ex-husband only once in the four years since the divorce: she received an unexpected telephone call from him in mid-1999. He reported that he was remarrying soon, and requested that Hatsumi no longer send a birthday present to her daughter since Maki would have a new mother. Hatsumi still sent a present. She heard from former neighbours that his new wife had brought her own daughter from a previous marriage, who was of a similar age to Maki, and that the new couple had recently added a son to this blended family.

HATSUMI: I always think about Maki ... but I can't bring myself to ask him to let me see her. I don't want to destroy their new family set-up.

(21 December 2000)

I asked if Hatsumi had considered approaching his new wife and explaining how she felt: that is, not wanting to affect their new family but still wanting to see her daughter. Hatsumi remained unconvinced about the effectiveness of such an approach.

Hatsumi remained pessimistic about regaining custody of Maki. Her position had strengthened; she was now living in proper accommodation and had held down a permanent full-time job for a few years. But she thought that her ex-husband's position had strengthened equally since his remarriage.

HATSUMI: I've almost given up recovering custody. It costs a lot. I can't provide a good environment for my daughter without a stable income.
KO: Have you completely?
HATSUMI: It's hard to give it up completely. Well, I don't want to move her again. I want to stay where we live and don't want to remarry, because my ex-husband may contact me about my daughter since he knows my current telephone number. I feel that I am passive just waiting, but I just hope that my daughter will eventually come and see me.

(21 December 2000)

Hatsumi was reluctant to seek legal aid service again, and was not hopeful that such a meeting would result in her gaining custody. When I mentioned the possibility of at least gaining the right to see her child regularly, Hatsumi said, 'After all it is up to my ex-husband. He may not want to let me see my daughter.' I suggested that her ex-husband's new wife might understand Hatsumi's wish since she herself was divorced.

HATSUMI: Mm ... I've been thinking about everything rather passively. I never thought of taking action myself [like contacting the new wife]. I just fear

that everyone will be unhappy if I make a move. I'm just so scared about
it. But I think it [seeing her again] is my goal. Well, I may not be able to
call this a goal, because it's so vague.

(21 December 2000)

When hearing about her ex-husband's remarriage, Hatsumi again regretted
her actions at the time of separation.

HATSUMI: At that time I came to dislike everything about him. You know
people get in that mood now and then? But now I regret it. You can
always get a divorce, but it is much more difficult to continue the marriage. Once divorced, there's no going back, you see. I regret that I couldn't
think more clearly and come up with another answer. I regret … I might
have ended up getting divorced, but I didn't have to divorce in such a
hurry.

(21 December 2000)

Hatsumi hoped that she had learned a lesson from this, and that she would
not repeat these mistakes in the future. She said she had abandoned the idea
of another relationship altogether, thinking it demanding (*shindoi*) and troublesome (*mendôkusai*) to get to know a new person from scratch and develop
a relationship. But Hatsumi later contradicted herself somewhat when she
said that it might be possible to cultivate a special relationship with someone
she already knew.

  Hatsumi continued working at the same office, and was just as unhappy
with the work. While she did not expect any job to offer everything she wanted,
she was considering resigning. She was concerned about the restructuring of
the office, and considered she was poorly paid at 150,000 yen per month. She
expected that her employer would not try to stop her from leaving, unlike
her first employer, since the organisation wanted to reduce staff numbers and
could employ younger workers at a lower salary. Having said that, she pre-
dicted that her chance of finding a better job would be slim, because of her
age (29) and what she considered to be her inadequate computer skills.
Mid-discussion, she paused a moment.

HATSUMI: You know, when I talk, I feel I've been talking only about nega-
tives. That's what I don't like about myself. I don't know why I always
do this. Is this because of my situation, or my mental state? I don't
know.

(21 December 2000)

At this point in our conversation I was taken aback, since I was feeling
exactly the same about her. I feared that she had noticed my reaction,
although I was simply responding to her story with what I judged to be
appropriate non-judgemental conversation-fillers (*aizuchi*). I suspected then

that she liked talking about herself to me or to anyone else who was interested in listening to her. I reasoned that many people liked talking about their problems as a way to release stress.

Reflecting on her 11 post high school years, Hatsumi was amazed at how her trajectory had altered from what she had originally hoped for. She also recognised personal limitations and external constraints more concretely than previously.

HATSUMI: Time has gone so quickly. My 20s have gone by so fast. So many things have happened to me. But because I had so many things to manage, I feel I haven't done anything important.

KO: I don't think so.

HATSUMI: I feel I have to do something, you know, like getting a skill or a qualification. I'm sure I've said this to you before. But I haven't been able to really achieve this. When I was much younger I felt anything was possible, like I want to do this and that, but now I can see my limitations, so I can't have such dreams.

KO: When did you start feeling like that?

HATSUMI: Perhaps it's to do with my age. When I was 27 or 28 – the year before last. This year, I feel more like I can't do it. Of course, I shouldn't blame my age. I didn't expect that I would be like this when I left high school ten years ago. I'd expected that I would be more successful.

KO: When you graduated from high school, how did you think you would be at 30?

HATSUMI: I thought I would be successful in at least one thing. Having a good job and earning good money – such a vague idea. I'd never thought I would be like this.

KO: Really? Looking back, when do you think your plan changed?

HATSUMI: I think, perhaps, with the divorce.

(21 December 2000)

How, then, did Hatsumi see her transition to adulthood over those years?

KO: Do you think you've become adult, say, compared to when you were at high school?

HATSUMI: You mean, in how I think? Of course, I've changed so much since then in that way.

KO: Does that make you feel you are an adult?

HATSUMI: Mm ... I'm not sure if I feel I've become an adult, maybe not. Rather, I just feel that I've changed my way of thinking a lot since the divorce. Without the divorce I wouldn't have changed so much. I'm not saying that divorce made my situation and thinking better, but it just changed them drastically.

KO: For example?

HATSUMI: Well ... how can I explain? I can't explain well, since it is so vague. For example, how I relate to others has changed.

KO: You mean you keep your distance more?

HATSUMI: That's also true. Before, I was selfish and self-centred. I was tense [*kitsui*], and didn't like losing, like at work. I still don't like losing. I only thought of myself, liked myself the best, and was convinced that I would be good at many things. I think I had that kind of arrogance, you know. Then I experienced failure [*zasetsu*] many times, including divorce. That, I feel, has changed how I see people and things in many ways. It's difficult to explain what those changes are.

KO: You mean you've lost that arrogance?

HATSUMI: Not completely, but to a degree. It's one of the changes.

(21 December 2000)

Hatsumi's personal journey after leaving school did not lead her to where she had expected she would arrive, but she acknowledged the changes that she had experienced in the journey.

Hatsumi's immediate future desires remained vague. In response to my question about what she wanted to be doing in five years, she said that she would leave her present workplace when she received the next summer bonus in seven months' time.

KO: What will you do then?

HATSUMI: You may think I'm dreaming, after I said that I can now face reality, but I want to focus on learning English. Not because I want to be an interpreter but because I just want to.

(21 December 2000)

Hatsumi intended to work part-time to implement this plan, which her mother was concerned about because she counted on Hatsumi's income. Hatsumi also wanted a stable income and to be in a situation where she could welcome her daughter, having her visit on Saturdays if possible. But again, Hatsumi did not seem to have any concrete strategies to make her wishes reality.

Part II
Themes from the stories

4 Initial entry into the wider adult world

This chapter focuses on the first two years after departure from high school, and will be followed by chapters examining specific domains: employment (and unemployment), relationships and friendships, marriage and divorce. I decided to study this period separately since it was in many ways distinct; the young adults were shocked by the sudden change from the protective environment of high school, where teachers softened the harsh realities of the outside world and where the students shared a relatively homogeneous working-class family background (Okano 1993). The young women began by comparing their new encounters in the wider world with the familiar world of school, but this point of comparison gradually receded over the two years. This chapter asks the following questions. How did 18–20 year olds make sense of their departure from 12 years of schooling and entry into the adult world? How did they learn to see themselves in this process in terms of class, gender and ethnicity?

Six months prior to graduation, when each student's job was finalised, they had mixed feelings. There was a sense of relief to know where they were going, but this was accompanied by a feeling of anxiety. Many wanted to stay at school longer, preferring the life they had as students. They saw that being a student meant a carefree existence with minimal responsibility.

At the end of their second year out of school, 17.3 per cent of Imai Tech High School graduates who entered employment and 9 per cent of those from Sasaki High had resigned from their first jobs. Their teachers stated that these figures were comparable with those of preceding years. Nation-wide, 35 per cent of 1990 high school graduates who entered the workforce had left their first jobs by the end of their second year of employment, and this figure remained stable in the 1990s (Yajima and Mimizuka 2001: 107). Of the 21 women in the study, five had already resigned from their first jobs. Three were married, one with a one-year-old child. At the time all but two of the unmarried women lived with their parents and families.

Making sense of the workplace

During the first two years out of secondary school, work featured prominently in the women's lives. Both their schools and companies repeatedly told them that full-time work granted them the status of *shakai-jin* (literally, society person, understood to be a fully fledged adult) (Roberson 1995), and that it demanded their commitment in terms of both time and focus. Many experienced an initial sense of dismay or even shock, as revealed by Hatsumi's comment in Chapter 3. Their interpretations of new experiences displayed both commonality and diversity, and were to direct their subsequent decision-making and actions.

The level of satisfaction with employment fluctuated over the two years, like 'waves', to quote Orie:

ORIE: Since I started work, many 'waves' have come and gone. I thought of quitting several times. But now [after two years] I feel a bit settled, and have not felt the 'waves' recently. I feel I go to work, as everyone else does – and this is because I have not found anything I strongly want to pursue.

(15 February 1992)

In general, the level of individual satisfaction with employment was determined by two factors: enjoyment, or otherwise, of the work itself, and workplace atmosphere (i.e. human relationships, *ningen kankei*). The latter was more important for many. If a woman found human relations at work pleasant, she was likely to continue even if the tasks were boring and commuting one way took up to two hours, as we shall see below. On the other hand, if both the job itself and human relations were unpleasant, there was little choice but to leave.

Initial training in the first full-time job

Early April, when cherry blossoms are in full boom, signals the beginning of official transitions in Japan: the nationwide commencement of the academic year when new recruits start in their workplaces. All women received initial training from April, when new recruits nationwide begin their employment. The women remembered this period fondly. The length of the initial training varied depending on the size of the company and the nature of the job, and ranged from two months for a government employee to three days in a small company. Training included lectures on being *shakai-jin*, the company profile and philosophy, generic skills such as answering the telephone and communicating with colleagues and seniors, and, later, specific job-related skills once they had settled into their assigned division, as has been observed in other studies (Matsunaga 2000: 55–74; Ogasawara 1998; Rohlen 1974).

Women found that the training was novel to them in two respects. First, they were paid during their training. Second, the women vividly observed that the training was provided separately for groups of male university graduates, male factory workers, female university graduates, and female high school and junior college graduates. It was understood that the content and duration of the training offered to respective groups varied and were related to career prospects within the company. The most enjoyable aspect of training for the young women was making new acquaintances with shared educational background and future aspirations. These new recruits encouraged and consoled each other later on when they faced difficulties.

Many experienced an initial sense of dismay, even shock, at the unexpected, when they were assigned to their first position after training and faced the reality of the work content, conditions and human relations. A few cried at work. Many more contemplated quitting sometime in the first year (as I will explain later), but gradually learned to see the workplace in a realistic and pragmatic way by comparing their experiences with those of their friends.

SHIZU: There were so many things that surprised me. Rough speech was one. I wanted to quit in the first three months because I didn't have much work to do, and when they taught me something I was slow in picking it up. Soon after I was assigned to the office one of my seniors harshly criticised my work. I went and cried in the toilet.

(2 February 1992)

Managing the disappointment: work content, annual leave and overtime work

The work content was disappointing to many of the women. Only three of them positively liked their tasks. Many more expressed an unambiguous dislike, while others accepted their lot without complaint as part of the reality of working life. Fumiko, a graduate of the interior furnishing course at Imai Tech High, was happy with her position since it entailed more than 'clerical work'. At the Mitsubishi subsidiary company that she entered through a connection of her self-employed electrician father, she was asked to do technical drawing, to learn new skills, and to take a leadership role in guiding her year's intake.

FUMIKO: The work turned out to be much better than I had expected. I'd thought that I would be serving tea, and turning up early to clean the office. I know that girls do things like that in other companies. We're different. Men also clean the floor. Everyone gets their own tea.

(16 February 1992)

Oriko, Fumiko's classmate, enjoyed producing drawings from draft plans of train carriage interiors in her work at the subsidiary of a prominent heavy industrial company. Kanako, another classmate, was fascinated with grading diamonds and pearls at a pearl jewellery company. The three were unusual among their peers in attaining a sense of achievement in their work from the outset.

Most of the women found they derived no fulfilment from work, or thought that their jobs were unsuited to their personalities. For the women who enjoyed good workplace human relations, or who from the outset had realistic expectations of their jobs, the disappointment was less acute. The ways in which the women addressed such dissatisfaction varied. Natsumi, a graduate of the interior furnishing course, took the most radical step – after six months she decided to leave the small bicycle company where she worked.

NATSUMI: I was doing clerical work in relation to insurance. The recruitment card sent to our school said the position was for a designer, and that's why I applied. At the beginning I accepted it, thinking that this was what everybody experienced, but then I started thinking that I didn't like the job. I tried to convince myself that it was my job [to do whatever was assigned]. But I thought I should study further in order to get the kind of designing position that I wanted.

(25 January 1992)

Natsumi left work after one year for further study at a private vocational college (*senmongakkô*) while working and living alone near the college. Her boss initially tried to dissuade her from resigning but, knowing her determination, had to accept it in the end. Her decision was a difficult one, since she liked the people she worked with, who gave her a warm farewell.

Transfer to other types of jobs within the same company was a solution for two women. Miyuki, a graduate of the interior furnishing design course, found her checkout job at a large co-op supermarket chain store physically draining and repetitive.

MIYUKI: In my second year I said to my immediate supervisor that I wanted to quit. Then somehow I was made an *âtisuto* [which involved designing window displays and drawing posters and price tags using lettering skills]. My supervisor, without me knowing, had managed to arrange my transfer to another branch as an *âtisuto*, saying that he knew of my desire for the *âtisuto* position! How did he know? I might have casually said I was more suited to *âtisuto* work, and he took the hint. After all, he didn't want me to quit. I think that it would have impacted on his own performance evaluation.

(6 February 1992)

Noshie, a third-generation Korean graduate of the commerce course whom we met earlier, obtained a checkout position at a chain restaurant through a connection of her father's, with a verbal promise that she would move to a clerical position in the same company in three months. For a while after the restaurant opened, the place was so busy that she worked from 10 a.m. to 10 p.m. with only a five-minute lunch break. She developed blisters on her feet. She eventually gained a clerical position after her father's intervention.

Other women who disliked the content of their work also expressed a wish to resign, but were persuaded to endure (*gambaru*) by their bosses and colleagues. A nurse trainee, Sekie, was physically exhausted every day and thought of quitting many times. She worked full-time as a live-in nurse assistant at a private clinic and attended nursing school every afternoon.

SEKIE: Both the working hours and wages were so different from those listed on the recruitment card. I was exhausted every day, and thought this was not what I had expected. I used to feel envious of the girls who worked in small clinics without hospitalisation facilities. They had no night shifts, no evening work, and sometimes earned more than I did. But I later noticed that I had learned a much wider range of tasks at our clinic than the girls at the small clinics, and I thought that this was not a bad thing.

(26 January 1992)

After 21 months in the job, and three months before the certification examination, Sekie started accepting her nursing career.

Yoshie also found a sales position in the furniture section of a large department store boring and physically demanding. Yet Yoshie was realistic about the job market, and reluctant to take a risk in quitting her current job.

YOSHIE: The work is not fulfilling, partly because not many customers come to the furniture department. It could be that I'm not suited to a sales position. The job is uninteresting. Also, my immediate boss is fussy about little things. But then I can't think of any other job. Realistically, there aren't so many great jobs. If I think of my leave arrangements and good human relationships right now, I hesitate to make a change.

(30 January 1992)

Being appointed a 'sister' (someone who guides new recruits) in her second year also gave Yoshie a sense of responsibility. She had recently unsuccessfully requested a transfer to the women's clothing section.

Women did not always receive encouragement for *gambaru* from their bosses. Tomoe, a third-generation Korean graduate of the data-processing course, hated the bank's policy whereby all female workers were required to sit an internal examination every six months, because, she claimed, some of the content was irrelevant and everyone, regardless of length of service, sat the same test. In the end she approached her boss about this situation, something few new recruits have the courage to do.

TOMOE: My boss said, 'This is the company's policy. Do you intend to receive a salary without accepting the policy?' I was irritated. I was not saying I wouldn't participate in regular testing, but I just didn't think the system was rational. Then I went on explaining why the system was unsound and how it could be modified. Then he just lost his temper, and we argued. He said, 'If that's the case, it may be better for you to resign.' I said, 'I agree.'

(1 February 1992)

Given the limited kinds of employment and chances for promotion that female high school graduates can expect, it is crucial to make the most of a job. The meaning of work depends on what one makes of that job (Corson 1985). While this message was conveyed in various ways in the final year of high schooling, the fact that so many women were disappointed suggests that the practice was not as effective as the school intended. The school's message (communicated also by family and other adults) that 'you will need to stick with a job for three years to know whether you really want to leave' seems to have contributed to some of the women deferring the decision to resign.

The women's concerns about working conditions during this period centred on two issues: annual leave and overtime. First, the women found it difficult to exercise their entitlement to annual leave. They said that they felt guilty, at inconveniencing their colleagues, and uncomfortable, unless the leave was for something socially important (e.g. a funeral). Even in an office where seniors took recreation leave, being the youngest and newest member of staff made it difficult to do the same, although some had developed what they described as the 'courage' (*yūki*) to do so.

TOMOE: Although we are theoretically allowed to take leave for whatever reason, we can't. Nobody takes a long period of leave. It is difficult to do; you just don't feel comfortable. I have not heard of taking leave for a trip. If you want to travel, you leave on Friday evening and return to work Monday afternoon [start work late on Monday].

(1 February 1992)

Moko was a clerical worker in the personnel department of a large steel company. Although she wanted to travel overseas, she was reluctant to take the necessary leave.

MOKO: Although our workplace is not busy, certain tasks need to be done daily. I do various tasks [she explains them in detail]. So I can't take annual leave. I mean, I can ask the person who used to do my job [to fill in for me for a day] but can't possibly ask her to cover for my absence when I am going on a holiday trip.

(1 February 1992)

Even when encouraged to take full annual leave, the workers felt uncomfortable about doing so.

HATSUMI: Since our office is the headquarters for the union, which advocates an increase in annual leave, our boss insists that I take more annual leave; but in reality I can't. If I take leave, I can't keep up with my work. Even now I can't complete all the assigned tasks on time.

(9 January 1992)

Unlike the others, Miyuki had strong views about her leave entitlement after her request to take a day off to attend a pop concert was rejected.

MIYUKI: My immediate boss told me that I lack common sense, since I had been on a holiday to the US several months before. Of course I knew that it would be a hassle. That's why I requested the day's leave a month ahead, so that he could get casual staff in plenty of time. Then I asked for a half-day off just to minimise the inconvenience, but he wouldn't give that to me either. For me, leave is meaningless if I can't take it when I want it, frankly speaking. If my friends are not available to go out with me, or if I can't go where I want, leave is meaningless. I work to live, not vice versa ... you know. Then I was told that I lack common sense! What sort of common sense is that? I don't follow his logic.

(6 February 1992)

Second, there were two aspects of overtime work that did not please the women. One was the large amount of overtime work required (except for Kanako, who welcomed this as an opportunity to earn more), and the other was underpayment or non-payment for overtime. Japan was still experiencing an economic boom during the period 1990–91, and there was a serious labour shortage. Not knowing what the norms were, many of the women worked as much as their bosses asked them, often exceeding the maximum hours set by each company in relation to the Labour Standards Act. Physically and mentally tired in their new environments, the women disliked it. Unlike men, who may see overtime work as an opportunity to demonstrate their commitment and/or develop relations with their bosses and seniors, the women did not associate such work with their promotion prospects. Indeed, many women envied those working for companies that adopted the policy of 'no overtime work'. Noshie was a clerical worker at such a company.

NOSHIE: My workplace is not bad. Our company doesn't have overtime work. If you interpret this in a positive way, you can go home at 5.30 p.m. But if you interpret it in another way, it means however much overtime you work you don't get paid for it.

(26 January 1992)

In fact, Noshie turned up for our interview over Sunday dinner on her way back from her office, where she had just completed a task due on the following day. She said that she was responsible for completing the task on time even if it meant working out of hours.

Furthermore, overtime was not fully remunerated. The women reluctantly accepted this situation as being beyond their control. Miyuki worked almost two hours' overtime every day but did not receive the appropriate payment.

KO: Why do they pay you fewer hours than you've worked? Do people in the personnel department make an adjustment? Can't you complain about it?

MIYUKI: (Laughs) No point! Everybody's in the same boat. If I raise the issue, I might get the blame. So I don't want to stick my head out. All companies are the same in this regard. But I think it is very strange [*hen*] though. If they can't pay us, why make us work overtime?

(6 February 1992)

A few women, however, developed their own justification for performing unpaid overtime work. Hatsumi, the union office staff member, worked about 30 hours overtime per month in the first year, more than the upper limit of 20 hours. She was instructed to claim for 20 hours of overtime, and the remaining hours under the heading of 'other allowance', and received a full allowance for the hours that she worked, at least initially.

HATSUMI: But I started feeling guilty at receiving so much extra pay.

KO: Why?

HATSUMI: I didn't think that I worked enough to deserve the overtime pay that the company gave me. I mean, I had to work overtime because I was not competent enough to complete the assigned tasks during regular hours.

KO: Who said that? Your boss?

HATSUMI: No, no one said that to me. We don't have time cards. So if you don't apply for overtime pay, you just don't get it. That is, if you don't apply, it means that you did not work overtime. So nowadays I just apply for ten hours.

(9 January 1992)

Hatsumi's voluntary overtime work was similar to Noshie's willingness to work extra hours. They somehow considered that they were not keeping up with their work through their lack of ability rather than an excessive work-load, and that they must make up for their shortcomings by working extra hours, without additional payment.

A new kind of 'human relations' at work

The human relations in the workplace were more complex than the women had ever experienced, although schools gradually prepared the young to enter the hierarchical relationships of the adult world through, for example, the existence of senior–junior relationships in club activities (LeTendre 1994; Rohlen 1983: 190–91). There was a hierarchy of workers: seniors were ranked by length of service, then came immediate supervisors and other superiors. There were different career tracks depending on one's education level and gender. There was the distinction of belonging: outsiders versus insiders. That is, an office would have permanent employees of the main company, employees of subsidiary companies, and temporary full-time workers (*haken*) sent from agencies (but who may have been working in the same workplace for over three years thanks to constant renewal of contracts). There was also a distinction between full-time and part-time workers. The women also learned how to interact with clients. While they learned appropriate formal language usage for different relationships (including various uses of honorific language),[1] it took them a while to adapt to the formal (e.g. with clients and superiors) and informal interaction patterns in the workplace. The women not only learned that they were required to maintain harmonious relationships at work, but also realised that it was in their best interests to do so.

Relationships with immediate bosses and seniors were extremely significant in determining the level of satisfaction with the workplace. Unpleasant relationships made the workplace virtually unbearable, and drove two women out, even if the work content was satisfactory. Oriko, a graduate of the interior furnishing course, was delighted to get an industrial designer's position at a subsidiary of a multinational heavy industrial company through her school's job referral system. She liked drafting train carriage interiors, but disliked her immediate boss.

ORIKO: He's very clever, but not flexible. So sure of himself that he would not listen to others. For example, if I worked really hard but couldn't finish a task, he made up his mind that I was lazy.

(3 February 1992)

She became desperate, crying in the toilet almost every day over the way her immediate boss spoke to her, which she considered to be 'bullying'. She approached his immediate boss and asked if she could resign since she could not endure the situation. He was sympathetic to her plight (given that her predecessors had suffered similar experiences working with the same man) and repeatedly asked her to stay (*gambatte*) by promising a change; but the change in her boss's behaviour lasted only one month.

ORIKO: It was partly my fault. My male colleagues advised me to express my anger and sadness more openly by, for example, ignoring my boss so that he would know that I was genuinely upset. But I'm not good at doing that. Ten minutes after I'd been crying, when he started speaking to me, I somehow managed to respond as if nothing had happened.

(3 February 1992)

In the end, after 21 months she was relieved to be able to resign by citing marriage as a reason, without causing loss of face to anybody. She was invited to return to work part-time after marriage, an offer she politely declined.

Fukuko was the top student in her class, and declined her teacher's advice to attend a local government university via the school's recommendation system. Instead, she secured a position in the national postal service through a competitive examination, in the hope of a job with short working hours so that she could devote herself to Jehovah's Witness missionary activities. (She had been a member of the Jehovah's Witnesses since her high school days, following in the steps of her mother.) After a few months of training given to hundreds of new recruits, she started working in a small post office with four staff. One of her senior workers was incompetent, which Fukuko, along with their postmaster and another female worker, compensated for by working late.

FUKUKO: Not only incompetence, she bullied me, saying things like 'Why do you make such a mess?' in front of customers. She often got angry at me. Since I didn't want to challenge her by saying 'It was not me' in front of customers, I just apologised. Then I gradually got stressed out. My dad said that I no longer laughed as much at home, and everyone around me noticed that I was mentally exhausted. So, although the branch manager tried to dissuade me from leaving, others did not.

(5 February 1992)

Fukuko liked the postmaster's caring and sympathetic approach towards the staff. But this approach to human relations, which Fukuko considered 'traditional', relied on colleagues accommodating one another by making up for individual weaknesses, and underpinned the postmaster's decision to take in the senior worker, whom no other branch office wanted. As Rohlen (1974: 79–80) notes, incompetence is not an excuse for dismissing someone, even in the private sector. Fukuko was encouraged by many customers, as well as by other new recruits (whom she met during the initial training) who wrote letters encouraging her to stay. But in the end, after 16 months in the job, she decided to resign, choosing a relatively quiet time to leave to cause the office minimum disruption.

Quitting within two years

Thirteen of the 19 who entered employment at least contemplated resigning when faced with difficulties in the first two years. However, within the same period only five had left their first employment. Two women resigned in pursuit of desired long-term careers. Natsumi left for further study at night school with the intention of securing an industrial designing position, while Fukuko, who was bullied, wanted to commit herself to Jehovah's Witness missionary work. The other three women cited marriage as the reason for resigning but, as I explain later, the realities were more complicated. In the first two years in the workforce, two others had recently informed their bosses of their decision to resign: Tomoe did so after heated discussion with her immediate boss, while Mutsuko had enrolled in a baking course at a private vocational school for the following year. Shizu and Hatsumi were still seriously considering resignation in the near future. When the women considered resignation, they first consulted their friends, family and close colleagues. Several expressed their wish to resign to their immediate bosses, but were in all cases encouraged to defer their decisions.

Hatsumi was stressed because she thought she was making too many errors in her job, and because she felt that her work excessively dominated her life.

HATSUMI: I feel that work eats up 80 per cent of my life. That is too much weight attached to work. My work is demanding and I am exhausted. If I worked part-time, it would be easier. We have six-monthly performance appraisal meetings with one of our bosses. In a meeting last December (after 20 months at the job), I asked him to let me resign in June. He asked me why. When I said, 'I am not able to perform as well as I like and have lost confidence,' he said, 'That is not a reason for resignation. Everybody lacks confidence in performing some tasks. Please persist [*gambatte*].'

(9 January 1992)

The women had not expected that their desire to resign would be opposed by the companies. In fact, companies typically attempted to persuade a woman to reconsider her decision to quit by instituting a lengthy process of resignation, and by having the woman's immediate bosses and other senior staff members attempt to dissuade her. Colleagues often became worried and discussed the matter with the woman, generally encouraging her to think again. As we saw, bosses tried to discourage even the two 'bullied women' (Fukuko and Oriko) from resigning.

Observing this happening to themselves or to others around them, the women noticed the difference between having a permanent full-time job and the casual part-time jobs (*arubaito*) that they held while at high school, and by extension felt a sense of being *shakai-jin*, whom they understood to have more responsibility.

ORIE: It's not as simple as quitting your *arubaito* job. You can't just stop coming to work tomorrow or even next week. Say, if I want to quit, the replacement person has to be recruited and I will have to supervise her training. It'll take at least three months to stop work.

(15 February 1992)

Even Tomoe, who was told to resign by her immediate boss after a heated argument, had difficulties getting other bosses to accept her decision to resign.

The women wondered why companies made resignation difficult. Oriko thought that her immediate boss might lose face through her leaving prematurely, and chose to resign by citing pending marriage as the reason. Miyuki suspected that her immediate boss actively arranged another position, which he considered to be more appealing to Miyuki, because he feared that the company would judge him negatively for an immediate subordinate's departure. Other women interpreted the boss's efforts to dissuade them from quitting as goodwill. They also wondered whether this applied to older workers, and whether companies considered young women too immature to make such a big decision.

The women's readings of their employers' reactions are supported by other studies. Rohlen (1974:73) states that irregular forms of quitting (i.e. other than retirement for men and older single women and resignation on marriage in the case of all other women) imply that the relationship between the individual and the company has failed and cause embarrassment to both parties. The immediate bosses have a particular stake in dissuading subordinates, since their reputation could suffer, which might result in their being transferred or demoted if several resignations occur (Rohlen 1974: 86, 88). Ogasawara's study (Ogasawara 1998: 166) on tertiary-educated female office workers supports Rohlen's view, suggesting that male workers' ability to work with female office workers is supposed to demonstrate a boss's management ability. Ogasawara's tertiary-educated white-collar female workers (popularly called 'OLs') understood this mechanism fully and used this fact to their advantage; but 17 to 20-year-old high school graduates did not.

In view of the difficulty of early resignation, marriage provided a legitimate reason for both parties (employees and bosses). Among the five who quit their first employment by the end of their second year, three cited marriage as their reason. However, post-marital resignation was not mandatory. In fact, Orie worked for a month after marriage so that she could receive an end-of-year bonus. Marriage in this case was a trigger, or a socially acceptable justification, for leaving employment that they were not happy with. Besides Kanako, who left in her third month in a job when she moved to a distant location as a result of marriage (triggered by pregnancy), the other two women were dissatisfied with either the work itself or with human relations at their workplace, and were pleased to resign.

ORIKO: Looking back, I think that I might have married in order to escape from that suffering; I mean, at least one of the reasons for marriage. I had long wanted to quit, but did not have a good reason. You know, it's a bit awkward to publicly state, 'I want to resign because I do not like my immediate boss.' Don't you think?

(3 February 1992)

Oriko did not think that her boss was aware that he was responsible for her resignation.

Making sense of one's class, gender and ethnicity at work

The workplace enabled the women to have contact with a wider range of people than ever before. This, I suspect, was first because of the relatively large scale of these women's employers (firms with at least 100 employees). Second, these women (except for Kanako, who was employed in a pearl jewellery factory for three months) worked in clerical or sales positions rather than blue-collar jobs. Both of these factors made the workplace more heterogeneous in terms of employee class and educational background, in comparison with, for example, small family-run businesses, retail stores and small factories. In the former workplaces, a working-class subculture is less likely to develop, in contrast to the small factory that Roberson studied, where a male blue-collar subculture prevailed (Roberson 1998: 309). Nationwide, less than 20 per cent of female high school graduates enter blue-collar work, as opposed to 57 per cent of their male counterparts (as we saw in Chapter 2; see Table 2.1); and this difference is likely to affect the ways in which young working-class men and women experience class-specific factors in the first years at work.

Awareness of class

The girls' decision to enter vocational high schools and then the workforce was at least partly guided by their class culture. They did not share the dominant middle-class pursuit of university education and jobs in large corporations. Instead they chose vocational high schools in their final year of junior high school (aged 15) because they believed vocational high schools would assist them to get a job, just as academic high schools focus on preparation for entrance examinations. The subculture at these vocational schools, where most students had similar family backgrounds, also influenced their plans for the future. Most women, for instance, envisaged their post-marital life as working part-time to supplement the family finances ('unless my husband's income is sufficient'), rather than becoming a full-time middle-class housewife, as described by Vogel (1978) and Imamura (1987).

Being constantly in a workplace made up of workers of diverse backgrounds, the women emphasised meeting 'new kinds of people' at work, which eventually led them to position themselves socially in relation to their co-workers and to heighten their own sense of place in the social hierarchy. For example, when coming into personal contact with four-year university female graduates, the women saw these unfamiliar women as coming from 'proper' families and living on the other side of town. It seems that the women almost automatically associated four-year university female graduates with family wealth, fathers' occupations, and place of residence, even though they were not fully informed about individual cases.

For many of these women, this was their first direct continuous personal contact with female university graduates. Naturally, the women may have had casual and one-off encounters with such graduates or aspirants in elite academic high schools, but they were now *required* to maintain pleasant daily contact with them. When referring to these women, they often used expressions such as *sodachi ga chigau* (literally, having a different upbringing), *ojôsan* (proper young unmarried ladies) and *uchira to chigau* (unlike us). They noticed differences but could not explain them effectively.

NOSHIE: When I talk to them in the way I used to with my classmates at high school, it is totally different. My workplace does not normally recruit high school graduates. The university graduates are from expensive schools like XYZ University. So they all come from nice families. You see, I was born and bred in the *shitamachi*, and only have high school education. I just can't keep a conversation going. For example, I would say, 'We used to do this and that while at high school.' They would say, 'Oh, we have never done that.'

KO: So are you making friends at work?

NOSHIE: I think they are all good-natured. But it's just that our conversation is awkward. You know, the way in which they play is different ... the atmosphere is different.

KO: How?

NOSHIE: Well, how can I explain? ... They do an extension of what they did while at uni, which is alien to us. Sometimes I don't understand what they are talking about, like doing this and that on their way back from uni. Well ... now some of us women who eat lunch together are planning to have an overnight trip and I am invited, but I don't think it will be fun [laughs]. I am sociable, but you know, I really don't want to go. I feel I won't be able to stand being with them all day long.

(26 January 1992)

While curious about and friendly with female graduates, the women felt at a distance from them. Orie, for instance, did not take up the opportunity to join the company-run English conversation classes since she did not feel it was for high school graduates like her. Many did not attempt to develop personal friendships with university women, because they felt *kyûkutsu* (uncomfortable). Nor did they feel a desire to be like them.

Perception of gender norms

While at high school, the girls knew that once they left what they considered to be a 'protected' environment their experiences would be more directly guided by their female gender. They learned, for example, that employment positions were allocated according to gender, that women did not have equal access to promotion, that married women were expected to take primary responsibility for the family, and that women (of their background) would work part-time to supplement the family income. While the school intervened in the ethnic minority students' decision-making about their post-school employment in the form of strong anti-discrimination messages and affirmative actions (Okano 1997), it displayed indifference to gender matters (Okano 2000).

The women's assumptions of gender-specific expectations were confirmed in the workplace in several ways. First, they saw that initial training was provided separately for groups divided by gender and education levels.

MOKO: The company employs so many men. For the entry ceremony all new recruits gathered at the head office, 100 women and over 500 men. But at the training we all said, 'Where are the men?' Men and women had separate training. Later we noticed that university graduates had gone to the research centre in another town and high school graduates to factories. We never saw them again.

(1 February 1992)

Second, they saw that task distribution was gender-specific: female workers and male workers were assigned different kinds of tasks at the outset. The men were allowed to work more hours of overtime than women; but given that the overtime hours were not fully remunerated, the women were not envious. Third, the women also observed that older women without tertiary education did not reach positions comparable with their male counterparts, and that even female university graduates could not attain the same positions as their male counterparts. Fourth, young women learned the reality of the famous M-curve of female labour participation, whereby full-time permanent female workers leave work for several years for child-rearing and return to work (but not necessarily to the same workplace) as part-time casual workers. While many post-industrial societies share this M-curve, the dip in the middle remains deep in Japan (see Figure 4.1). Such expectations were expressed in casual conversations.

MOKO: At a party one of the bosses advised us that we should travel overseas while still young. I said, 'Since I can't afford to travel on my salary, I will go overseas with the 300,000 yen coupon that the company gives workers for 35 years' service.' Then everyone said, 'Really! You must be joking. Do you intend to work that long?' [Laughs]

(1 February 1992)

Family responsibilities interfered with women's work arrangements. There were very few older regular female workers. Many women gave up work when they married or had children, although employers often did not impose such restrictions. Female university graduates also followed this path. They learned of *kotobuki taisha* (resignation with congratulations), whereby the marrying female worker given a warm send-off by colleagues and bosses with their

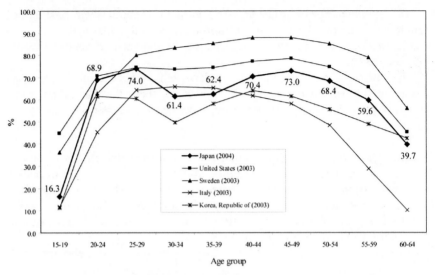

Figure 4.1 Female labour participation by age group: international comparison and the percentage for Japan in 2004.
Source: ILO (2005).

good wishes. The women's perception of their future in the company was pessimistic. They were fully aware that they would stay in clerical jobs until retirement. Many considered working until marriage or the arrival of their first child, and did not have long-term plans.

In view of these observations, it is not surprising that the women learnt to see their paid employment as being less important than that of men. Two competent women willingly quit their permanent positions and relocated themselves to suit their husbands' needs.

YAYOI: Well … since I'm a woman, I am not fussy about my job, and it will take care of itself somehow. But my husband's job is different; it is for life.

(31 January 1992)

This was despite the fact that both husbands were unable to hold down jobs. Consequently, Yayoi supported her husband by undertaking part-time work. Kanako and her husband had to borrow heavily, and lived with his parents for almost a year after marrying.

Women did not necessarily regard limited opportunities at work as deplorable. Seeing the differences in career paths between men and women, several of them thought that men's lives were physically and mentally more demanding and that their lot was better. Middle-class women shared this view (Iwao 1993).

NATSUMI: I often think, because men have the responsibility of being the breadwinner, they must think about the long-term future. So even if they have their own 'dreams', they can't realise their dreams so easily, don't you think? ... Yeah, the men's lot is more demanding.

(25 January 1992)

Despite perceptions of a less than favourable future at work, some women at the age of 20 were starting to consider a longer-term commitment to the company than they had initially intended – staying on for five years or until the age of 23. Sekie, a nurse trainee, and Fumiko, a clerical worker, started thinking of strategies to gain the same career prospects as 'them', those with university qualifications.

Third-generation Koreans

When third-generation *zainichi* Koreans were deciding on employment in their final year of high school, their Korean background was the major consideration because *zainichi* Koreans still faced barriers in terms of access to and promotion in the mainstream Japanese employment market (Okano 1997). They were encouraged to choose Korean-friendly mainstream companies, but some, like Tomoe, chose (against her teacher's advice) an ethnic Korean company in search of what she called 'comfort'. At a new workplace, awareness of one's ethnic background was again heightened. Entry into mainstream employment forced two of the three *zainichi* third-generation Korean women to make decisions, yet again, as to how to project themselves: whether as *zainichi* Korean or as Japanese. This situation was not new to them. They had faced this dilemma frequently whenever they encountered a group of new people; for example, when introduced to friends' friends or when joining a club. To date, both had usually opted to remain silent on their ethnic background. At school they had adopted Japanese names and revealed their ethnic background only to selected friends.

Once at work, the women gave more serious consideration to the choice than usual, because they would be interacting with their colleagues almost every day. While both Orie and Noshie decided to continue their use of Japanese names at work, each adopted a different approach. Orie decided to announce her *zainichi* background to her immediate office colleagues at Mitsubishi Heavy Industries from the outset, since she preferred that to being 'found out' behind her back. Her mother suggested that she subsequently adopt her Korean name on the basis that such a public announcement would make the continued use of her Japanese name meaningless, but Orie decided against that as she felt, to quote her words, 'My Japanese name represents myself more accurately, and suits me.'

Noshie decided against such a public announcement about her ethnicity but did not actively cover up her Korean origin. As we saw in Chapter 3, it was only when she casually mentioned her *zainichi* background in the context of the general election that she discovered her colleague's knowledge of her nationality. The colleague and others avoided referring to Noshie's nationality since they believed that Noshie would prefer it that way. Noshie understood the complexity involved – since she had adopted a Japanese-sounding name, people might well have interpreted this as her desire to hide her Korean background. Although everyone now knew about her *zainichi* background, Noshie never considered adopting her Korean name at work. These women's perception of themselves is in contrast to that of *zainichi* Koreans educated in the North Korean ethnic schooling system in Japan (Ryang 1997) and tertiary-educated South Koreans, who are more likely to adopt Korean names (Fukuoka 2000).

The third Korean girl, Tomoe, did not face this decision. She chose to work in a Korean-run bank for South Korean residents, thinking that she would feel more comfortable working there than in a non-Korean organisation. She was not entirely enthusiastic about the decision, but she considered it to be a safe option at the time; it was also supported by her father, who was a member of the North Korean organisation (Chongryun), and by her elder brother and his wife, who were active members of the South Korean organisation (Mindan).[2] The bank provided her with an all-*zainichi* environment for the first time in her life. All of her colleagues and bosses were South Korean *zainichi* who, Tomoe said, understood her situation. Tomoe liked that aspect of the workplace, but disliked the employment practice that treated female workers as temporary staff with an employment period of, at most, three years. This, she claimed, was typical of Korean firms and worse than the treatment of women employees in Japanese companies.

The three *zainichi* women's confidants (who were Japanese) heard these stories and vicariously experienced their friends' lives as *zainichi*. At the Kobe-city Adult Day ceremony, hosted for and attended by young people who had turned 20 during the previous 12 months, Noshie and Tomoe wore colourful *chogori* ethnic costumes like most *zainichi* Korean participants. Orie decided to wear kimono at the last moment, to her mother's displeasure; and was a little concerned about how other Koreans might see this decision. The photo that Orie took showed a group of happy ex-Sasaki High girls dressed in kimono and *chogori*. By virtue of mixing at the ethnic boundary, these close friends developed an understanding of what it meant to be a *zainichi* Korean and, by extension, to be mainstream Japanese. This sense of difference in ethnic background did not deter them from sharing a long-lasting friendship, as well as a sense of solidarity of class background: They still referred to themselves as 'us', as distinct from female university graduates.

Income, consumption and leaving home

A permanent full-time job brought the women a regular personal income. They earned about 100,000 yen (approximately US$ 800 in 1992) per month after tax, insurance and superannuation payments, and received several times that for each of the twice-yearly bonuses. However, a regular monthly wage and bonuses did not give these women much more extra money for their immediate use than they earned in part-time jobs (*arubaito*) while in high school. Several women contributed a token amount (*kimochi dake*) to their family budget. Tomoe contributed 45,000 yen per month to her household (her stay-at-home mother and four sisters); her two elder sisters each contributed 50,000 yen. Hatsumi also made a major contribution.

KO: Does the money that you earn make you feel *ichininmae* [adult]?
HATSUMI: Yes, I think so, maybe because my family's been poor. It did make a difference. I can now give some money to my parents, save for myself, and buy my own clothes. I give 30,000 yen to the household budget. When I receive a bonus and on New Year's Day I give pocket money to my parents. I think they like it.

(9 January 1992)

Some parents deposited their daughter's contributions into special savings accounts created for the daughter's future. Regardless of their input to the household budget, the women were forced by their parents to save over half of their monthly salary and bonuses. This meant that many had saved over one million yen in two years.

One's own money, however, has more significance when combined with freedom from school regulations and the supposed adult status granted by a permanent full-time job. School regulations prohibited the wearing of make-up and accessories on school grounds, and discouraged it outside school. Now that they no longer faced such restrictions, and had legitimate reasons to purchase clothes for work (even though most wore uniforms once at work), the young women started to experiment in creating their personal images through consumption.

But the 'freedom' from school regulations came with another restriction – that of limited time for recreation. This affected the kind of activities that the women could enjoy, making shopping a popular pastime. Many obtained a full set of cosmetics and new clothes. Yayoi bought a fur coat that she had long wanted, and Fumiko a small car. These women did not show particular interest in European 'brand' products favoured by middle-class junior college students (McVeigh 1997). Tomoe spent 10,000 yen each month at the hairdresser, and took up golf at a golf-driving range. Travelling was also fashionable, but was indulged in only by those who had the 'courage' to use their annual leave for such purposes. Two women went overseas with their friends, while others opted to spend their annual leave skiing, for which they purchased 'proper' gear. Two women attended English conversation courses – Hatsumi wanted to go on a working holiday overseas, while Norimi was planning to take a language course in the US. Consumption became one of the available forms of self-expression and an attempt to create an identity (Clammer 1997: 153–67). However, the producers of the goods and the media, for example women's magazines, also guided their consumption patterns.[3]

The changes brought by such consumption varied from the extreme to the almost unnoticeable. Yayoi's case was described by her high school friends as *shakai-jin debut*, whereby, they claimed, she underwent a complete change through consumption, triggered by a new group of 'friends'. Yayoi was a simple and studious student at technical high school, and went out with a student one year her senior at the school, whom everybody assumed she would marry. As we saw in Chapter 3, during the one-month initial training at a large electronics chain store, Yayoi encountered what she described as glamorous (*hanayakana*) girls, found them 'refreshing', and simply enjoyed the kind of after-work activities that they participated in as a group, such as socialising with young men at restaurants until late at night. Her parents were not happy but considered it a passing phase. Fukuko was at the opposite end of the continuum. Her lifestyle had not been affected by the regular income and freedom that came with a full-time permanent job.

FUKUKO: I don't go out much, and am pretty much self-sufficient. I am just stingy! I don't understand why young women spend so much money on brand products.

(5 February 1992)

Lifestyle changes were drastic for those who started living alone. Apart from Sekie, who was required to stay in the clinic's nurse accommodation from the outset, Natsumi was the only woman who started living on her own in the second year out of school. She did this in order to combine work with a designing course at a private vocational college, after quitting her first permanent job. Her budget was tight. While her parents paid the tuition fee, she supported herself, spending half of her salary on rent. When I met her ten months after she left home, she was stressed and had started to consider returning home.

NATSUMI: After I started living on my own, I felt a strong sense of gratitude towards my parents, and how lucky I've been. I even miss my parents getting angry at me.

(25 January 1992)

Several women revealed their desire to live away from their parents, which they believed would encourage the independence they saw themselves as lacking. They were also aware that their parents would not allow them to do this. Yoshie's family life had not changed from her high school days, even after she started working as a sales person at a large department store.

YOSHIE: Unless I live alone, I won't feel I need to do housework. My mother does everything and I don't have any chance to cook or do laundry. She's very efficient. When I think of doing some of the housework, it's already done.

(30 January 1992)

Fumiko, the ambitious clerical worker, faced a dilemma in wanting a certain degree of independence while also wanting to keep the comforts that she had long enjoyed. She was planning to leave home and live with her boyfriend later that year.

KO: Now that you earn a salary, do you feel a sense of independence [*jiritsu*]?
FUMIKO: Not yet, because I still live with my parents. If I leave home, I will feel a sense of independence. My mum cooks for me and does everything. I've saved a lot, over one million yen. I would feel insecure if I didn't have any savings. I don't like depending on my parents, but am not ready to be independent yet.

(16 February 1992)

Many women did not like being seen as immature, in particular by their parents. In order to overcome this, they wanted to live away from home.

ORIE: My parents always say I'm not a grown-up yet. I myself don't feel that I am one, and they interfere. I say to them, 'I'm working now and have my own life, so please leave me alone.' Then my dad says, 'What are you talking about? It is natural to interfere since you aren't yet a grown-up. If you don't like it, you can leave this house.' I can't talk to him sensibly, you know.

(15 February 1992)

Hatsumi had been taking English conversation lessons as a means to achieving independence.

HATSUMI: I just want to be more independent [*jiritsu*]. That's why I want to go on a working holiday. I want to learn English and then be independent. Then I can leave home. I think I am unreliable [*tayorinai*]. I am frustrated with my attitudes and actions at work. At home I am told that I am immature and undependable. I don't like it. I want to do everything myself and gain more self-confidence.

(9 January 1992)

Fukuko initiated a saving plan for her parents' anniversary trip in the face of their refusal to accept her contribution to the household budget, since she did not want to be considered immature.

Late-teen marriages and relationships

These working-class women were not under the kind of pressure to find and keep a boyfriend as experienced by their counterparts in the UK and the USA, at least in the first two years out of high school (e.g. Cockburn 1987; Griffin 1985; Skeggs 1997). I did not observe any strong desire on the part of the women, nor social pressure, to get married, in contrast to the case of factory women and office ladies (so called 'OLs') in Lo's 1985 study (Lo 1990). This may have been due to the tendency for relatively late marriage among Japanese. The average ages of first marriage in 1970 were 26.9 for males and 24.2 for females; but were 29.6 and 27.8 respectively in 2004 (Japan-Kôseirôdô-sho 2005c), a point I return to in a later chapter on marriage. Another factor was that the women still lived with their parents, rather than in crowded company dormitories, which, Lo said, encouraged women to marry in order to be able to move out (Lo 1990). The influence that their parents could exercise on the 18–20 year olds seems more substantial than in the case of their Anglo-Western counterparts, as shown, for example, by the women's willingness to follow their parents' advice to save half of their salary. Nor did they project themselves as sensual beings, for example, in their dress and deportment, in comparison to Anglo-Western women of the same age. White's description (M. White 1993: 170) that 'teens in Japan, to American eyes, seem cute, innocent, perhaps asexual' seems to apply to these young women. The number of births to women under 20 remains small in Japan, a point discussed in Chapter 7.

Three women married during this period. We met two of them in Chapter 3, Kanako and Yayoi. Kanako married a high school sweetheart after finding she was pregnant within five months of graduating from high school. Kanako's parents were not happy. Her husband was a job-hopper and was unemployed for some time, but Kanako gained a sense of stability from living with his mother and her family, who supported the couple financially for almost 16 months. During this time, she gave birth to a premature baby girl and suffered her husband's affairs and gambling, but moved to a rented flat once he settled into a fishing job on his uncle's boat. Although the family had a large debt (including fishermen's union fees, a car loan and expenses) and she asserted that they lived 'in poverty', Kanako and her husband seemed happy. Several of her friends from high school wondered if she really was, as we saw earlier. Fumiko, another friend from high school, was more concerned with the level of debt that Kanako and her husband had accumulated over two years.

Yayoi was married to a delivery-man whom she had met at work, and had moved to a provincial city where her husband and his parents lived. He was a first son. When I visited the newlyweds in 1992, Yayoi was 'managing' a difficult situation; her husband had been unemployed for several months, and her part-time work supported the household.

YAYOI: To tell the truth, I tasted how miserable it was to have no money in the house. I really wanted to lead a 'normal' life. That wish was always in my mind. Then I thought, 'Why have I had to put up with so much since I got married?'

KO: You didn't ask for your parents' help?

YAYOI: No way. I could never ask them to lend us money. Honestly, it was also so hard to pretend that everything was all right.

(31 January 1992)

Yayoi was also coping with in-laws that she came to dislike. Nonetheless, she continued to project herself as content with the situation, both to her own family and to close friends.

Nineteen-year-old Oriko's marriage to a man 20 years her senior met uncompromising opposition from her parents. Oriko was the top student in the class at Imai Tech High, a good friend of Kanako, and the only student in her class with a tertiary-educated father, a real-estate agent. Her parents believed that she was unnecessarily taking on a difficult future, financially, physically and emotionally. Reminding her that the man was an only son with three elder sisters from a relatively poor family, her parents warned that she would soon have to care for her prospective husband's elderly parents, who were already in their 70s. Her own mother had been caring for her demented mother for several years, and did not want Oriko to take on such a demanding role at a young age. The strains placed on women caring for elderly relatives in Japan are well documented by Long (1996). Oriko's parents emphasised the fact that her boyfriend's parents lived in a municipal housing complex for lower-income families, and that he, at almost 40 years of age, had yet to purchase a house to accommodate both his family and his parents.

ORIKO: My father said, 'The conditions for this marriage are the worst that I can think of. Don't choose the worst. Please marry an ordinary man.'

(3 February 1992)

Oriko pleaded with her parents, and managed to persuade them to agree to the marriage. Oriko was genuinely shocked by her parents' reaction to a relationship which to her was an innocent and romantic development between two individuals. She had never heard her parents referring to others as 'poor' and had not expected them to be as materialistic as to show grave concern with the lack of her future husband's savings. She had expected her parents to be happy for her. At the time of interview in the husband's company flat, Oriko looked content with her honeymoon pregnancy.

None of the parents welcomed the three marriages. They expressed their opposition quite frankly. The parents of Kanako and Yayoi cited the men's personality problems and income-earning capacity. Oriko's parents were concerned with her fiancé's family background. All considered the late teens too early for marriage. Those who married were now members of a new 'convoy', and were coping with the beginning of a 'long engagement' (Plath 1980). Kanako and Yayoi found this extremely demanding and difficult, and wondered why they had entered marriage so early. They stressed that the in-laws were 'different' from their own families, but were unable to articulate the nature of this difference in general terms; referring, rather, to numerous concrete examples that annoyed them. Kanako was still trying to make sense of and conform to what she called the 'fishermen's way of life', which was quite different from her upbringing. The 'fishermen's culture', according to her, included a clear gender-based division of tasks, both on the boat (e.g. women did not dive) and onshore (women mended the nets). The men's lives also included hard drinking and gambling, fighting and violence, mutual lending of cash, and characteristic speech patterns. The fishermen's community maintained close-knit relationships, extending across generations and often involving family relationships. Yayoi, who had been married only three months when I met her in early 1992, was still trying to come to terms with seemingly incomprehensible actions on the part of her in-laws.

Four women were dating casually and having fun. Dating for them was 'just for play's sake' (*oasobide*). As long as dating remained 'play', they did not need to be concerned with complexities (*gotagota shitakoto*). The complexities included their own awareness of class differences (*sodachi no chigai*) and *zainichi* backgrounds, and their partners' and their own families' reactions, to which I shall return in Chapter 6.

Comparison with school experiences, and differentiating themselves from others

Between the ages of 18 and 20, two distinct processes influenced how the working-class women learned to perceive themselves. The first process involved comparing their new experiences with their past as a high school student. The second process involved differentiating themselves from people with whom they had to maintain continuous contact. In both processes, the women found the workforce to be the most important factor in the development of their adult identities. I shall explain the two processes in turn.

Transition from school to the workplace was a significant departure after 12 years of schooling. The women were often surprised by new experiences, and reminded of the fact that they were no longer students. They learned socially appropriate behaviour while at work, including not claiming for overtime or taking annual leave. They were puzzled when some of the recruits (including themselves) were not readily released from their job if they decided to leave. This brought home to them the fact that this work differed from the casual part-time jobs (*arubaito*) that they had held while at school. Two women found their bosses and seniors so unbearable that they resigned because of them. While earning their own money was not new, freedom from school regulations allowed them to spend their income, and to experiment at creating their own self-images through consumption. However, patterns of consumption were limited by the restricted time available for recreation, and by the limited amount of disposable income after contributing to family budgets and allowing for forced saving. Korean women departed from their past practice of not publicly revealing their ethnic identity, and made renewed decisions as to how to project themselves. For the few who married during this period, becoming a married woman and a nominal member of the husband's family brought socially expected roles and the responsibilities of wife and daughter-in-law. So did becoming a mother. The women could not fail to notice these normative expectations from their own families and relatives, as well as from their in-laws. They thus continuously saw themselves in comparison to what they had been as a high school student, and recognised that important changes had occurred to them, whether in the workplace or through marriage.

The second process involved differentiating themselves from other people they encountered. The resulting identities were not a group identity based on the workplace, as was the case with male workers in large companies in Rohlen's study (Rohlen 1974). Instead, the women found individual identities that distinguished them from their co-workers in terms of social class (*sodachi no chigai*) and gender. The workplace provided the women with direct personal exposure, often for the first time, to a wide range of people with diverse past experiences (e.g. family backgrounds and educational levels). The women noted not only that gender and educational qualifications determined task distribution, training and promotion, but also companies' assumptions about gender-specific family responsibilities as represented in *kotobuki taisha*. Furthermore, it was their continuous contact with female university graduates in the workplace that had the most significant impact on the women's perception of their own class backgrounds. They perceived these graduates, who came from middle-class families from different parts of the city, as 'new kinds of people'. The women saw that the graduates' past experiences and futures both in the workplace and in their private lives (e.g. choice of marriage partner, route to marriage, and full-time housewife role) were quite different from those they were familiar with in their close urban *shitamachi* community of a relatively homogeneous working-class population. While the women were friendly with the women university graduates, they continued to feel uncomfortable in their presence. 'New kinds of people' also entered the women's lives via dating and marriage. Marriage was particularly significant in forming new 'convoys' in their lives. The reactions of, and their relations with, their in-laws and their own relatives brought opportunities aplenty to discover themselves in comparison to 'others'.

During those two years, the 18–20-year-old women faced a new set of experiences and people, while constraints remained in the background. Their self-perception was changing, becoming more refined, detailed and concrete, but clearly remaining under a broad and unarticulated umbrella of 'working-class woman'.

5 Paid employment

From permanent to non-standard jobs

In the previous chapter, we saw how the young women managed to settle into the wider social world in the first two years after leaving high school. Their experiences during those years involved a distinctive series of events, and an unmistakable awareness of the status change from being a student to a full-time permanent employee. This process is widely referred to as a transition to *shakai-jin* (literally, society person), but as we saw earlier, being a *shakai-jin* is not identical to being an adult. This chapter examines the experience of employment after the initial years.

Let me first briefly locate the employment experience of this age group (19–30 years) in the life cycle of women. After schooling, women move to paid employment; some leave after childbirth while others stay on, and some of those who leave return to work when their children reach school age. While this trend has been observed in many post-industrial societies, Japan displays the sharpest drop in female workforce participation in the middle years. This trend in Japan is referred to, because of its shape, as an 'M-curve'. There is a strong contrast with social democratic nations in Scandinavia, where women continue working through child-bearing age (see Figure 4.1). But this is not the whole story. Japanese women differ from their sisters in other post-industrial nations in that they rarely return to full-time permanent jobs after childbirth (Yu 2002). The percentage of women in full-time permanent employment does not increase when women return to work after a break (see Figure 5.1).

Any jobs that are not full-time and permanent are considered 'non-standard' employment. Employment status categories in Japan differ slightly from those in the Anglo-West. First, the distinction between 'standard' (or 'regular') and 'non-standard' employment is the most significant in determining working conditions and in examining employment experiences in Japan. The Japanese labour market assumes full-time permanent employment to be 'regular' or 'standard' (*seiki*); it normally offers job security, lifetime employment, wage increases based on length of service and various forms of firm subsidies. Permanent part-time employment or fractional permanent appointments, whereby a worker holds a permanent job, works at a fraction of full-time hours and is paid pro rata, is almost non-existent. Second, non-standard forms

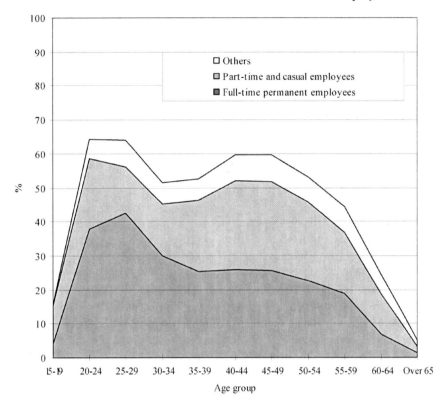

Figure 5.1 Percentages of female workers and full-time permanent employees by age group (2002).
Source: Japan-Kôseirôdô-shô (2005b: Figure 2–33).

of employment include *pâto, haken, shokutaku, keiyaku, rinji koyô* and *arubaito.* With no nationally accepted definition for each of these employment types, their boundaries remain obscure, and different employers, agencies and regions adopt different terms to describe the same category of work (Housemand and Ozawa 1998). *Pâto* generally refers to employment of less than 35 hours per week, but some 'part-timers' work more hours. *Haken* (literally, dispatching from an agency), *shokutaku* (literally, asking someone to work unofficially) and *keiyaku* (contract) are often close to full-time work, but involve fixed short-term contracts and are likely to be exempt from firm subsidies and fringe benefits (Yu 2002: 495). *Arubaito* and *rinji koyô* generally refer to casual work paid by the hour.

There is a national trend for female workers to move from full-time permanent jobs to non-standard employment over their life cycle. Over 70 per cent of those aged 20–24 are in full-time permanent jobs, while 46 per cent of 45–50 year-olds are in non-standard jobs (see Figure 5.2). The trend

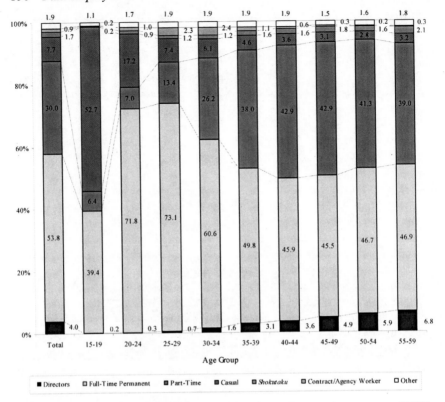

Figure 5.2 Distribution of different types of female employment by age group (1997). Source: Japan-Rôdô-shô (1999: Figure 2–5).

reflects the experiences of the women in my study: 73 per cent of those in the 25–29 age group were in standard employment. Other trends among female workers have been a general shift from large-scale companies to small to medium ones, and from white-collar to blue-collar jobs (Shirahase 1995: 2001).

To enhance our understanding, I decided to place the employment experiences of the young women in my study in four categories: (1) at their first company for 11 years; (2) in a permanent full-time job, but not at their first company; (3) agency, contract and part-time workers; and (4) casual employees. These categories are not mutually exclusive, but the young women seemed to make distinctions between them. Other than those who still held their first full-time permanent job, the women passed through different categories of employment status over the 11 years. Yayoi, for example, resigned from a permanent full-time job in order to marry, became a full-time homemaker, re-entered the workforce via casual work to support the family, was divorced, worked casually again in a fresh start, and then finally settled into another permanent full-time job. Some women were in two categories simultaneously: for example, having a casual job at weekends while holding a full-time permanent position during the week.

My informants' categories of employment altered over the survey period (see Table 5.1). In April 1990, one month after graduation from high school, 19 started their first full-time permanent job and two commenced tertiary education (one at a four-year co-ed university, and one at a two-year women's junior college or *tandai*). These two women had gained a place through school recommendation rather than taking the well-publicised competitive entrance examinations, as is often the case with mediocre students at non-elite academic high schools or vocational high schools (Okano and Tsuchiya 1999). By late 1997 (aged 25 or 26), the two tertiary students had obtained their first permanent employment after graduation. In early 2001 (aged 29), seven of the group of 21 were still in their first permanent full-time job, and three were in their second standard job.

In early 2001, the daily routines of those in paid employment still centred on the workplace, while those with children had shifted their focus to family life. Others placed priority on their 'lifestyle' or recreational activities. The patterns of their work experiences were thus influenced by their private lives. Why did some women stay in their first job, even for as long as a decade? For those who did, what were their future career plans? What was their experience of promotion? Why did some quit their first job? If they did, how did they find another job? Why was non-standard employment such as agency, contract and casual work attractive? Did their perception of agency and casual work change over the years? If so, how and why?

Staying with the first full-time permanent job

Of the seven people still in their first job in early 2001 (after ten years), all experienced at least some dissatisfaction with aspects of employment, such as work content, instrumental gains (working conditions) and human relationships. Often only one of these three aspects was acceptable and different individuals could place different values on each of them. For some, human relationships were the most important aspect. Those who possessed realistic expectations tended to be more satisfied, and more readily accepting of the situation they found themselves in.

Nationwide, the average length of employment with one employer for female workers has been increasing gradually. It was 9.0 years in 2004, an increase from 6.5 years in 1984 and 7.6 years in 1994 (Japan-Kôseirôdô-shô 2005b). This results partly from the recent trend towards late marriage. The national average for male workers was 13.4 years in 2004. In 2004, 22 per cent of female workers had worked with one employer for 5–9 years, 18 per cent for 1–2 years, and 15 per cent for 10–14 years (see Figure 5.3).

Table 5.1 Employment status of the women in the study in 1990, 1992, 1997 and 2001 (by number of women in each employment category)

	April 1990	January 1992	December 1997	January 2001
Permanent employee at first company	19 Ⓐ Ⓑ Ⓒ Ⓓ Ⓔ Ⓕ Ⓖ Ⓗ Ⓘ Ⓙ Ⓚ Ⓛ Ⓜ Ⓝ Ⓞ Ⓟ Ⓠ Ⓡ Ⓢ plus 2 other students (Ⓣ Ⓤ) who took up full-time tertiary studies	14 Ⓐ Ⓑ Ⓒ Ⓓ Ⓔ Ⓕ Ⓖ Ⓗ Ⓘ Ⓙ Ⓚ Ⓛ Ⓜ Ⓝ Plus 2 tertiary students (Ⓣ Ⓤ)	10 Ⓐ Ⓑ Ⓒ Ⓓ Ⓔ Ⓕ Ⓖ Ⓣ Ⓤ Ⓗ Satoko (married 1993, 2 children)	7 Ⓐ Moko Ⓑ Orie Ⓒ Miyuki Ⓓ Fumiko (divorced 1995) Ⓔ Saeko (married 1999) Ⓕ Yoshie (married 1999) Ⓗ Satoko (2 children)
Permanent employee but not at first company	0	0	6 Ⓟ Yayoi (divorced 1994) Ⓞ Natsumi Ⓚ Hatsumi (married 1993, divorced 1996) Ⓛ Sekie Ⓜ Shizu (married 1996) Ⓝ Mutsuko	4 Ⓟ Yayoi (divorced 1994) Ⓚ Hatsumi (divorced 1996) Ⓛ Sekie (married 1998) Ⓙ Tomoe
Agency worker	0	0	2 Ⓘ Norimi Ⓙ Tomoe	2 Ⓘ Norimi Ⓟ Sachiko

Table 5.1 (continued)

	April 1990	January 1992	December 1997	January 2001
Casual worker	0	3 Ⓟ Yayoi (married 1991) ◎ Natsumi ◎ Fukuko	1 ◎ Fukuko	4 ◎ Fukuko Ⓝ Mutsuko ◎ Natsumi Ⓡ Oriko (married 1991, 2 children)
Not in paid employment	0	2 Ⓡ Oriko (married 1991) Ⓢ Kanako (married 1990, 1 child)	2 Ⓡ Oriko (married 1991, 2 children) Ⓢ Kanako (married 1990, 3 children)	4 Ⓢ Kanako (married 1990, 3 children) ◎ Noshie (married 1998, 1 child) Ⓤ Sayaka (married 1997, 1 child) Ⓜ Shizu (married 1996)

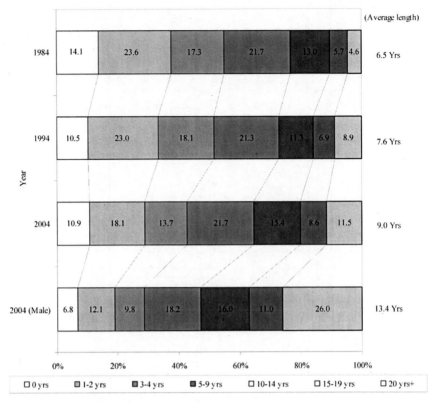

Figure 5.3 Distribution of female workers' length of employment with one employer.
Source: Japan-Kôseirôdô-shô (2005b: Figure 1–13).

Intrinsic satisfaction from work content

Fumiko, a graduate of Imai Tech High's interior design course, originally entered a Mitsubishi subsidiary company as an assistant to a designer of electrical circuits (*denki haisen kairo no zu*). Within the few first few months, she was asked by her boss to undergo extra training in design, which made her feel that she was being put on a faster career track than the other girls. In her second year, Fumiko was appointed leader of a newly created girls-only group designing software to manage a drainage system. She experienced a steep learning curve but enjoyed it. Some of her female contemporaries who could not keep up eventually became her assistants. Fumiko attributed her rise to her sound understanding of what the company valued in workers.

KO: Why do you think your seniors saw potential in you? Were you good at technical drawing? I don't recall that you were at high school. (Laughs)

FUMIKO: (Laughs) You've got a good memory. I wouldn't say I'm good at it. I was just quick. It is better to be quick in the job than to be good at it, once you are at work. However well you draw, if you can't make it on time, it's no use. At high school I used to draw things for Yayoi for 500 yen. I'm good at *tenuki* – doing a slack job in such a way that people don't notice it.

(21 November 1997)

If we consider Fumiko to be *yôryô ga ii* (tactful), as she described herself, her former classmate Natsumi lacked this attitude. Natsumi wanted to take time completing a job to her satisfaction, but her work was not always appreciated. In 1996 (her sixth year at work), Fumiko was promoted to the university graduate career track, and started working as a designer rather than as an assistant. This involved frequent trips to other cities, and more responsibility for her work and for her assistants. She liked the challenge of her work content, and managed human relationships effectively. She was also lucky. She considered that clients excused her mistakes more readily because she worked on public works projects. Clients from the electricity generation industry, however, were not so generous, and requested male staff members at the outset. Fumiko was the only one in the study who continuously liked her work content over the 11 years.

There were also experiences of ups and downs with the same employer over the years. Miyuki, for example, was satisfied with her situation in late 2000, precisely because she saw it in light of a series of struggles at different branches in the previous years. She liked her current position, which had little overtime work and pleasant relationships with colleagues. 'Artist' work was much more interesting than the checkout work that she initially did, and her skills in lettering and display gained at high school were appreciated. Miyuki's happiness at work perhaps derived from her realistic expectations of work and the workplace, the lack of the kind of inferiority complex that Hatsumi had, and an attitude that she called '*wagamichi o iku*' (going one's own way). Miyuki planned to continue working at the current workplace, while studying through a distance education program. She knew that she could not have everything that she wanted in a job; that a job came as a package of likes and dislikes.

Orie, a third-generation Korean woman, remained in the accounting department of a large firm, Mitsubishi Heavy Industry, for 11 years. In late 2000, she was happy with the workplace, although there had been times earlier when she had hated it and this had affected her health. Regular rotation of tasks among the department's 60 workers seemed to help. Orie was rotated about every two years, which, she thought, suited her.

ORIE: Well, when you do the same job for two years, you get bored. When you get a new task, it is demanding for about half a year, but … Mid-last year I had another change of work in the department. It was the most difficult and demanding job that I'd ever had. I was given a task that only men had done before. I hated it for a month. I don't think that my boss taught me well, either. I was so stressed out that I ended up going to hospital in an ambulance in the middle of the night. I had what they called 'excessive breathing' [*kakokyû*] and a convulsive attack [*keiren*], and I couldn't breathe. Apparently it was caused by psychological pressure. I don't have it any more. It was just a one-off.

(22 November 1997)

Orie understood that rotation was intended to assist workers to learn various tasks, but she also thought that it would prevent inappropriate actions such as favouring particular clients or misappropriation of money. Besides the job content, Orie was happy with the human relationships that a large company offered. The company, in Kobe-city, employed 6,000 regular workers, with many more workers seconded from its subsidiaries, and agency workers. The large number of workers enabled Orie to be 'choosy' without feeling guilty or embarrassed.

ORIE: There are about 60 people working in our office. I don't need to talk to people I don't like. I maintain surface relationships with a wide range of people. For example, I eat lunch with girls who entered the company in the same year as me [*dôki no hito*] in other departments. After work, I may go out with girls from our department. I don't eat with the same people every day. I feel as if I have found comfortable zones in different areas at work. I'm with X this time, I'm with Y that time, and so forth.

NOSHIE: That's great.

ORIE: I was stressed out when I had to eat lunch at my desk in our office for a few months after the earthquake, because the company cafeterias had been destroyed. I couldn't work out why I was so stressed, you know. Later I realised that it was because I was eating lunch with the same people every day! Then for the first time I understood what my sister was going through – she had been eating at her desk all that time.

(22 November 1997)

Orie also appreciated the generous working conditions that a large company offered women. Both maternity leave and child-rearing leave were available. But she also understood that this leave was not used much, and that an 'unwritten agreement' existed that an individual should not exercise her full leave entitlements. She did not think, for example, that she would be allowed to take one year off for family responsibilities. She said, 'I've no intention to push that far' (*sokomade yaru tsumori nai*).

Nationwide, the system of childcare leave (*ikuji kyûgyô*) of 12 months or more was available at about 36 per cent of companies in 2003. Larger companies were more likely to offer it: for example, 44 per cent of companies with more than 1,000 employees (Rôdô-Seisaku-Kenkyû-Kikô 2004). (See

Table 5.2.) However, as Orie and her friends observed, employees did not utilise the system effectively. Only 30 per cent of female employees of companies offering at least 12 months' childcare leave reported that they had taken advantage of this (Japan-Kôseirôdô-shô 2005b).[1]

We see a similar trend in relation to aged-care leave (*kaigo kyûgyô seido*) of three months or more. In 2003, this leave was offered by 45 per cent of all companies and 57 per cent of companies of over 1,000 employees (Rôdô-Seisaku-Kenkyû-Kikô 2004). However, only 10 per cent of female employees took advantage of the leave (Japan-Kôseirôdô-shô 2005a).

Work isn't great but human relationships keep me there

While not enthusiastic about the work content, some women were reasonably happy with their work. They all worked for a large company and enjoyed better-than-average working conditions. Moko and Saeko both considered the clerical work to be uninteresting but easy enough to manage.

MOKO: I have been doing the same job since I started eight years ago. But on paper I am working as a loan employee [*shukkô*]. That is to say, the personnel department is now a separate company. I am on the payroll of Saki Steel Company, but I work in a company called Saki Personnel Centre. But Saki Personnel Centre does exactly the same job as the department that I entered. It is strange and complicated.

KO: So the work itself is easy? You don't have to learn new things all the time?

MOKO: Yes. It is easy going in the sense that I don't have to learn many new things. But we rotate jobs.

(14 November 1997)

Moko was the only one among her friendship group of four who was still with the same company, for which she was teased by others.

Table 5.2 Companies offering aged-care and childcare leave by company size

Company size (number of employees)	*Percentage of companies offering aged/family care leave of more than 3 months (%)*	*Percentage of companies offering childcare leave of more than 1 year (%)*
Less than 100	32.0	28.0
100–299	41.3	36.2
300–499	43.4	34.8
500–999	45.2	26.8
1,000+	56.8	44.3
Total	44.6	35.7

Source: Japan-Kôseirôdô-shô (2005a: Furoku 2–1, Table 20).

KO: So, you see no reason to quit?

NORIMI: Well in that case, don't you have a lot of *otsubone-san*? [literally, a lady-in-waiting who served in the aristocratic court or feudal lord's household and had considerable power. In this context the term is used to describe an older unmarried female worker who gains power over other female workers by remaining in the same workplace for a long time.]

MOKO: Well, an *otsubone-san* who used to be in my workplace when I entered the company recently returned. She was on a secondment elsewhere until the present subsidiary personnel company was formed. I'm now working on secondment from the parent company at this subsidiary company.

(14 November 1997)

Moko was curious about agency work, which Norimi and Tomoe were involved in, and interjected with many questions. I had an impression that Moko, still in her first job, was somewhat envious of her friends' seemingly carefree lifestyles, but at the same time was scared of leaving the security of the large company where she had worked for years. While Moko complained about what she considered to be a low monthly income (195,000 yen before tax), she was able to holiday in Asia on company-organised trips.

Saeko was unsure why she had continued in her present job as a clerical worker despite disliking the work content. Commuting by train took her almost two hours one way, and she had also faced various unpleasant experiences over the years.

SAEKO: Well … it may be that, on balance, human relationships are good. There is something comfortable about the place, which is why I haven't left. There are many holidays. I work five days a week, there is a summer holiday and other days off. We get a long holiday of nine to ten days three times a year. I'm not too sure why, but I've heard that because it's a huge factory, it's better to shut off the electricity for a long time than just for a day or two, if that is necessary.

(8 November 1997)

Saeko was also happy that her overtime work (20 hours per month) was paid accordingly. She had looked for jobs closer to home, but found none that matched the working conditions at her current job. Since she regretted not investigating the location of the company more thoroughly while at high school – she knew that A-city (where the company was located) was next to Kobe-city where she lived with her parents and assumed that it was close by, without realising that A-city also extended north – Saeko was determined to check every aspect of any potential new job, including location.

However, the issue of the long commute to work was resolved in Saeko's favour when she married a colleague and the company underwent restructuring in 1999. When the company decided to move the section where Saeko worked to a provincial city 100 kilometres away, it moved all female workers who lived nearby to other sections so that they did not have to travel long distances. Saeko, living far from work in the first place, was to be moved to the provincial city, but since she was to marry a colleague and live in company accommodation on the current site, she was excused. The work in the new section turned out to be much less demanding time-wise, and recently married Saeko was happy with the arrangement. The company offered 10 months' childcare leave, which Saeko had started thinking of utilising in the future.

Yoshie, a sales assistant, had worked in the interior furnishing section of Sogo Department Store in the city centre for almost eight years, but still saw herself as a novice sales assistant in that section, calling herself *hiyoko* (literally, a chick).

YOSHIE: In other sections like women's clothing, I would be called a veteran, having worked in the same section for eight years. But not in our section. Many of us there have been there well over ten years!

(13 November 1997)

The section had many workers from manufacturers on the floor, who, according to Yoshie, were experts and taught her about particular furniture and general trends. While she had worked hard, she still felt that customers trusted her less because of her age, in particular when purchasing large items of furniture and Japanese-style items. In the first few years, she had requested transfer to another department, without success.

YOSHIE: There are very few transfers for girls. It may happen if a woman works really hard and is head-hunted, or if she is hopeless and is kicked out of the section! ... Or if she has serious problems with her boss.

(13 November 1997)

By 2000, she had abandoned her wish for a transfer, and started noticing the merits of the furniture department. She reasoned that the work was boring but less physically demanding than in other departments (because of the small number of customers). The section had about 30 workers, with fewer than ten women. Only four workers were younger than Yoshie. The staff turnover in the section was low, partly because the store had stopped hiring new recruits in 1995 because of the recession. Yoshie was now the oldest female permanent worker in the section, although three married female agency workers were older and more experienced than her.

The predictability and stability was something she valued about her work. She was never enthusiastic about her work, but saw no better alternative. She was happy with the stable staff members, who provided her with familiarity. She also liked the arrangement of receiving extra time off for working overtime, as she considered time for herself more important than money. The stability and trusting relationship that she had developed with her colleagues turned out to be a valuable asset when she married in late 1999. Her colleagues encouraged her to go home early. Marriage did not affect her work substantially. In fact, when she experienced conflicts with her in-laws, the work acted as a great diversion from her private life, as we will see later.

KO: Are you glad that you've continued working?

YOSHIE: Of course. If I stayed home after being told off like that by the in-laws, I would go mad. It is a good diversion [*ki ga magireru*] when I joke and laugh with my colleagues.

KO: Does your husband say anything about you working?

YOSHIE: He seems to wants me to quit, but knows that it would make our financial situation tough.

(28 December 2000)

The department store faced financial problems, closed down many branches all over the country, and conducted 'restructuring' in late 2000. While her high school friends were concerned about Yoshie's employment, Kobe branch stayed open. Yoshie had been seconded to another branch's closing down sale when I met her in late 2000. She was fatalistic about her employer's future.

Unhappy, but what's next?

Some long-timers found no satisfaction in any aspect of their work and workplace, but still persisted. Satoko, whom we met in Part I, typified the case where a family breadwinner saw it as her responsibility to continue in a job that she disliked for the sake of her family. Satoko's husband was a self-employed truck driver who drove the truck that she had bought for him with her loan. Her two children were still young. She commuted a long distance (two hours each way), leaving home at eight in the morning and not getting home until after ten at night. She suffered from chronic fatigue. And yet, in view of other options available to her, she felt that the current arrangement was the best for the time being. Satoko considered herself fortunate in that she worked for a large company that offered childcare leave (*ikuji kyûgyô*) and flexible working hours (*henkei rôdô jikan*), which allowed her to start and finish late. Not all companies offered flexible hours. Table 5.3 reveals that the number of employers offering flexible working hours grew eightfold during the period 1988–2003 and that large-scale companies spearheaded this trend.

It was not only Satoko who suffered from work-induced health problems. In her third year at work, Sayaka, a graduate with a four-year degree, also found the job physically demanding, and was genuinely concerned about her deteriorating health. When job-hunting as a fourth-year student in 1993, she

Table 5.3 Proportions of companies offering flexible working hours in 1988, 1993, 1998 and 2003

Year	Companies offering flexible working hours as a percentage of all companies (%)	Percentage of companies with more than 1,000 employees, that offer flexible working hours (%)
1988	7.0	24.1
1993	27.4	58.4
1998	54.8	65.7
2003	57.1	69.4

Source: Japan-Kôseirôdô-shô (2005a: Furoku 2–1, Table 15).

had found very few jobs for female graduates because of the economic downturn. She went for many positions that she found in recruitment magazines as well as those to which she was introduced by her university, but was unsuccessful. It was tough. She was not in a position to be choosy, after receiving many replies from companies to the effect that they would not recruit female graduates that year. Only two companies responded positively to her inquiries. One was located far from home, however – a one-hour train ride and a 20-minute bus ride away.

SAYAKA: I thought that I'd better choose a job that I was more likely to stay in, work for at least three years, and save.
KO: And then what were you planning to do?
SAYAKA: Then I would think about something else. Like, I'd get some skills and experience there, and then go for agency work or something.

(15 November 1997)

Her relatives and friends were not impressed with the position she finally obtained in a small *shitamachi* inner-city company. Sayaka was realistic about what she could get that year and thought that it would serve as a stepping-stone to something else when the economy picked up. On the first day, the company president reminded Sayaka that she was employed in the university graduate career track.[2]

SAYAKA: That unpleasant company president showed me the pay scales. He said, 'Look at the salaries of private post-secondary vocational education institution [*senmongakkô*] graduates and high school graduates who entered the company with you. There are differences in expectations.' It seems that high school graduates do much the same jobs, but university graduates in the career track are told to do new things all the time; there's so much to learn. They told me that if I did the same work all the time, it would be a waste of their money!

(15 November 1997)

Sayaka's work involved receiving orders from overseas and arranging exports (often of leather or chemical-synthetic material made in Japan), in the trading division of the small company. The company employed 50 people, with ten in the trading division. Sayaka managed the export section of that division, along with another new recruit and the division manager. She explained that Asian companies wanting to export to Japan wanted Japanese-made materials preferred by Japanese consumers. Often these Asian companies were subsidiaries of, or associated with, large Japanese firms, who employed local labour to manufacture goods for Japanese consumers. She found many Asian clients were 'aggressive', and finished work late every day because of the time difference with other Asian nations and to continuous revisions of their orders. The company did not officially recognise overtime, which meant that she was not paid for the extra hours worked. Sayaka felt pressured to perform. Her boss assured her that upcoming restructuring (*risutora*) would not affect her, and that her bonus would not be halved as in other departments that had been making losses. But the prospect of restructuring made human relationships in the company awkward. Worried about her inability to juggle a demanding job and housework when she married in several months, and with health concerns, Sayaka planed to continue working for only another three months at the most when I saw her in late 2000.

Unlike Satoko, who could not find a better job, and Sayaka, who had made plans to get out of a miserable situation, Sachiko was unsure what she wanted to do after resigning from her current job. After graduating from a junior college, where she had studied nutrition, Sachiko obtained a clerical position at an insurance company through a referral from the college. She described herself as a '*nandemoya*', somebody who does miscellaneous tasks such as photocopying, serving tea, communicating with clients, and whatever else she was asked to do. While she was not entirely happy with this, Sachiko did not know what she wanted in her next move, which was why, she said, she had stayed in the job for five years. She also felt that married women took advantage of the 'family-friendly' conditions that the company offered them, and that single women like her carried the extra workload.

Resigning from their first permanent job

Two-thirds of the women had already resigned from their first full-time permanent job by early 2001 (11 years after graduation). Nationally, most high school graduates who leave their first regular job do so within three years of leaving school. Figure 5.4 shows that of the high school graduates of 1990 (my actors' cohort), 22 per cent left within one year and a further 13 per cent in their second year, rising to almost 45 per cent by three years, and that the percentages have not changed substantially over the years (see Figure 5.4). Among 'young people' (defined as 15–24 years old), 20 per cent

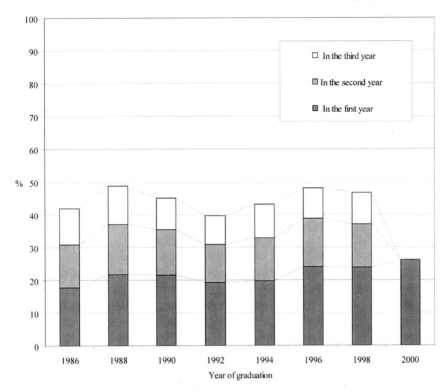

Figure 5.4 Percentages of high school graduates who left their first jobs within the first three years between 1986 and 2000.
Source: Japan-Kôseirôdô-shô (2002).

and 27 per cent left their regular jobs in 1990 and 2000 respectively (Yajima and Mimizuka 2001: 108).

Women in the study resigned from their first jobs for various reasons. If it was to pursue their dreams, young women had clear ideas about, and plans for, the future. Others left their first job in order to escape from working environments or conditions that they could no longer tolerate. For others, marriage or pending childbirth triggered resignation. Young adults' reasons for leaving their first full-time regular job varied depending on the age group. Human relationship problems (33.9 per cent) and unsuitable job content (24.4 per cent) were dominant reasons for 15–19 year olds. In addition, 18.3 per cent of 20–24 year olds gave health/marriage/family issues as a reason for resignation (Yajima and Mimizuka 2001: 110). (See Table 5.4.) If we see female employees as a whole, marriage and child-rearing accounted for 14.4 per cent of those who quit in 1994, slightly lower than the 19.3 per cent in 1980 (Japan-Rôdô-shô 1999).

The consequences of resigning the first job were rarely happy. How and why did some women manage to find a comfort zone in the workplace, while

Table 5.4 Reasons for leaving initial full-time permanent employment among 15–29 year olds (unit: %)

Age group	Not satisfied with job content*	Health, family-related reasons (incl. marriage)	Difficulty maintaining relationships in the workplace	Not satisfied with working hours and leave	Not satisfied with pay	Unhappy with the company's prospects	The company bankrupted or being dismissed	To take over the family business	To start one's own business	Others	Unknown
Total	27.2	15.2	13.0	10.7	7.9	5.7	2.1	1.2	0.2	16.1	0.6
15–19	25.2	2.3	33.9	14.9	0.3	0.2	1.8	-	4.5	14.0	2.8
20–24	32.1	9.5	13.3	13.4	7.2	6.1	2.1	0.7	0.3	14.9	0.5
25–29	24.9	18.3	12.3	9.3	8.4	5.7	2.1	1.4	0.1	16.8	0.6

Source: Yajima and Mimizuka (2001: 110).
Note: *This category includes those who found the work content unsuited to themselves, those who could not apply their particular skills and abilities in the workplace, and those who were not given any responsible duties in the workplace.

others were continuously disappointed with their employment? What did they learn from their experience of quitting?

In pursuit of one's dreams

When young people discovered something that they were determined to pursue, they left seemingly stable jobs even if they thought that the work itself was acceptable. It was a courageous act since they were leaving the predictable and secure for the unpredictable. If the person did not like her workplace, the decision was easier.

Fukuko left her first job at a local post office since she had trouble relating to her senior colleague, and work was impinging on the Jehovah's Witness missionary activities that she wanted to pursue. Although she enjoyed a good relationship with her colleagues, Natsumi left her first job in the second year to obtain qualifications that would enable her to work as a designer. The small bicycle company closed down several years after Natsumi left, because of the recession.

Mutsuko quit her first job (a clerical position) after two years in order to attend a one-year full-time cake-baking course at a private vocational college (*senmongakkô*). It was not that she disliked her job, but she wanted to do what she felt passionate about at the time. She borrowed money for the tuition fee from her parents, but as late as 1997 had not paid them back. It was an expensive exercise – on top of the tuition fee, there were other costs including materials and equipment. Mutsuko enjoyed the course and felt a sense of achievement, and after qualifying, found a job at a cake bakery.

Norimi's dream was cultivated and planned for three years before she decisively implemented it. Working as a clerical worker at a large manufacturing company for three and a half years, she saved enough to study English in the USA for a year. Once focused on this project, she had no hesitation in leaving her job.

Seeking better working conditions

Sekie, whom we met in Part I, left her first employer as soon as she completed her obligatory time there. After obtaining an assistant nurse qualification in early 1992, she completed *orei hôkô* (service for gratitude). Although it is not legally binding, under *orei hôkô* newly qualified assistant nurses were expected to work for one year at the clinic where they had received their practical training while attending nursing school. Sekie disliked the clinic; working conditions were hard and human relationships were unpleasant. She searched employment magazines, and applied for and gained a position at a small clinic. In 2001, she had been there for eight years.

Several women cited physical exhaustion as the reason for leaving a job. Shizu resigned from her first job, a clerical position in a large shipping company, in order to escape from physical exhaustion that she no longer could endure. She had no thought of where she would go next, nor was she concerned about whether she would find another permanent job.

SHIZU: I didn't think much ahead. I just wanted to get out and have a rest for three months or so. I mean, to give my body a rest. It had been very demanding [*shindoi*] – a lot of overtime, like working until eight at night every day. Before the bubble burst, it was worse. I worked until ten o'clock. We were told not to record all the overtime hours since it would go over the hours allowed for women. If that happened, the company would be in trouble. But the money wasn't an issue for me.

(8 November 1997)

Shizu finally reached her decision to leave in December 1994, but the earthquake delayed the implementation. She quit three months later, and was happy to be unemployed for a while in order to recover from her exhaustion.

Mutsuko also found the work at a cake bakery, her second regular job, too physically demanding, and lasted only nine months.

MUTSUKO: I quit because it was so demanding physically. I stood for 14 hours a day without a rest.

NORIMI: It was terrible. She complained to us a lot.

MUTSUKO: For the first year, workers only do the front work and help with the *shikomi* tasks [baking preparation]. I was always moving around. After leaving the job, I couldn't do much, I was so absent-minded.

(14 November 1997)

After leaving the bakery, Mutsuko did casual jobs for several months.

Pay was rarely mentioned as a reason for quitting. This is partly because the monthly salary did not vary significantly across companies for this age group. Salary disparities became more conspicuous once workers were over 40 years old. But it was a serious issue when an employer simply could not pay workers. Natsumi faced such an employer and worked without pay for over six months.

Natsumi completed a two-year course in interior design at a private vocational college (*senmongakkô*) after resigning from her first regular job (which she gained through her high school's referral system). While taking the course, she supported herself doing various *arubaito* jobs. She felt a sense of achievement in completing the course, and was excited when she landed a job at an architect's office (*kenchiku sekkei jimusho*) through an introduction by one of her lecturers. It was a small office; the owner employed two young workers. Natsumi did clerical work, drafting, word processing and also donned a hard hat to assist in building-site management. She initially loved the job, being part of a team that designed a building in response to a client's wishes. The boss expected the young aspiring architects to work without substantial pay, because the four years' experience that they gained at the office was required for second-grade certificate holders (such as Natsumi) to gain a first-grade qualification. She received only 50,000 yen per month for the first year, half of what she had earned in her first job. In her second year, the owner paid her 100,000 yen per month but no travel costs (she spent almost 50,000 yen per month on commuting from home). She continued in this poorly paid job because she loved the work. However, after she was not paid for six months because of the company's failure to win projects, Natsumi started to experience serious financial hardship. Her parents were not happy.

NATSUMI: If I was from a wealthy family, I would be happy to work and learn without being paid, in order to get necessary experience for the first-grade architect qualification. But in my case, I just can't survive. I've managed so far [without being paid], since I live with my parents. I also do casual jobs on weekends, to pay my fares. Sometimes I can't cover the cost myself. Besides, I feel as if I'm a burden [*katami ga semai*] at home.

(13 October 1997)

She did not contribute to household expenses since she spent most of her salary on commuting. When Natsumi first expressed her wish to resign in June 1997, her boss became angry. She felt awkward, in particular about wanting to resign in such circumstances given that she had obtained the position by way of introduction from her lecturer at the college. She resolved to persevere further. Two months later, Natsumi brought up the issue with her boss again.

NATSUMI: I said that I couldn't continue, since financial difficulties had become too much for me. I have borrowed a lot from my parents, and I can't ask for more. But he got angry again, saying, 'Aren't you an adult? You're over 20 years old. Why do you talk about your parents?' He said that this was my family's problem. I was hoping that he would ring my parents and explain the situation, and thus ease the tension at home. But he said he would do no such thing. He also wanted me to understand his situation – he was mentally exhausted – and blamed me for being inconsiderate in bringing this up at such a bad time. Then I said that I would think about it again. I became confused and unsure of what I wanted to do then. That was a month ago. I'm thinking more calmly now and still think that I can't continue this way – working without being paid.

(13 October 1997)

Natsumi's parents were supportive of her decision to resign, but were annoyed at her inability to carry out her decision. She went to see the lecturer who had introduced her to the job, explained the situation, and announced that she had decided to resign. He understood the situation, which gave her some relief.

Escaping from troubled human relationships

We have seen that human relationships were extremely important for happiness in the workplace. Even though some women disliked their work, if they liked their colleagues and bosses they would stay on. By the same token, if young people could not manage human relationships well, they were likely to leave their workplace despite enjoying the work itself. Emotional stresses also affected physical well-being.

We saw earlier that unhappy human relationships frequently drove some young workers to tears. Fukuko was extremely stressed by her strained relationship with her senior colleague, which affected her appetite and mental state. Encouraged by her parents and convinced that she could support her missionary activities with casual jobs, she quit in her second year. Oriko's father also suggested that she resign when she was depressed by her relationship with her bullying boss. Tomoe's reason for resignation was twofold: she did not like the company policy and the arrogant attitude of her immediate boss.

Shizu's case differed slightly in that she was much older (in her late 20s), married and in her second regular job. After quitting her first employment through physical exhaustion, she worked for a small trading company for five years. She attributed her stress to the changing nature of human relationships. When Shizu started at the small company, male seniors were often out of the office and she worked with a senior female worker who was meant to guide her. When the woman left, a new junior college graduate (four years younger than Shizu) joined the company, and Shizu now found that she was expected to guide the new recruit. Whenever the boss found fault with the new recruit's work, he would instruct Shizu to show her what was expected.

SHIZU: At the beginning, it wasn't that bad, but the longer it continued, the more stressful it became for me to 'guide' the new recruit. I asked my immediate boss to tell her directly, saying, 'It puts a strain on our relationship when I comment on her work directly, since we are in the office together all day.' I tried to refresh myself every day after work so that I did not feel stressed out the following day ... In the end, I stopped complaining about her minor errors, which made our relationship much better. But my boss was not happy. In the end I decided to quit, telling him that I wanted to focus on being a housewife.

(30 December 2000)

It was two years after Shizu started first feeling stressed that she made the decision to resign. She did not inform her boss of the real reason for resignation.

SHIZU: Well ... what could I say? It was difficult to say that. Maybe because I thought there would be no change even if I did give the real reason. So there was no point. I didn't want to make the workplace uncomfortable and then quit. So I just left like that. The boss wasn't happy, and said, 'We will be in trouble,' but he didn't object.

(30 December 2000)

In the end, the company recruited Shizu's junior from her first employer to replace her. Her husband was supportive, leaving the decision to her, saying: 'Either way is fine by me.' After this traumatic experience, Shizu no longer wanted to work for small companies, although this aspect had at first been a welcome change from her original workplace, a large firm. Her perception of the workplace changed once she had more experience and held a different position within the company – she was no longer a novice worker just out of school. She did not want to be in a position that required her to guide others, it seemed.

SHIZU: It was OK to work in a small company when I was at the lower rank but not now. I've also learned human relationships are more difficult to manage in a small company. With my first employer [a very large shipping company], even when I didn't get along well with one person, I could just keep my distance. Big companies have manuals for everything. The small company didn't have any, and individual workers had to learn by themselves. I didn't get good training from my senior female colleague when I started.

(30 December 2000)

As we saw earlier, this particular merit of a large firm in easing human relationships was also recognised by Orie, who maintained loose relationships with her colleagues at Mitsubishi.

Triggered by marriage and childbirth

There were no companies that demanded that employees resign because of marriage or pending childbirth. While by early 2001 three women had resigned from their first jobs because of marriage and two because of childbirth, in all cases they could have continued working if they had been determined to. Their perceptions of realistic conditions led them to decide otherwise.

Three women left their first permanent employment because of marriage in the first two years. Oriko saw marriage to a colleague (19 years her senior) as a way to escape from a workplace that was becoming increasingly unbearable. Yayoi was required to uproot herself to move to a provincial city to join her husband, and had no regret in leaving a job that she did not like anyway. In contrast, Kanako liked her work sorting pearls in a factory; but after falling pregnant, which preceded a formal marriage, their precarious financial situation forced them to move in with her in-laws who lived far away from the factory. All three companies had instituted unpaid maternity leave.

In the two cases of resignation in the later years at work, the women made their own decisions not to continue at work after childbirth and resigned while pregnant. Noshie feared that she would be unable to work to her full capacity as a private secretary's assistant, and that her kind colleague (whom she liked) would need to cover for her. While her husband left the decision to her, she decided to resign when she was five months pregnant. Hatsumi's decision was based on her husband's wish to have her at home, and on her less than positive view of her job. These two women were acutely aware that the chances of gaining similar jobs after having a baby were slim, and that the household budget would need their income. All of these women who resigned as a result of marriage and pending childbirth were irregularly in paid casual employment by early 2001.

Finding work

After resigning from their first permanent jobs, those who wanted a 'rest' from physically demanding jobs spent a few months just doing that, not attempting to find employment. Others were less fortunate financially and started looking for a job soon. Job-seeking in the mid-1990s employment market was grim. The recession had made the situation very different from the late 1980s when the women had found their first jobs. Besides, all of them had found their first permanent jobs through the school-based referral system, where the school acted as a mediator between employers and students in a maternalistic and protective way. This was the first time that they were independently looking for a job, for which they had no prior experience.

Nationwide, in the period 1998–99, of female job-seekers aged 29 and under, 12 per cent obtained work within six months, almost 40 per cent within one year, and 86 per cent within 18 months. The equivalent figures for males were 13.2 per cent, 43.8 per cent and 94.2 per cent respectively (Japan-Kôseirôdô-shô 2005b: Figure 2–58). There was a general trend for the women who left regular employment (permanent, full-time) to obtain non-regular (casual and/or temporary) employment. Of those who resigned from regular employment, the majority (70.9 per cent) went into irregular jobs. This trend was more sharply observed among female workers who resigned to have children (Japan-Kôseirôdô-shô 2005b: Figure 2–67).

After resigning, women typically got casual work in their neighbourhood through informal networks (e.g. a sales position in a small retail shop, or an unskilled position in a small business) while deliberating on their next move. Those who were born and brought up in the close-knit *shitamachi* area were able to enjoy this kind of informal employment more readily. Tomoe, for example, having resigned from the Korean bank, worked as an assistant at a local hairdresser's until she found agency work.

There were four channels for seeking employment: the Public Employment Security Office (PESO), commercially produced employment magazines, contract job agencies and informal social networks. People often resorted to different channels at different points in time. The women found that the process of individual job-seeking was far more demanding than the systematic and protective school-based job referral process that they underwent when seeking their first regular employment. Many jobs obtained through their own hard work were often unsatisfactory, which gradually led them to reassess and adjust their expectations regarding the kinds of work that they could find. Natsumi had the most extensive experience of 'job hunting' in the 11 years after graduating from high school, as seen in Table 5.5.

Natsumi's journey indicates how she changed her views on employment. While she was studying in the evening course, a job was simply a means to earn a living and support her studies. She was fully aware that she could not be financially dependent on her parents. Natsumi initially hoped to hold a design position but soon realised that this was difficult to achieve. She also learned that combining a full-time permanent job during the day and studying in the evening (which also required completing assignments) was impossible, and chose the least demanding casual job locally so that she could reduce her living cost by living with her parents. The successful completion of her course did not lead to the kind of employment that she had long hoped a new qualification would bring. She had also developed a sense of distrust towards job agencies and employment magazines, often making comments like 'You can't believe what they say.'

Women generally trusted the PESO more than commercial employment magazines and agencies. Hatsumi used the PESO on two occasions to find employment. The first was a part-time clerical position at a post-earthquake construction site. The other was when she desperately sought a permanent full-time position after her divorce. She considered herself lucky to find a full-time permanent clerical position, in particular as the PESO ensured that her employer took account of her previous work experience in determining her salary. Tomoe went to the PESO when she decided to obtain a full-time permanent job after being an agency worker for several years. She was happy to obtain a regular clerical job at a local shoe warehouse. Her salary was less than she had hoped for but the proximity to her home made the job convenient.

At the time there were numerous commercial employment magazines, which were particularly applicable to job-seekers in metropolitan areas. Women who used them, however, variously mentioned that these magazines created a false illusion that there were plenty of jobs in the market if one was not fussy. Descriptions of positions and companies were somewhat exaggerated and rosier than the reality, according to those who applied for jobs in these magazines and went to interviews. All such jobs started as casual, at least for the first three months, or were contract-based, and might eventually lead to permanent positions. Sekie was the only one who was able to obtain a permanent full-time nursing position after a probationary period. Sekie had been in the same job for over seven years and was still happy. Others were less fortunate. Natsumi found two casual jobs through these magazines but did not last long in either.

Table 5.5 Natsumi's employment trajectory April 1990–January 2001

Year and month	Event
1990 April	Started a full-time permanent design position at a small bike company. Resigned in March 1991.
1991 April	Started an evening course in interior design at a private vocational school. Began a full-time permanent clerical job in a real-estate company obtained through a connection of her father's (a construction site manager).
1991 August	Left the job because of strained human relationships caused by the company's poor business performance and restructuring. Applied for three designer positions through an employment magazine. Also applied for one design position through a job agency, but was told that they did not want a woman. Although she asked the agency to contact her about suitable positions, she never heard from them.
1991 December	Obtained a casual clerical job in a stockbroking company (*shôkengaisha*) through an employment magazine. Stayed only briefly since the commuting distance was excessive.
1992 January	Obtained a full-time permanent clerical position in an interior design company through a newspaper advertisement. Stayed only six months, after finding it difficult to combine work and study and being told by the employer to abandon studying.
1992 July	Obtained a casual sales assistant job at a local dry-cleaning business to support herself, while living with her parents.
1994 April	After completing the course in March 1994, obtained the type of designer's position she had been aiming for, through her lecturer's introduction, and initially greatly enjoyed the work. Resigned after a few years as the employer had not been able to pay her for many months. During this time she also held a casual sales position at a local bakery in order to earn a living.
1998 March	Unemployed and on benefits for a few months. Held various casual jobs.
1998 October	Through the PESO (Public Employment Security Office), obtained a one-year-contract clerical position at a company managing several post-earthquake construction sites.
1999 November	Unable to find a job through the PESO, so applied for jobs in commercial employment magazines. Obtained a casual clerical position at an interior design company. Resigned on being told to accept a 50 per cent pay cut.
2000 February–2001 January	Obtained a casual job at an agency company for architects through a newspaper advertisement.

Informal social networks dominated the casual job market, but sometimes led to permanent employment as well. Yayoi had been waitressing casually at a neighbourhood coffee shop (a job which she also found through her friends) for almost a year when her uncle found her a clerical position at an arcade company, which she did not think she could decline, given the economic circumstance at the time. She took the job as a casual position for the first year, with the hope that it would become a permanent position if her performance was deemed satisfactory. This happened eventually. Shizu was approached for a regular clerical position by a small company run by one of the clients of her previous employer. She was not keen, since she wanted to have several months of well-deserved rest, but took the job up in the end, tempted by the good working conditions (generous pay and holidays, no overtime work, and proximity to home).

Mutsuko, after quitting a full-time permanent job at a cake bakery because of physical exhaustion, obtained a clerical job through her friend Tomoe. Tomoe mentioned that her cousin was looking for someone for clerical work at a newly opened Kobe-city branch of a Tokyo clothing company. The clothing company had manufacturers make the products, which the company then sold to retail shops. Mutsuko received orders and sent requests to the manufacturers. She worked there for six years until late 2000, when the branch was closed because of the recession.

KO: Do you like the job?
MUTSUKO: Well. I can do whatever I like when the work is not busy, like reading my favourite books or studying. Few visitors come to the office. I am normally alone. Tomoe's cousin sometimes comes to the office, but he is usually involved in marketing, away from the office.
KO: Does Tomoe visit you?
MUTSUKO: Sometimes.
NORIMI: Always. It's comfortable since the office is an ordinary residential flat in a nice inner-city area with telephone and fax machine.
TOMOE: I try on some of the dresses in the office [laughs].
MUTSUKO: It's relaxed. No stress.
TOMOE: If you want to study or have something you want to do, it is great.
KO: Are you studying?
MOKO: Yes. She has French dictionaries beside her desk.

(14 November 1997)

Mutsuko had been studying French since Norimi took her to Europe earlier that year. Her friend, Moko, found this useful for her own work when she received an invoice or receipts in French.

Attractions of non-standard work

We saw earlier that the proportion of the total workforce in non-standard forms of employment had gradually increased over the 1990s, and that most of those workers were female. An historical survey of non-standard employment reveals that it has long existed, both formally and informally, with its prevalence determined by, and fluctuating in accordance with, changing economic conditions (e.g. Gottfried and Hayashi-Kato 1998). For instance, during an economic boom when there was an acute shortage of labour in certain occupations (e.g. construction), numerous non-standard jobs were available for illegal guest workers. The majority of women returning to work entered non-standard forms of employment because of the systematic barriers to older women, who were simply not offered regular jobs or who faced rigid requirements such as upper age limits and long working hours (Yu 2002). Some writers consider that non-standard employment was a neglected pillar of the Japanese employment system which contributed to Japan's economic 'miracle', and that it was designed to maintain gender-based employment practices (Brinton 1989; Gottfried and Hayashi-Kato 1998). Others argue that this system was not designed to exclude married women but unintentionally discouraged them from entering the regular labour market (e.g. Yu 2002). Non-standard jobs had thus long absorbed older married women who wanted to enter the employment market.

After quitting a standard job, female workers usually found employment again in the non-standard workforce. Nationally, approximately three-quarters of women who gave up regular jobs ended up going into non-standard jobs. This trend was stronger among women with children. The use of different categories of non-standard employment (*pâto, keiyaku, haken, arubaito*, etc.) varied among employers and agencies, and young women only vaguely understood their boundaries. One trend was for workers in non-standard jobs to stay with an employer for a shorter period, with that period becoming even shorter over the 1990s. The number of those who stayed with an employer for less than a year jumped from 12.5 per cent in 1992 to 24.8 per cent in 2002; those staying over five years went down from 45.2 per cent to 23.6 per cent in the same period (see Figure 5.5). My actors' trajectories of employment reflect how individuals, both workers and employers, create such national trends. Since the women's understanding of differences in non-standard forms of employment was limited to *haken, arubaito* and *keiyaku*, I will focus on those here.

Agency *(*haken*) and contract jobs*

The vast majority (90 per cent) of registered agency workers ('temps') are females under 35 years old. Companies are often reluctant to hire older workers. Temporary worker agency services were legalised with the Temporary Worker Law of 1985 (which was later revised in 1999). During the boom period of the 1990s, when some of the women in this study chose this option, the number of agency workers increased, but it was concentrated in service industries in metropolitan areas. (For a detailed study, see Weathers 2001.)

Some young people preferred the lifestyles offered by non-standard forms of employment; for others this type of work was the only viable option given the kind of commitment usually required by standard forms of employment. Normally, a job-seeker first registered her name for a particular type of job at an agency. If she did not like a particular job, she could leave without any animosity. The contract lengths varied. Even a three-month contract could be renewed to one year. As of early 2001 (when they were aged 29), two of

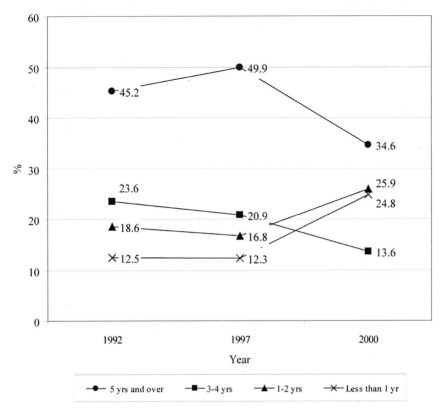

Figure 5.5 Percentages of female part-time and casual employees in terms of the lengths of their employment in 1992, 1997 and 2000.
Source: Japan-Kôseirôdô-shô (2005b: Figure 2–43).

the women were working for an agency, while the others had decided to return to a full-time permanent job.

The attraction of agency work was its flexibility in terms of job content, human relationships and time. A woman could leave a job readily if it turned out to be uncongenial. This freedom could be a liberating experience. Having worked casually at a local bakery after resigning from her first regular clerical job, Tomoe took up a clerical job at a mobile phone company through an agency. It was initially a three-month contract, but continued to be renewed for almost three years, making her the longest-serving agency worker in the host company. She later took up several agency clerical jobs, as this suited her leisure plans and gave her the flexibility and sense of freedom that she had long wanted. She travelled in Japan and overseas between the agency jobs. She could quit a job that she did not like without undergoing the sort of lengthy process she had endured with her first employer, a Korean bank, as we saw in Part I.

Norimi worked in her first regular job for three and a half years, and saved more than enough money to study English in the United States for a year and to spend another six months in Europe, where she met her boyfriend. After returning to Japan, instead of visiting the PESO, she went straight to an agency and immediately obtained a clerical job. She wanted a job that enabled her to save money quickly and travel to Europe to see her boyfriend.

NORIMI: I like this lifestyle, since I want to go to Europe at least twice a year. Being an agency worker, I can easily take time off. The last time I took Mutsuko to Europe with me. Agency work is much more flexible. The other day I took a one-week break for the second time in a year at the same host company. Then the boss of the company got angry. It's not as if my being away was going to inconvenience their work.

TOMOE: That's selfish. We're agency workers.

NORIMI: I was so angry. I work as an agency worker because I want that kind of flexibility, right? I really wanted to tell him to leave me alone. The boss said, 'Other workers asked why only you get long holidays twice a year and your absence has a bad influence.' I told the agency that I wouldn't work for that company. Then the company complained to the agency. Can you believe it? I think the other workers said those things because they don't know I'm an agency worker.

(14 November 1997)

In early 2001, Norimi was still enjoying the lifestyle offered by agency work – flying to Europe every six months to see her new boyfriend.

Norimi is possibly correct in assuming that her permanent worker colleagues in the same office did not know of her agency worker status. Even if they had been aware, they might not have understood the working conditions of agency workers. Many permanent workers who were still in their first jobs – Yoshie, Fumiko, Saeko and Orie, for instance – did not have much knowledge about the conditions. That was why Moko, a permanent worker who was still employed at her original company, was extremely curious about these conditions when our discussion turned to the topic. She wanted to have firsthand information from her friends, Norimi and Tomoe.

The pay for an agency work was lower than that for a permanent worker in terms of annual income. But the former's monthly salary was much higher because an agency worker did not receive biannual bonuses and could opt not to contribute to superannuation and various insurances. For instance, Tomoe, as an agency clerical worker, earned 250,000 to 260,000 yen a month in a busy month and 200,000 yen in a slow month. In contrast, her friend Moko, a permanent clerical worker at a large company, was paid 195,000 yen gross and just over 100,000 yen after tax and other deductions.

Some agencies offered opportunities to join various insurance, superannuation, health and unemployment schemes. Often they are only available as one package. Tomoe subscribed to some of these schemes but recently discontinued her contributions. Norimi decided from the beginning not to join.

TOMOE: Often those with long-term contracts take up these insurance schemes. But the premium, in particular for superannuation, is very high. There's no guarantee that you'll receive the superannuation – I may not live that long. Besides, by the time I am entitled to it, the recipients' age might be raised to 70. We don't know how much we get, either, certainly not as much as old people are getting now. So I was starting to think it would be better to take up life insurance, and then I lost my job. If you don't work for over one month, superannuation expires. It's been already one month since I last worked! So I'm not going to take up the superannuation.

(14 November 1997)

Tomoe also discovered that it was difficult to receive the unemployment benefit. In order to be eligible to apply for it, she had to wait one month after completing a contract job and see whether the agency offered her another job. She then had to wait a further seven days to apply, and then for one month before receiving the first payment.

TOMOE: It's very unlikely that you would not find a job during that time, since there are so many short-term contracts. You can't receive the benefit that easily. That's why I'm thinking of stopping paying the 800 yen monthly payment for it. Yesterday I went to apply for the benefit and said that I had one-week contract job, and I was told to come back after that job finished. What a nuisance!

(14 November 1997)

In order to receive the benefit from the PESO, one must have contributed while employed. Tomoe went to the PESO with a form (*rishoku hyo*) from her previous employer, which listed the details of her wages for the year, the reasons for leaving the job, and other relevant details. The PESO then calculated the amount of benefit to be paid to her while she looked for a job. The length of the previous employment determined the period of benefit, and the reasons for leaving the previous job determined the length of the waiting period for the benefit. She then had to visit the PESO every week to demonstrate that she was unemployed. Tomoe and Norimi considered these requirements far too demanding. That was why, Norimi said, she did not even bother going there to claim benefit in the first place.

In recent years, the recession has meant that some fresh graduates have started their working life after school as agency workers (Japan-Kôseirôdô-shô 2005a: Figure 2–13). Some employers and job-seekers consider that this trend has damaged the reputation of agency work, since agencies originally employed those with some work experience with an expectation that they had the basic work skills. Some employers claim that the quality of *haken* workers has declined. For instance, Moko, a permanent worker at a large manufacturing company, noted that many agency recruits had to be given basic training by the companies to which they were sent. Some of them were permanent employees of the agency company, rather than those who had registered with the company itself. Moko observed that her company no longer recruited permanent clerical workers, but had its subsidiary companies or employment agencies employ permanent workers and then send their workers to its offices. Tomoe understood that this was cheaper for the employers.

Casual work (arubaito)

The women saw casual work either as a source of income or as a diversion from staying at home. As a source of income it was never considered ideal or a main source. Casual work was a convenient stop-gap source of money in the face of suddenly changed circumstances. Many women took on casual work when they resigned from a full-time job and were unsure of the next step. While the media has reported a trend for an increasing number of young people to live on casual work, called *frîta* (e.g. Tachibanaki 2004; Mimizuka 2005; Kosugi 2002; Miyamoto 2004), none of the women in this study saw this as their first choice. Tomoe worked casually at a hairdresser's after quitting her first job, until she decided to get agency work, which she thought offered better pay. For Natsumi, who studied interior design at a vocational college after leaving her first employment, casual work was the means to support herself, supplementing what her parents provided. Some women took up casual week-end work in addition to their full-time work during the week, in order to increase their income. Moko worked casually as a waitress at a nearby café, something she had done since high school days, for extra money.

Yayoi initially found a casual job a convenient diversion from home, where she was a full-time housewife, having married and moved to a provincial city where she knew very few people. She later found herself having to support her husband and herself when her husband was often out of work. She later worked as a casual bar hostess in order to earn needed cash quickly to cover up her husband's misappropriation of money at work.[3] After returning to her natal home following her divorce, Yayoi took up another casual waitressing job at a neighbourhood coffee shop, which gave her a new outlook on life. Yayoi became more forward-thinking when seeing her colleagues (mainly university students) enjoying themselves and planning for a future other than marriage. Kanako also worked casually to support her three daughters when her husband was hospitalised for a few months. She took up a hostessing job at a nearby bar at night, where she enjoyed talking with a wide range of clients.

For some, a casual job could be an escape from the routines of being a full-time housewife, as we saw with Yayoi. Hatsumi was at home with a one-year-old child, and felt constantly watched by her in-laws, who lived nearby. With her husband often away, she felt trapped.

HATSUMI: I just wanted a place that I could escape to. I wasn't good at housework. My in-laws and other people told me to do this or that. I tried hard, but nothing seemed to go well. When you feel like that, you just need a place to escape. If I was working, I thought my husband would support me even if my housework is inadequate.

(24 October 1997)

She found a solace and happiness in her mundane clerical job at a construction site.

Moving up career ladders? Long-term career plans

Among those in full-time permanent jobs were some who had climbed career ladders, taking up further responsibilities and medium-level management positions. The others remained in clerical jobs that provided job security but few opportunities for further promotion. The difference did not necessarily result from deliberate individual actions. Nor were those who had moved up career ladders necessarily happier than those who had not. The career trajectories of these women reveal what sort of limited opportunities were available to high school-educated young women during the 1990s recession, how some took up these opportunities, while others did not, and what consequences each of them faced. In January 2001, almost 11 years after leaving high school, four women found themselves advancing in their careers.

One of them was Fumiko, who in her second year of employment had begun to nurture an ambition for promotion to the university graduate track (via an internal examination). Of my actors, she was the only one who deliberately sought promotion. In the year she planned to attempt it, the company abandoned internal examinations and introduced a new system whereby promotion was determined by one's superiors' assessment. Fumiko was successful in gaining promotion under the new system. She felt that the company's system of performance assessment worked in her favour in this regard. At the beginning of every year, a worker had a performance interview with his or her boss and division manager, and agreed on individual annual goals. Thereafter, every month, the employee met with the boss and discussed progress. Fumiko thought that she was good at marketing her achievement in these interviews, and also that the system allowed female workers a better chance of promotion. In a 1997 interview, she deplored the fact that many of her female colleagues had abandoned career advancement even before they attempted it.

Once in the graduate track, Fumiko could work longer hours (the restriction on female working hours no longer applied) and earn much more, but her workload increased. She enjoyed the work. The promotion occurred in 1996, shortly after her divorce, and provided her with a needed diversion from the traumas in her private life. Her promotion to the university graduate track also changed her relationships with her colleagues.

FUMIKO: Once in the graduate track, people changed in how they related to me. Well, I felt that way. You know, all the girls are assistants in our design department. Even my seniors [*senpai*] are now assistants to me. I have to be very careful about what I say and do. I can't talk about my salary, for instance. Previously, people were sympathetic to me, saying, 'You have so much work to do [for your pay]!' Now they take it for granted that I have a heavy workload. Girls take turns in collecting and delivering documents to and from other departments, and ask why I'm not doing it. My boss told me not to do it, since the company is not paying me to do that kind of thing. But I pleaded that I wanted to do it in order to keep harmony with the girls. Yes, I'm happy that my salary went up, but human relationships became more complicated. But I do have close colleagues and friends at work, so I can put up with the odd unpleasantness. After all, I don't want to make anybody feel unhappy, do I?

(21 November 1997)

The subsidiary company employed about 5,000 people nationwide, and its Kobe branch 600. In her department (of public work engineering), there were 70 permanent workers (30 of them female) and 30 workers contracted from elsewhere. Many of the female workers joined the company through their fathers' social networks; most were high school graduates and a few were junior college graduates. The majority of male permanent workers were four-year university graduates, and there were a few graduates of *kôsen* (five-year national government vocational schools for 15 to 20 year olds) or technical high schools. Other than Fumiko, there was only one female in the university graduate track, a woman seven years her senior.

However, in late 2000, Fumiko had no desire to move further up the corporate ladder, thinking that she had advanced as far as she wanted to. She explained her feelings as follows. First, the next promotional step, group leader, mostly went to local employees, but although this position involved no increase in salary there were added 'troublesome matters' (*yakkaigoto*), such as taking leadership of the group and managing subordinates and the budget. She did not consider it worth the effort. Second, Fumiko did not see much prospect for promotion from the group leader position. Since her employer was a subsidiary engineering company of Toshiba, ex-employees of the parent company occupied most higher management positions.

KO: But don't you want to continue your present work?

FUMIKO: I do want an income, but I'm not sure if I want to keep this job. If I didn't have to earn a living, I would like to be a novelist. I can't write while doing the present job. I just don't have time. As I said, I sometimes work until midnight. If a publisher or an internet company offers me a flexible job with good pay, I would be happy to quit.

(14 November 1997)

While she was keen on promotion in 1992 and still deplored her female colleagues' lack of interest in career advancement in 1997, by late 2000 Fumiko was happy with her current position and had no further interest in promotion. She wanted to focus on something more personally satisfying. Given that she remained single after her divorce, Fumiko had no apparent external constraints to pursuing her dream to be a novelist

In contrast to Fumiko, others achieved promotion to middle-rank positions in the company hierarchy without conscious planning or ambition. Miyuki, initially employed as a cashier at a large co-op chain store, obtained an 'artist' position creating advertisements and producing displays. She had worked diligently, and in late 2000 reluctantly accepted a middle-rank management position vacated by her senior, who was leaving the company. Miyuki considered herself 'middle-rank' in the company, and acknowledged an increased responsibility and workload. She neither wanted further promotion nor wished to continue working there in the long term.

Yayoi, who joined an arcade construction company as a clerical worker after divorce at the age of 24, was transferred to the design department for training in order to increase the company's capacity to respond to massive demand during the post-earthquake reconstruction boom. After six years in early 2001, she was working in an equal capacity with male graduates of technical high schools and female university graduates. She understood the inner workings of the company, and saw herself as no longer at the bottom of the company hierarchy (*shitappa*). However, Yayoi had no wish for further promotion, but was concerned about her long-term career, thinking that she would face physical and intellectual limitations in five years' time. She thought of taking up study to enhance her skills for employment past her mid-30s.

The assistant nurse, Sekie, also achieved career advancement, not in terms of moving up the company hierarchy (since she was the only nurse in the clinic) but as a professional. She became the only nurse in the clinic after a senior nurse left. Sekie had been more ambitious when she was struggling as a trainee assistant nurse. Being encouraged by lecturers and senior nurses at teaching hospitals, she wanted to study further at a professional nursing school after finishing her assistant nurse qualification, in order to become a fully qualified nurse (*seikan*) who could work in theatres, since an assistant nurse (*junkan*) could perform only a limited range of tasks or work in a small private clinic. The fully qualified nurses who supervised her had an impact on her at the time; their professionalism impressed Sekie and they mentioned that the system of assistant nurses might not last long because of the high level of knowledge and skills required for modern medial treatment. However, on the completion of her assistant nurse qualification, she was so exhausted that she wanted to have a 'rest'. By 1997, Sekie was unsure if she wanted to pursue further qualifications since she was comfortable with the lifestyle that her job at a small clinic provided. By 2000, she had completely abandoned the idea, convinced from her own experience of nursing that assistant nurses would be needed by the medical system because of their lower cost, and that 'not all jobs need *seikan*'s skills'. In late 2000, she was more interested in pragmatic aspects of career planning. She planned to move to a large hospital with maternity leave and childcare facilities before she became pregnant, so that she could take advantage of them.

Changing priorities: job content, human relations and instrumental gains

A starting place in the labour market was given to 18-year-old girls by their first full-time permanent jobs gained through the school-based job referral system. Young women started these jobs immediately after graduating from high school. The following ten years (April 1990–January 2001) coincided with the end of the bubble economy and the subsequent recession, which led to changes in employment practice whereby non-standard forms of employment became more readily available.

Some of the women continued with their entry jobs for 11 years, finding an intrinsic satisfaction in the job content, feeling comfortable with human relations at work although the job itself was boring, or being unable to find what they saw as 'better options' and/or what they wanted to do next. Others resigned from their first jobs at different points in time in order to escape from intolerable human relationships, to pursue their dreams (e.g. further study) or what they saw as more interesting jobs and better working conditions, or to prepare for pending childbirth. Those who resigned had to seek jobs in the adult labour market for the first time, through the Public Employment Security Office, commercial employment magazines, agencies or informal channels. The women who had moved up the career ladder by early 2001 were all in standard employment; but none wished for further promotion. Non-standard forms of work (*pâto*, contract, agency and casual work) were attractive to some women, who combined different forms of non-standard employment to suit their lifestyles and leisure or to accommodate family responsibilities. Such work also provided necessary stop-gap employment when women faced changed circumstances.

The ways in which they saw employment altered over the 11 years. When thinking of a job, women considered three aspects: job content (e.g. intrinsic satisfaction, the level of difficulties), instrumental gains (e.g. working hours, salaries, the extent to which it was easy to exercise leave entitlements) and human relationships. The work content and human relationships initially featured strongly in determining the level of job satisfaction. As the women gradually combined employment with other interest and responsibilities, however, such as their families, relationships and leisure, instrumental aspects became important. Thus non-standard employment was more appealing at some stages than at others, depending on circumstances. Such circumstances included their private lives. This is what I now turn to in the following chapters.

6 Forming relationships

While at high school, very few of the women announced that they had steady boyfriends. They mixed with other girls and formed close-knit friendship groups. I recall being surprised to find that having a boyfriend or a girlfriend was not as important to them as to their Australasian counterparts, some of whom I had taught as a high school teacher in both Australia and New Zealand. The girls were in many ways 'asexual', to quote from Merry White's book *The Material Child* (2003). They did not dress in a way that emphasised their feminine sexuality, and boys did not display the kind of masculinity that prevailed in Australasian schools in the form of physical strength and a macho subculture. I saw several boys bringing to school what seemed to be very cute lunchboxes and water bottles decorated with the Snoopy (cartoon characters). Neither girls nor boys disparaged these actions. But this did not mean that none were sexually active. Nationally, about 40 per cent of young people are sexually active by the time they graduate from high school at the age of 18, a substantial increase from less than 10 per cent three decades ago (Iwamuro 2005). Some of the students at the two high schools where I spent one year were no exception, but did not let others know about their sexual activity. Kanako was one of them; she eventually married her boyfriend. Yayoi had a steady boyfriend, a graduate of the same high school, whom everyone thought she would marry.

Young people today have considerably more time than their parents to experiment and enjoy relationships before entering marriage. The age at first marriage has gone up considerably over the years. In 1970, the average age for first marriage for males and females was 26.9 and 24.2 respectively; in 1995 it was 28.5 and 26.3 (Nihon-Fujin-Dantai-Rengôkai 1996: 236). The average age of a woman when she had her first child also went up from 25.4 years in 1960 to 27 years in 1990, and in 2000 it was 28 years (Nihon-Fujin-Dantai-Rengôkai 2001: 267). My actors were aware of this and intended to enjoy this period of relative freedom. From the daily conversations at the high schools, I realised that the girls had been exposed to many cases of early (i.e. late-teen) marriage among family friends or relatives, and that many of them did not want to follow this path. They said, 'I want to have a good time before having kids.' I wondered at the time how they would meet people to form relationships with and what kinds of marriage arrangement they would pursue in the years to come.

This chapter examines the women's experiences of relationships. These were important aspects of their understanding of the 'real world'. While relationships include marriage and divorce, I have decided to exclude them here. They will be examined separately in the following chapter, since marriage brings a distinctive set of social expectations and experiences, such as those stemming from extended human relationships. This chapter instead focuses on relationships outside marriage, some of which eventually led to marriage. Relationships affected, and were influenced by, employment experiences. Firsthand experience of the large earthquake in early 1995 also affected individuals emotionally and materially, directing existing relationships more clearly towards marriage or exposing their fragile nature. How did the women find partners? What did they want from relationships and marriage? Did these expectations differ between individuals? How did unmarried women change their expectations of marriage over the years? How did class, ethnicity and institutions affect decisions about relationships and marriage?

The women experienced varying types of relationships: a steady relationship; marriage (with or without children); divorce; a post-divorce relationship; and no steady relationship. Table 6.1 shows how the women experienced different types of relationships over the years (1990, 1992, 1997 and 2001).

In early 1992, two years out of school, three of the 21 women had married at the age of 19 or 20. One had an 18-month-old baby. In the next five years, four more of the women married, and more babies were born. At the age 24 or 25, Oriko and Satoko had two children, and Hatsumi had one girl. While some were content with their marriage (which entailed partner, sometimes children, in-laws and other relatives), others were not. Indeed, between 1992 and 1997 three marriages resulted in divorce. In January 2001, the women were 29 and almost ten years out of high school. Nine of the 21 were married, five with children. Two were engaged to marry soon. Five had a steady partner, including the two who were divorced and in new relationships. Four of the women had no boyfriend.

Below I will examine how the women formed relationships, why some of them found themselves partnerless, and how they perceived arranged meetings with a prospect of marriage. I will then turn to how the women assessed a marriage proposal, and the distinctive experiences of ethnic minority women in relationships.

Forming relationships and having fun

All the relationships started as casual friendships. Many of the women met their future boyfriends as work colleagues, at outings organised by workplace or colleagues, at parties or through mutual friends. Some renewed childhood friendships after meeting former classmates from primary school. When I

Table 6.1 Relationship status, April 1990–January 2001

	April 1990	January 1992	December 1997	January 2001
Steady boyfriend	Yayoi Kanako	Fumiko	Tomoe (6 months) Norimi (3 yrs) Saeko Sekie (2 months)	Norimi Natsumi Mutsuko
Engaged	Nil	Nil	Sayaka Noshie	Tomoe (to be married in late January 2001) Orie
Married	Nil	Kanako (1990, 1 child 1990) Oriko (1991) Yayoi (1991)	Kanako (3 children, aged 7 yrs, 5 yrs and 4 months) Oriko (2 children, aged 5 yrs and 1 yr) Satoko (married 1993, 2 children, aged 3 yrs and 1 yr). Hatsumi (married 1993) Fumiko (married 1994) Shizu (married 1996)	Kanako (3 children, aged 10 yrs, 8 yrs and 3 yrs) Oriko (2 children, aged 8 yrs and 4 yrs) Satoko (2 boys, aged 6 yrs and 5 yrs) Shizu Sayaka (married 1998; 1 child 1999) Noshie (married in 1998; 1 child 1999) Sekie (married 1998) Saeko (married 1999) Yoshie (married 1999)
Divorced	Nil	Nil	Yayoi (divorced June 1994) Fumiko (divorced 1995) Hatsumi (divorced 1996)	Yayoi Fumiko Hatsumi
Post-divorce relationship	Nil	Nil	Yayoi (affair) Fumiko	Yayoi (affair) Fumiko
No steady boyfriend	All except for the above two	Miyuki, Natsumi, Sachiko, Moko, Orie, Mutsuko, Fukuko, Hatsumi, Yoshie	Miyuki, Natsumi, Sachiko, Moko, Orie, Mutsuko, Fukuko, Hatsumi, Yoshie	Miyuki, Sachiko, Moko, Fukuko, Hatsumi

met the women two years after they left school, four were dating casually and having fun. None of the four seriously considered marriage. Dating for them was 'just for play's sake' (*oasobide*). As long as dating remained 'play', they did not need to be concerned with complexities (*gotagota shitakoto*). The complexities included their own awareness of class differences (*sodachi no chigai*) and *zainichi* backgrounds, and their partners' and their own families' reactions.

The meaning that the women attached to a steady relationship altered as they aged from their early into their late 20s. For some, relationships remained 'play', a 'game' and 'fun', a source of entertainment. Yoshie, a sales person at a large department store, twice confessed her romantic interest to a man four years her senior in the same company (but not in the same section), but he politely declined to go steady with her. Yoshie had not given up, and when her friend Oriko tried to match her up with one of her colleagues at a large manufacturing company, Yoshie declined, saying that she was still pursuing her man. If the other party became serious about marriage, it could ruin the relationship. Others, once satisfied with a steady relationship, started contemplating the possibility of marriage. As they became older, their interest in marriage increased, perhaps partly because of social pressure from parents and family members.

The women debated with close friends the pros and cons of their boyfriends as possible marriage partners. They clearly distinguished marriage from a relationship. The requirements of a happy marriage differed from those of a happy relationship. In Part I, we saw Tomoe making a 'rational' assessment with her close friends of her boyfriend, whom she considered 'indecisive and immature'. Sekie, very popular among men according to her friends, decided to turn down a visiting doctor's proposal of marriage when she was a 19-year-old trainee nurse, since she was convinced that such a marriage would not work because of her perception of class differences. She enjoyed relationships for 'play' and had a different boyfriend almost every six months; she made a clear distinction between a relationship and a marriage. Norimi, below, felt the same way about her relationship.

Norimi

When I saw her in late 1997, Norimi had maintained a long-distance relationship with a man in Europe for three years. She was excited to explain her encounter with the man while holidaying in Europe, after studying English for a year in the USA in 1993.

NORIMI: In a town I was visiting he came up to me. He invited me to go to a flower market there. Since there were not many people there who could speak English, I was happy to have him around. We became close then, and lived together for a month. Then I returned to America, and tidied up my belongings and then went to Europe again to live with him. Then there was the earthquake in Kobe-city. When I rang my parents, I was told to wait there for a while until things were sorted out in Kobe-city. So I spent almost six months there. My parents then asked me come home. By then I'd spent almost all my money, so I was thinking of going home anyway.

(14 November 1997)

After returning to Japan, Norimi visited her boyfriend in Europe a few more times. In order to maintain this lifestyle, she chose to work as an agency worker, an arrangement that she liked. On her last trip she took her friend Mutsuko with her. Mutsuko described him: 'Although he is 39, he looks young. We don't feel the age difference that much.' Norimi planned to visit him for a month, return to Japan and save, then visit him in summer again with Mutsuko. Norimi had a realistic view about marriage to the man, because of what she described as his lack of earning capacity (*seikatsuryoku*).

KO: Would you see yourself marrying your boyfriend?
NORIMI: I don't think so. It's impossible. I feel insecure since he doesn't have much earning capacity [*seikatsuryoku*].
MUTSUKO: I wouldn't either.
KO: Do you think you would manage OK with him?
NORIMI: Of course. No problems with everyday life. We get along well.
MUTSUKO: Well ... If he doesn't drink too much and if he doesn't spend too much money, that is [laughs].

(14 November 1997)

Both Norimi and Mutsuko were puzzled that he was unemployed and yet seemed to have a comfortable lifestyle.

KO: But you can work and provide for yourself, can't you?
NORIMI: It's impossible there. There're no jobs.
MUTSUKO: No jobs. Everyone drinks during the daytime. Everywhere in town we saw unemployed people. We couldn't stop thinking, 'Why don't they have jobs?' You know, we always work.
NORIMI: We were puzzled, how could they survive like that? In Japan we have normal jobs or casual jobs [*arubaito*]. I would marry him if he had a regular job and a fixed income. Yes, I would like to marry him.
KO: Is he interested in marriage as such?
NORIMI: I don't think so. He's divorced. He doesn't seem to care about marriage or, you know, about having kids. Actually, people over there just live together if they like each other.

(14 November 1997)

Both Norimi and Mutsuko looked forward to their trip to Europe the following year.

Saeko

Saeko was a quiet, self-effacing yet pragmatic girl. Her friends were surprised when she left her boyfriend of six years ('a nice man' by her description) in order to make a move towards another man whom she found attractive. She was 25 years old. Saeko's first boyfriend was one of her office colleagues, and one year her senior. It was an 'approved and public' relationship, and people treated Saeko as 'his girlfriend'. She enjoyed it in the beginning. However, people at work, his parents and friends soon started to assume that the two would marry. Whenever she visited his parents' place, they talked about marriage. She felt that she would have to marry him and started planning the wedding date.

Then, when she delivered a document, she happened to meet a man, one year her junior, who was working in another section of the company. She liked him and the fact that people in his section, unaware of her six-year relationship with the current boyfriend, treated her as what she called 'an independent individual', rather than as 'someone's girlfriend'.

SAEKO: I thought about it a lot. I already had a man whom I once thought I would marry. Everyone around us assumed that. I had no idea if the new man would like me. I asked myself, 'Is it worth taking a risk and breaking up with a boyfriend I've had for six years for such an uncertain future?' But then, I thought I would regret it if I didn't take that risk but married my old boyfriend instead. Once married, you can't do much about it, right? That would be a disaster, don't you think? I hated the idea that I might be regretting something all my life. So I said to my former boyfriend, 'I have somebody else I love.'

KO: Wow ... You were brave!

SAEKO: He said that I should think it over. So we didn't see each other for a while. I was very lonely because I had been spending so much time with him, and was tempted to go back to him. Then I would *ganbaru* [persevere]. And that paid off in the end. I got my new boyfriend three months later.

(8 November 1997)

Sachiko, a good friend of Saeko's, recollected fondly the time when Saeko was struggling with this decision-making. Saeko was glad that her friend Sachiko unexpectedly encouraged her to pursue the new man, since she had expected Sachiko to oppose such a move. After all, Sachiko knew her ex-boyfriend very well, and he was a very kind and likeable young man.

SAEKO: I was so glad to hear what Sachiko had to say at that time.

SHIZU: Well, Sachiko is like our big sister!

SAEKO: We didn't tell Shizu about this until after it had all happened. It was around the time of Shizu's wedding, and I didn't want to consult her about such a thing – I mean parting – although in the end it worked out well.

(8 November 1997)

When I saw Saeko in 1997, she was unsure of the future of the relationship. Two years later I received a wedding photo from her.

During interviews and conversations, it emerged that the most divided view on partners was to what extent and in what ways a male partner should take the lead and be decisive. We saw in Part I that Tomoe wanted her boyfriend to be more decisive and tell her what he wanted to do, and idealised a man as someone 'who tells me to follow him' (*ore ni tsuitekoi*). Her friends, hearing this, expressed differing opinions.

MOKO: I also like the kind of man who tells me to follow him.
NORIMI: If he's your type, that is.
TOMOE: But if he's thought about my wishes, and then tells me what to do ...
NORIMI: I mean, I don't like it if he insists on doing things that I don't like.
KO: How about you, Mutsuko?
MUTSUKO: I can't accept 'follow me' from a man. A man who says things like that thinks he's superior – I can't stand it. But I don't like an indecisive man, either – I want him to consult me.
TOMOE: He should say, 'I think this way, what do you think?' rather than 'What shall we do? What shall we do?'
MUTSUKO: Yeah, I don't like 'What shall we do?'
NORIMI: He should have some idea before asking you.
MOKO: You guys are demanding a lot! (Laughs)

(14 November 1997)

Some women liked their partners to make decisions. Shizu was in such a relationship, which eventuated in a marriage she was contented with. For others, such a one-sided relationship was unthinkable. Miyuki was one of those, having left relationships and returned to her girlfriends, with whom she enjoyed talking much more.

A related question was to what extent a woman was expected to adapt to the partner, which they described using the term 'compromise'.

MOKO: Would you compromise?
NORIMI: Not me.
MOKO: None of us wants to compromise. Tomoe would be most prepared to. Don't you think?
TOMOE: I know that I am very adaptable.
MUTSUKO: Yeah, sometimes I feel you shouldn't compromise so much.
TOMOE: My friends say, 'Why can't he satisfy you when you're the easiest to get along with [*atsukaiyasui*]?'
MUTSUKO: Exactly. I totally agree.
TOMOE: You know, I agree easily to what he says, and compromise.
MUTSUKO: I've often thought that you've been too accommodating.

(14 November 1997)

Being indecisive also applied to the women. In late 1997, Natsumi said that she wanted to marry before she turned 30. She wanted a man with a strong sense of direction in his life, and was frustrated with her first boyfriend, who was 'indecisive', according to her best friend Miyuki. Natsumi met him in late 1997 while working at a post-earthquake reconstruction site in Kobe-city. She was a casual clerical worker and he was the site manager. He was four years her senior, and the two went out together every day. But as a manager of a small-scale construction company, he was expected to move from one site to another (including distant locations) almost every three months. Then the two met only every three months but frequently talked on the phone. Natsumi liked him because he was easy to talk to, which was a novelty to her, she said, since she had been poor at communicating with men in general. 'He is not handsome, and I don't like his appearance. But I just feel so comfortable being with him' (18 December 2000). When I met her in late 2000, Natsumi genuinely wanted to marry her boyfriend and have children; but he had not discussed marriage. She was unsure how she could make him aware of her feelings, since she was reluctant to ask him herself.

Miyuki had encouraged Natsumi to ask her boyfriend if he was interested in marrying her. Ever the pragmatist, she also suggested that, given Natsumi's interest in marriage and children, Natsumi should drop the man and find someone more promising if he was not interested in settling down.

NATSUMI: But isn't it unusual to ask such a question out of the blue?
KO: Not really.
MIYUKI: Tell him that you met an old friend from high school [i.e. KO], who asked you if you were marrying him, and this made you wonder what he thinks of you.
NATSUMI: So direct?
MIYUKI: What about saying that your doctor told you to have babies before you turn 30 since your health isn't great. [Natsumi's doctor had given her this advice a few weeks previously.]

(20 December 2000)

Natsumi had not yet introduced the man to her best friend, Miyuki, whom she met every month. She was afraid Miyuki would be judgemental about him. She had not revealed her three-year relationship to her parents, either:

NATSUMI: Because things will get complicated. Mum would tell me to bring him home. I don't want him to feel the relationship is getting complicated [*mendokusai*].

(18 December 2000)

She feared that her mother, a devout Sôkagakkai member, would not be happy.[1] Her father had once been involved in the religion, and all the children had been forced to attend the religious meetings when young. Natsumi had told only her younger brother about her boyfriend. Strangely, she seemed to cherish the status quo of the relationship, despite the fact that she was eager to move towards marriage.

Not having a steady relationship

In late 1997, nine of the women did not have a steady boyfriend at the age of 26. One remained partnerless after a divorce, while four had broken off a relationship. Hatsumi was divorced. The other four had never had boyfriends. Miyuki and Sachiko were no longer interested in relationships. The other partnerless women wished for a steady relationship, but on their terms. This was partly because, in their late 20s, they felt they needed to consider the possibility of marriage. None of them showed a sense of desperation; they were 26, just after the 'Christmas cake' age.[2]

Miyuki found a steady boyfriend soon after she entered the workforce, but in retrospect realised that she was just interested in having a boyfriend rather than in him as an individual. She left him because the relationship became boring and she preferred being with her close girlfriends, with whom she could discuss anything. As we saw in Part I, Miyuki later became preoccupied with preparation for her university study through a distance education program; once this started, she had neither time nor energy, let alone any interest, in finding a boyfriend. In addition, she also was not being pressured by her parents to find a marriage partner.

Sachiko's lack of interest in intimate relationships derived from her long-term observation of her parents' marriage, which she considered unhappy and miserable.

SACHIKO: I don't have partners because I don't think I'm enthusiastic [*sameteiru*] about romantic relationships. My parents have fought since I was small. It always stayed in my mind and I felt I didn't want to be like that. At the moment their relationship is settled. My father is not strict, but we are not very close. I'm not too close to my mother either. Because my younger sister was always attached to my mother, I would have felt sorry for my father if I had also turned to my mother.

(8 November 1997)

In the past, Sachiko had gone out with men but was not serious about these relationships, nor did she see herself getting married in the future. Saeko, her close friend, also grew up seeing her parents unhappy with each other. But in her case, their miserable marriage made her determined to seek happiness in a relationship. This was one of the reasons, she thought, why she took the risk of leaving her six-year relationship for a younger man, as we saw earlier.

In contrast to the indifference shown by Miyuki and Sachiko, Moko made it known that she was keen to have a boyfriend. She had never had a steady boyfriend, and attributed this to her job. Her life centred on her work, but there were very few young men at her workplace. She was conscious of her colleagues' recent marriage.

MOKO: My sister often teases me: 'When I was your age [26], I already had a child.'

TOMOE AND NORIMI: (Laugh)

MUTSUKO: Ah well, we're 26 already.

MOKO: There's a 'marriage rush' going on among my work colleagues. This year, as many as six managed to get married [*ganbatte kekkon shita*]. Until now almost all of us have been single, but ...

NORIMI: Are they [the married ones] still working?

MOKO: The only person who quit was the one who married a man in Okayama [another prefecture]. Half of them married work colleagues [*shanai kekkon*].

NORIMI: Don't you have any chances like that?

MOKO: No, unfortunately. I'm now thinking of being a rarity, a permanently single person ... Because my present work suits me.

ALL: [Laugh]

(14 November 1997)

Moko was unwilling to compromise (*dakyô*), and wanted a marriage on her own terms. Her response to a meeting for a possible arranged marriage demonstrated this, a point to which I will return soon.

For Yoshie, the present arrangement of living with her parents was too comfortable to think of alternatives, unless she found someone that she felt passionate about. In late 1997, at the age of 26, she had never had a boy-friend. She did not hesitate to say that she was eager to marry because of her age, but she saw the situation with a sense of detachment and calculation. She liked her present lifestyle, and this was reinforced when she started seeing many 'problems' associated with marriage, through her elder sister's and her friends' circumstances. Yoshie's elder sister, two years her senior, married a subway station attendant at 22. Although the man was the elder of two boys, his parents had already decided that the younger brother would become head of the family and encouraged the couple to live on their own (rather than with the husband's parents). Yoshie's sister was delighted and considered herself very lucky. However, the situation changed after the younger son left the family home; the parents now expected the elder son to look after them in their old age. Besides unwelcome expectations and inter-ventions on the part of the in-laws, Yoshie's sister disliked staying at home without earning her own money. Yoshie and her mother were forced to listen to the sister's complaints day after day, which led Yoshie to question the desirability of a marriage like her sister's.

Yoshie had begun to contemplate strategies to have it all – a husband and children – without the difficulties. A husband marrying into her parents' house (*mukoyôshi*) might be a good option, she thought.[3] She considered that her parents' newly built house (which they had paid for with money they received for selling a small piece of land in *shitamachi* Sakura-ward to Kobe-city, as part of the post-earthquake redevelopment) could be an attraction for a potential *mukoyôshi*. However, Yoshie was not confident about the prospect, saying, 'I don't even have somebody who wants to marry me, let alone somebody who is willing to become a *mukoyôshi*!' Her parents wanted to see her marry, and regularly made this known to her very clearly, which made Yoshie feel uncomfortable.

YOSHIE: My mother always complains that I'm not married.
KO: She doesn't want you marry just anyone, does she?
YOSHIE: I think she does. She says that so and so's daughter is married. Next month so and so's daughter is having a wedding! It's like 'Please marry somebody for our sake!'

(14 November 1997)

Yoshie was approached by one of her father's relatives to meet someone with a view to marriage, but declined to attend since she did not want to leave Kobe-city. Such meetings (called *omiai*) are a way for single people to find a partner, but their popularity has declined over the last several decades.

Arranged meetings with a view to marriage (*omiai*)

An *omiai* can be arranged by a relative or family member, or even one's boss, who acts as an intermediary to arrange a meeting. The intermediary is expected to match two young individuals with what he or she considers compatible characteristics, such as family background, level of education and income, interests and personality. If both parties agree to meet on the basis of viewing respective CVs and photographs, the intermediary arranges a meeting between them, often at first with both parties' parents present, in a restaurant, café or hotel; later the prospective couple are left alone to talk. If the young people express a mutual interest, further meetings are arranged to assess the prospect of marriage. There is little coercion throughout the process, and either party can withdraw at any time.

Japan is unique among post-industrial societies in that there are a large number of couples married through such an arrangement. Almost half of the existing married couples first met in this way. Arranged marriages are gradually being replaced by marriage according to individual choice ('love marriage'), as seen in Figure 6.1. In 1945–49, only one-fifth of couples chose to marry in love marriages. In 1965–69, more couples had started marrying for love, and in 1998 this type of union accounted for 87 per cent of the marriages that took place that year.

Many of my actors saw *omiai* as a middle-class activity, which was not personally applicable to them: 'It's not for the likes of us.' They explained

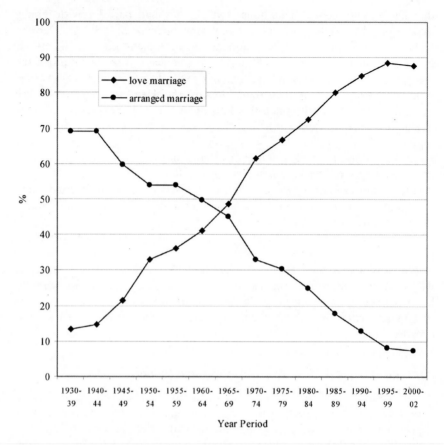

Figure 6.1 The relative percentages of arranged and love marriages between 1930 and 2002.

Source: Kokuritsu-Shakaihoshô-Jinkômondai-Kenkyûsho (2002).

that *omiai* was intended to match two families with something at stake (like wealth and social status), and that it was not relevant for families such as theirs with relatively little wealth or social position. Few of the young women's extended family members had married through *omiai*. Arranged marriages emphasise 'suitability' and 'compatibility' between two individuals and families, rather than romantic love. Mutual affection and respect are expected to grow from sharing married life together.

SACHIKO: I know some of my friends from junior college have their mothers bring *omiai* photos. But since we are 'common and ordinary' people [*shominteki*], it is not like that for us. Families have to be proper [*chantoshita*] to have *omiai*.

(8 November 1997)

YOSHIE: Even if I tried *omiai*, I would have nothing to say. I mean, things like being able to play the piano, practise flower arrangement, and the tea ceremony. There is nothing that I can boast about. Besides, I think you need to be at least a junior college graduate; my parents think so as well. They say that I will have to find somebody myself.

(30 January 1992)

Several years later, when her parents became desperate to find her a partner, Yoshie was approached by a relative of her father for an *omiai* meeting. The prospective partner was a school teacher on a remote island off the southern end of Kyûshû. Yoshie's father was from Kagoshima Prefecture and had many relatives there. Yoshie was not interested in leaving Kobe-city, preferring to continue with her present work at the department store.

Moko had a similar experience to relate. She projected herself as wanting a boyfriend, and regretted never having been in a steady relationship. She thought that an *omiai* might offer her an opportunity to establish a relationship. She was reasonably happy with the candidate, who was a graduate of a well-known private university in the area; he was 29, and worked at a small family-run company. He looked handsome to her, and also to her friend Norimi (who saw his photograph at the time).

MOKO: He was a second son, and had his own house. People around me thought he was a good catch. But he was in K-city (a small city in a distant prefecture). I said that I wouldn't be interested since I would have to quit my job. I said that for the time being I want to work. At my present workplace I have my own job in personnel-related work, rather than making tea and photocopying. I enjoy working there. But my mother wasn't convinced by what I said. She wants me to marry as soon as possible, and let the future take care of itself [*toriaezu*].

NODA: If the man lived in Kobe-city, you could have stayed in your job.

MOKO: Yeah, I would've considered this *omiai* more seriously.

TOMOE: If you both worked, you could employ a housemaid [*kaseifu*], couldn't you?

MUTSUKO AND NORIMI: Yes. Then you wouldn't have to do housework at all.

MOKO: I do all the housework now. I do the lunchboxes for me and my younger brother.

(14 November 1997)

Moko was thus the main housekeeper in the household, looking after her ill mother and a younger brother. This contrasted with many of her contemporaries, who were looked after by their mothers, which made their lives too comfortable to abandon. Ethnic Koreans perceived an arranged marriage differently, as we will see later.

Decision-making: responding to a marriage proposal

We saw above how the women held different expectations of relationships and marriage. When they faced a proposal of marriage, their reactions were pragmatic in that they weighed the pros and cons, sought advice from their close friends and family members, and gave 'counter-conditions' to their partners before accepting. They underwent what I would consider a rational *process* of decision-making. Whether their choices were rational remains open to debate since this question enters the domain of values, which is beyond the scope of this book. There was only one case of a rejected proposal: Sekie, the 19-year-old trainee nurse who received a proposal from a visiting doctor. Family responses varied.

Nationally, a higher number of love matches (as opposed to arranged marriages) does not simply mean that young adults find marriage partners randomly. People still choose those with occupational and educational backgrounds similar to their own as marriage partners (Sugimoto 2003: 170). Shida and his colleagues (Shida et al. 2000: 167, 170) demonstrated this trend in terms of fathers' occupations and education levels. The advent of love matches initially led to the opening up of the marriage market across class boundaries, but in recent years more young adults are choosing to marry into a similar class background. Comparison of marriages in four different post-war periods (pre-1955, 1956–70, 1971–85 and post-1986) found that inter-class marriage (as measured by fathers' occupations) increased until 1985 but decreased thereafter (Shida et al. 2000: 166). Intra-class marriages, in terms of young adults' education levels, remained strong across the four periods. In other words, parental background no longer features as strongly as it used to, but the individual's education level does. I suspect that this trend has emerged at least partially because of changes in occupational structure (from agricultural jobs to manual jobs and then to white-collar jobs) and the general rise in educational levels over the last five decades. It is interesting that inter-class marriage patterns are more prevalent in present-day arranged marriages than in love marriages; this could be due to the fact that arranged marriages are used by a limited group of people who cannot find partners on their own (Sugimoto 2003: 170). As we saw earlier, the prospective partners proposed for Yoshie and Moko to consider were university graduates, a high school teacher and an heir to a prosperous family business.

How and why do young people continue to marry those with similar class background? An influential factor appears to be the place a young person is likely to encounter potential partners. According to a 1998 survey, about 34 per cent first encountered their partners at work, 27 per cent through siblings and friends, and 10 per cent at educational institutions (Kokuritsu-Shakai-hoshô-Jinkô-Mondai-Kenkyûsho 1998). It could be that the chance of being in the same place as a potential partner is influenced by one's educational and family background, which in turn is likely to result in choosing partners with a background similar to one's own.

Below we shall see how young people choose partners of similar background to their own in the name of 'comfort', and if they do otherwise, how they justify their decisions despite concerns expressed by significant others. We shall explore the detailed process of decision-making that is involved.

Sayaka

Sayaka was one of the few students in Sasaki High's commerce course who proceeded to a four-year university. She wanted to go to a nearby prefectural university of commerce through her school's recommendation system, but was told by teachers that her marks were too low. During her first two years at a private university, Sayaka had enormous difficulties in adjusting to the new lifestyle and surroundings and, worse still, suffered from health problems that included a long period of hospitalisation. When I saw her in 1992, she talked about these negative past experiences in a positive light, and was relieved that her life had returned to normality.

Five years later, in 1997, she was very happy. She had recently become engaged to her boyfriend, Ken, whom she had been dating for five years. The wedding was to take place in six months' time. Sayaka had met Ken at the university's taxation study club (*zeiri kenkyûkai*) when she was in her third year. A senior (*senpai*) in the club, who was supposed to teach Ken word processing, suddenly realised this commitment clashed with his *arubaito*, and asked Sayaka, who happened to be walking by, to teach Ken on his behalf. Sayaka was skilled in word processing from high school. One year later, the two began to go steady, although Sayaka was initially reluctant and declined his request several times.

SAYAKA: I didn't think I could get along with Ken ... when I thought about my environment and his environment.
KO: Like?
SAYAKA: Like the environment where I grew up. I just didn't think we were suited to each other.

(15 November 1997)

Sayaka then graduated and entered the workforce as a graduate-track employee in April 1994. Ken went on to postgraduate study in order to obtain a qualification as a licensed tax accountant and started working for a relatively low salary in a tax accountant's office. When Ken started mentioning marriage Sayaka was not keen.

SAYAKA: Because he was going to the graduate school, he would have a chance to meet other women. I thought I'd find somebody more suitable for me as well. You see, his father is in medicine.
KO: You mean his father is a doctor?
SAYAKA: Yeah. He is also a professor of medicine. My family is an ordinary employee's ['salaryman's'] family, you see. No way the two are suited to

each other. I thought it would be demanding [*shindoi*] for me to go there. By then I'd heard about his mother as well ... like playing tennis, taking English conversation lessons and other sorts of classes. His mother seems to do whatever she likes and is so different from my own mother. Later on I had a chance to talk to her directly on the phone; my guess was right. She sounded cold and formal.

(15 November 1997)

Sayaka gradually became more confident in managing her relationship with her future in-laws. She was introduced to Ken's parents in the third year of the relationship, and a few times after their engagement. She was also asked to accompany Ken and his parents to see his ailing grandfather in a remote city. Sayaka's own parents were worried about the differences between the two families, but in the end supported her decision.

Besides the relationship with the in-laws, Sayaka worried about how the couple would manage their budget and how she would balance full-time work and home responsibilities. The two were fully aware that, if she did not work, they would not be able to cover their household expenses. Ken was yet to become a fully qualified tax accountant, and earned much less than Sayaka. For instance, Sayaka received three times the bonus that Ken received that year, because she had been working as a graduate-track employee for two years longer. Ken's parents were fully aware of their financial situation, and suggested they live with them in their apartment in a wealthy suburb of Kobe-city, but Sayaka was reluctant. Then Ken's parents offered the couple their apartment rent-free – the parents would move to another property that they owned. Sayaka was not willing to accept this offer either. She told Ken that they should build up their own assets themselves. She was later persuaded by Ken to accept his parents' second offer for the sake of their future children, and because Ken was, after all, the first son of the family. Sayaka reluctantly accepted, on condition that she would continue working at least until they had children and that they would reconsider the arrangement if her relationship with her in-laws became difficult. This resolution made her feel much better, in that she would still be contributing to the family budget.

Sayaka did not mind staying at work. Although the job was physically demanding, it gave her a sense of achievement. But given her health problems, she was seriously worried whether she would be able to manage both her demanding job and her family responsibilities once she was married.

SAYAKA: I have problems with my shoulders and don't feel well. I have to go to my osteopath [*sekkotsuin*] regularly. I think using a computer every day is affecting my condition. Also, I don't have much appetite. When I get home from work, I just want to have a nap. After that, I have dinner, a bath and go to bed. Right now, I'm looked after by Mum. She cooks for me and tells me what I should be eating. She does my laundry. When she says, '*Ganbatte,*' I feel encouraged. She keeps my life going. Look at my room. It's so messy. Mum pretends not to notice the mess. But, you know, that messy room will be the reality for my married life.

(15 November 1997)

Seeing this, her mother, who initially encouraged Sayaka to keep working after marriage, started advising her to resign so that she could better look after herself. Sayaka had already mentioned the impending marriage to her boss. The boss wanted her to continue working. But the more Sayaka thought realistically about her health, the less convinced she was about juggling work and home responsibilities. Would it be wise to continue working at some risk to her health? She then decided to keep working at least three months after the wedding, have a break, and start working part-time elsewhere, since she felt awkward about leaving the company so suddenly. On the other hand, she reasoned, her slackness regarding housework (about which she was not confident) would be excused if she worked full-time.

SAYAKA: It also reminds Ken and his family that we can't survive unless I continue working like this. I may fall pregnant, though. We won't have to pay rent, so we should be able to save some money. With the rent-free accommodation I won't have to force myself to work so hard.

(15 November 1997)

The wedding day was set six months ahead. Sayaka was happy talking about the wedding, and felt much more confident in coping with her future in-laws. After all, they were not going to live with her. She was keen to move into the large apartment. Ken's parents were happy and her parents felt comfortable about the marriage now.

Shizu

Shizu was a quiet and friendly girl while at high school. Her close friends at the time, Sachiko and Saeko, had remained her best confidantes. Neither Sachiko nor Saeko had expected that Shizu would be the first of them to marry. They had expected Saeko, who had been dating the same man for several years, to be the first bride.

Shizu married Haruo, an ex-colleague two years her senior, in late 1996. She was 27. Shizu's initial job after finishing school was as a clerical worker at a large shipping company. She had wanted to leave, since the work was demanding and mentally and physically exhausting. This situation became worse during a boom period in the early 1990s when she worked until 10 p.m. almost every day. She was glad when the recession came since it relieved her workload. By December 1994, Shizu had had enough and decided to resign. Then the earthquake happened. Her family house was ruined, and her family was forced to reside in Kobe-city's temporary accommodation for 12 months before returning to their repaired house. Shizu deferred her resignation in the midst of the upheaval of her private life, but finally quit after several months, with the hope that she could 'rest' for at least three months at home before starting another job. A client of her old employer offered her a job in his small family-run company, which she decided to accept.

One year after the earthquake, Shizu's boyfriend, Haruo, whom she had been dating for almost three years, unexpectedly proposed to her. She was unprepared. Shizu was still learning the new job and hoping to settle back into her family home, which she hoped would bring some stability to her life; she did not want to face another big change at that time.

SHIZU: It seems that the earthquake triggered him into thinking about marrying me after dating for three years.
KO: What happened?
SHIZU: Well, the earthquake forced him out of the company's bachelors' dormitory into its family accommodation. He found it difficult on his own. Then he started thinking that it was high time he got married – as simple as that! [Laughs] I wasn't convinced by this. I mean, it wasn't a good reason for marrying someone, don't you think? I thought, 'Is it right to decide to get married for such a simple reason?'
KO: But hadn't you thought about whether you could marry him before this happened?
SHIZU: No. I'd never thought about marrying him. I was surprised. I immediately rang Saeko and Sachiko for advice.

(8 November 1997)

Saeko recalled Shizu's phone call: 'Shizu was anxious, but I sensed she was anxious at having to go through yet another change. I mean, after too many recent changes like moving house more than once after the earthquake and changing jobs, she shouldn't have to worry about Haruo. I think I said something like 'You'll have to follow your feelings. If you think it's too much to consider another change right now, don't go ahead with it. Wait and see.' Shizu's parents were not supportive, claiming that the family backgrounds were too different.

SHIZU: My father said, 'Don't marry a first son from the country. You will suffer as a result. Since our family isn't a "normal family" [in that the family is not headed by someone in regular employment], you're going to have problems with Haruo's family. I don't want you to go there. I don't want to see you suffer. Marry someone with a similar family background to ours – I mean, from the *shitamachi*.'

(8 November 1997)

Her parent's comment increased Shizu's anxiety about Haruo. She was fully aware that Haruo had grown up in a different family environment. His parents both had full-time positions in the civil service, in contrast to her parents, who had always been in irregular employment. Haruo had been to a four-year university, which Shizu said he described as being a third-rate new university with low entry requirements. She considered that the lifestyle would be so different that she might not be able to adjust. Sachiko also said, 'Well, we have a perception that people in the civil service are conservative, rigid and inflexible' (8 November 1997).

After weighing up the pros and cons with her friends, Shizu trusted her instincts in the end.

KO: What do you think made you decide finally?
SHIZU: Hmm … I wonder. He promised me that he would always consider my well-being first. I think that he has kept his promise so far.

(8 November 1997)

Shizu and Haruo organised a small wedding. While Haruo invited many relatives, Shizu had only her parents, sisters and Saeko and Sachiko. They had a honeymoon to Europe one year after the wedding. Shizu looked happy in the photos of their wedding and honeymoon.

Both Sayaka and Shizu were concerned with differences in family background (*katei kankyô* or *sodatta kankyô*) when contemplating marriage proposals and compatibility. Class differences were not well articulated but strongly felt. It also emerged that all the women had varying understandings of class differences. Sekie, for instance, distinguished between material wealth and intangible family social status when talking about rejecting a marriage proposal from a visiting doctor: 'If he had only been rich, it would have been OK.' Shizu saw the difference in terms of lifestyle when she described her boyfriend's family – civil servants in a provincial city (who were respected in the community) – rather than in terms of wealth. Sayaka saw the difference in terms of lifestyle, social status and wealth. Hatsumi, though, saw class difference purely in terms of relative material wealth in comparison to her own family. Oriko did not notice the difference in class, until her father pointed out that her boyfriend's parents still lived in municipal housing and had no money; and that her boyfriend would have to buy a house for them. For Noshie, ethnic differences overrode class differences. The women did not exhibit an overt desire to 'marry up', which they feared would bring discomfort.

The women separated marriage and romantic relationships, and understood that romantic love alone was insufficient for a good marriage. An appropriate marriage, to them, involved parental approval on both sides and similar social status. Indeed, magazines for teens convey this 'traditional' message about marriage. The women also distinguished social status from wealth, with differences in social status being more problematic and intimidating.

Responses of parents when consulted about a marriage proposal revealed what many parents wanted for their daughters' marriages. Given that all my actors' marriages were so-called 'love matches' as distinct from 'arranged marriages', the parents offered their views only after their daughters had received a marriage proposal. The process of negotiation then took two stages: initial response and final support, which was sometimes given reluctantly.

Those who considered marrying very young (i.e. under 22) were all advised that they were too young to make such an important decision. Kanako, who eventually married her high school sweetheart, was told by her parents that Umeo was 'unreliable' and would not be a sound provider. Kanako was then already pregnant. Oriko's parents were fiercely against her proposed marriage to Saburo, a man 20 years her senior, saying that it was the worst scenario that they could imagine. He was almost 40 (Oriko was 19), living with his parents in municipal housing, and the only son, with four married elder sisters. Saburo would have to buy a house and care for his aged parents, who were already in their 70s; since he was already 40, Saburo did not have many years left to work in his present company. Oriko's father was furious at Saburo for enticing such a young innocent girl who could not possibly consider the situation in a rational way. Another woman who married young, Yayoi, was advised that the man would not be able to offer her a secure life; she refused to listen to her parents and went ahead with the marriage, which ended in divorce a few years later.

Having fallen pregnant, Hatsumi found herself in what she perceived to be an 'impossible situation'. She wanted to have an abortion, which her boyfriend did not support. Her parents said that if she wanted to have an abortion she should end her relationship with her boyfriend. Her father also commented that a chef's lifestyle was different from an ordinary salaryman's, and that Hatsumi did not properly understand this. As we saw above, Shizu's parents expressed concern with what they saw as differences in family background (urban versus provincial, and civil servant versus irregular employment). Sayaka's parents were also concerned with what they saw as class difference (a medical professor's family versus an ordinary salaryman's family).

How a daughter had met the man also caused some anxiety. Yoshie's relationship with her boyfriend was initiated by her high school friend Oriko. He was Oriko's husband's nephew. Her parents warned that becoming related to one's old friend endangered the friendship, which at the time Yoshie laughed at; but this was to become reality in a few years. The others (Satoko, Fumiko, Noshie, Sekie, Saeko) did not face any objections from their parents to their intended marriages.

Parents wanted their daughters to marry, but not anybody. They wanted their daughters to have 'comfortable' marriages. A 'comfortable' marriage includes financial security and stability, and comparability between the two individuals and in family background. They believed that financial difficulties would strain the relationship. Comparability of family background encompassed wealth and occupation, which affected consumption patterns and lifestyles. They had no wish for their daughters to 'move up' the social ladder by marriage, which they considered would bring their girls unhappiness. The women themselves were aware of these considerations. Those who married against their parents' initial advice had to make extra efforts to make the marriage 'comfortable'.

Pressure to marry within the ethnic group: *zainichi* Koreans

Just as marriage to a person from one's own class background was considered desirable, so was marriage within one's own ethnic group. All three third-generation ethnic Korean women wanted to marry Japan-born Koreans (*zainichi*), but were realistic about their prospects. Nationally, the majority of Japan-born Koreans marry Japanese, despite parental wishes for a *zainichi* partner. Just over 30 per cent of Korean marriages involved Japanese partners in 1960, but over a half did in 1980. In 1995, in 82.2 per cent of Korean marriages, the partners were Japanese (Fukuoka 2000: 35; see also Table 6.2).[4]

Except for Tomoe, who worked in the *zainichi* bank where all workers were *zainichi*, the other two *zainichi* women had few chances to meet *zainichi* men. 'How do we pick out *zainichi* men? They do not wear *zainichi* name-tags wherever they go,' said Orie.

ORIE: I have gone out with a few men, but they were all Japanese. My mother told me to go out with Korean men. My parents insist that I marry a Korean man. I was so sad when I heard what happened to one of my cousins. She went through the Korean school system, but fell in love with a Japanese man at work and got pregnant. The Japanese family, as they always do in this kind of case, wanted the two to marry immediately and arranged the wedding, but our relatives didn't attend it. The couple now live with the Japanese man's parents. Another cousin, who had just had an *omiai* meeting, told me to go out with Korean men, because she said it would be me who would eventually get hurt if I fell in love with a Japanese man. My dad is adamant. I think I'll have to elope if I desperately want to marry a Japanese man.

(15 February 1992)

Table 6.2 Marriages of Koreans to non-Korean partners as a percentage of all marriages of Korean people, 1956–94

Year period	%
1956–60	29.9
1961–65	32.6
1966–70	40.4
1971–75	48.7
1976–80	54.7
1981–85	66.1
1986–90	78.6
1990–94	82.5

Source: Morita (1996: 179).

Indeed, when Orie looked around her, all her relatives were married to Koreans through family arrangements. Orie's mother frequently suggested that she attend youth meetings of the Association of South Korean Residents in Japan (Mindan) to meet Japan-born Korean men. Orie did not like her parents' interference but understood their concern:

ORIE: My parents don't want me to experience hardship because of my nationality. Even if everything is fine at the beginning of marriage, there will be a time when conflicts arise. That's when the in-laws will start talking about my Korean nationality. My parents said, 'We couldn't bear it if you were miserable.'

(15 February 1992)

When Orie was 20, her relatives began encouraging her to participate in *omiai*, but she declined, saying that she was still too young to marry.

We met Noshie, a third-generation Korean, in Part I. She went out with her Japanese boyfriend, Oki, for six years, after which the pair decided to get married. Noshie and her family had long expected that Oki's family would oppose such a marriage because of her Korean nationality; but given that the family had not raised the issue over the six years she entertained some hope that it was not a concern to them. This proved to be naïve.

NOSHIE: His father in particular was stubborn. I visited him and talked about it and two weeks later he agreed.
KO: You must have impressed them.
NOSHIE: I don't think so. I'd visited his house many times over the six years. I'd never hidden the fact I was a Korean. They'd known about my Korean background so long and yet didn't say anything. What were they thinking? Our family was prepared to hear that his family might not like my background; but didn't understand why the family hadn't told me that to me much earlier. We were upset because the family all of a sudden started talking about it. Because of this, my family still feel somewhat disappointed.

(22 November 1997)

While Noshie was more optimistic about her marriage in late 1997, she could not hide her disappointment with the way she and her family had been treated.

In many ways, Noshie's family was relatively flexible in their expectations. Noshie's school friend, Orie, had much stricter expectations from her family. Orie attributed this difference to the fact Noshie's father was Japan-born with Japanese schooling, in contrast to her own father, who immigrated from Korea. Noshie's father's mother arrived in Japan from Korea when she was three. Noshie had been living with her paternal grandmother since her parents separated. The grandmother, according to her, was very 'enlightened' (*hirakete iru*) in that she considered one's nationality irrelevant. But her grandfather was strict. Many of Noshie's uncles had married Japanese.

NOSHIE: Since I am a woman, they are more eager to see me marry a Korean man. They think that Korean women married to Japanese men have a hard time.

(22 November 1997)

Zainichi women, as well as being pressured to marry *zainichi* men, were also encouraged to marry earlier than their Japanese counterparts.

It was because of this that Korean women perceived an arranged marriage differently from their Japanese friends, who saw it as a middle-class activity. *Zainichi* women saw *omiai* as useful because of the lack of opportunities for *zainichi* to meet one another. All three *zainichi* women were pressured to attend arranged meetings for the purpose of marriage, often organised by senior relatives. Noshie was forced to attend one in order to diffuse relatives' constant pressure, and Orie attended three such meetings. Both felt sorry for the men, since they attended such meetings just to please their relatives, without any intention to marry. In the case of Noshie, she already had a steady Japanese boyfriend, Oki, to whom she eventually became engaged.

Orie was under greater pressure to attend an *omiai* after her younger sister married a Japanese at the age of 23. Her relatives said that she should not take *omiai* as seriously as she did and should just see what the man was like – advice that she followed. She was nervous at the first meeting, but not at the following ones. She disliked herself afterwards.

ORIE: People had been telling me to do an *omiai* since I was 23. I felt that I should be more serious about finding a partner. After these meetings, I did not like myself. I felt that I had hurt these men. If I attended an *omiai* seriously looking for a partner and the other party was not inter-ested in marriage, I would be furious. So I explained this feeling to my mum, and she understood.
NOSHIE: I felt the same way after an *omiai*. I did it once – I had a boyfriend already. But my relatives were insistent, and I just went to the meet-ing to please them. I didn't expect anything would happen [*shitemirudake shitemiyô*].
ORIE: Yeah, they say, 'Just do it for the sake of doing it [*surudake shiteminasai*].'
NOSHIE: Exactly. But this is not such a simple matter. It's not just meeting him to have a chat over lunch, you know. I felt sorry for the man.
ORIE: Me too.

(22 November 1997)

The women were aware that their parents wanted them to marry a Korean, and that an arranged marriage was one of the few ways to meet eligible Korean men.

Orie's father was adamant that her sister would not marry a Japanese at the beginning, but in the end he agreed after the man persistently visited her parents to plead his case. Orie was surprised at how much her father had changed since then. Orie hoped that his experience with her sister's marriage would smooth the way for her eventual marriage. Even so, she suspected that her father had not come to terms with her brother having a Japanese fiancé. It was different for the heir to the family. Parents feared that a Japanese woman would not be able to carry out the various Korean customs (*shûkan*).

At this point our conversation shifted to differences between Japanese and Korean customs, and then to diversity within so-called 'Japanese customs'. As we saw in Noshie's story in Part I, the two Korean women realised Korean customs too were changing. When they were small, the *hôji* and other customs were very lavish and everyone was expected to contribute enormously. In recent years, many of these events were simplified. They noted that fewer people came to their families' *hôji*, that the events were on a much smaller scale, and that ready-made dishes could now be offered, rather than requiring the women to start preparing the food two days in advance. For instance, Orie's family now conducts *hôji* at New Year and mid-summer, instead on respective anniversary dates. From that year (1997), Noshie's family started visiting relatives in Korea instead of holding *hôji*.

ORIE: On New Year's Day I am very busy cooking from early morning till night. So I can't travel with friends around that time. Even if we go somewhere on New Year's Eve, I have to make sure I return early in the morning. Even if I want to visit a shrine or a temple on New Year's Day [*hatsumôde*], I can't go.

NOSHIE: We have to go home immediately for *hôji*. We are busy on New Year's Eve too.

ORIE: We have to help cook all day for both of these days.

(22 November 1997)

While Orie and Noshie had never attended the same *hôji*, they clearly related to each other's descriptions and experiences of the custom, suggesting that their experience is widely shared by the women in this age group.

Like the other two *zainichi* women, Tomoe had always maintained a strong wish to find a 'suitable' Korean husband. This, in reality, was difficult to achieve. The man had to be Korean *and* somebody she liked. Unlike their grandmother's generation, the women were not prepared to marry somebody simply because he was Korean. That was why Tomoe and her family were delighted at her brother's marriage to a *zainichi* woman. Indeed, her family considered that his wife was too good for him, and that he was extremely lucky. They were even grateful to her that she married their son. Tomoe and her sisters, however, had not been successful in finding Korean boyfriends. Two of her sisters had Japanese boyfriends. As we saw in Part I, Tomoe dated a Japanese man, to whom she eventually became engaged. He had very little knowledge about *zainichi*, but she felt that he understood her situation. Her elder brother also had a serious talk with her fiancé to inform him about the realities of being a *zainichi*. Tomoe planned to wear a Korean ethnic costume at the wedding.

Relationships for *asobi* (play), and marriage for *igokochi* (comfort)

The women clearly differentiated relationships from marriage. Relationships were supposed to be for fun and amusement, without having to consider 'complexities'. A marriage was a destination that all of them, at first, wanted to reach eventually; but they wanted to have a carefree time beforehand. While the majority indicated in their last year of high school the desire to be married by the age of 23, only a minority (five) of the 21 women followed this plan. The women understood that raising the subject of marriage with their boyfriends might bring up various 'complexities', such as compatibility in family background and parental approval, and that such complications might ruin their carefree and happy relationships. The meaning that the women attached to relationships gradually altered as they moved into their late 20s, when they started to seriously contemplate marriage.

In this context, not having a partner did not seem to bother these women to the same extent as it might their Anglo-Western counterparts. I suspect that this was in part because social activities are not organised on the basis of participation principally by couples. At 26 (the national average age for female first marriage) nine (out of 21) were partnerless, either having left previous relationships or never having had a boyfriend. With their late 20s looming, the women increasingly wanted relationships on their terms, and preferred not to be involved with men if this meant more compromises. They enjoyed female company. At the same time, having relationships for the sake of fun became increasingly difficult to maintain, since social expectations of marriage impinged on them.

The process of decision-making in the face of a marriage proposal was pragmatic. The women consulted extensively with significant others regarding the 'complexities' involved in marriage. Not all parents were happy with the proposed marriage and provided various suggestions. They wanted their daughters to enter a marriage where they would feel 'comfortable' (*igokochi ga ii*), rather than wanting them to progress socially through marriage. The women and their parents sought compatibility between the two individuals' lifestyles, comparability in family background or upbringing (*soddata kankyô*), financial security, positive responses from both parents, and a consensus on care for aged in-laws and parents. The women came to accept these views as they moved into their late 20s. Ethnic Korean women wanted to marry within their own ethnic group; but found it difficult to realise this since they met few eligible Korean men. For this reason, among Koreans arranged meetings with a prospect of marriage (*omiai*) were encouraged. Two of the women attended such meetings with Korean men in order to alleviate on-going pressure from family members, but ended up feeling guilty for participating with no intention of marriage. By January 2001, all three Korean women were either married or engaged to Japanese men, reflecting the national trend.

Those who married had conventional weddings at hotels or wedding halls (except pregnant Kanako) and honeymoons. After a short period of initial novelty and excitement, they were to learn what marriage involved beyond two individuals living together. This is the focus of the following chapter.

7 Marriage and divorce in their 20s

We saw in the last chapter that the women expected something different from marriage than from relationships. The latter were seen as play, *asobi*. As long as a relationship remained *asobi*, it was a form of leisure and amusement (and a learning experience) and did not require the women to consider 'complicated' aspects of the real world. Such aspects included what they vaguely understood as class difference (although they did not articulate this as such), ethnic background, income level, employment status and potential in-laws. These complexities entered the relationship once the couple considered marriage.

At 20, the women regarded marriage as a state that they would eventually enter, but they lacked a realistic view of it, seeing marriage as a distant destination that they would somehow be able to control, as is seen in this conversation.

NOSHIE: Some of my friends married soon after graduating from high school and already have kids. One of my friends says that she has more freedom to enjoy herself [*yoyū*] now that her kids are at school. When I have kids and am living on a tight budget, they may invite me on a trip or something – but then I won't be able to go!

SEKIE: The demanding years of marriage don't last for ever, so it may be better to marry early, don't you think?

ORIE: People say that if you marry early, you'll have an easier time in middle age as well.

SEKIE: Yeah, you'll be more comfortable when you're older. I guess it's up to you which one you like better. You may think it's better to have a comfortable life later, but …

NOSHIE: One of my aunts, who married early, now has grown-up kids. She enjoys a comfortable life and can go on overseas trips. She says to me, though, that she doesn't get excited by overseas trips – that it's different from going overseas when you're young. You know, she's not fit enough for some of the activities she wants to do. If you're young, you can hike and walk long distances, and can better experience the whole thing.

SEKIE: When you're young, you can get a lot out of your experiences, even if you don't have much money. But once you're old, you'll be miserable without a certain amount of money.

ORIE: Many of my aunts had babies soon after marriage, and couldn't enjoy themselves because their life revolved around children. They say that I shouldn't have babies straight away but enjoy married life first.

(22 November 1997)

Both Noshie and Sekie eventually married at 26, within a year of this interview.

As in post-industrial Western societies, Japanese are increasingly marrying at later ages. In 1970, the average age for first marriage was 26.9 for males and 24.2 for females, but in 2004 it was 29.6 and 27.8. (See Figure 7.1.) While class-specific marriage partner selection has persisted, the age gap between newly married spouses has become increasingly variable in recent years. In the last three decades, the number of same-age couples and couples in which the wife is older has doubled. (See Table 7.1.) This, I suspect, was influenced by the gradual replacement of arranged marriages by love marriages, as was seen in the last chapter. The selection of partners in arranged marriages tended to follow conventional ideas of age-appropriateness, whereby husbands were considerably older. In love marriages, shared interests and values are more important.

Late marriage has likewise delayed childbirth. The number of teenage mothers was always low in post-war Japan; and has declined further in recent years. In 2005, only 1.67 per cent of births were to women under 19.

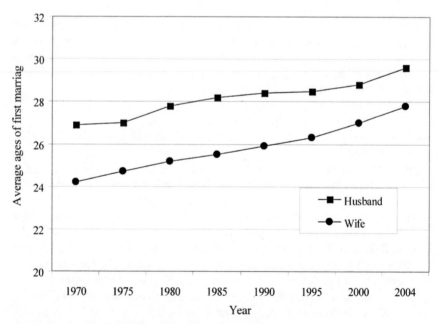

Figure 7.1 Average age of first marriage for each partner, 1970–2004.
Source: Japan-Kôseirôdô-shô (2004a: Table Konin-4).

Table 7.1 Age gaps between spouses between 1970 and 2004

Year	1970	1980	1990	2000	2004
Wife older than husband (%)	**10.3**	**11.7**	**14.3**	**21.9**	**23.1**
4 yrs and over (%)	1.8	2.0	2.5	4.7	5.5
3 yrs (%)	1.2	1.4	1.7	2.9	3.1
2 yrs (%)	2.3	2.6	3.1	4.8	5.0
1 yr (%)	5.0	5.7	6.9	9.4	9.5
The same age (%)	**10.1**	**12.8**	**15.9**	**19.2**	**19.2**
Husband older than wife (%)	**79.5**	**75.4**	**69.8**	**58.9**	**57.7**
4 yrs and over (%)	41.9	38.0	33.5	24.6	24.9
3 yrs (%)	13.2	12.2	10.5	8.7	8.3
2 yrs (%)	12.7	12.6	12.2	11.1	10.5
1 yr (%)	11.7	12.7	13.7	14.5	14.0

Source: Japan-Kôseirôdô-shô (2004a: Table Konin-6).

Over 70 per cent of women give birth to their first child between the ages of 25 and 35. (See Figures 7.2 and 7.3.)

This chapter examines how the married women in this study negotiated their relationships with their husbands and in-laws, and created a household. Their children were often born within two years of marriage. What roles did the women choose to take on in a household, and how did they manage family and work responsibilities? How did they develop relationships with newly acquired relatives while maintaining connections to their natal families? What were the financial situations of young married couples in the 1990s? How did they try to solve 'problems' in their marriages? I shall also examine the process of divorce in the context of 1990s Japan, when the number of divorces increased.

Patterns of marriage

There seem to be three main types of roles that wives took within a newly created household. In the first, the wife became the main income-earner and the manager of the household; she exerted most influence in household-related decisions and all housework. In the second, both husband and wife worked full-time and shared household duties in what we may call a 50–50 marriage. This was often the case in the early stages of marriage before children arrived. The third pattern was what was popularly considered as conventional: the husband was the main earner and the wife either stayed home or worked part-time. Most marriages with young children took this form, although there were variations in the extent to which wives dominated household decisions.

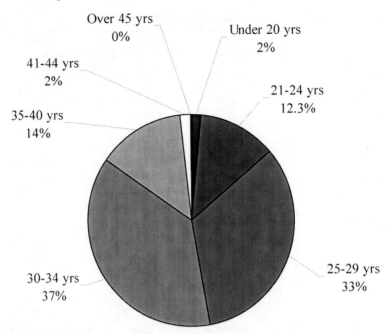

Figure 7.2 Percentages of births by mother's age group in 2005.
Source: Japan-Kôseirôdô-shô (2005c).

Female breadwinners

When a wife took on a breadwinner's role, her life became extremely demanding, both physically and emotionally. Three women in this study became both breadwinner and homemaker, since their husbands were in precarious employment and were also unwilling to take on the homemaker's role. As we saw in Part I, various strains led Yayoi and Fumiko to question whether it was worthwhile to be in such a marriage and eventually to initiate divorce. Satoko held on to her demanding marriage. Was this the type of marriage that they wanted for themselves? I don't think so. These women had never intended to become the main income-earner. While at high school, they had envisioned a conventional marriage in which the husband would be the breadwinner and the wife would supplement her husband's income by part-time work. Why and how did they find themselves in such a different situation?

One cause was unforeseen changes that occurred after marriage. Satoko's husband had a permanent job when they married, and there was no reason for her to suspect that he would become unemployed in the near future. Satoko's husband quit his work shortly after the marriage, citing problems with human relationships. It could be that Satoko's secure permanent job at Matsushita Electronics, a large company, made it easy for him to consider

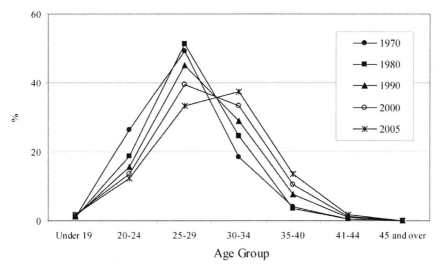

Figure 7.3 Percentages of births by mother's age group between 1970 and 2005.
Source: Japan-Kôseirôdô-shô (2005c: Table 4).

this option. Satoko then took out a mortgage and bought him a truck so that he could work as a self-employed truck driver. Thinking that her husband's income would then be less stable than hers, Satoko saw no choice but to be a reliable income-earner, in particular since the couple soon had two infant boys.

The other cause was wishful thinking on the part of the women. Contrary to her expectations, Yayoi's husband had been transferred to a company branch in his home town far away from Kobe-city. But a few months before their marriage, he quit the job because of 'human relationship problems'. She had trusted that he would soon settle into stable employment, and undertook an elaborate pretence of his employment during the wedding. Fumiko's case resembles Yasuko's in that the former believed that her fiancé would settle into working with her father after he relocated from a distant city to marry her.

Fumiko

In early 1992, two years out of school, Fumiko was enjoying her work, with the ambition of obtaining a transfer to the university graduate track through an internal examination. She was planning to live with her boyfriend, Satoshi, whom she had first met at middle school. The two had continued corresponding while at high school, after Satoshi moved to the eastern part of Japan through his father's work. The correspondence eventually led to romance. While dating in 1992, she proudly told me that Satoshi had promised to support her career ambitions. Upon deciding to marry, he resigned his blue-collar position at a Hitachi subsidiary company (which he did not like anyway, according to Fumiko) and moved to Kobe-city to live with her. Fumiko, in hindsight, regretted that she had not noticed problems then.

FUMIKO: He had a mother-complex. He could not do a thing. He only did what I told him.

KO: You mean housework?

FUMIKO: Everything. He let me to do whatever I liked, because I was running in front and he was simply following me; I can see that now. Once we decided to live together, I had to do everything, finding a place to rent and so on. But I thought it was OK since I am more practical than him. He didn't have much saved up either. So I used my savings to rent and furnish the place.

(21 November 1997)

Prior to Satoshi's relocation, Fumiko arranged a temporary job for him with her father's small electric-wiring business until he found something more permanent. But Satoshi was not interested in – or, as Fumiko saw in retrospect, not capable of – going out and finding a job himself. His father had arranged his first post-high school job.

Living in a de facto relationship turned out to be less than ideal for Fumiko, who held a demanding full-time job. The fact that she kept the nature of their relationship from her workplace added a further strain, but the couple thought that this would be alleviated by a formal marriage in six months' time. Fumiko arranged the wedding and honeymoon. The post-marital situation did not improve, however, which she attributed to two factors. First, once the first flush of happy marriage was over, Satoshi continuously complained about her family, in particular her father, with whom he worked. Fumiko became impatient with this and pleaded with him to stop. In addition, his daily phone calls to his mother continued. Second, Fumiko suffered from physical exhaustion, due to her 'double shift' of working full-time and looking after her husband. She cooked a traditional Japanese breakfast for him before leaving for work. When she returned from work at midnight, he still expected her to cook dinner for him. She would go out to buy takeaway food at a convenience store.

FUMIKO: In the end I collapsed. I had a fever over several days. Mum came to cook for us. Guess what he said: 'I don't like your mum's cooking.' I was angry. On the following day, I thought I was getting better and turned down Mum's offer to cook again. But I ended up sleeping all day. When he returned home, he asked, 'What about our dinner?'

(21 November 1997)

She disliked the expectation from Satoshi and his mother that she would *look after* him. His dependence on Fumiko and what she considered his selfishness became increasingly irritating. One Saturday, when he was expected at work, Fumiko failed to wake him up. He became furious at her, and she apologised, but he was still angry. This event made Fumiko stop and think. After heated arguments over this incident he apologised, and life went back to normal. But the last straw came at the time of the earthquake. Fumiko was in bed with influenza at the time, and the flat ended up in chaos with things strewn from shelves and cupboards, and the refrigerator toppled over on the floor. They had no water, electricity and gas for weeks. According to Fumiko, Satoshi just stood amid the chaos, not knowing what to do. Fumiko had to drag herself out of bed to tidy up the flat. Hearing how other wives were pleasantly surprised by their husbands' clean-up and restoration efforts after the quake, Fumiko was even more irritated by her husband's helplessness. Thus many small incidents accumulated to leave Fumiko in a constant state of irritation. Then Satoshi's relatives started blaming her for his unhappiness. She begged him to make changes but nothing happened. Fumiko's friends were concerned about her well-being and urged to consider her own happiness. In the end, she suggested that they separate for a while to think things over. When Satoshi wanted to return to her, she refused to have him, and suggested divorce. This was the beginning of her 'nightmare', which we will return to later in this chapter.

Not all wishful thinking turned out to have negative consequences. We met Sekie, the nurse, who supported her husband for a year shortly after they married. He had never had a secure job, and both saw limited prospects in his job as a branch manager of a pizza restaurant chain. On her suggestion that he acquire a qualification and make a career change, he decided to study electric wiring in a vocational institution (*shokugyô kunren gakkô*). He studied diligently in the evening, while working casually as a small delivery-van driver during the day. After completing the course he secured a permanent full-time job at a cable television installation company, to Sekie's relief. The two then enjoyed a financially secure life. Sekie's employment and income remained secure, which enabled them to have the double-income 50–50 relationship discussed below. It seems that Sekie's support, with that of her family, including making lunch and dinner for her husband when he was coming home late, helped him through a demanding time.

Double-income marriage

Most of the women continued working after marriage and until they were heavily pregnant. Kanako and Orie were exceptions, leaving work around the time they were married. There were no company regulations requiring the women to resign because of marriage or pending childbirth; indeed, many decided to resign shortly before childbirth as a result of a pragmatic assessment of their personal situation. So what some of the women regarded as a double-income 50–50 marriage was only a temporary arrangement until the couple had a child.

We saw this development with Saeko, who perceived her marriage to a colleague as a 50–50 marriage until she took maternity leave. Shizu also enjoyed this arrangement until she resigned from her work because of psychological exhaustion and the need to 'enjoy being a full-time housewife' for a while. Naturally, their decisions were made possible by their husbands' secure employment. Sekie, the nurse, and Yoshie, a permanent full-time salesperson at a large department store, were still enjoying this type of arrangement in early 2001. With both partners working full-time in an almost equal capacity, the couples tended to share household tasks. Husbands did not expect wives to do what they would expect from a full-time homemaker. Two incomes also enabled Sekie and her husband to purchase a house at the age of 28, with a 35-year mortgage at an interest rate of 0.3 per cent, a special offer for the earthquake victims. The couple felt settled, and enjoyed mutual hobbies like guitar lessons, English conversation classes and overseas trips.

Saeko moved into a company flat when she married a co-worker in late 1999. The two continued working and shared the housework. The company expected her husband to work overtime, which Saeko did not mind since she preferred having a relaxing time at home to working late like her husband. Saeko's base salary was slightly higher than her husband's, since she had started working one year earlier, but his gross salary was higher because of overtime allowances and 'family allowance'. He started receiving 'family allowance', 20,000 yen per month, when he married Saeko, even though she worked at the same company and earned more than he did. Saeko found this a strange arrangement – the company's assumption seemed to be that a male would be the breadwinner, regardless of the salary level. For each child, her husband would receive 5,000 yen 'dependents' allowance'. It may have been their comparable salaries that made it easy to share housework more evenly in the following daily routine.

Saeko usually finished work at 5 p.m., and reached home, on foot, 15 minutes later. She tidied their flat and prepared an evening meal while putting a load of washing through the washing machine. After her husband arrived home at 7.30 p.m., they had dinner and spent the rest of the evening relaxing, going to bed at around midnight. They both got up at 7 a.m., which Saeko considered a great improvement compared with her single days, when she was living with her parents and used to be up at five o'clock to catch the train.

SAEKO: On Saturdays, he normally goes to work. I've decided that Saturday is a cleaning day. I change the sheets, vacuum and mop the floor, and then choose one household task, like cleaning windows, to do in a leisurely manner over the rest of the day. He comes home around half past five. I don't cook on Saturdays. We go out, get a takeaway or buy *obento*. I want to have a rest on Saturdays and Sundays. We've decided that Sunday is his housework day. He cooks breakfast and dinner. In the afternoon we do the grocery shopping for the week. Sometimes we go to *pachinko* for about three hours before shopping. *Pachinko* is a pastime for both of us.

(23 December 2000)

Saeko was happy with her marriage, which she did not think constrained her activities. She continued to go out regularly with her female friends, Shizu and Sachiko for example, for regular weekly activities like yoga or swimming.

Her friend Shizu's transition to married life a few years earlier was also relatively smooth.

SHIZU: My married life was hard at the beginning, since Mum had been doing everything for me, and suddenly it was me who was doing everything around the house. It took several months before I got into the routine. My work is not demanding, and I have Saturday to myself.

(8 November 1997)

Shizu often went out with Saeko and Sachiko. The three had attended aerobics together the previous year, and had recently started yoga classes. Saeko and Sachiko felt somewhat guilty towards Shizu's husband for inviting Shizu out with them.

SACHIKO: Shizu has not fundamentally changed since she married ... but I do feel that she's often thinking about housework [laughs].
SAEKO: Before she got married, I used to be more light-hearted about inviting her out. But I must say, I'd still invite her out even if she became a housewife [KO: Shizu works full-time], although I do feel guilty about [taking her away from] her husband [laughs].
SACHIKO: Both of us feel sorry ...
SAEKO: But we tell each other that it's OK to feel this way since Shizu still works and earns her own money.

(8 November 1997)

It seems that Shizu's employment made her outings with her friends easier to justify.

Full-time housewives

Becoming a full-time housewife was a widely chosen option, at least when children were of pre-school age. While having a seemingly happy and uneventful routine, the housewives had many concerns and problems, such as a husband's infidelity, health problems, the prospect of caring for elderly parents and in-laws, the need to purchase a house, strained relations with their own family members, difficulties with in-laws, and financial worries, to name a few. Unlike for many middle class full-time housewives, financial constraints were real for these working-class women. How did these housewives manage emerging issues, and what did they learn from them?

Oriko

When I met Oriko in early 1992, she was three months pregnant with a honeymoon baby, after marrying a colleague 20 years her senior. She received no support from her parents to start with, who considered the man 'the worst possible case', but eventually won their approval. In 1997, at 25, she had a five-year-old boy at kindergarten and a two-year-old girl. Oriko was a happy and contented housewife, whose main concern centred on her boy's relationship with his kindergarten teacher. I went on a picnic at a nearby nature reserve with Oriko, her daughter and Oriko's friend Ako, who she introduced as an old friend of hers from middle school. Ako drove us to the park, since Oriko was still taking driving lessons. Ako was a member of the Jehovah's Witnesses church, which Oriko's mother had recently joined. For six years since her marriage Oriko had lived in a three-room flat in the housing complex provided by the large heavy industrial company where her husband worked. She got along well with her neighbours and saw her parents frequently, as they lived nearby. The family income was reasonable, much higher than that of her friends' husbands, since Oriko's husband was already 46. But this meant that the couple faced greater pressure to buy a house soon as they had less time to pay off the mortgage before his retirement. As the first son, Oriko's husband, with Oriko, took it as his responsibility to care for his ageing parents, who were living in a municipal housing complex. The couple had just bought a house for themselves and his parents by taking out a loan, and were looking forward to moving in within several months. If they were unable to pay off the housing loan before Oriko's husband retired, the couple would use a portion of his retirement package. The house was 20 years old – according to Oriko, a new house (which she initially wanted) was out of their reach.

Oriko was content with her husband. They had arguments; but when these happened it was Oriko who became emotional and loud. He always remained silent, which tended to put a stop to conflict. Somehow they would end such arguments by apologising to each other. Oriko appreciated that her husband had changed greatly to accommodate family needs. For example, he began staying at home at weekends when the first child arrived, instead of playing badminton, baseball and the other sports he had enjoyed during his long bachelorhood. Oriko told him that he could still go out with his friends, but he wanted to be with his children. She also felt that she had overcome her concern at their age difference.

ORIKO: I often tease him over his long bachelorhood. I say to him, 'You dated so many women, travelled to so many places with them, but you were my first man!' I think he understands how I feel. I feel that our family has one parent (her husband) and three kids, maybe because of our age difference. He treats me as if I were a child, and I like that. I am *amaenbo* [someone who assumes dependence on others], and grew up surrounded by my parents' affection. I feel that I moved from my parents' protection to my husband's protection. So my life has not essentially changed. Basically I am good at *amaeru* [being dependent on others] – my seniors at work used to tell me I was.[1] When I didn't know what to do, I just asked around rather than looking it up myself. Even now I tell my husband what I want, and expect him to do it. It is so demanding to guess what others want from me.

(27 October 1997)

Oriko's children were her greatest joy. While appreciating how demanding child-rearing (*kosodate*) could be, she enjoyed playing with her children 'as if she were a child'. She wanted another child but her husband was not in favour of this since he was now 46, and said that there were already three children at home.

ORIKO: I can't think of my life without my kids. I sleep with a child on each side, and I feel sad when I think that this will not go on for ever because they'll grow up. I was especially happy to have my second child, a girl. When she grows up she'll be my confidante [*hanashi aite*]. My husband was very happy that we had a girl for the same reason.

(27 October 1997)

Oriko's son was now attending a kindergarten two days a week, and she cherished the time that she spent with her daughter. Besides that, driving lessons and planning for the big move to their first home currently occupied her. Oriko's biggest concern now was how her son was getting on at kindergarten. She talked at length about an incident that involved him and his classmate, and criticised the way the kindergarten teachers handled the matter.

By late 2000, to supplement the family income, Oriko had started working part-time as a receptionist at a local recreation centre while her children were at school and kindergarten. Her father-in-law had died recently, which left her mother-in-law to decide whether she would move into Oriko's household. Oriko had maintained pleasant relations with her in-laws, but her friendship with Yoshie, who married Oriko's husband's nephew, was strained. In many ways, Oriko represented the young stay-at-home suburban mother of small children, who outwardly led a comfortable life but who was aware how transient this peace was: a peace that could easily be interrupted by sudden change, such as having her in-laws move in.

Marriage finances

The financial situation of married couples was determined by a combination of factors, such as the main income-earner's age, stability of employment, single or double incomes, and number of children. Some saw it as a 'struggle', while others managed. Perceptions of one's own financial situation were often influenced by the individuals' prior experiences. The women's perceptions sometimes differed from mine. Indeed, perceptions of their financial situations tell us more about them (and me).

'Financial struggle', as I call it, is a very subjective expression. While I saw some situations in those terms, the women did not necessarily see their situations in that way, or were perhaps too occupied with keeping the household together to think about how they might describe their financial circumstances. Women who married young (18–23 years of age), and resigned from their permanent full-time jobs for the sake of marriage and pregnancy, were especially likely to face financial constraints. To start with, they had not had time to build significant savings. As we saw in Part I, Kanako, who married her high school sweetheart at 18 after becoming pregnant, underwent almost a year without income because her husband had no stable employment; they had to live with his biological mother and her in-laws. Yayoi, who had married at 19, was desperate to maintain the household income through part-time work; she had resigned from her first permanent position to join her husband in another city, and he subsequently became unemployed. In order to cover for his misappropriation of the company's money, she worked in an office during the day and as a bar hostess at night. Lack of sleep undermined her health, which she believed contributed to a miscarriage. Hatsumi, who married at the age of 21 after becoming pregnant, also had difficulties managing the household budget on a low income.

Others did not struggle but managed to survive financially. Although Oriko had married young at 19 and resigned from her job, since her husband was 20 years her senior and accordingly had a higher salary, she was able to maintain a reasonable standard of living. This was also the case for Noshie, who had married at 26. While Noshie found a single income with an infant difficult to manage, the rent-free accommodation provided by her husband's parents was helpful. In both cases, the husbands provided a secure income. Fumiko, while marrying young at 21, managed the household budget satisfactorily because she had held on to her job and had no children, even though her husband had irregular employment.

Better placed were the women who managed to maintain a reasonable financial situation. Given that this was not easy in a family with children and a single income, it was not surprising that the only one who succeeded was Sayaka, a four-year university graduate, whom we met earlier. She married her boyfriend at 26 and resigned from her job shortly before giving birth to their first child a year later. While she said that the family's finances were 'very tight' with her husband on a low salary as a newly recruited tax accountant, the family had the benefit of living in a rent-free, spacious flat owned by his parents in an exclusive suburb. Her husband's long-term salary prospects were also good.

The women who kept their full-time permanent jobs managed well financially while they had no children. Shizu had married at 24 and Saeko at 27; both lived in very inexpensive company accommodation provided by their husbands' employers, which enabled them to save for the future. Sekie, the nurse who married at 26, had saved an amount sufficient to purchase a flat in the same year. The couple enjoyed overseas trips, and guitar and English conversation lessons. Yoshie, who married a university graduate at 27, also had a reasonable standard of living. It seems that university-educated husbands brought home slightly better salaries.

Relationships with in-laws and natal families

Marriage brought a new set of relationships with the husbands' family members, relatives and friends. Japan has remained unique among post-industrial societies in that a substantial portion of elderly care is still provided by family members (Sugimoto 2003: 175). Almost a half of older people (aged 65 and over) continued to live with their children, relatives and others. (See Table 7.2.) Nonetheless, changes are observable. Nationally, the percentage of three-generation households had declined to less than one-tenth of total households in 2004. The percentage of nuclear family households remained steady, while that of single households increased. (See Table 7.3.) There was still an expectation that aged care would be provided by one's children, preferably sons and their wives, but daughters now play an increasingly significant role in the care of ageing parents. Today, aged parents often have sufficient superannuation not to require financial assistance from their children, but need emotional and practical support. Many are more comfortable accepting this support from their daughters than from their daughters-in-law. This is reflected in changes in parental preference for their children's sex; in 1972, over half of the people surveyed desired a boy if

Table 7.2 Distribution of types of household with individuals who are 65 years old and over, 1980–2005

Year	Number of people 65 years and over (% of the total population)	Individual living alone (%)	Couple living alone (%)	Living with children (%)	Living with other relatives or non-relatives (%)
1980	10,729 (9.2)	8.5	19.6	69.0	3.0
1985	12,111 (10.1)	9.3	23.0	64.6	3.0
1990	14,453 (11.8)	11.2	25.7	59.7	3.5
1995	17,449 (14.7)	12.6	29.4	54.3	3.7
2001	16,367 (35.8)	19.4	27.8	41.2	11.6
2005	17,864 (38.6)	20.9	29.4	38.3	11.4

Source: Nihon-Fujin-Dantai-Rengôkai (2001: 272); Japan-Kôseirôdô-shô (2004b).

Table 7.3 Distribution of household types, 1975–2004

Year	Single family household (%)	Nuclear family household (%)	Three-generation household (%)	Others (%)
1975	18.2	58.7	16.9	6.2
1985	18.4	61.1	15.2	5.3
1995	22.6	58.9	12.5	6.1
2004	23.4	60.6	9.7	6.3

Source: Nihon-Fujin-Dantai-Rengôkai (2001: 272); Japan-Kôseirôdô-shô (2004b).

they were to have an only child, but in 1992, this figure was less than a quarter (Japan-Sôrifu 1995: 16). It is in this national context that the expectations and experiences of the women in this study need to be understood.

The women had vaguely expected that their relationships with their in-laws would be difficult to manage. At the time of marriage, five women were aware that, in marrying a first or only son, they were expected to care for their aged in-laws eventually; they accepted this expectation somewhat fatalistically, but not necessarily willingly. As the relationship with the in-laws unfolded, they gradually formed more realistic views about the prospect. The level of willingness to live with in-laws varied among the women.

At one end of the continuum was Oriko, who remained the most optimistic about caring for her aged in-laws. Her relationship with her in-laws was relatively smooth. Her husband's parents were already in their late 70s when the 19-year-old Oriko married a man 20 years her senior. Oriko's parents' most serious concern was that Oriko would have to take on the care of his elderly parents, who were living in a rented apartment in a municipal housing complex. Oriko and her family regularly visited her husband's parents, although her husband's elder sisters kept in much closer contact with them. When Oriko and her husband bought their first house, they invited his parents to come and live with them. The elderly couple declined, saying that they wanted to live by themselves while they were healthy enough to do so (Oriko's father-in-law died in 2000). Oriko thought that her in-laws were happy in the public housing complex since their three daughters lived nearby, but knew that the present situation would not last.

ORIKO: I am prepared to take care of his parents when they want to move in with us. They say this will only be when they are no longer healthy, but I am also anxious about it. I often think that now is the easiest and most comfortable time of my life, and that greater responsibilities are to come.

(27 October 1997)

Nevertheless, she looked happy and maintained an optimistic outlook.

Oriko also now realised that she would be responsible for her own parents in their old age. Both her elder brother and younger sister were overseas. Her elder brother had dropped out of Imai Technical High School, worked as a construction worker and later as a site supervisor for several years, and eventually married. On their honeymoon, the couple liked Canada so much that they eventually migrated there. Her brother dreamed of becoming a park ranger in a national park; but for the time being did various unskilled jobs to survive. Oriko's younger sister, a university graduate, had obtained a job in Italy through a friend of her father's, and had married an Italian. She showed no sign of returning. The sister, according to Oriko, was a career-woman type. Since Oriko was the only child living near their parents, and now that Oriko and her husband had bought a house nearby, the sense of responsibility was even more acute. Oriko did not see her mother very often despite their proximity. Oriko's mother was caring for her own mother, who was 93, bed-ridden, and had suffered from Alzheimer's disease for over ten years.[2] Oriko was also taking driving lessons, thinking that being able to drive would ease her tasks.

ORIKO: I have been telling her that she should get someone else to do things. She does not have to do everything herself. She is always tired. I worry about her. But she won't listen to me.

(27 October 1997)

Perhaps the kind of care that Oriko planned to offer her in-laws would differ from that provided by her mother for her grandmother. Oriko's suggestion that her mother use paid caregivers was pragmatic, given the availability of home-care services; but it remained to be seen how Oriko would manage when her time came.

Noshie, on the other hand, became increasingly doubtful that she would like to live with her in-laws. As we saw in Part I, Noshie and her husband, Oki, lived with his parents shortly after their wedding, which made Noshie extremely uncomfortable. The couple then moved to a prefabricated house that Oki's uncle's family had built for themselves on Oki's parents' land as temporary accommodation immediately after the earthquake. (The quake destroyed Oki's parents' house.) Noshie and Oki did not pay rent, which helped their financial situation. Noshie was initially genuinely grateful for his parents' gesture, but grew irritated at her mother-in-law's unwelcome interventions in what Noshie saw as the couple's business. The more upset she became, the more clearly she started to see Oki's parents' 'strategy' (her word). She began to want to move out of the house and rent a modest flat, suspecting that her husband's parents wanted the couple to leave the 'temporary' accommodation (which by its nature was uncomfortable) and live with them. While they continued to live in the prefabricated house, she felt that they were incurring a debt to Oki's parents, and that the longer this situation continued the more difficult it would be for the couple to establish a separate household. She felt that they had been *amaeru* (dependent) on his parents, and that they would have to pay a price for this in the future. Since their single income did not allow them to pay rent, Noshie was determined to find part-time work once her children were a little older.

Two other women, Shizu and Sayaka, showed similar objections to generous assistance from their husbands' parents. They also felt uncomfortable at their husbands' willingness to accept such assistance; and believed that a couple should start their life together humbly, and build their assets gradually. Notwithstanding, each woman accepted the offer after being persuaded by her husband.

Even if a woman found her mother-in-law acceptable, other relatives, often called *gaiya* (literally, outfielders, in baseball terminology), could pose problems. Yoshie's was one case. Yoshie's problems with her in-laws were complicated by the fact that her husband was a nephew of her close friend Oriko's husband and Oriko had introduced them. When I met her in late 2000, Yoshie was not on speaking terms with Oriko. She retrospectively appreciated her mother's warning before her marriage: 'If you marry a relative of your friend, you will end up losing your friendship.' Yoshie was happy with her mother-in-law (a single mother), whom she found to be quiet and reserved, but hated the mother's elder sisters, who continuously commented on and intervened in what Yoshie considered to be the couple's own business. Worse, Yoshie was convinced that the aunts' negative comments resulted from information that Oriko inadvertently revealed to them, and that Oriko in fact sided with them.

KO: You mean, Oriko is one of your aunts-in-law?
YOSHIE: Exactly. She is one of the naughty aunts-in-law!
KO: You mean, she has become one of their family?
YOSHIE: Yes. She might have been talking badly about me [laughs].
KO: But why would she do that? What does she get out it?
YOSHIE: I don't know. But I guess she has no choice but to side with them. These three aunts are her sisters-in-law and she lives near them and sees them all the time. They are much older than her – almost her mother's age. She probably feels she has no choice but to go along with their conversation. Being the youngest, her status is weak [*tachiba ga yowai*], so she just has to go with the flow of the conversation. I don't think she can say, 'Yoshie is not like that.' She would be isolating herself. You never know, she may really be thinking badly of me.

(28 December 2000)

While Yoshie's irritation grew at what she saw as constant criticism from the aunts-in-law, the last straw was two particular incidents that infuriated her so much that she left her husband for her natal home. One was her husband's act of giving his salary to his mother without consulting her and the other was what she saw as the aunts' public condemnation of Yoshie's behaviour at her husband's grandfather's funeral. I was taken aback by Yoshie's emotion when revealing this, since I had never seen her so upset.

As soon as she was married, Yoshie tried to put money away as she had used all her savings for the wedding (of which she paid half, three million yen), the honeymoon and new furniture for their flat. She was relieved when her parents paid the airfares for her fathers' relatives, who were from an island off the southern tip of Kyushu, when they attended the wedding. Then Yoshie discovered that her husband Nobita had already told his mother (without consulting Yoshie) that he would continue to contribute 40,000 yen monthly to her household expenses. Yoshie was unhappy with this arrangement but accepted it on the condition that she would give her own parents the same amount, to which he reluctantly agreed. Since Yoshie's family subsequently declined her offer, she instead saved that money 'for a rainy day' (*watashi no hesokuri*). Nobita handed Yoshie his full monthly salary, out of which she gave him 70,000 yen (40,000 yen for his mother and 30,000 yen for his pocket money). Yoshie casually mentioned this financial arrangement to her friend, Oriko.

YOSHIE: Then, guess what happened next? These aunties rang their sister [Yoshie's mother-in-law] and learnt that she had not received any money since the wedding. They thought that I was lying! Can you believe it? Then they rang me and accused me of pretending to look 'nice'! I was so angry. I then found that he hadn't been giving the money to her! I told him that I was leaving him for a while and went back to my mum.

(28 December 2000)

Then came Nobita's grandfather's funeral. Yoshie tried hard to perform what she believed to be her duties as a new member of the family, accepting offers of drink and food. Then she was reprimanded by her aunts-in-law for her 'misbehaviour'; that is, eating and drinking too much. Yoshie's own mother, who also attended the funeral, noticed the strained relationship between Yoshie and her aunts-in-law and was sympathetic to her plight. When Yoshie was criticised, her husband failed to take her side. Yoshie was so angry that she told him off and went home to her mother again.

Shizu thought that her relations with her in-laws had been just acceptable, at least so far. Her parents-in-law were close to their daughter, who was married with children and lived in the same provincial city. Shizu liked the natural environment in the country, but did not feel particularly comfortable with her in-laws, since she had little in common with them.

SHIZU: I think they're basically nice people. But I get nervous. Whenever I go there, I catch a cold afterwards. I go there several times a year, including mid-summer and New Year's Day – and always I get sick after I return!

(30 December 2000)

She felt that her in-laws were slightly interventionist. They were also too willing, in Shizu's view, to offer monetary assistance to the couple. Shizu's husband intended to return to his home city after his retirement, if he continued to work at the present company. He might even return earlier if he changed jobs. Shizu wanted to remain in Kobe-city.

Of all the married women, Satoko was the only one who developed an extremely close and understanding relationship with her in-laws. As we saw earlier, her husband's parents and aunt looked after her pre-school-age children after picking them up from childcare. Although her husband was the first son, his parents were willing to let him and his family move in with Satoko's mother, a cook at a hospital, who was to retire soon, so that she could look after the grandchildren once they started school. Satoko was very grateful for their understanding.

There were also those who kept a distant relationship with their in-laws. Both Saeko and Shizu had in-laws living in other cities, and visited them only a few times every year. Sekie's husband's parents lived nearby, but he did not want to have much contact with them. Even though Sekie encouraged him to visit them often, she gave up in the end following his continued refusal to do so.

While the women developed new relationships with an expanding circle of relatives and friends after marriage, their relationships with their own parents underwent changes. Mothers often became sounding boards and offered assistance to their daughters. Kanako's mother and her sisters were always available to assist in baby-sitting Kanako's children, and after the birth of a new baby. Fumiko's mother was concerned with her daughter's health, and came to the couple's flat daily to do the housework when she was bed-ridden. Physical proximity assisted Sekie and Oriko to maintain close relationships with their own parents. Sekie and her husband bought a house next to her parents' place, and often had dinner there, along with her younger sister and her husband. Oriko frequented her parents' home with her children during the day. Sayaka's parents, who originally opposed her marriage to a man she met at university because of what they saw as class difference, remained supportive of Sayaka throughout. Sayaka returned to her parental home on a few occasions when she argued with her husband. Her mother always welcomed her.

Shizu was the only one whose relationship with her natal family became strained after marriage. She visited her parents only two or three times a year, even though they lived nearby, and phoned only once a month. One of her two elder sisters was divorced and had returned to her parents' home with two children, aged six and four. The sister had fallen out with her parents before her marriage, but after the earthquake the family members were reconciled. Another elder sister also lived in the parental home. Six people in total thus lived in a house that had been half-destroyed by the earthquake. The bathroom had not been repaired, so they had to go to a nearby public bathhouse. The house belonged to Shizu's mother, who had been given it by her parents, but the family rented the land, having done so since immediately after the war. Unfortunately, no lease document existed. To add to an already difficult situation, Shizu's father was unable to support the family on his earnings, and her mother had always worked.

SHIZU: I don't like them. No, I like them, but I don't like their lack of seriousness [*fumajime*] and not working. When I think of us, I feel upset and angry. I think they should realise that this is not the time to be *fumajime*. But no one there understands what I mean. I can only say this to my mum.

KO: You mean, she is the only one who understands?

SHIZU: Yes.

KO: But do you really say things like 'Why don't you work?'

SHIZU: Yes I do.

KO: To your mother?

SHIZU: No, to the others. I also said so to my dad. But it made no difference. I like them, but since I got angry with them, I haven't been near them. I tried to change Dad's mind, like writing him a letter and visiting him at his workplace, but it made no difference. A father at least should be able to support himself, right? He can't do this. So my mother has been *ganbaru* [persistently working hard].

KO: So your mother has been working all the time?

SHIZU: Yes. But when she lost her job after the earthquake, she couldn't find other work because of a duodenal ulcer. I was sending 40,000 yen every month until I quit working. Mum doesn't complain because that stresses her out more. I used to get stressed when I was living with them, but I wasn't brave enough to leave home then.

(30 December 2000)

Her mother, aged 57, had been making shoes, but had recently found a new job sorting toys. Shizu felt completely helpless and unable to help her mother.

Marriage 'problems' and their perceived solutions

All women mentioned 'problems' in their marriages. These problems included not only issues related to the couple, but also those more to do with the extended family and human relationships with in-laws. When faced with problems, women discussed them with their husbands and consulted with their friends and family. These problems led four women (Yoshie, Sayaka, Hatsumi and Fumiko) to return to their parental homes for a while. Their husbands often pleaded with them to return. More serious problems resulted in separation and subsequent divorce, as we shall see later.

YOSHIE: I went home in such a state that my mum initially said, 'If he's such a cold person, you can always leave him and come home.' Then he came and apologised to me and my mum. He was barred from my mum's house for a while. She said to me, 'Don't bring him home again.'

(28 December 2000)

On this particular occasion, Yoshie stayed at her mother's home for over a week. In the end, her mother asked her to leave, since the neighbours had started noticing that there was something wrong.

YOSHIE: She said, 'You can leave him if you want, but don't plan on living here. Please live somewhere else – of course you can visit us!' Then I had several calls from him asking me to return. Mum again asked me to go home [to him]. So in the end that's what I did. Since then I haven't stayed overnight with Mum. We only visit.

(28 December 2000)

Yoshie, in her second year of marriage, seemed reconciled to the idea that her marriage could be worse. I also had an impression that the couple communicated their dissatisfactions well.

YOSHIE: Well ... I can't complain about him. If only I could protect him from his nasty aunts. His pay could be better, but I can't complain really.
KO: There's no perfect husband, is there?
YOSHIE: Exactly. He helps me with the housework. He's understanding about my work commitments. Maybe better than many other men.

(28 December 2000)

Fortunately, Yoshie got along with her mother-in-law, and accepted the prospect that the couple would live with her in her old age. Her mother-in-law was divorced and had no husband to look after, so Yoshie also felt that she would be of great help if she, Yoshie, decided to go back to work after she had a baby.

Some women learned to accept 'problems' that they felt they had little chance of resolving. A case in point involved the serious problems that Kanako faced, such as her husband's extramarital affairs, his gambling and his unemployment in the first two years of their marriage. Later, she faced his health problems, which arose from excessive drinking and violence, yet held on to the marriage while arguing continuously with him. I continued to be struck by her sense of optimism whenever she talked about her family. Her high school friends were awed by Kanako's endurance and persistence, saying, 'Why does she have to put up with that?' Later, they came up with the explanation that Kanako wanted to be needed by, and to look after, someone. She was the eldest of the five girls in her family and had always looked after younger siblings. In the tenth year of their marriage, Kanako and her husband were happy, with three children and a new flat that they had recently purchased with a special loan for earthquake victims. According to the couple, the husband's 'problems' had been resolved to a degree.

In another instance, Satoko was unhappy with the chronic state of physical exhaustion that resulted from juggling a demanding job and caring for her children, but she was calmly resigned to the fact that this situation would continue unless her husband brought in a regular income. (She held little realistic expectation of this, however.) So she kept going.

How did these women learn to accept their problems? They did not articulate the process well, simply saying, 'There's no choice' (*shikata ga nai*). Sayaka explained the process that led to her accepting a marriage as it was.

SAYAKA: I went back to my parents' house with Aki [her one-year-old son] for a week. I thought about divorce as well. But in the end I bowed deeply [*dogeza shite*] and apologised to my husband and my mother-in-law, although my mother-in-law said that I didn't have to do that.

KO: That's very dramatic. How did this happen?

SAYAKA: Well, let me think. It was triggered by his kicking me when we were arguing. We were arguing because I was angry at his mother for criticising me, but of course other things that I didn't like had been building up, and they all came out then.

KO: Like?

SAYAKA: She always says that they've been so nice to give us this flat. I'd heard enough of that. She would often come in to look for things that she'd left here, as if this place still belonged to her. And I just couldn't stand my husband's strange money-sense. I mean, his spending habits are inappropriate for his level of salary as a newly employed tax accountant. You see, he was brought up in a decent [*jôhin ni*] way and wants to buy nice things. For example, when he went on a business trip he bought a very expensive glass object. He bought a new French car, when I said that a second-hand Japanese car would be fine. He tells me to buy this and that, but his salary just doesn't go that far. Then, my mother-in-law often says that they lived in a company house first and gradually built up their assets, you know.

KO: What made you decide to return home?

SAYAKA: I decided to apologise [to my husband and my mother-in-law] and return, since my husband said that he was to blame and said sorry. I also couldn't stand looking at my father's sad face. Besides, I felt that if I went for a divorce then, I would be denying everything that I had done, like going to university and getting a good job. I don't like my mother-in-law, but I know she is very intelligent and capable. So I told myself it would be up to me what I made of it, and decided to endure [*nintai*].

(22 December 2000)

Since the incident, Sayaka had been reasonably happy with the family arrangement. While recognising that she disliked some aspects of the marriage, she was prepared to endure them in order to enjoy its positive aspects.

At this stage, as long as they had their husbands on their side in disputes with their in-laws, the women were prepared to make do with the relationship. As we saw in Part I, Kanako's husband took her side when the relationship with his step-mother became difficult, which resulted in the couple severing contact with his father and brother. Noshie's husband also played a subtle role in managing her dissatisfaction with her in-laws. But there were women who opted for divorce in order to escape from an unhappy marriage that they could no longer endure.

Divorce

The divorce rate remained low in post-war Japan in comparison with post-industrial Western countries. It started increasing in the late 1980s and reached the level of France in the late 1990s, but was still lower than in the USA and UK (Fuess 2004: 144). The rate rose from 1.28 divorces per 1,000 people in 1990, to 2.15 in 2004 (see Figure 7.4). Divorce within five years of marriage still accounts for almost one-third of all divorces, although divorce later in marriage has increased in recent years, as shown in Figure 7.5. It is widely observed that with the increase in the divorce rate, the social stigma attached to divorce has weakened (Fuess 2004: 152). National opinion surveys support this and reveal, for example, that those who approved of divorce in cases of partner dissatisfaction accounted for 21.2 per cent of the sample in 1972, 30.3 per cent in 1984 and 44.4 per cent in 1992 (Japan-Sorifu 1995: 38–39). Younger people were more likely to support divorce, in particular those in their 20s (63.8 per cent of females and 52.3 per cent of males) (Japan-Sorifu 1995: 39). I suspect that changes in attitudes have made divorce a more viable option for unhappy couples.

In recent years wives have more often initiated divorces than husbands. The media has exaggerated this trend by creating the image of 'unsuspecting

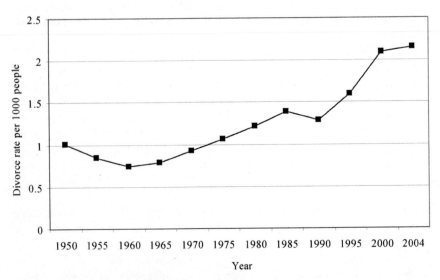

Figure 7.4 Divorces per 1,000 people between 1950 and 2004.
Source: Japan-Kôseirôdô-shô (2004a: Table Rikon-4).

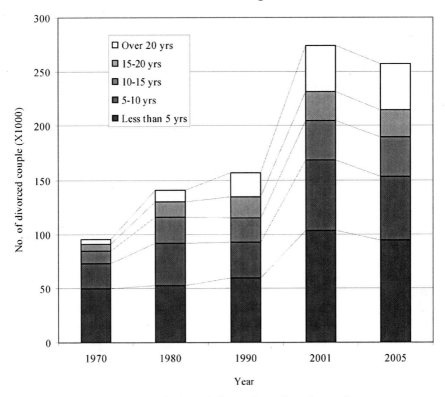

Figure 7.5 Duration of co-habitation of divorced couples prior to divorce.
Source: Japan-Kôseirôdô-shô (2004a: Table Rikon-1).

men as the surprised victims of divorce' (Fuess 2004: 165); the reality, however, remains elusive and complicated. Both Yayoi and Fumiko initiated divorce, but whether their husbands could be regarded as 'victims' is open to debate, as we shall see below. A distinctive change is noticeable in child custody in the post-war period. Mothers have gained custody of all their children in over 70 per cent of cases since the early 1990s; however, in the 1950s, husbands gained custody of all children in over 50 per cent of cases (Japan-Sôrifu 1995: 38). Hatsumi's case was a minority one in that her husband retained custody of their daughter.

Three women in the study, Yayoi, Hatsumi and Fumiko, underwent divorce. All of them married relatively young (20, 21 and 23 respectively) and were divorced within three years. We see desperation, misery, sadness and ingenuity in the process leading to divorce, although each case has its own trajectory. Yayoi and Fumiko share features: both initiated separation and subsequent divorce and had no complications involving children. Both in the end obtained most of what they wanted; and, as I see it, came out of the process somewhat empowered, in the sense that they gained self-confidence.

In addition, the two were able to convince people around them that the separation was the result of their husbands' deficiencies and that they had persevered to try and save the marriage. In other words, people saw the two as 'victims'. Hatsumi's case differed greatly. Her husband initiated separation and divorce. Also, a child was involved. In retrospect, Hatsumi did not get what she wanted – she lost custody of her daughter. At that time, once her husband had initiated the separation she was unsure of what she wanted and thought only of getting out of the marriage. She had difficulties in portraying herself as a victim. Many people saw her husband as being betrayed by her affair with a colleague. Hatsumi lost self-confidence through the process and felt helpless in the following few years.

We followed Yayoi's case in Part I. She left her husband in desperation after trying hard to cover up the fact that he had been misappropriating his employer's money. In separating, she had moral support from her employer and her family. After a lengthy negotiation, she managed to persuade her reluctant husband and his family to agree to the divorce. Yayoi did not go through the formal family court procedure, since there were no shared assets involved.

Fumiko, on the other hand, underwent a formal mediation process at a local family court at her husband's family's insistence on this. Fumiko's request for a divorce sparked heated arguments between both families. Fumiko had never expected that a divorce would be so difficult to achieve. Her husband Satoshi's mother proposed that the fathers conduct a formal negotiation, telling Fumiko, 'Since you hurt my son, I will not let you speak to him.' Fumiko's father responded, 'My daughter became ill so many times because she was overtired! It's your son's fault.'

FUMIKO: Then Satoshi's family started saying that this was a case of defamation [*meiyo kison*] and said that they would go to the court with a lawyer. So, I made all the correspondence into *kumonjo* [official documents, whereby a postmaster keeps copies of the documents]. In any case I learned a lot in the process. When I was desperate, my sister gave me a newspaper article about legal aid [*hôritsu sôdansho*]. So I went to Kobe-city's legal aid office to consult about the mediation [*chôtei*], since I had no idea what I had to do to get a divorce.

(21 November 1997)

Fumiko was advised by the legal aid office that having a lawyer would not give her much advantage in the case of mediation, and that she should visit a court to obtain detailed information about the process, which she did immediately. In the end, Fumiko herself attended the mediation process, as well as Satoshi's lawyer. They were called twice.

FUMIKO: I never saw his lawyer since each of us went there separately. Basically, the mediator reported what the other party said, asked what I would do if they said this and that, such as regarding property and assets. I said that I just wanted a divorce – I didn't need any consolation money [*isharyô*], and wouldn't ask for any money, even though I paid for the wedding, honeymoon and so forth. But I did make it clear that I wanted the apartment that we'd bought shortly before we got separated, and I would repay half a million yen that his parents paid as part of the deposit.

(21 November 1997)

When Fumiko and Satoshi bought the apartment, she paid 1.5 million yen and Satoshi's parents paid half a million yen, because they wanted Satoshi to be seen to be contributing as well. The apartment was not yet in their possession. Satoshi's parents then asked where Satoshi's savings (from his salary) were, which offended Fumiko greatly. According to Fumiko, Satoshi was so careless in spending his money on himself – by, for example, buying an expensive watch, playing *pachinko* and drinking – that he had saved nothing. She had to create documents about his salary and outgoings, and provided these to the mediators to convince them that she had not gained any money from her husband's salary. 'It was Satoshi who was spending my money,' said Fumiko, but she did not raise this issue, fearing that the divorce process would take longer. She just wanted to end the marriage quickly. The money was not important, as long as she could buy the apartment from him. In the end, Satoshi's family agreed. Fumiko was happy.

Fumiko was relieved when Satoshi returned to his parents' home in the east of Japan, far away from Kobe-city, since she thought he would be secure there. This made her feel 'safe'.

FUMIKO: I was scared of him, to tell the truth. Since he is vulnerable, I thought he might commit suicide, not being able to handle all this. Once, when we fought over something, he sped off in his car and almost had an accident. I also saw some of his violent aspects. He was never physically violent towards me, but I was scared when he hit doors, threw plates, kicked things, and incited a fight with strangers on the street. I was scared of being dragged into his violent actions. That's why I often hid kitchen knives. At the same time, I was scared about him committing suicide, you know. I didn't want him to die because of me! I think because of his parents' over-protection, he was weak psychologically and emotionally [*seishintekini*], and became violent when he didn't get his way. My parents were glad that he returned to his parents' house, because they told me that they were fearful for my safety, too.

(21 November 1997)

It took six months after they had started living separately for the divorce to come through. By then Fumiko had already started going out with one of her colleagues, who was sympathetic to her plight. Work offered her a comfortable diversion, and she became a more committed career woman. She was happy to own her own apartment independent of her parents at the age of 24. She had lived all her life in a rented flat in a municipal housing complex. Luck was on her side when she gained the sole ownership of the apartment from her ex-husband. She was able to take advantage of a special housing loan available to earthquake victims. She took out a 35-year loan.

Fumiko felt that she had learned greatly from this unpleasant experience.

FUMIKO: It's strange to say this, but I've learned so much out of this. I represented myself at the family court, did everything when buying a property, and now have more confidence in myself – like I can survive independently. Of course I had a lot of support from my family. A funny thing is that the more confident I've become about myself the more I want to be gentle and nice to somebody. That person is now my mum. I want to make my mum happy. I also volunteer as a counsellor for an internet counselling service [*nayamigoto sôdan*]. I experienced a terrible marriage, a divorce and so forth. I'd like to think that another young person can find my comments useful.

(21 November 1997)

Fumiko's experience was thus also empowering. She was happy that she was out of the marriage, that her family had been wonderful, and that she had recently received a promotion at work. Her life did not centre on relationships any more. It was her work that dominated her life and provided a needed diversion from the traumas that she had undergone in the course of her marriage breakdown.

In contrast to Yayoi and Fumiko, who despite their trauma felt somewhat empowered through their experience of divorce, Hatsumi felt helpless. She regretted the fact that she had lost custody of her daughter, which she attributed to her inability at the time to take a long-term perspective when considering her options. She still thought that her daughter believed that her mother had left her for another man, and not being given an opportunity to explain her side of the story saddened her.

Post-divorce independence

We saw in Part I that Yayoi had a few relationships after her divorce, but ended them once her boyfriends mentioned marriage. She wanted to avoid the kind of relationship that would lead to marriage, since she feared that marriage would involve relationships with in-laws and lead to her husband being dependent on her. At the company where she obtained a full-time permanent job one year after her divorce, she developed a steady relationship with her boss, who was married with teenage children. She enjoyed the relationship precisely because there was no prospect of marriage, but she was fully aware that her parents would not approve of it. Later, she surprised herself when she bought a flat in order to enable her elder sister (who was then divorced and bringing up a young daughter) to move into her room in her parents' house. The purchase was triggered by the generous housing loan offer to earthquake victims, without which Yayoi did not think it would have been possible. This gave her a sense of independence and confidence, in particular, since she felt a great sense of indebtedness to her family for their support during the divorce procedure.

Fumiko had also gone out with two boyfriends, both colleagues at work. The impetus for a new relationship was her unhappy marriage. At that time, Fumiko and her husband had a 'yo-yo' relationship; for example, they would fight, Fumiko would get upset and leave him alone so that he would calm down, and then they would get back together again. In retrospect, she considered that her interest in her colleague contributed to her proposing to her husband a long-term separation 'to think it over', which eventually resulted in divorce. After the divorce was finalised, Fumiko did not immediately embrace a new relationship. She felt uncomfortable about becoming involved with work colleagues, since she feared it might confuse the personal with the workplace, but in the end she could not resist temptation.

FUMIKO: But once we became intimate, he [one year her senior] started complaining about the workplace. I hated it. So I said that we should go back to just being friends. I didn't want to hear his complaints about my other colleagues. I was indecisive though. I was still attracted to him, you see. I don't think he liked me being indecisive. In the end he told me that he had someone else in mind and we parted. I still like him. I liked it because I felt that the two of us were going for what we thought to be ideal or had a purpose. He had high ideals and goals, and was always working to achieve them. I loved that aspect of him. But at the same time, he was always stressed out and disappointed because he always sensed a gap between his ideals and the reality. Then he kept complaining.

(21 November 1997)

In addition, Fumiko felt that he was jealous about her promotion to the university graduate track, where he was, immediately after her divorce. He said, 'Women are always lucky – they are recognised even for a little bit of merit.'

After parting from him, Fumiko found another man (30 years old) who was interested in her. She was not initially interested, but because he was simply 'nice and kind' she started going out with him. He was an employee of another computer company, seconded to work in her office. He was not ambitious to move up the career ladder and was generally content with what he had achieved but, according to Fumiko, lacked high ideals, which disappointed her. It was precisely because of this, she suspected, that he did not see a gap between his ideals and reality and was generally happy with himself. He was also genuinely concerned with her well-being, listened to her worries and about her past relationships, and was willing to drive her home when she worked late at night. Fumiko was aware that she was confused about what she wanted in a relationship or marriage.

FUMIKO: I know I like my former boyfriend better. I've read various books on relationships since my divorce and have come to understand him. I misunderstood him – now I think he's a 'typical man'. If we get back together, we may be able to have a different kind of relationship from what we had before. But he will be demanding to live with, both mentally and physically. My current boyfriend would be much easier to be married to. He is so happy with himself!

(21 November 1997)

Fumiko had been reading non-fiction books, in particular about psychology and relationships, in order to make sense of what happened to her marriage. One was Deborah Tannen's *You Just Don't Understand: Women and men in conversation* (in translation), and Fumiko was keen to share and discuss her views with me. For the time being, however, she had decided to enjoy her independence, living in the flat she had bought and visiting her mother, who lived nearby. She was also committed to her work, after achieving the transfer to the university graduate track.

While Yayoi and Fumiko came to enjoy their renewed independence after divorce, Hatsumi remained unsure. She had not had any relationship during the four years since the divorce. The reasons for her reluctance were complicated. She always feared that a new relationship might negatively affect her chance of regaining custody of her daughter. She was not confident in developing a new relationship, since, she claimed, she did not know what she wanted from one. She was also unsure if she would be able to remain rational once she became emotionally involved. Gaining a place in a municipal housing complex gave a sense of permanency to Hatsumi, her mother and a younger sister, as they had been living in temporary accommodation for earthquake victims (*kasetsu*) for over a year. Hatsumi had obtained permanent full-time employment which meant that she could support herself and her mother, but she felt no commitment to the job.

Managing a new web of relationships

We have seen how young women aged in their 20s developed their roles in their newly created households and learned to accept the responsibilities that went with those roles. In the working-class women's marriages that I studied, I found three types. One was the wife who took on the roles of breadwinner and homemaker because of her husband's precarious employment. The second was the wife who worked full-time and earned the same level of income as her husband, who for his part participated equally in the housework; this was often the scenario before the couple had children. The third was the full-time housewife, perhaps with a casual part-time job, who looked after pre-school children. Some of these working-class women faced considerable financial constraints in contrast to their university-educated middle-class counterparts. Financial problems sometimes became a source of the women's dissatisfaction with marriage.

For most of the women who married in their 20s, marriage provided the first opportunity to move out of their parents' home. Although this gave the women a sense of independence from their parents, they simultaneously saw themselves entering another web of relationships with in-laws and relatives. They needed to learn the 'rules of the game' in the new relationships fast, often through trial and error and accompanied by trauma and tears. Problems with in-laws were frustrating and irritating, causing some women to return temporarily to their parental home in the first three years. However, over the years, the women gradually learned to perceive problems with their in-laws in a wider and longer-term context. They learned to understand that marriage came as a package of the pleasant and unpleasant; that an inevitable part of any marriage package was in-laws and relatives; and that in-laws perhaps did not have malicious intentions towards them and might some day offer intangible benefits to them as well as to their children. A great deal of pragmatism seemed to play a part in this process. The women communicated their agonies with their in-laws extensively to their friends. Those who chose divorce as a solution to their marriage problems initially questioned whether their actions were wise, but were forced to move on. Natal family support was crucial in facilitating this process. Some came out of divorce empowered and with a sense of independence, and succeeded in establishing their own single-person household after a period of dependence on their parents.

A sense of independence was thus felt when they left the parental home to establish a new household through marriage. Marriage brought a range of responsibilities socially expected of a wife, mother and daughter-in-law. Forced to juggle these in daily routines without consciously planned strategies, the women learned to maintain what they considered a balanced and happy life, to differing degrees. In early 2001, approaching the age of 30, the women were in different stages of the life cycle. Those who had started a family young already had children at school; some had just got married or engaged; others had no plans for marriage in the near future. Three were divorced. Importantly, the friendship groups still kept in touch.

8 Decisions and their consequences in paths to adulthood

Seeking 'comfort' (*igokochi*)

The final chapter draws together the preceding discussions and examines several transitions to adulthood simultaneously (e.g. leaving school and entry into the labour force, employment, relationships and leisure, family, marriage and parenting). There is merit in illuminating the interface of multiple transitions (rather than examining them separately, as much prior work has done) since young adults' experiences in these transitions are often interlinked: for example, women's decisions about their work are closely related to their domestic situations in marriage and parenting (Thiessen and Looker 1999: 62). In so doing I ask the following questions. How did young working-class women conceive the transition to adulthood and what adulthood entailed? How were their trajectories to adulthood shaped by individual decisions and actions on one hand, and by structural conditions on the other?

We saw in Chapter 4 how young women experienced entry into full-time employment from high school and learned to manage what many saw as a radical departure from 12 years of schooling. This included finding meaning in mundane work, managing workable relationships with colleagues and planning their future. Chapter 5 revealed how they made sense of their experiences of employment and unemployment, and how their understanding of employment altered over the period. The next two chapters turned to the young women's private lives. We saw how they developed romantic relationships and decided on permanent partners, and how they negotiated relationships with their husbands and in-laws in the marriage, and in some cases in separation and divorce. We also learned how they maintained relationships with their natal families throughout these experiences.

I will first discuss the women's subjective understanding of young adulthood; and then examine their trajectories to adulthood in terms of individual decision-making, actions and external circumstances (including institutional factors). I will then attempt to show how their trajectories to, and understanding of, adulthood are guided by urban working-class status and, for some, ethnic minority status.

Young adulthood

In earlier chapters (in particular, Chapter 1) I briefly discussed recent trends involving young adults in the West, and institutional features that guide transitions to adulthood, as a global backdrop to my stories. Japan displays some of the features of southern European welfare regimes in that the state expects families to play a role in providing welfare for their family members. The link between what youth learn at school and employment is strong for vocational high schools, which my actors attended. Vocational high schools provide their students with job contacts though an institutional system of school-based job referral, which is built on a long-tem relationship between a school and a large number of employers. As in the West, we saw that Japanese young people experience transitions to adulthood quite differently from two decades ago; and the public is concerned with the increasing lack of conformity that young people display towards the old norm of linear progression from full-time study to full-time regular employment. At the same time, young people now question the normative notion of adulthood that they attribute to older generations and regard as being inappropriate in the present circumstances that are beyond their control.

The young women in this study, having started permanent full-time jobs through a predictable link with their schools, found that having a job was alone not sufficient for engendering a sense of adulthood. Since they had obtained permanent full-time jobs under the guidance of protection of the school-based job referral system (as explained in Chapter 2), the job itself and the income it brought were not given primacy in their transition to adulthood. It may also be that those who have completed a transition role (e.g. securing employment) do not attach as much importance to the role as those who have not, as was shown in a study on Swedish youth (Westberg 2004).

It was the nature of the employment experience that mattered to these young Japanese women; it had to enable them to formulate concrete personal goals to pursue. A permanent full-time job, though seemingly a top priority when one does not have one, did not bestow for them a sense of adulthood. Second, unlike the Australian young people mentioned earlier, many of these women, after almost two years at work, had not yet had opportunities to explore priorities between work and private interests. They were too preoccupied with finding ways to adjust to their work, which many thought required more commitment than they were willing to offer. Some, like Miyuki, whose leave application was rejected, did question the expectations of what she saw as excessive commitment to her employer. Also, the women started assessing and balancing their priorities much later, in their late 20s, not because the absence of a permanent full-time job forced them to seek alternative paths to self-fulfilment, but as a result of reflecting on their extended experience of permanent full-time employment.

Similar to the situation in the West, my actors' narratives suggest that they comprehend 'adulthood' in terms of intangible, individualistic features. They also reveal that their understanding derived from comparison with their past, with the extent and point of comparison changing over the years. Comparison with one's past was most prominently expressed when I saw them two years after graduating from high school in 1992. Everyone expressed a strong awareness of changed status from full-time high school student to full-time permanent employee, with the accompanying changes in expectations and responsibilities, as we saw in Chapter 4. This, I suspect, was partly because of the shared memories that the women and I had of my year at their high schools, and partly because of their departure from 12 years of schooling. When I saw them next in 1996–97, the point of comparison was no longer high school days, but their circumstances when I had last seen them in 1992. They no longer talked about how the workplace differed from school, but of their experience of recent events (at work and in relationships), which they interpreted via the cumulative pool of their own past experiences. This was one of the reasons why I decided to create a separate chapter (Chapter 4) on the initial two years.

Three themes stood out in the women's understanding of adulthood. They were: (1) having 'a sense of concrete and achievable purpose' (*mokuhyô*), (2) acceptance of responsibility, and (3) independence (autonomy). The last two were also generally agreed criteria for adulthood in the eyes of young adults in the West, but what these young Japanese meant by these terms seemed to differ slightly, as I shall elaborate later. While 'a sense of concrete and achievable purpose' and acceptance of responsibility were considered to be features that the young could achieve during earlier phases of young adulthood, independence (both financial and decision-making) was understood to come at much later stages. I will elaborate on these three features in turn.

Having a goal (*mokuhyô*) was frequently mentioned soon after leaving school. While none of the women considered herself to be a 'fully fledged adult', since having a permanent full-time job alone was not sufficient for becoming one, many did recognise their own growth (*seichô*) in concrete ways. The women cited specific workplace experiences when pressed to consider their path to adulthood. Their recollections of these events were always accompanied by the qualification 'although I am not an adult yet'. They may seem insignificant to others – many said to me, 'You may think this is trivial' – but they were major events for the individuals concerned, who enthusiastically recollected each one in vivid detail. Sekie, as a nurse trainee, experienced a moment of 'enlightenment' at work, which gave her the motivation to persevere in the face of difficulties.

SEKIE: Yes, I do feel somehow that I've grown recently. You know I'd hated the job, and wanted to quit many times. But that was until the final practice placement last December. During that placement at a teaching hospital, something happened to me – nothing special, but important for me. When I was taking care of a patient with shoulder paralysis, an idea of supporting her without hurting her occurred to me, and I told my supervising nurse, since we had to report everything to her. She said to me, 'It's an excellent idea. You have been observant and very thoughtful.' I thought, 'This is nursing, noticing the needs of a patient that ordinary people don't, and helping her.' Then, I started to feel good about myself and my job. I started thinking that I had complained too much about my work, without trying to understand my job. Then, I started feeling a sense that I had grown – I mean that I was becoming an adult.

(26 January 1992)

Noshie experienced some joy in her seemingly mundane clerical job.

NOSHIE: When I saw for the first time an advertisement that I had created at a branch restaurant, I felt, 'Wow!' I can't explain the feeling well. It's strange, because when my boss said that my work was good, I didn't feel this, but when I saw with my own eyes my work being used, you know, I got motivated [*yaruki ga detekita*].

(26 January 1992)

For Orie, a clerical worker, being asked to teach senior colleagues gave her a sense of self-importance and growth.

ORIE: Well, although you may not think this is important, I felt different when I was asked by my superiors to give a workshop. I put a lot into preparation at home, and when I finished delivering it in a large conference room, I felt 'Wow, I have come a long way to be able to do this,' although I still don't think I am *ichininmae* [a fully fledged adult].

(15 February 1992)

These specific experiences of permanent full-time work were all highly personal and individualised. They helped the women develop short- and long-term goals and the motivation to achieve them. A sense of growth and fulfilment derived from finding, and pursuing, these goals. These goals were 'realistic' and concrete in that the young women saw them as achievable in the given time frame.

Goals that the women set in later years were wider ranging. Miyuki, who became a display designer after working as a checkout clerk at a co-op supermarket, felt a sense of achievement when her Valentine's Day chocolate display won a prize. At the end of her second year in employment, she proudly showed me photographs of her various seasonal displays. Five years later (eight years after leaving school) her personal goal shifted to studying design in a correspondence course at a junior college (*tanki daigaku*, a two-year tertiary institution) of fine arts. She had surprised herself.

MIYUKI: Eight years is a long time, but I've changed my thinking gradually, and I'd like to think I hadn't wasted those years. Without them, there wouldn't be this 'me' who wants to study. So even if this challenge doesn't work out, I will feel satisfied – I did something that I had come to want over the last eight years. You know, I've learned a lot over these years. My attitudes to people have changed. Of course they're not perfect, but I've come to understand more about myself. I'm a slow learner who needed those eight years, and I'm still learning!

(23 October 1997)

Three years later Miyuki was determined to complete her course by achieving a difficult balance with full-time work (where she had gained a middle-management position) although she fully understood that the qualification would not bring much benefit to her present work. Fumiko's goal trajectory included becoming a group leader and gaining a transfer to the university graduate track at work, trying to save her marriage, gaining ownership of the flat in her eventual divorce settlement and then enjoying a relatively peaceful and uneventful period. Few personal goals included individualistic qualities such as 'independence' and equality that American young people see as prerequisites for the transition to adulthood (Arnett 1997). Perhaps these qualities were too vague for the women to pursue as their concrete goals.

Having a goal was not new to these women: their teachers had guided them closely throughout school to develop goals. LeTendre (2000: 95) showed that, in contrast to their American counterparts, Japanese middle school teachers see as their paramount task getting their students to find goals or activities, preferably related, however indirectly, to academic success, and that such goals provide organisation in a young person's life that helps their adolescent development. For example, long-term participation in a sports club is assumed to cultivate endurance, tenacity and perseverance, which are required for academic success. At the vocational high schools that the women attended, teachers collectively provided their students with information and systematic guidance to help them find and decide on their occupational destinations in a manner that I have described as maternalistic (Okano 1993). Now the women had to find, and strive for, a personal goal without the kind of assistance hitherto received. And it is precisely achieving this task that seemed to enable the women to feel a sense of growth. There was no big event that transformed each of the women into adults. Rather, a series of small experiences (which may seem trivial to others but nonetheless enabled them to find a personal goal) seemed to constitute a gradual and cumulative process of moving towards adulthood. Adulthood as seen by these women was a vague destination to which a series of personally significant experiences gradually led them over a long period.

'Responsibility' can also mean different things to different people. Some see responsibility for oneself as sufficient (Arnett 2004: 15), while others may include responsibility for 'other people' as a sign of maturity. My actors considered that responsibility and concern for 'others' was as important as for oneself. Questions then arise as to who was included in the 'others' that they were expected, or wanted, to be responsible for, and to what extent: immediate family members, immediate work colleagues, close friends, former school friends, a network of relatives, or even civil society as a whole? They took it for granted that a mother took responsibility for her young children by sacrificing her own needs; but the extent to which they felt responsible for their colleagues varied.

We saw how the women were concerned with the 'inconvenience' that their actions might cause to their colleagues at work. This concern discouraged many of the women from applying for annual leave that they were entitled to, and made them carefully consider the timing of resignation. Although she was encouraged to stay on, Noshie decided to resign from her private secretary's position when she was five months pregnant since she felt that her condition was imposing an extra burden on her senior, whom she had come to respect. Hatsumi endured the discomfort of pregnancy and worked until shortly before giving birth, despite her husband urging her to resign, since she felt obliged to teach the job content to a new recruit who was to replace her. Fukuko chose the quiet time of the year to resign from a clerical position at a small postal office, where she had been bullied, since she did not want to inconvenience her boss, whom she respected. Tomoe opted for short-term agency work, since she planned an overseas trip with her friends in several months and did not want to inconvenience her colleagues by leaving the job after such a short time. Norimi willingly chose short-term agency work so that she could travel to Europe to visit her new boyfriend twice a year without feeling uncomfortable about causing problems for her colleagues and boss. The women thus frequently used the expression, 'without causing inconvenience to others' (*hokano hitoni meiwaku o kakenai*), when making employment-related decisions.

I am not sure whether the women's seemingly successful internalisation of this trait (of seeking to avoid inconveniencing others) derived from school or from family members. Their high schools strongly conveyed this message to students in their final year when I observed them making decisions about, and obtaining, post-school destinations. The message was framed in such a way as to indicate that an individual student's careless actions might unfairly affect other students, as well as future students, in recruitment examinations and interviews at companies to which the school referred them. Students were given details as to what to do and what not to do when attending recruitment examinations and interviews; and when a student failed to abide by this, teachers immediately took action to apologise to the companies and make amends (Okano 1993: 122–25). This was understandable given that the school's pool of jobs for its graduates depended on its long-term relationships with various employers. Students were further advised by the school to persist with their first full-time permanent job for at least one year, and preferably for three years, because, they were told, it would normally take three years for them to make an objective assessment of the job and workplace. They were also advised, if they considered quitting, to contact their former homeroom teacher or the guidance teachers, to see if the school could help in resolving employment difficulties through liaison with the employer (for example, by discussing with the employer the possibility of transfer to a different section in the company). Only some students followed this advice.

The third feature of adulthood is independence, represented by the term *jiritsu*. The term literally means standing on one's own, and often refers to financial independence from one's family of upbringing. It implies independent decision-making, as distinct from being obliged to follow the advice of parents and teachers. The women talked about independence as a long-term future goal, rather than an immediate one; something that came at much later stages of development than finding personal goals and achieving a balanced sense of responsibilities. This is consistent with the widely held observation that youth in Japan undergo a longer period of adolescent-type dependency on their significant adults and the educational institutions they attend than do their peers in the Anglo-West (Rohlen 1983; Okano 1993), and that Japanese society values interdependence among individuals and groups over the individual independence idealised in the Anglo-West (Reischauer and Jansen 1995).

We saw in Chapter 4 that having a regular income of one's own was not as significant a step as holding a full-time permanent job in the initial two years after leaving school. Several reasons contributed to this. Income itself was not novel, since many of the young women had already earned money from casual jobs while at high school. A regular income did not guarantee the women much more money for their immediate use. For example, some of them contributed to the budget at home and others were forced by their parents to put aside half of their monthly salary and most of their biannual bonuses in a term deposit 'for the future'. Although parents discouraged the women from pursuing immediate financial independence and what they considered an immature independence, they were encouraged to aim for an independence understood as a long-term process to be achieved when they were ready for it. It was for this reason that many of the women were asked to save a substantial portion of their income for the future, rather than contributing to the immediate family budget. Parents believed that their daughters would eventually work out what their 'future' entailed. 'The future' could be anything. While many of their parents expected it to involve marriage, the women had diverse ideas about their futures. Miyuki, in her ninth year at work, used all her savings for the tuition fee for her correspondence tertiary course. Norimi used her savings to study English in the USA in her fourth year at work.

Such expectations on the part of parents and the women's acceptance of them were perhaps also due to pragmatic considerations. Their families, though working class, were not financially desperate. Both the women and their parents were fully aware that high school graduates would have financially stretched living conditions, even with full-time permanent jobs, and needed further care or guidance under the family umbrella. In this context, parents wished to provide both material and emotional support when their children underwent the transition to the workforce. Most women thus lived at home with their parents until they married and created their own household, but this does not mean that they did not desire to leave home. As we saw in Chapter 4, a few women, like Orie and Hatsumi, genuinely wanted to leave home in order to gain recognition of their independence, but after assessing the pros and cons of such a move decided against it.

The literature suggests that parents, family members and wider kinship relatives can play important roles in facilitating transition to adulthood. The family's role in the transition is three-fold. First, it provides socialisation with adults and nurtures intimate and trustful relationships with caregivers during childhood. Second, it offers financial and material support during transitions. Third, it offers an emotional and psychological support base during those transitions. An examination of American high school graduates in their early 20s suggests that the family can act as a facilitator for the transition to adult economic security, and that the prolonged dependency of youth on their families is an adaptive strategy in response to changing economic conditions (Aquilino 1999: 168–75). The average amount of material assistance from families to 18 to 34-year-old Americans during the transition to adulthood is over $38,000; and this amount is correlated with parental income levels (Schoeni and Ross, 2005). Inequalities in support available from families are likely to contribute to cumulative advantages and disadvantages. Studying British youth, Morrow and Richards (1996) commented that specific groups with limited family assistance are disadvantaged and vulnerable at this crucial stage of life. Perhaps the state needs to provide institutional mechanisms to discharge a collective responsibility for young adults.

Decision-making (*jibunde kimeru*) is also another aspect of independence. The process of independent decision-making can differ between individuals. While some may seek a literal independence in order to feel 'adult-like', others see decision-making based on extensive consultation with significant others as being independent. The latter approach characterised my actors. In particular, in relation to marriage, which they believed to be a union of two families rather than two individuals, they consulted extensively before they made decisions concerning potential marriage. The 'rational process of decision-making' that vocational high schools tried to instil when students studied the job market and decided on employment positions in the final year of schooling might have had some impact on them (Okano 1995a). Young adults' independent decisions and actions can be enhanced by a healthy relationship with their parents, providing them with the resilience to adapt to changing circumstances and the ability to establish stable intimate relationships with others (Kenny and Barton 2003: 374–75).

Decisions and their consequences: agency and structure

In the proceeding chapters we saw how young adults exercised agency in the context of external conditions that were beyond their control. They did this in interpreting changing circumstances, making decisions and acting on them, and in relation to employment, further education/training, families, relationships and leisure. How were their life trajectories shaped by individual decisions and actions on one hand, and by structural conditions on the other?

Studies have suggested that structural forces remain influential in shaping the transition to adulthood. Their focuses include social class (e.g. Bynner et al. 1997; Maguire et al. 2001; Johnson 2002; Johnson and Elder 2002; Ferri 1993; Morrow and Richards 1996; Plug et al. 2003), ethnic background (e.g. Wulff 1995) and gender (e.g. Griffin 1985; Gaskell 1992; Leadbeater and Way 1996; Valli 1986; Thomson et al. 2004; Fussell and Gauthier 2005). Any combination of the three in a specific national or regional context creates a set of experiences that differ from the privileged mainstream (e.g. Connolly et al. 1992; Shorter-Gorden and Washington 1996; Skeggs 1997; Mirza 1992; Walkerdine et al. 2001; Olsen 1996; McRobbie 1978: Mahaffy 2003). Class, ethnic background, gender and geographical region collectively shape the transition process directly by providing a concrete range of opportunities and conditions (social, cultural and material), and indirectly by influencing young people's long-term aspirations, immediate expectations and plans, as well as their daily decision-making.

In what ways were the Japanese women's trajectories shaped by individual decisions and external conditions? In order to assist this examination, I propose four analytical domains where the young women's significant experiences occurred. They are: (1) employment, (2) further education, (3) family (or domestic, which includes marriage and divorce) and (4) relationships and leisure. Although boundaries between these domains are sometimes blurred by the overlapping and interconnected nature of experiences in real-life situations, this does not diminish the value of these categories as analytical framework. For example, Yayoi's employment experience cannot be understood separately from what occurred in her relationships and family. She quit her first full-time permanent job in order to marry her boyfriend. Once married, however, she saw no choice but to work at the same company as her husband, which her often-unemployed husband begged her to do. She believed that her presence might help him to remain employed. Her entry into night bar hostessing was prompted by her desperate desire to raise cash to cover up her husband's misappropriation of the company's money before it was discovered by his colleagues. She managed to win the terms of her working conditions (whereby she received a cash advance on the basis of a verbal contract) by appealing to her employer's sympathy for her peculiar family situation. It was then her parents-in-law who, upon finding out about her job, forced her to resign, claiming that it brought disgrace on the family name. For Norimi and Miyuki the employment and relationship domains were interconnected. Norimi chose agency work because it enabled her to pursue her romantic relationship in Europe. She could work in between a few overseas trips a year without feeling guilty towards her bosses and colleagues.

Employers often created space for leisure by organising parties and trips, formally or otherwise, in which many of the women participated. Miyuki met her first boyfriend at one such event.

These domains thus help us to understand the different choices that women made (sometimes without much planning) and the strategies that they devised in order to pursue what they considered to be their priorities at the time. They also illuminate an individual's 'changes of plans' as her priorities altered over months or years. Some changes were deliberated and well planned, while others were carried out on the spur of the moment, saying, 'I just felt like it.'

Within each of these domains, there were three aspects that individuals assessed: (a) instrumental to the individual, (b) intrinsic to the individual and (c) human relationships. These aspects were pursued as benefits to the individual at one end of the continuum, or rejected or avoided as losses to the individual at the other end. One woman may value most in her job a generous income that allows her to be independent (an instrumental aspect of employment). Another woman may benefit more from the intellectual stimulation and sense of achievement that her work bestows (intrinsic aspects). Yet another woman, while finding no intrinsic satisfaction in the job itself, may simply be happy at work mainly because of the close relationships she has with colleagues. These aspects are not mutually exclusive. A woman may like going to work, despite disliking the job content, because she needs the income for her leisure activities and finds it less boring to be with her colleagues than staying at home. Some aspects, such as the unexciting nature of the job content, were beyond the actors' control through external constraints on high school-educated young women, yet they were able to devise strategies to emphasise positive aspects of their jobs in order to make their employment bearable. I will explain these three aspects in turn.

The first is the instrumental aspect. In the domain of employment, positive aspects include a regular income, the prestige associated with particular employers, and various company-sponsored benefits. Negative aspects include low pay and the demanding nature of the particular work (e.g. physical exhaustion experienced by cashiers Miyuki and Noshie). For example, Satoko, who worked for Matsushita Electronic Corporation, disliked the work content, the long commuting hours and her colleagues, but appreciated the income to support her family (in particular since her husband's income was irregular), the availability of childcare leave, the flexible working hours, and the fact that the company's prestige secured a loan to purchase her husband's truck. It was instrumental benefits in the form of a high income and flexible working conditions that drove Norimi towards agency work, which she could quit and pick up in between her regular visits to her boyfriend in Europe. In the domain of further education, a diploma could be instrumental in securing a higher level of pay. In the domain of the family, instrumental aspects included free accommodation, meals and laundry service. As we saw, both Yoshie and Orie wanted to leave their parents' homes to be recognised as being independent, but they could not bring themselves to do this for fear of losing the instrumental comfort that they enjoyed at home (I am sure that their families provided intrinsic comfort as well). In the domain of relationships and leisure, a boyfriend, such as Fumiko's, acted as a 'taxi driver', provided the pleasure of sexual activity, and supplied luxury items that Fumiko could not afford.

The second is the intrinsic aspect. The content of a job can be creative and fulfilling. Natsumi was passionate about the job content of a design position at a small architect's office. She had obtained the job after completing an interior design course at a private vocational college. Her commitment to her job was such that she worked for the employer (whom she disliked) for several months without proper payment when he was unable to win projects by tender. Fumiko enjoyed working on public works design and was transferred to a university graduate-track position. It was partly in order to maintain this intrinsically fulfilling work that she married her then boyfriend, who promised to support her career ambitions. (Later, an instrumental aspect of this work emerged as prominent for Fumiko, by providing a diversion and a source of confidence when she was suffering in her divorce.) Further training and education could also provide intrinsic satisfaction. For example, Miyuki enrolled herself in a correspondence course in design at a tertiary institution; and for the first time in her life enjoyed studying, which she had disliked while at school. Families often provided a sense of peace, belonging and intrinsic security to the women. Yayoi found a much-wanted sense of peace and stability by staying at her parents' home after her divorce was finally settled. Relationships and leisure activities provided the women with intrinsic pleasure. Yayoi's life in the first six months after high school centred on her *shakai-jin debut* (a complete change from a studious student to a playful woman) and leisure activities. For Norimi, her twice-yearly visits to her boyfriend in Europe determined her decisions regarding jobs, opting for contract jobs that allowed such flexibility.

The third aspect is human relationships. Human relationships (*ningen kaikei*, as the women commonly referred to it) featured prominently when the women made decisions in all domains. The reason they cited most frequently for leaving a job (as did Japanese workers in general, according to a nationwide survey quoted in Chapter 5) was unpleasant or unbearable relationships with their boss or colleagues. For the same reason, some women, like Saeko and Moko, continued in uninteresting jobs (clerical work) with poor working conditions (two hours commuting one way) because they found the human relationships at work comfortable. Human relationships were also widely discussed when a woman married and entered the spouse's network of relatives. We saw in Chapter 7 a number of cases where newly married women struggled to manage peaceful relationships with their in-laws. While Noshie initially appreciated a rent-free prefabricated house offered by her husband's parents (an instrumental gain), she later wanted to move from there because she felt increasingly upset by her relationship with them, seeing the arrangement as a kind of debt that allowed the parents to intervene in the couple's decision-making. Romantic human relationships could originate and develop in leisure activities.

A woman's assessment of the different aspects of a domain often depended on her assessment of them in the other domains. For example, a conflict-ridden marriage led Hatsumi to value what she saw as a supportive human relationship aspect in her part-time job. For Hatsumi, the money was not why she re-entered the workforce as a part-time clerical worker, leaving her one-year-old child in a childcare centre and being blamed for her decision by her in-laws. An individual thus carried and assessed a package (combination) of aspects in each of the four domains, and made decisions in the light of this package.

For example, Table 8.1 shows the package that Satoko carried in 1997. She continued to work for Matsushita Electronic Company although she disliked the work content. Her life as a package was acceptable to her, since her family gave her intrinsic and human relationship satisfactions. What Satoko considered positive and negative are indicated respectively by '+' and '-' in front of the various elements listed in the table.

The longitudinal nature of the study illuminates the ways in which the women carried and assessed the package, and how the package changed over the years. We saw earlier that the intrinsic aspect of employment was important for many at the initial entry into full-time permanent work, but that many were left disappointed with their workplace. Later, they gradually learned to see other aspects of employment (such as human relationships and instrumental aspects) as equally or more important. For some it was the realisation of the limited possibilities in job content for female high school graduates like themselves that prompted changes in how they approached

Table 8.1 Satoko, 1997 (26 years old)

	Instrumental aspects	Intrinsic aspects	Human relationships
Employment: eighth year at Matsushita Electronic	+ Good income + Company prestige + Company-sponsored benefits	– Dislikes work content	– Dislikes colleagues
Further education	N/A	N/A	N/A
Family: Married with two children, and living next door to in-laws	+ In-laws' assistance in child-rearing – Husband's unstable income	+ Feeling that children are safe + Feeling that she is wanted	+ Pleasant + Satisfying
Relationships and leisure	– Too busy for leisure	– Too busy	– Too busy

employment. For others, like Norimi, whose priority gradually became her frequent trips to Europe, instrumental aspects of employment (i.e. a high salary without insurance payments, short-term jobs) became the most important consideration. We will see these changes in Sekie (whom we met in Part I) in Tables 8.2, 8.3 and 8.4.

How can we effectively understand these changes over the years? First, they were partly in response to changing external circumstances and conditions. Included were changes in job content and working conditions, transfer to other branches, promotions, encounters with people whom the women respected, breaking up with a boyfriend, marriage proposals, events associated with family members and close friends (divorce, death, illness), needs of partners (e.g. unemployment, vocational training, frequent transfers) and of family members (e.g. recently divorced sister). The earthquake caused displacement and forced many people to live in transit accommodation for earthquake victims for several months. It also offered some a chance to sell land at a high price to the city council for development. Noshie obtained a private secretary's position at the company where she worked when the previous occupant of the position resigned after the earthquake destroyed her flat and she was urged by her parents to return to her home town. While the Hanshin–Awaji earthquake was a natural disaster, its impact was felt most strongly among the disadvantaged living in western inner-city suburbs, like the women in this study (this resonates with the case of Hurricane Katrina, which hit the USA ten years later in 2005).

Table 8.2 Sekie, January 1992 (20 years old)

	Instrumental aspects	*Intrinsic aspects*	*Human relationships*
Employment: Live-in nurse trainee at a clinic (almost two years with this employer)	– Low income – Long working hours and physically demanding work content + Satisfies the requirements for assistant nurse qualification	– Finds none	– Dislikes the head of the clinic and supervisors Colleagues are OK
Further education: Enrolled in assistant nurse training course at a nursing school	+ Required for her employment in the future	+ Fulfilling	+ Likes lecturers and classmates at the school
Family: Lives away from home	+ Resting place when off-duty	+ Psychological support	+ Peaceful. Gets on well with family members.
Relationships and leisure:A series of boyfriends	+ Diversion from demanding employment	+ Fun	+ Enjoyable

Table 8.3 Sekie, November 1997 (26 years old)

	Instrumental aspects	Intrinsic aspects	Human relationships
Employment: Permanent nursing position at a small medical clinic (fifth year with this employer)	+ High income + Convenient location + Convenient working hours + Physically easy job	+ Sense of responsibility being the only nurse. + Sense of fulfilment	+ Likes the head of the clinic and colleagues
Further education: Still contemplating upgrading her qualification by attending a course	N/A	N/A	N/A
Family:Lives with her family	+ Free accommodation, meals and laundry	+ Psychological support	+ Peaceful
Relationships and leisure:A series of boyfriends, friends, overseas trips, golfing, swimming	+ Opportunities to find a permanent partner	+ Fun + Offers learning experiences	+ Enjoyable

Second, changes also derived from the fact that, through their own internal awareness and through reflecting on their own experiences and their reading, the women gradually developed and modified ways of perceiving and assessing their immediate circumstances and social conditions. We see this when the same external event led different individuals to amend their priorities in different ways. That is to say, material circumstances alone were not sufficient to change how an individual carried the package of aspects. The individual needed to perceive and make sense of the material circumstances in a certain way in order for certain changes to result. When an opportunity arises, some may see it as a chance to pursue a long-term goal, but others may not.

It was not, however, that external circumstances unilaterally shaped decisions and actions by posing constraints. Individuals' past decisions and actions at one point in time brought consequences and circumstances to be faced later. Decisions and actions, often in combination with other factors, created or restricted a set of future opportunities, and influenced the women's material and social conditions and circumstances in the future. Past decisions and actions and the observation of their consequences also affected how the women perceived the world around them. This set of opportunities and circumstances (resulting partly from past decisions and actions) and a renewed scheme of understanding the world guided the women in their further decisions and actions. This process repeated itself over time; through it, the women experienced and negotiated young adulthood in their 20s.

Table 8.4 Sekie, December 2000 (29 years old)

	Instrumental aspects	Intrinsic aspects	Human relationships
Employment: Permanent nursing position at a small medical clinic (eighth year with this employer)	+ High income + Convenient location + Convenient working hours + Physically easy job	+ Sense of responsibility as the only nurse. + Sense of fulfilment + Sense of being trusted by the doctor	+ Likes the head of the clinic and colleagues
Further education: No longer contemplating upgrading her qualification	N/A	N/A	N/A
Family: Married in 1998, with no children	+ Double income + Purchased their first home – Increased housework load + Natal family helps with housework	+ Marriage gives a sense of being settled and calmness + Natal family gives emotional support	+ Peaceful with her own family – Distant with her in-laws
Relationships and leisure:Overseas trips, swimming, English conversation	+ Provided a sense of being settled.	+ Fun + Offers learning experiences	+ Enjoyable

For example, Sekie, by declining a marriage proposal from a visiting doctor, was able to have a longer career as an assistant nurse and marry another man later. Deciding to defer having children for several years after marriage enabled the couple to establish their financial base, enjoy leisure activities, and purchase a house with the assistance of the special loan for earthquake victims. Yayoi's refusal to consult with, and seek financial assistance from, her own parents when having problems with her marriage led inevitably to her ill health, a miscarriage and prolonged emotional suffering. It was Hatsumi's greatest regret that she signed a divorce document out of desperation and lost the custody of her one-year-old daughter. When this was coupled with the earthquake, which destroyed her mother's home, the prospect of gaining custody became remote. The decision by Tomoe, a third-generation Korean, to work for a *zainichi* South Korean bank introduced her to the world of the Japan-born Korean community in the city, with its particular restrictions and possibilities. Kanako, by giving birth to three girls when very young, suffered financial strain because she was out of the paid workforce.

We thus see the interface of structure and agency that was constantly present throughout these working-class women's trajectories via their mundane routines. They exercised agency in undertaking rational decision-making by considering a wide range of available options, assessing pros and cons in the light of their 'preferences' (what an individual wants as an outcome) and acting on them. This was done under a set of circumstances and conditions that were to varying degrees influenced by the structural conditions and their place in the social relations of hierarchy. Their 'preferences' were also shaped by their past experiences, which tended to reflect their positions in the society and be specific to class, gender, ethnic background and region.[1]

I would suggest that at the core of individual preferences for these women is being able to 'feel comfortable'. In contemporary Japan, incentives to move up the social ladder are no longer strong or overt, as a result of widespread affluence and increasingly diversified lifestyle choices. In this context, 'feeling comfortable' often acted as a more significant consideration for the young women in making decisions, both long-term and short-term, than did instrumental gains (e.g. better pay or marrying up). This is not new. Everyone has a comfort zone, and feeling comfortable is important. I have shown cases of high-school students choosing a job against their teachers' advice because they wanted to work in the place where they would automatically feel comfortable (Okano 1993). What is different in comparison with schooldays was that the young adults no longer had the input of adults with assumed authority who guided them with middle-class values. In this sense, I suspect that young working-class adults' decisions became more specific to class, gender and ethnic background as they grew older. Being in an educational institution may indeed assist young people form views less specific to their own class, gender and ethnic background, since the institution often contains adults in authority who promote generally dominant middle-class views. Young people can also be exposed to views different from their own at other heterogeneous places. For instance, in the period immediately after her divorce Yayoi was encouraged by her interaction with university students her own age at a café where she waitressed.

Working women in their 20s

The existing literature on women aged in their 20s has centred on their working experiences, often based on a specific workplace. These studies have examined two main groups: (1) university graduate white-collar female clerical workers of middle-class family background, and (2) blue-collar female workers of working-class background without tertiary education. My informants, high school graduates from working-class backgrounds, differ from both groups in that they all worked in white-collar office jobs or in sales, except for Kanako (a pearl factory worker). These individuals therefore represent a particular group of young women aged 18 to 29, and my study of this group complements the existing understanding of women in this age bracket.

High school-educated young women of working-class background have appeared as blue-collar factory workers in various studies that are based on workplaces: for example, at a large machinery company (Lo 1990), a large textile factory (Roberts 1994), a small machinery factory (Roberson 1998) and a small family-run confectionery factory (Kondo, 1990). These studies, although focusing more on older female workers (since nationally the majority of female blue-collar workers are married and work part-time), do refer to a minority of younger full-time workers. Young female blue-collar workers (and also retail workers in Matsunaga 2000) in large companies come from lower-income families in the country and live in the company's paternalistic dormitories, which they wish to escape through marriage (Lo 1990). They were also aware, seeing their co-workers, that they could continue full-time regular work into middle age if they wished, or obtain part-time positions after a child-rearing break. My actors lived in a metropolitan area and lived comfortably with their parents until they married; and they did not feel compelled to marry. Their income level was lower than for university graduates, some contributing to household budgets and/or saving substantial sums in preparation for their weddings. Unlike rural young women who lived in dormitories, my actors seemed to hold a strong emotional (and perhaps pragmatic) attachment to their city. As we saw, they were unwilling to leave their city for marriage.

Studies suggest that female factory workers perceived a class difference in relation to 'Office Ladies' (OLs). For example, Lo's young factory workers did not wish to work for the same company as OLs, whom they perceived as being more strictly required to conform to the company's human relationship norms and feminine roles (e.g. serving tea to male workers) (Lo 1990: 101). Blue-collar workers in Kondo's small confectionery factory expressed class distinction in terms of 'people who work with their hands, not with "paper and pencil"' (Lo 1990: 284). My actors also distinguished themselves from university-educated female co-workers; but not in terms of such clearly observed differences in work content as seen by Kondo's factory workers. Being white-collar office workers themselves, like the university graduates, my actors saw class distinction in terms of more intangible aspects such as lifestyles, past experiences, family backgrounds, speech patterns and promotion prospects.

My actors, while working in offices and therefore called 'OLs', differed from the 'Office Ladies' in Lo's machinery company (Lo 1990) who were all tertiary-educated and of middle-class background. Lo's OLs lived with their parents, and eventually married and became full-time housewives. Many of the 'Office Ladies' in Ogasawara's bank were also university educated and of middle-class background; and the author noted 'tensions' among OLs because of differences in educational background (Ogasawara 1996: 50–53). What stood out among Ogasawara's university-educated OLs was their insightful understanding of the power dynamics of human relationships in the office. They understood that male co-workers and bosses in pursuit of promotion needed co-operation from OLs in order to demonstrate their management skills, and employed manipulative strategies to influence and control male workers' actions in their favour (Ogasawara 1998: 166). Such strategies included ignoring or declining to do work for male co-workers and bosses who were not nice to them. They could adopt such strategies precisely because they were in peripheral positions excluded from promotion prospects, and because employment did not have a central place for their life course, unlike the men (who are socially expected to be family providers). My actors were either unaware of their potential power over male co-workers or chose not to exercise it. Ogasawara's OLs were more self-confident and aware of their entitlements in the workplace than my actors, who were also OLs.

The boundaries of career promotion opportunities seem negotiable, in particular at smaller-sized companies. We saw this in Fumiko's transfer from high school graduate clerical track to 'career track' for university graduates in her seventh year at a subsidiary engineering company of a major corporation. Yayoi was promoted from a clerical position to a technical design position when her employer (an arcade manufacturing company) recognised her designing and technical drawing skills, and she later worked with university graduate colleagues on an equal capacity.

What we learn here is that high school-educated young women of working-class backgrounds experience employment and workplaces quite differently from their tertiary-educated middle-class counterparts. They did not articulate the kind of frustration with gender-based discrimination that we saw in Rosenberger's study (Rosenberger 2001: 182–213) of tertiary-educated young single women in the 1990s. I suspect that my actors accepted their peripheral positions as non-tertiary-educated, and that absence of non-tertiary-educated male co-workers in the office made it difficult to assess their situation in relation to male counterparts. But at the same time, my actors shared with Rosenberger's young single women an attitude to work whereby they valued its instrumental aspect (e.g. money) or human relation aspects in order to sustain their interest in work, which did not hold a central place in their lives. Young women's experiences of work vary, depending on whether they work in a factory or in an office. Even among those working in offices, the size of companies seemed to have an influence on their experiences. There is also diversity in the experiences of OLs, despite being popularly considered a homogenous group, since OLs vary in their goals and education levels. My actors illuminate the gradations of young women's experiences of work in their 20s.

Working-class trajectories to adulthood: seeking 'comfort'

The young women's trajectories to adulthood have been guided by their working-class background, and by ethnic minority background for *zainichi* Koreans. There is divergence within their experiences, contingent not only on differences in external conditions, but also on their deliberate strategies, their past decisions and their consequences. I have discussed the class-specific nature of the women's trajectories throughout the book. Here I shall attempt to summarise important aspects that differentiated their trajectories from those of middle-class counterparts, and significant divergence between the working-class young women.

Working-class parental resources

The volume and nature of parental resources that working-class young people can rely on guide many aspects of their trajectories to adulthood. Parental resources are not limited to economic resources in the form of money and assets, but also include social resources in the form of personal and social networks, and cultural resources in the form of information and knowledge about how the society operates and strategies that they devise based on their past experiences.

Young people's awareness that they cannot rely on their family economic resources variously guided their decisions about themselves in both their public (employment) and private lives (e.g. marriage, children). For a start, many of these girls chose vocationally oriented senior high schools since they vaguely understood that they would enter the workforce without going on to tertiary education and recognised the merit of such schools in providing employment contacts. Their enrolment in vocational high schools subsequently restricted the chance to proceed to tertiary institutions.

Immediately after graduation from high school, they joined the bottom ranks of workplaces, which for many was the first experience of the 'wider adult world' where they encountered 'unfamiliar' kinds of people. Middle-class girls, on the other hand, encounter new experiences and unfamiliar kinds of people from a wider geographical area and varied family back-grounds at junior colleges and universities. In many ways tertiary institutions provide sites for personal exploration while young people are still relatively carefree without normative responsibilities. By the time university and junior college graduates enter the workforce, they would have enjoyed a longer period of personal exploration and are more likely to have experienced the wider adult world though part-time employment and by socialising with their new friends. Such experiences help preparing them for managing the unfamiliar, as well as foster more effective interpersonal skills.

Working-class girls could not resort to the kind of family personal net-works that would enable them to enter employment at so-called 'desirable companies'. Once in full-time employment, they were expected to save a substantial part of their income for 'future use' (including for marriage, since their families would be unable to pay all the costs involved), while others contributed a quarter of their income to the household budget. All of the young women who married paid for their weddings from their own savings.

The experiences of young working-class women illuminate the need to discuss the 'parasite single' phenomenon in relation to social classes. As discussed in earlier chapters, the term refers to unmarried full-time employed young adults in their 20s and 30s living at home with their parents (Yamada

1999: 41). In many ways it is a choice available mainly to middle-class young people. 'Parasite single' is a negative description of young people who enjoy expensive leisure activities (e.g. overseas trips) supported by good disposable incomes (as a result of living at their parents' home) and having their mothers take care of washing and cooking. It assumes a full-time housewife mother who looks after her full-time worker children, but the mothers of my informants themselves worked full-time or a substantial number of hours in order to supplement limited household incomes. The case of Sayaka was akin to being a 'parasite single'. She was a university graduate in a career-track position at a small trading company, always exhausted from long working hours and overwhelmed by responsibilities. Her mother, working part-time while caring for her own aging father-in-law, still did housework for her daughter, and was concerned with Sayaka's deteriorating health (due to overwork), advising her to quit working before marriage.

While some of my informants mentioned the term 'parasite single' (the phenomenon was widely discussed in the media), they did not identify themselves as such. When they talked about it, it was often in referring to male 'parasite singles' who they were determined to avoid marrying because, they claimed, these young men would be too spoiled by their mothers. So although the term 'parasite single' is gender-neutral, it seems to gain more negative edge when applied to young men (Dale 2005). A similar trend was observable in relation to the term *frîtâ* (those who go through a number of casual jobs rather than settling into a permanent full-time position). While they did not think highly of young male *frîtâ*, they were sympathetic to young women choosing this path. Indeed, many of my actors underwent periods of being *frîtâ* at some point during the 12 years after graduating from high school, often when 'resting' from, and considering other, full-time jobs. Others like Norimi and Tomoe, as we saw earlier, chose casual or temporary jobs, to suit their current lifestyles. Judging from the media and casual conversations, such gender-specific perception of both 'parasite singles' and *frîtâ* (i.e. acceptable for women but not for men) seemed popularly assumed. I suspect that this gender-specific perception of these two phenomena is indicative of the dominant expectations of gender-specific roles. The dominant male life trajectory is the corporate warrior model which involves dominance of work over private time (family and relationships), long working hours, acceptance of workplace rules (e.g. forgoing the full annual leave entitlement) and being a reliable family provider. Both 'parasite single' and *frîtâ* existences overtly reject this model, or preparation for it. In contrast, the dominant view of the female life trajectory does not assume such a central place for full-time work and being a family provider. This allows women to have more opportunities to pursue self-fulfilment through non-work activities such as relationships, leisure pursuits and voluntary charity work (Iwao 1993). There are always some options as a back-up.

Lack of family financial resources, on the other hand, has driven some of the young women to build assets independent of their families. Both Fumiko and Yayoi bought flats by obtaining housing loans at the relatively early age of 26, when divorce forced them to accept the possibility that they may never marry again (and therefore be unable to count on a provider). They had never imagined that they would purchase flats (in particular Fumiko, whose parents lived in public housing). The impetus came from the municipal government's offer of special housing loans for earthquake sufferers.

Consequences of not going on to tertiary education

Entry into the workforce without tertiary education entailed significant consequences, both short-term and long-term. Lack of the degree itself determined the initial entry level of employment and income, and subsequent opportunities for a wider range of promotion. The absence of professional knowledge and skills that some tertiary courses offer restricted the kind of employment obtainable. But this is not the whole story.

The women's employment was limited to peripheral positions of the workforce because of their lack of tertiary qualifications. They were, for example, excluded from career-track positions for university graduates that lead in due course to managerial positions. All women were aware of this workforce structure before entering it, but were further reminded of it in initial training at their workplaces where the new recruits received different training depending on their academic qualifications, as we saw in Chapters 4 and 5. However, Fumiko accomplished a transfer from a high school graduate clerical position to a university graduate career-track position through internal assessment, which had replaced external examinations.

Universities and junior colleges offer young people the chance to expand their world beyond their neighbourhood and high school community. They encounter the unknown and unfamiliar circumstances, try out new activities, make friends with new kinds of people, and thus are able to develop personally, in a carefree and tolerant environment, without pressure to conform to particular social roles. In many ways, the university experiences, including transgressions, are seen as a trial-and-error learning process and therefore 'good experience' in preparation for adult responsibilities. Many young middle-class women enjoy similar freedoms and exploration at private junior colleges. We see some of these 18 to 19-year-old junior college female students learning to become 'ladies' in McVeigh's study (McVeigh 1997). At four-year universities, some young women (aged 18 to 22) pursue their study, romantic relationships, sports clubs or political activism, while others focus on a series of casual jobs. The women in my study sample did not undergo this process of self-exploration. Instead, they went from a vocational high school (where students tend to come from similar family backgrounds and pursue similar post-school destinations) straight into permanent full-time jobs. Many of my informants perceived a 'difference' between female university-graduate colleagues and themselves, and confessed feeling uncomfortable about having to maintain pleasant daily interactions with them. Their stories revealed that the lack of experience with a wide range of leisure activities (e.g. skiing, various sports, overseas experience) and unfamiliar kinds of people contributed to forming stereotypical ideas about these graduates: for example, that they were all proper ladies from wealthy families. It also contributed to their uneasiness with the unfamiliar that I think resulted from a lack of the kind of human relationship skills that are useful when encountering strangers. Young working-class women, once in full-time employment, were required to accept the rules of the workforce (e.g. working long hours, forgoing annual leave) and did not have as much time and space to explore themselves and to develop a wide range of interests and leisure activities as did the tertiary students. Recall Noshie's comment, 'I think they are nice people but I don't know what to talk about with them.' At the same time, the young women found it difficult to make new friends with colleagues since they were expected to maintain the proper collegial relationships in the workplace.

An individual develops a 'comfort zone' based on his or her past experiences (e.g. in the family, at school, in the neighbourhood community, in local sports clubs). When my group are compared with the 'international young Japanese women', in a study by Kelsky (2001), the contrast is illuminating. Kelsky's highly educated career women, dissatisfied with what they perceived as the patriarchal institutions of work and the socially expected female life course, sought self-fulfilment by turning to the West in careers and romantic relationships. Kelsky's women are adventurous and self-confident, and equipped with the necessary skills (such as the English language) to seek unknown challenges in the West in order to escape from familiar barriers in Japan.

Getting married: the working-class way

The young women's decisions regarding marriage were discussed in Chapters 6 and 7. Some of my actors married relatively young, in comparison with their university-educated middle-class counterparts and the national average of 27.8 (Okano 2004: Figure 6.1). For example, Kanako, Yayoi and Oriko were all 19 to 20 years old, when their middle-class counterparts were still at university. Of the 21 young women that I studied, five married before they turned 25. Three of these marriages resulted in divorce. In January 2001, the year they turned 29 or 30 years old, nine were married, and the remaining 12 women were single (with three divorced).

Almost all the women considered an arranged marriage an option for a middle-class woman. It was thought suitable for those who have family assets and social status at stake or those who have something to 'show off', like academic qualifications (e.g. at least junior college graduation, some women mentioned) and 'feminine' skills like playing the piano. Two women, Moko and Yoshie, were approached by relatives for an arranged meeting with the prospect of marriage in their late 20s. Both cases were initiated by relatives in the regional prefecture from which one of their parents originated.

In both cases the male candidates were university graduates of appropriate age, with secure employment and reasonable incomes, but living in a regional area far from Kobe-city. Both women found the candidates appealing and would have considered them seriously if they had lived locally precluding the need for them to quit their current permanent jobs and leave Kobe-city.

Young ethnic Korean women did not see an arranged marriage as solely an option for middle-class couples, but as a valuable route to marrying an ethnic Korean, since it was difficult to meet young Korean men without personal involvement in ethnic Korean activities. None of the three young Korean women in my study strongly desired an ethnic Korean husband, and this was the wish of their parents, who suggested participating in arranged meetings with the prospect of marriage. Noshie and Orie attended such meetings in order to diffuse parental pressure. All three chose and married Japanese men in the end. If they had been through the North Korean school system (e.g. Ryang 1997) or had been actively involved in ethnic youth organisations like Tomoe's elder brother, they might have been more likely to have married ethnic Koreans.

Young women found marriage partners themselves at parties, through mutual friends, or by developing friendships from primary or middle school into romantic relationships. Among the various considerations surrounding potential marriage partners the most important for the women was that they should feel comfortable (*igokochi*) with the man, and hopefully with his family members.

The women did not show any desire for 'marrying up'. When at high school, some indicated prior desires (*akogare*) for becoming middle-class full-time housewives; but subsequently assessed the pros and cons of such an option and decided that it was not worthwhile. We saw Sekie, a 19-year-old trainee nurse, declining a marriage proposal from a visiting doctor since she felt uncomfortable marrying someone with superior family background and sorry for her mother, who would not be able to cope with relationships with such a family. Contrast these young women with Kelsky's 'international career women' who desired marriage with Western men in order to escape from what they saw as oppressive Japanese social institutions and norms. My group sought neither opportunities for upward social mobility nor excitement or passion, but 'comfort' (*igokochi*) in marriage partners: someone who related to their background and upbringing and who could effectively manage relationships with their own family. The ways in which these women considered potential marriage partners in their late 20s were grounded in their observation of relatives' experiences and were extremely pragmatic, as shown in earlier chapters. They were fully aware of their own positions in a hierarchical society, and their possession or lack of particular attributes, and conducted rational calculations of the consequences of marriage for themselves and their families. My actors' choice of marriage partners is consistent with the national trend whereby intra-class marriage prevails.

This does not mean everyone married non-tertiary-educated working-class young men. Sayaka married a trainee tax accountant, the son of a medical professor whom she met at university; Shizu married her colleague, the son of local civil servants in a provincial city; and Noshie married a construction site supervisor, a friend from her *shitamachi* middle school. It was Sayaka who most felt a difference in class, living close to her in-laws and receiving financial assistance from them in the form of a rent-free upmarket condominium in a middle-class suburb. Noshie's husband, though a university graduate, was from a working-class family, which made it relatively easy for Noshie to adjust. Shizu visited her in-laws (who lived in a distant prefecture) only twice a year.

Financial constraints and working-class lifestyles in marriage

Young working-class women's marriages often started with financial constraints within the marriage itself. Those who married young to working-class men of a similar age experienced most hardship, when they set up a new household and started paying rent. If a child came along and the wife stopped working, the situation became extremely difficult. Women who married in their late 20s with substantial savings were able to avoid such hardships. Of course, many middle-class women also subjectively experience a sense of financial deprivation soon after marriage, if they had previously been living with their parents and using their income for leisure activities. But the reality of financial constraints is much more serious for young working-class women.

Having said that, not all of them experienced hardship. The financial situations in the initial stages of marriage are contingent on a number of factors. The number of years of pre-marriage employment for both women and men, and their money-saving strategies, make a difference. The younger one marries, the less personal savings one possesses to counter any potential hardship. Kanako's case illuminates this difficulty. She married her 19-year-old boyfriend after both had been in full-time employment only for several months and with no savings. She left her job when they moved into his parents' house, located far from her workplace, since his income alone could not afford rent. He was job-hopping and she soon had a child; and they continued to live with his parents.

This situation could be avoided if a woman married a much older man receiving a much higher salary (in accordance with his length of service) and with substantial savings, or if a woman deferred marriage until she was established and had made long-term plans to defer having children. Recall 19-year-old Oriko's marriage to a 40-year-old man. They moved into a flat in an inexpensive housing complex, arranged by her husband's employer, soon started a family, and then purchased a house several years later. It is worth noting that Oriko's husband is a factory worker at a large well-known company that provides such facilities as company housing and housing loans. All the women who married men whose employers offered company housing for newly married couples (normally only for five to ten years) made use of it. Sekie, an assistant nurse, married in her late 20s with substantial savings and planned not to have children until her mid-30s. She supported her husband while he was training to be an electrician, and later bought a house.

Another important factor is the degree to which parents of newly married couples can provide the couple financial assistance; but my working-class actors were not able to count on it. They were also reluctant to receive such assistance from their parents or in-laws. Sayaka, who married a man of middle-class background, was offered a rent-free upmarket condominium by his parents when they realised that their 26-year-old son's income as a trainee tax accountant could not afford rent even if Sayaka worked. Sayaka claimed that without such help they could not achieve the kind of lifestyle that he wanted. Shizu's in-laws, middle-class civil servants, were also willing to offer financial assistance when she quit working. She was initially reluctant to accept their help, but was later persuaded by her husband for the sake of their children. The fact that these women could not, or did not want to, accept the kind of financial assistance that middle-class parents readily made available thus at least partially distinguished working-class marriages.

Ethnic Koreans

For Japan-born ethnic Koreans, their minority background guided decision-making, within the constraints of working-class trajectories. It was the major consideration when deliberating on post-school employment destinations, because of the perceived (and real) barriers that existed for them.

Entry into the wider world beyond their neighbourhood community after leaving school provided them with opportunities to interact with new people (who, unlike their classmates and local acquaintances, were ignorant about the history of *zainichi* Koreans), which enabled them to continue learning how the mainstream society perceived ethnic Koreans. At their workplaces, the young ethnic Koreans did not experience the deliberate bullying and discrimination that they had feared; and all decided neither to actively conceal nor to publicly announce their ethnic identity. Their colleagues tried to avoid referring to their ethnic background in daily conversation, assuming that the women would prefer this. The women in turn considered their colleagues well-intentioned but this avoidance hindered the development of close relationships with workmates.

Young ethnic Korean women also continued to revise how they perceived themselves in relation to what they saw as an increasingly diverse *zainichi* community, ranging across those educated and actively involved in the Japan-based North Korean community (Chongryun) and those who aligned with the South Korean counterpart (Mindan) to those who are members of neither. None of the women in my study sample were actively involved in ethnic community activities, but it did not mean that their *zainichi* identity was any weaker than those who were involved. The young women developed their own ways to define themselves as *zainichi* Korean. They also recognised that what they understand to be 'the Korean traditional customs and cultures' were diverse and changing, and that they could freely decide whether and how they might participate in those customs and cultures.

This sense of freedom became particularly important when all three Korean women married Japanese men. While their parents typically wished their daughters would marry *zainichi* Korean men, my actors chose marriage partners who were Japanese (with the eventual blessing of their families). They were aware of the challenges which marriage to Japanese men might bring, but appreciated the comfort that they found in their relationships with their chosen partners. These women are now in a position to create their own sense of ethnic identity, as mothers of 'Japanese national' children of Korean descent.

Working-class women's transitions to adulthood

There is much that Japanese young adults share with those in Western industrialised societies when making transitions to adulthood, both in their experience and in how they view the process of reaching adulthood. At the same time, we also saw some distinctive features of young Japanese. I suggest that these features result at least partially from institutional differences under which young people make choices. The young women in this study, obtaining their first permanent full-time job through an institutional link with their school, found that the job itself and the income it brought were not necessarily primary in the transition to adulthood.

The young women understood adulthood by comparing it with their past. We saw changes in the extent to which, and at what point in their history, they compared their present experiences and thoughts. The women's biographical narratives on adulthood over the 12 years revealed three frequently occurring themes: a sense of concrete and achievable purpose (*mokuhyô*), balanced acceptance of responsibility (*sekinin*) and a mature sense of independence (*jiritsu*). It was understood that a mature sense of independence would come once they felt comfortable with having concrete goals and finding a balanced way of discharging various responsibilities.

The women's trajectories to adulthood were shaped by the interaction of individual decisions and actions with external conditions and circumstances (including institutions). Seeing their trajectories in terms of how the young women assessed three particular aspects (instrumental, intrinsic and human relationships) in each of the four domains of experience (employment, further education, family, and relationships and leisure), we were able to understand why the women made certain decisions and the consequences of the decisions, and to clearly identify changes in the priority accorded the aspects in the four domains over the years. In the process of decision-making, an individual's preference remained important – indeed, often more significant than instrumental gains – and 'feeling comfortable' formed the core of that preference.

The young women's trajectories to adulthood have been guided by their working-class background, and in the case of *zainichi* Koreans by their ethnic minority background. At the same time, divergence existed within their experiences, contingent on differences in external conditions, their deliberate strategies, and past decisions and the consequences of them. I have summarised aspects of the young women's paths to adulthood that are specific to working-class and ethnic minority background, in terms of the nature and volume of parental resources, work experiences, consequences of not undertaking tertiary education, choice of a marriage partner, and financial constraints and lifestyles in marriage. The young women pursued what they considered 'comfort' (*igokochi no yosa*) rather than aspiring for upward social mobility or radical 'adventures' through employment or marriage in charting transitions to adulthood. What constituted comfort was highly personal, having developed through each individual's past experiences (including family, school, neighbourhood community, friends, leisure activities and workplaces) and reflected in their class and ethnic background.

Conclusions

The book started with four major questions. How do young people make transitions to adulthood in Japan? How do they conceive of adulthood? How are their trajectories to adulthood shaped by individual decisions and actions on one hand, and by structural conditions on the other? How are their trajectories to, and understanding of, adulthood guided by urban working-class status, and for some, ethnic minority status? We followed the lives of a group of young women from April 1989 to January 2001 as they matured from the age of 18 to almost 30 years old, starting from a one-year ethnographic study at their high schools, which developed into a 12-year biographical study. Following detailed chronological portraits of eight individual women in Part I, I discussed four separate themes, building on Part I and introducing the experiences of other women, while locating these experiences in the context of national and global tends in the 1990s.

In this process, readers have also come to know me. A longitudinal qualitative study like this has its own methodological issues involving the researcher, and I will reflect on them here. The shared experience of the year's ethnographic fieldwork allowed us to have a degree of shared assumptions and a shared frame of reference in subsequent interviews. During the interviews the women often referred to small events that we both experienced at their high schools. Interview questions and answers assumed prior knowledge of each other and of other actors (e.g. other students, teachers, friends' boyfriends), reflected shared experiences of their final year of high schooling and subsequent interviews in intervening years. I used to have lunch with these girls at the high school canteens, met their mothers at school functions, knew how each of them was regarded by other students, and heard how teachers assessed their achievement and potential. They told me how they felt about school and themselves, their aspirations, jobs, family, success and disappointments at different points of time. This long-term joint frame of reference has contributed, I think, to forming a stronger rapport and understanding which promoted a shared sensitivity between us. Second, my memories of the ethnography and previous interviews differed from theirs. This of course occurs in any ethnographic interviewing because actors and researchers occupy different positions, but to a greater extent in a longitudinal study since the researcher constantly revives and reconstructs her memories through extensive reading, analysing, reflecting and writing up the previous fieldnotes and interview scripts.

Third, the year-long ethnography and repeated interviews in the subsequent 12 years enabled me, and each woman, to chart their life stories as they experienced the transition to adulthood. In so doing the women were able to create their own biographies, interpreting their current lives and reflecting on their respective past thoughts and experiences. We learn: (1) how they reinterpret elements of their pasts in the act of recalling it (e.g. 'I thought I loved him but in fact I now think I just wanted to have a boyfriend'), (2) their past views of themselves (e.g. 'I thought I hated and wasn't good at studying at school'), (3) their past projections of the future (e.g. 'I thought we would make a good marriage because he supported my career ambitions, but ... '); and (4) the future that they foresee now (e.g. 'I'll get a job at a teaching hospital so that I can leave my child at the on-site childcare centre'). This is because in the research process the women were asked to reflect on their past, their interpretations at the time and of the future, and present interpretations of the past and projected future. We were thus provided with a rich picture of the reflexive process of growing up at different points in these women's lives.

I was struck by the range and intensity of agency that the women exercised as they explored and experimented their paths to adulthood. While acutely aware of (and often deploring) the limitations and constraints facing them, the women initiated significant changes and commitments in their lives, including moving from one employer to another, leaving a job to undertake further education at significant expense, initiating separation and divorce, and purchasing a house.

They also exercised agency in creating a personal sense of happiness and hardships. An individual devises his or her own notion of what constitutes happiness, based on past experiences and circumstances. This is common sense, but I occasionally forgot it. Recall Kanako's swift response to counter my casual comment: 'You do have such a demanding life' (considering her husband's earlier unemployment and illness, his affairs, three small children to support on a low income, and a strained relationship with her in-laws), by replying, 'Not really, I think I somehow live to please myself' (*so demo nai. Kekkô dôrakuni ikinuiteru kotobakari*). It reminded me that I might have come to see some of them as victims of external circumstances, and that the women themselves often created their own biographies that were much more accurate than mine, and in which they felt increasingly confident.

Drawing on a one-year ethnography and subsequent interviews, I have suggested that working-class Japanese women in their 20s understood their transitions to adulthood in terms of intangible aspects or what seemed almost like 'feelings', rather than in terms of their self-assessment against the normative notion of adulthood. While similar observation pertain to their middle-class counterparts in the West (e.g. Arnett 2004; Cote 2000), the

women's understandings are rooted in sets of institutions and social expectations specific to Japan. The intangible and individualistic feelings of becoming an adult seemed to comprise three distinctive parts. First, they needed to
experience a sense of finding and maintaining a concrete and achievable
purpose (*mokuhyô*). It was through concrete, personally significant experiences that gave the young women a sense of achievable goals, as well as the
motivation required to reach them (*yaruki*), that many recognised their own
growth (*seichô*) towards adulthood. Second, they felt a sense of 'becoming
an adult' when they learned a balanced sense of responsibility (*sekinin*),
embracing groups they were members of, significant others (e.g. workplace
colleagues, friends, relatives and family members) and personal needs. They
were more likely to feel this balanced sense of responsibility after finding a
concrete and achievable personal purpose and motivation. Without a sense
of personal direction, as was often the case with many young women in their
first year out of school, a balanced sense of responsibility was hard to
achieve. Often the women placed their responsibility for their employers and
colleagues over that for their own needs, and experienced frustration. Many
wanted to leave their first jobs since they could not find an appropriate balance. Third, the women wanted to feel a sense of independence, which they
considered they could aim for after finding a concrete purpose (*mokuhyô*)
and achieving a balanced sense of responsibility. Independence can be both
financial (although there was disagreement on its extent among the women)
and in terms of decision-making; and was understood to be a long-term goal
that individuals would gradually work towards over the years and eventually
achieve at their own pace. Their families extended their 'protection' over the
women, considering that high school graduates are not ready for economic
independence, even with a full-time permanent job, and that the young
needed further support or guidance under the family umbrella. A few women
initially disliked this as paternalistic; but many appreciated their mothers'
practical support and caring when their jobs became stressful.

Feeling a sense of adulthood in their 20s was thus a gradual and individualised process that centred on the three aspects mentioned above. Over the 12
years the women's understanding of adulthood involved a continuous process
of reinterpreting immediate circumstances, deciding what was important to
them in the light of their perceived options, and acting accordingly. At a first
glance, this process looked vague and unplanned. A closer examination suggests
that the women seemed to distinguish four specific domains of importance:
(1) employment, (2) further education, (3) family (including in-laws) and (4)
relationships and leisure. Relative importance attached to the respective
domains differed among individuals, and how an individual saw relative importance also differed at different points in time. Some were able to assess the relative importance of each domain by considering both long-term and short-term
priorities, while others did not distinguish such differences clearly.

When considering these four domains in decision-making, the women
seemed to have their assessment on three broad aspects: (a) instrumental to

the individual, (b) intrinsic to the individual, and (c) human relationships. Individual woman pursued each of these aspects as personal benefits at one end of the continuum, or rejected or avoided the aspect as a loss at the other end. We can see this when one of the women values most in her job a generous income that allows her to be independent (an instrumental aspect of employment), while another woman benefits more from the intellectual stimulation and sense of achievement that her work bestows (intrinsic aspects). Yet another woman, while finding no intrinsic satisfaction in the job itself, may simply be happy at work mainly because of the close relationships she has with colleagues (human relationship aspect). Some aspects, such as the unexciting nature of the job content, were beyond the actors' control because of external constraints on high school-educated young women; yet they were able to devise strategies to emphasise positive aspects of their work in order to make their employment bearable. One woman's assessment of different aspects in one domain often depended on how she perceived the remaining domains. We saw this, for example, when a difficult marriage led Hatsumi to value a supportive human relationship that became part of her employment and leisure domains.

Following the women over the 12 years, we saw that the relative importance attached to respective domains (i.e. employment, further education, family, and relationships and leisure) by an individual altered over time. These changes were partly in response to changing external circumstances and conditions, such as job opportunities, workplace reorganisation and transfers, and the earthquake. Some of the changes in circumstances and material conditions, however, resulted from the women's own past decisions and actions. The changes in priority domains were also partly because the women gradually developed different ways to perceive and assess immediate circumstances, social conditions, and the workings and constraints of the society.

Here we see an interface of structure and agency throughout these women's trajectories via their mundane routines. They exercised agency in making decisions and acting on them under a set of circumstances and conditions that were beyond their control. This was done in the light of their 'preferences'; but their 'preferences' were also shaped by their past experiences, which tended to reflect their positions in the society and be specific to class, gender and ethnic background. Their decisions and actions in turn had consequence in guiding their subsequent trajectories to adulthood by creating or restricting future opportunities and by influencing their material and social conditions in following years. I have suggested that the core of individual preferences for these women is a sense of 'comfort' (*igokochi no yosa*).

Working-class background and, in the case of *zainichi* Koreans, their ethnic minority background have guided young women's decisions and actions, leading to trajectories that are distinctive from those of young middle-class women. For example, a lack of certain parental resources restricted their opportunities for tertiary education (e.g. by not possessing sufficient financial resources, and by being uninformed about the workings of the education system). Lack of tertiary education restricted the range of possible employment and promotion prospects, and deprived them of opportunities for personal exploration as university students without pressure to conform to particular social roles. The young women chose marriage partners with whom they (and their families) felt 'comfortable', and showed little desire to marry someone in pursuit of opportunities for upward social mobility, romantic adventures or alternative lifestyles. Young married couples (some with children) often faced financial constraints in the early stages of marriage, because of limited income levels and because they could not count on parental financial support, and devised ways to manage their situations.

It is through this process that young adults learn to feel more confident in their decisions and actions, to become more capable of finding future directions, and to care for the needs of others in their immediate surroundings. The young women in my study have become more reflexive about themselves; but did not display the kind of insightful self-reflection offered by middle-aged people in Plath's study (Plath 1980). Plath's subjects perhaps had the benefit of longer-term hindsight, more time to themselves and a 'settled' feeling that completion of child-rearing and retirement from full-time work might have brought. My actors were in the midst of finding themselves and making transitions to adulthood. Their experiences of growing up after leaving school exhibited a range of continuities from their schooldays – they were encouraged to strive for similar personal qualities (e.g. consideration of other people, conformity to group norms, discovery and pursuit of personal goals, long-term perspective). But these qualities were more concrete and contexualised in the diverse settings in which they found themselves, and they no longer received the kind of systematic guidance that teachers had provided in their secondary school years (LeTendre 2000; Rohlen 1983; Okano 1993).

This book is a product of my interaction with these young women over the 12 years. I was privileged to share their stories of growing up and negotiating adulthood through their 20s, and feel that I have made a belated transition to adulthood with them. I still continue our relationship and my research. While this book covers the lives of the women between 1989 and 2001, at the time of completing this manuscript in 2006 the women are now in their mid-30s; many of them are preoccupied with family responsibilities, while others try to juggle family with career development. Still others are unmarried (intentionally or otherwise) and exploring futures in which they will be independent and self-supporting. Someday in the future, I hope I will share with the reader their stories of their maturation in mid-adulthood.

Notes

Introduction

1 The habitus is said to be created and constantly reformulated through one's past and on-going experiences (first in the family, later in the wider community, including school). These experiences are guided by the conditions of one's everyday life (i.e., material circumstances, cultural resources and social networks), all of which are strongly influenced by family position in a stratified society where resources are unequally distributed. Once embodied, the habitus gains a history and generates thinking, appreciation, perceptions, and actions. As such, the habitus *tends to* create practices that reflect and reproduce the agent's objective social position.

2 A longitudinal ethnography

1 The atmosphere and lifestyles in Tokyo *shitamachi* are detailed in Bestor (1989) and Kondo (1990).
2 The *buraku* people are descendants of an outcaste population. While the institutionalised caste system was abolished in the mid-nineteenth century, the *buraku* people still face symbolic discrimination, but there has been an improvement in their social mobility and educational attainment. The presence of Koreans in Japan is a direct result of Japan's colonisation of the Korean Peninsula from 1910 to 1945. The original Koreans fled to Japanese cities in pursuit of employment after being dispossessed of their farming lands by the Japanese colonial authorities, or (from 1937) were shipped to Japan as forced labour. Under Japanese colonisation Koreans were Japanese subjects, but in 1952, when Japan regained sovereignty at the end of the post-war occupation, Koreans living in Japan unilaterally became foreign nationals. See Okano and Tsuchiya (1999: 110–18).
3 Naturally, female university graduates have a wider choice, for example, between career track and clerical track positions.
4 A local academic, Hirayama (2000), argues that this disparity in post-quake recovery was caused by the social inequality that predated the earthquake; and by the local government's continued adoption of the 'dual model' housing policy which was centred on 'self-help'.
5 See *Toshiseisaku* volume 98 (January 2000), which offers a collection of articles that examine the economic recovery of the city.

3 Portraits of selected women

1 The floors of traditional Japanese rooms are covered by *tatami* mats, which are made of woven rushes and straw. They are rectangular, having a standard size of 180 cm x 90 cm, and a thickness of 5 cm.

2 *Pachinko* is a popular pinball game played in purpose-built 'parlours' housing rows of *pachinko* machines.

4 Initial entry into the wider adult world

1 Japanese honorific language has two functions. One is to acknowledge hierarchical relationships by expressing respect for others and self-effacement. The other is to recognise a distinction between group membership and non-membership. These two functions are expressed in terms of varying nouns and pronouns for individuals, and differing verbs and verb endings. See Wetzel (2004) and Niyekawa (1991) for the details of Japanese honorifics.
2 I initially considered it strange to see different members of the same family living peacefully together and belonging to the North and South Korean organisations, given their ideological divide. But this is not uncommon. Tomoe explained that her brother likes being 'Korean' but not the North Korean ideology that their father has long espoused.
3 Women's magazines play an important role in this. Popular magazines for young women (late teens and early 20s) cover fashion (how to co-ordinate clothes and where to buy them), food (recommended metropolitan restaurants and menus and recipes), overseas and domestic travel (where to visit, eat and stay, etc.) and romance. While Tanaka (1998) argues that these magazines try to offer young women instructions and recommendations about these matters through 'prescriptive' language, Sakamoto (1999) contends that they offer young women the chance to explore their new identities, rather than imposing a particular version of an ideal type of women.

5 Paid employment

1 Kôseirôdô-shô calculations are based on the Rôdô-Seisaku-Kenkyû-Kikô (2004).
2 Companies offer two tracks of white-collar employment: a clerical track and a career track. The latter became open to female four-year university graduates after the 1986 Equal Opportunity legislation, and offers the same training and promotion prospects as for male graduates.
3 Anne Allison (1994) details the nature of 'bar hostess' in her anthropological study.

6 Forming relationships

1 Sôkagakkai is a new religion derived from a sect of Buddhism. The religion has a large number of followers among the working-class population and supports a political party, the Kômei Party (Clean Government Party). See James W. White (1970).
2 Christmas cakes are sought after and retain their full prices at shops until the evening of 24 December. After 25 December they lose their value and the shops sell any remaining stock at a discount price. The term 'Christmas cakes' was often used in Japan to refer to marriageable women after they had reached 25 years of age. The term is becoming less relevant since the average age of first marriage for women has gone up in recent years.
3 The term *mukoyôshi* describes a man who marries into his wife's household and takes her family name. This practice happens when the family has only female children.
4 The increasing incidence of mixed marriages will produce more Japanese nationals with a Korean ethnic background. The 1984 legislation, which granted Japanese nationality to children with at least one Japanese parent, will accelerate this

process. A forecast based on demographic information suggests that by the mid-twenty-first century the number of Korean nationals with special permanent resident status (*tokubetsu eijûsha*) will have decreased to zero (Sakanaka 2000). The trend is already observable. The population of original Korean settlers and their descendants has been decreasing by 10,000 a year, although the total number of Korean nationals remains stable since this loss is replaced by Korean newcomers (Jyung 2000). A substantial number of Japanese nationals with a Korean background already exist and this number is set to increase rapidly. Among children this trend is clearer. For example, although Tokkabi Children's Club, an active ethnic Korean children's club, started in 1974 with all participants being Korean nationals, two-thirds of current members are Japanese nationals with a Korean ethnic background (Jyung 2000: 62). The increasing proportion of Japanese nationals with a Korean ethnic background (we may call them 'Korean Japanese') within the general Korean population calls for a more inclusive definition of *zainichi* Koreans (Jyung 2000; Pak 1997). Older Koreans had long considered Korean nationality (not having Japanese nationality) as the core of their ethnic identity; and Koreans who chose Japanese nationalities were often considered to be traitors or lacking in ethnic pride (Pak 1997).

7 Marriage and divorce in their 20s

1 *Amae* has been translated as 'dependence' in the literature. It has been widely assumed that this notion is specific to Japan, and that it lacks the kind of negative connotation that we might attach to 'dependence' in the Anglo-West. See, for example, Doi (1973).
2 Long (1996) provides the social and cultural constructions of aged care and its practice in Japan. Women over 50 predominantly provide aged care.

8 Decisions in paths to adulthood

1 Bourdieu (1984) presents a convincing analysis of how an individual's 'taste' is a product of class-specific experience.

Bibliography

Allison, A. (1994) *Nightwork: Sexuality, pleasure and corporate masculinity in a Tokyo hostess club*, Chicago: University of Chicago Press.

Aquilino, W. S. (1999) 'Rethinking the young adult life stage: prolonged dependency as an adaptive strategy', in A. Booth, A. C. Crouter and M. J. Shanahan (eds) *Transitions to Adulthood in a Changing Economy: No work, no family, no future?* Westport, CT: Praeger.

Arnett, J. J. (2004) *Emerging Adulthood*, New York: Oxford University Press.

—— (1997) 'Young people's conceptions of the transition to adulthood', *Youth and Society*, 29(1): 3–23.

Asano, S. and Guo, F. (1999) 'Kobe kakyô no hisai hinan fukkô to sôgo enjo', in N. Iwasaki, K. Ukai, M. Urano, K. Tsuji, K. Nitagai, T. Noda and T. Yamamoto (eds) *Hanshin Awaji Daijishinsai no Shakaigaku, Volume 2 (Hinan seikatsu no shakaigaku)*, Kyoto: Shôwadô.

Ball, S. J., Maguire, M. and MacRae, S. (2000) *Choice, Pathways and Transitions Post-16: New youth, new economies in the global city*, London: Routledge.

Bernstein, G. (1983) *Haruko's World: A Japanese farm woman and her community*, Stanford: Stanford University Press.

Bestor, T. (1989) *Neighbourhood Tokyo*, Stanford: Stanford University Press.

Bocknek, G. (1980) *The Young Adult: Development after adolescence*, Monterey, CA: Books/Cole Publishing.

Booth, A., Couter, A. C. and Shanahan, M. J. (eds) (1999) *Transition to Adulthood in a Changing Economy: No work, no family, no future?* Westport, CT: Praeger.

Bourdieu, P. (1984) *Distinction: A social critique of the judgement of taste*, Cambridge, MA: Harvard University Press.

—— (1977) *Outline of a Theory of Practice*, Cambridge: Cambridge University Press.

Bradley, H. and van Hoof, J. (eds) (2005) *Young People in Europe: Labour markets and citizenship*, Bristol: Policy.

Breen, R. and Buchmann, M. (2002) 'Institutional variation and the position of young people: a comparative perspective', *Annals of the American Academy of Political and Social Science*, 580: 288–305.

Brinton, M. C. (1989) 'Gender stratification in contemporary urban Japan', *American Sociological Review*, 54(4): 549–64.

Broadbent, K. (2003) *Women's Employment in Japan: The experience of part-time workers*, London: Routledge Curzon.

Bynner, J., Ferri, E. and Smith, K. (1997) *Twenty-Something in the 1990s: Getting somewhere, getting nowhere in the 1990s*, Aldershot, UK: Ashgate.

Cicchelli, V. and Martin, C. (2004) 'Young adults in France: becoming adult in the context of increased autonomy and dependency', *Journal of Comparative Family Studies*, 35(4): 615–26.

Clammer, J. (1997) *Contemporary Urban Japan: A sociology of consumption*, Oxford: Blackwell.

Cockburn, C. (1987) *Two-Track Training: Sex inequalities and the YTS*, London: Macmillan.

Connolly, M., Roberts, K., Ben-Tovim, G. and Torkington, P. (1992) *Black Youth in Liverpool*, Voorthuizen, The Netherlands: Giordano Bruno Colemborg.

Cook, T. and Furstenberg, F. F., Jr (2002) 'Explaining aspects of the transition to adulthood in Italy, Sweden, Germany, and the United States: a cross-disciplinary, case synthesis approach', *Annals of the American Academy of Political and Social Science,* 580: 257–87.

Corijn, M. and Klijzing, E. (eds) (2001) *Transitions to Adulthood in Europe*, Dordrecht: Kluwer Academic Publishers.

Corson, D. (1985) 'Education for work', *International Review of Education*, 31: 283–302.

Cote, J. E. (2000) *Arrested Adulthood: The changing nature of maturity and identity*, New York: New York University Press.

Creighton, M. (1996) 'Marriage, motherhood, and career management in a Japanese "counter culture"', in A. E. Imamura (ed.) *Re-Imaging Japanese Women*, Berkeley: University of California Press.

Dale, L. (2005) 'Lifestyles of the rich and single: reading agency in the "parasite single" issue', in L. Parker (ed.) *The Agency of Women in Asia*, Singapore: Marshall Cavendish Academic.

Doi, T. (1973) *The Anatomy of Dependence*, Tokyo: Kôdansha International.

Du Bois-Reymond, M. (1998) '"I don't want to commit myself yet": young people's life concepts', *Journal of Youth Studies*, 1(1): 63–79.

Dwyer, P. and Wyn, J. (2001) *Youth, Education and Risk*, London: Routledge Falmer.

EGISR (European Group for Integrated Social Research) (2001) 'Misleading trajectories: transition dilemmas of young adults in Europe', *Journal of Youth Studies*, 4 (1): 101–18.

Ferri, E. (1993) *Life at 33: The fifth follow-up of the National Child Development Survey*, London: National Children's Bureau.

Fuess, H. (2004) *Divorce in Japan: Family, gender and the state, 1600–2000*, Stanford: Stanford University Press.

Fujimura-Fanselow, K. and Kameda, A. (eds) (1995) *Japanese Women: New feminist perspectives on the past, present and future*, New York: Feminist Press.

Fujita, M. (2001) 'Hanshin daishinsai no nakadeno kôkôseitachi no katsudô to rentai', *Kôkôsei no Hiroba*, 40 (June): 44–47.

Fukuoka, Y. (2000) *Lives of Young Koreans in Japan*, Melbourne: Trans Pacific Press.

Furstenberg Jr, F. F., Cook, T. D., Sampson, R. and Slap, G. (eds) (2002) *The Annals of the American Academy of Political and Social Science, Special Issue*, 580.

Fussell, E. and Gauthier, A. H. (2005) 'American women's transition to adulthood in comparative perspective', in R. A. Settersten Jr, F. F. Furstenberg Jr and R. G. Rumbaut (eds) *On the Frontier of Adulthood: Theory, research, and public policy*, Chicago: University of Chicago Press.

Gaskell, J. (1992) *Gender Matters from School to Work*, Milton Keynes: Open University Press.

Goldstein-Gidoni, O. (1997) *Packaged Japaneseness: Weddings, business and brides*, Honolulu: University of Hawaii Press.

Gordon, T. and Lahelma, E. (2003) 'From ethnography to life history: tracing transitions of school students', *International Journal of Social Research Methodology*, 6 (3): 245–54.

Gottfried, H. and Hayashi-Kato, N. (1998) 'Gendering work: deconstructing the narrative of the Japanese economic miracle', *Work, Employment and Society*, 12 (1): 25–46.

Griffin, C. (1985) *Typical Girls? Young women from school to the job market*, London: Routledge and Kegan Paul.

Hamabata, M. M. (1990) *Crested Kimono: Power and love in the Japanese business family*, Ithaca: Cornell University Press.

Heinz, W. R. (1999) 'Introduction: transitions to employment in a cross-national perspective', in W. R. Heinz (ed.) *From Education to Work: Cross-national perspectives*, New York: Cambridge University Press.

Hirayama, Y. (2000) 'Collapse and reconstruction: housing recovery policy in Kobe after the Great Hanshin Earthquake', *Housing Studies*, 15(1): 111–28.

Hodkinson, P., Sparkes, A. C. and Hodkinson, H. (1996) *Triumphs and Tears: Young people, markets and the transition from school to work*, London: David Fulton Publishers.

Honda, Y. (2005a) *Wakamono to Shigoto: Gakkô keiyu no shûshoku o koete*, Tokyo: Tokyo University Press.

—— (2005b) 'The danger of obsession with academic ability', *Japan Echo*, 32(3): 16–20.

Housemand, S. and Ozawa, M. (1998) 'What is the nature of part-time work in the United States and Japan?', in J. O'Reilly and C. Fagan (eds) *Part-Time Prospects: An international comparison of part-time work in Europe, North America and the Pacific Rim*, London: Routledge.

Imamura, A. E. (1987) *Urban Japanese Housewives: At home and in the community*, Honolulu: University of Hawaii Press.

International Labour Organization (ILO) (2005) *LABORSTA, Yearly Data*. Online. Available HTTP: http://laborsta.ilo.org (accessed 15 January 2006).

—— (2002) *LABORSTA, Yearly Data*. Online. Available HTTP: http://laborsta.ilo.org (accessed 15 January 2006).

Ioka, T. (2000) 'Hanshin daishinsai kara shakaifukushi ga manandamono', *Shakai Fukushi Kenkyû*, 78(1): 18–25.

Irwin, S. (1995) *Rights of Passage: Social change and the transition from youth to adulthood*, London: University College London Press.

Ishida, H. (1993) *Social Mobility in Contemporary Japan*, London: Macmillan.

Iwamuro, S. (2005) *Eizu Seikansenshô*. Online. Available HTTP: www.taishukan-sport.jp/d00/002/002000006.htm (accessed 10 December 2005).

Iwao, S. (1993) *The Japanese Woman: Traditional image and changing reality*, New York: Free Press.

Iwasaki, N. (2000) 'Role and functions of local communities in earthquake rescue, shelter administration and reconstruction', *International Journal of Japanese Sociology*, 9: 111–19.

Japan-Kôsei-shô (1996) *Heisei 8-nendo Kôseihakusho*, Tokyo: Gyôsei Shuppan.

Japan-Kôseirôdô-shô (2005a) *Heisei 16-nendoban Rôdô Keizai no Bunseki*. Online. Available HTTP: http://wwwhakusyo.mhlw.go.jp/wp/index.htm (accessed 15 December 2005).

—— (2005b) *Heisei 16-nendo Hataraku Josei no Jitsujô*. Online. Available HTTP: www.mhlw.go.jp/houdou/2005/03/h0328 (accessed 15 December 2005).

—— (2005c) *Heisei 16-nendo Jinkô Dôtai Tôkei*. Online. Available HTTP: http:// wwwdbtk.mhlw.go.jp/toukei/cgi/sse_kensaku > (accessed 15 December 2005).

——(2004a) *Jinkô Dôtai Tôkei Nenpô: Shuyô tôkei hyô*. Online. Available HTTP: www.mhlw.go.jp/toukei/saikin/hw/jinkou/suii04 (accessed 12 December 2005).

——(2004b) *Heisei 16-nen Kokumin Seikatsu Kisochôsa*. Online. Available HTTP: www.mhlw.go.jp/toukei/saikin/hw/k-tyosa/k-chosa04 (accessed 12 December, 2005).

——(2002) *Shinki Gakkô Sotsugyô Shûshokusha no Shûshoku Rishoku Jôkyôchôsa*. Online. Available HTTP: www.mhlw.go.jp/houdou/2002/03/h0305–1b.html (accessed 15 December 2005).

Japan-Monbu-shô (1991) *Heisei 3-nendo Gakkô Kihon Chôsa Hôkokusho: Shotô chûtô kyôiku kikan, senshûgakkô, kakushugakkô*, Tokyo: Monbu-shô.

Japan-Monbukagaku-shô (2002) *Heisei 14-nendo Gakkô Kihon Chôsa Hôkokusho: Shotô chûtô kyôiku kikan, senshûgakkô, kakushugakkô*, Tokyo: Monbukagaku-shô.

Japan-Rôdô-shô (1999) *Heisei 10-nendo Hataraku Josei no Jitsujô*, Tokyo: Rôdô-shô, Josei-kyoku.

Japan-Sômuchô-Tôkeikyoku (2004) *Japan Statistical Yearbook*, Tokyo: Sôrifu.

Japan-Sôrifu (1995) *Josei no Genjô to Seisaku*, Tokyo: Sôrifu.

Johnson, M. K. (2002) 'Social origins, adolescent experiences, and work value trajectories during the transition to adulthood', *Social Forces*, 80(4): 1307–41.

Johnson, M. K. and Elder, G. H. (2002) 'Educational pathways and work value trajectories', *Sociological Perspectives*, 45(2): 113–38.

Jyung, Y. (2000) 'Zainichi gaikokujin o dô kyôikusuruka (2)', *Rôdô Keizai Junpô*, 54 (1653).

Kadowaki, A. and Sataka, M. (2001) *Otona no Jôken: Shakairyoku o tou*, Tokyo: Iwanami Shoten.

Kariya, T. (ed.) (2006) *Ima Kono Kunide Otona ni naru to iu koto*, Tokyo: Kinokuniya Shoten.

Kawai, H. (1996) *Otona ni narukoto no muzukashisa*, Tokyo: Iwanami Shoten.

Kelsky, K. (2001) *Women on the Verge: Japanese women, Western men*, Durham: Duke University Press.

Kenny, M. E. and Barton, C. (2003) 'Attachment theory and research', in J. Demick and C. Andreoletti (eds) *Handbook of Adult Development*, New York: Kluwer Academic.

Kerckhoff, A. (1990) *Getting Started: Transition to adulthood in Great Britain*, Boulder: Westview Press.

Kobe-shi (Kobe-city) (2004) *Heisei 16 nendo Kobe-shi Tôkeisho*, Kobe: Kobe-shi.

—— (1997) *Heisei 9-nendo Kobe-shi Tôkeisho*, Kobe: Kobe-shi.

—— (1989) *Dai 66-kai Kobe-shi Tôkeisho*, Kobe: Kobe-shi.

Kokuritsu-Shakaihoshô-Jinkô-Mondai-Kenkyûsho (2002) *Dai 12-kai Shussei Dôkô Kihon Chôsa (Fûfu Chôsa)*. Online. Available HTTP: www.ipss.go.jp (accessed 20 December 2005).

Kondo, D. (1990) *Crafting Selves: Power, gender and discourse of identity in a Japanese workplace*, Chicago: University of Chicago Press.

Kosugi, R. (2003) *Frîtâ to iu Ikikata*, Tokyo: Keiso Shobô.

—— (ed.) (2002) *Jiyû no Daishô: Furîtâ – Gendai wakamono no shûgyô ishiki to kôdô*, Tokyo: Nihon Rôdô Kenkyû Kikô.

Lam, A. (1992) *Women and Japanese Management: Discrimination and reform*, London: Routledge.

Leadbeater, B. and Way, N. (eds) (1996) *Urban Girls: Resisting stereotypes, creating identities*, New York: New York University Press.

Lebra, T. S. (1992) *Above the Clouds: Status culture of the modern Japanese nobility*, Berkeley: University of California Press.

—— (1984) *Japanese Women: Constraint and fulfilment*, Honolulu: University of Hawaii Press.

LeTendre, G. (2000) *Learning to be Adolescent: Growing up in US and Japanese middle schools*, New Haven: Yale University Press.

—— (1994) 'Guiding them on: teaching hierarchy, and social organization in Japanese middle schools', *Journal of Japanese Studies*, 20(1): 37–59.

Lo, J. (1990) *Office Ladies, Factory Women: Life and work at a Japanese company*, New York: M. E. Sharpe.

Long, S. O. (1996) 'Nurturing and femininity: the ideal of caregiving in postwar Japan', in A. E. Imamura (ed.) *Re-imaging Japanese Women*, Berkeley: University of California Press.

MacDonald, R. (1998) 'Youth, transitions and social exclusion: some issues for youth research in the UK', *Journal of Youth Studies*, 1(2): 163–76.

McRobbie, A. (1978) 'Working class girls and the culture of femininity, in Centre for Contemporary Cultural Studies (ed.) *Women Take Issue*, London: Hutchinson.

McVeigh, B. (1997) *Life in a Japanese Women's College: Learning to be ladylike*, London: Routledge.

Maguire, M., Ball, S. J. and MacRae, S. (2001) 'Post-adolescence, dependence and the refusal of adulthood', *Discourse*, 22(2): 197–211.

Mahaffy, K. A. (2003). 'Gender, race, class, and the transition to adulthood: a critical review of the literature', *Sociological Studies of Children and Youth*, 9: 15–47.

Mathews, G. and White, B. (2004) *Japan's Changing Generations: Are Young People Creating a New Society?* London: Routledge

Matsumoto, K. (2000) 'Sûji de miru hanshin daishinsai', *Chihôgyôsei*, 9242 (20 January 2000): 12.

Matsunaga, L. (2000) *The Changing Face of Japanese Retail: Working in a chain store*, London: Routledge.

Miller, L. and Bardsley, J. (eds) (2005) *Bad Girls of Japan*, New York: Palgrave Macmillan.

Mimizuka, H. (2005) 'Yureru gakkô no kinô to shokugyô shakai eno ikô: Kyôiku shisutemu no henyô to kôsotsu mugyôsha', in Shakai-seisaku-gakkai (ed.) *Wakamono: Chôkikasuru ikôkito shakai seisaku*, Kyoto: Hôritsu Bunka Sha.

Mirza, H. S. (1992) *Young, Female and Black*, London: Routledge.

Miyamoto, M. (2004) *Posuto Seinenki to Oyako Senryaku: Otona ni naru imito katachi no henyô*, Tokyo: Keiso Shobô.

Modell, J. (1999) 'When history is omitted', in A. Booth, A. C. Crouter and M. J. Shanahan (eds) *Transitions to Adulthood in a Changing Economy*, Westport, CT: Praeger.

Morita, Y. (1996) *Sûji ga Kataru Zainichi-kankoku-chôsenjin no Rekishi*, Tokyo: Akasho Shoten.

Morrow, V. and Richards, M. (1996) *Transitions to Adulthood: A family matter?*, York, Canada: Joseph Rowntree Foundation.

Mortimer, J. T. and Larson, R. W. (eds) (2002) *The Changing Adolescent Experience: Societal trends and the transition to adulthood*, New York: Cambridge University Press.

Mugikura, T., Mun, J. and Urano, M. (1999) 'Esunikku komyunitei no hisai jôkyô to kyûen katsudô', in N. Iwasaki, K. Ukai, M. Urano, K. Tsuji, K. Nitagai, T. Noda and T. Yamamoto (eds) *Hanshin Awaji Daijishinsai no Shakaigaku Volume 2 (Hinan seikatsu no Shakaigaku)*, Kyoto: Shôwadô.

Naitô, M. (1999) 'Kasetsu jûtaku niokeru seikatsu jittai', in N. Iwasaki, K. Ukai, M. Urano, K. Tsuji, K. Nitagai, T. Noda and T. Yamamoto (eds) *Hanshin Awaji Daijishinsai no Shakaigaku Volume 2 (Hinan seikatsu no Shakaigaku)*, Kyoto: Shôwadô.

Nakata, T. (1996) 'Budding volunteerism', *Japan Quarterly*, 43(1): 22–27.

Nihon-Fujin-Dantai-Rengôkai (2001) *Josei hakusho*, Tokyo: Horupu Shuppan.

—— (1996) *Fujin Hakusho*, Tokyo: Horupu Shuppan.

Nihon-Rôdô-Kenkyû-Kikô (2000a) *Wakamono no Shûgyô Kôdô no Henka o Kangaeru*, Tokyo: Nihon Rôdô Kenkyû Kikô.

—— (2000b) *Furîtâ no Ishiki to Jittai: 97-nin eno hiaringu kekka yori*, Tokyo: Nihon Rôdô Kenkyû Kikô.

Nishida, Y. (1999) 'Hinansho to natta gakkô ni okeru kyôshokuin', in N. Iwasaki, K. Ukai, M. Urano, K. Tsuji, K. Nitagai, T. Noda and T. Yamamoto (eds) *Hanshin Awaji Daijishinsai no Shakaigaku Volume 2 (Hinan seikatsu no Shakaigaku)*, Kyoto: Shôwadô.

Nishiyama, S. (2005) *Borantyia Katsudô no Ronri: Hanshin-Awaji Daishinsai kara sabushisutensu shakai e*, Tokyo: Toshindô.

Niyekawa, A. (1991). *Minimum Essential Politeness: A guide to the Japanese honorific language*, Tokyo: Kôdansha.

Ogasawara, Y. (1998). *Office Ladies, Salaried Men: Power, gender and work in Japanese companies*, Berkeley: University of California Press.

Okano, K. (2004) 'Japanese working-class girls in their first employment: transition to adulthood', *Journal of Education and Work*, 17: 421–39.

—— (2000) 'Social justice and job distribution in Japan: class, minority and gender', *International Review of Education*, 46(6): 545–65.

—— (1997) 'Third-generation Koreans' entry into the workforce in Japan', *Anthropology and Education Quarterly*, 28(4): 524–49.

—— (1995a) 'Rational decision making and school-based job referrals for high school students in Japan', *Sociology of Education*, 68(1): 31–47.

—— (1995b) 'Habitus and intraclass differentiation: nonuniversity-bound students in Japan', *International Journal of Qualitative Studies in Education*, 8(4): 357–69.

—— (1993) *School to Work Transition in Japan: An ethnographic study*, Clevedon, Avon: Multilingual Matters.

Okano, K. and Tsuchiya, M. (1999) *Education in Contemporary Japan: Inequality and diversity*, Cambridge: Cambridge University Press.

Olsen, C. S. (1996) 'African-American adolescent women: perceptions of gender, race and class', *Marriage and Family Review*, 24: 105–21.

Ozawa, Y. (2000) 'Dêta ni miru Kobe keizai no genjô to kadai', *Toshi Seisaku*, 98 (January): 3–16.

Pak, J. (1997) 'Zainichi kankokujin no kokuseki mondai saikô', *Gendai Korea*, 37: 60–69.

Pharr, S. J. (1981) *Political Women in Japan: The search for a place in political life*, Berkeley: University of California Press.

Plath, D. (1980) *Long Engagements: Maturity in modern Japan*, Stanford: Stanford University Press.

Plug, W., Zeijl, E. and Du Bois-Reymond, M. (2003) 'Young people's perceptions on youth and adulthood: a longitudinal study from the Netherlands', *Journal of Youth Studies*, 6(2): 127–44.

Raffe, D., Brannen, K. and Croxford, L. (2001) 'The transition from school to work in the early 1990s: A comparison of England, Wales and Scotland', *Journal of Education and Work*, 14(3): 293–313.

Reischauer, E. O. and Jansen, M. B. (1995) *The Japanese Today: Change and continuity*, Harvard University Press.

Renshaw, J. R. (1999) *Kimono in the Boardroom*, New York: Oxford University Press.

Roberson, J. E. (1998) *Japanese Working Class Lives: An ethnographic study of factory workers*, London: Routledge.

—— (1995) 'Becoming shakaijin', *Ethnology*, 34(4): 293–313.

Roberts, G. (1994) *Staying on the Line: Blue-collar women in contemporary Japan*, Honolulu: University of Hawaii Press.

Roberts, K. (2003) 'Change and continuity in youth transitions in Eastern Europe: lessons for Western sociology', *Sociological Review*, 51(4): 484–505.

Rôdô-Seisaku-Kenkyû-Kikô (2004) *Rôdôsha no hataraku iyoku to Koyôkanri no arika ni kansuru chôsa*. Tokyo: Rôdô Seisaku Kenkyû Kenshû Kikô.

Rohlen, T. (1983) *Japan's High Schools*, Berkeley: University of California Press.

—— (1974) *For Harmony and Strength*, Berkeley: University of California Press.

Rosenberger, N. R. (2001) *Gambling with Virtue: Japanese women and the search for self in a changing nation*, Honolulu: University of Hawaii Press.

Ryang, S. (1997) *North Koreans in Japan*, Boulder: Westview Press.

Sakamoto, K. (1999) 'Reading Japanese women's magazines: the construction of new identities in the 1970s and 1980s', *Media, Culture and Society*, 21: 173–93.

Sakamoto, M. (2001) 'Crisis management in Japan: lessons from the Great Hanshin–Awaji Earthquake of 1995' in A. Farazmand (ed.) *Handbook of Crisis and Emergency Management*, New York: Marcel Dekker.

Sakanaka, H. (2000) 'Zainichi kankoku chôsenjin no kako genzai mirai', *Gendai Korea*, 40: 30–41.

Saldana, J. (2003) *Longitudinal Qualitative Research: Analyzing change through time*, Walnut Creek: Altamira Press.

Sato, I. (1991). *Kamikaze Biker: Parody and anomy in affluent Japan*, Chicago: University of Chicago Press.

Sato, T. (1998) *Otona ni naru to iu koto (Iwanami Junia Shinsho)*, Tokyo: Iwanami Shoten.

Schoeni, R. F. and Ross, K. E. (2005) 'Material assistance from families during the transition to adulthood' in R. A. Settersten Jr, F. F. Furstenberg Jr and R. G. Rumbaut (eds) *On the Frontier of Adulthood: Theory, research and public policy*, Chicago: University of Chicago Press.

Settersten Jr, R. A., Furstenberg Jr, F. F. and Rumbaut, R. G. (eds) (2005) *On the Frontier of Adulthood: Theory, research, and public policy*, Chicago: University of Chicago Press.

Shakai-Seisaku-Gakkai (ed.) (2005) *Wakamono: Chôkika suru ikôki to shakai-seisaku*, Kyoto: Hôritsu Bunka Sha.

Shanahan, M. J. (2000) 'Pathways to adulthood in changing societies: variability and mechanisms in life course perspective', *Annual Review of Sociology*, 26: 667–92.

Shibata, K. (1999) 'Hinansho no katsudô no tenkai', in N. Iwasaki, K. Ukai, M. Urano, K. Tsuji, K. Nitagai, T. Noda and T. Yamamoto (eds) *Hanshin Awaji*

Daijishinsai no Shakaigaku Volume 2 (Hinan seikatsu no Shakaigaku), Kyoto: Shôwadô.

Shida, K., Seiyama, K. and Watanabe, H. (2000) 'Kekkon shijô no henyô', in K. Seiyama (ed.) *Jendâ Shijô Kazoku (Nihon no Kansô Shisutemu 4)*, Tokyo: Tokyo Daigaku Shuppan.

Shirahase, S. (1995) 'Diversity in female work: female part-time workers in contemporary Japan', *American Asian Review*, 13: 257–82.

Shorter-Gorden, K. and Washington, N. C. (1996) 'Young, black, and female: the challenge of weaving an identity', *Journal of Adolescence*, 19: 465–75.

Skeggs, B. (1997) *Formation of Class and Gender*, London: Sage.

Sugimoto, Y. (2003) *Introduction to Japanese Society*, Cambridge: Cambridge University Press.

Tachibanaki, T. (2004) *Datsu Furîtâ Shakai: Otonatachi ni dekirukoto*, Tokyo: Toyo-keizaishinpo-sha.

Tamaki, F. (2002) 'Hanshin Daishinsai kara 7-nen: "saigai jakusha" ga kataru shinjitsu' *Shio*, 516 (February): 270–79.

Tanaka, K. (1998) 'Japanese women's magazines: the language of aspiration', in D. P. Martinez (ed.) *The Worlds of Japanese Popular Culture: Gender, shifting boundaries and global cultures*, Cambridge: Cambridge University Press.

Tanayama, K. (1999) 'Hinansho unei o meguru kyôin borantyia hinansha no kankei', in N. Iwasaki, K. Ukai, M. Urano, K. Tsuji, K. Nitagai, T. Noda and T. Yamamoto (eds) *Hanshin Awaji Daijishinsai no Shakaigaku Volume 2 (Hinan seikatsu no Shakaigaku)*, Kyoto: Shôwadô.

Tannen, D. (1991) *You Just Don't Understand: Women and men in conversation*, London: Virago.

Thiessen, V. and Looker, E. D. (1999) 'Diverse directions: young adults' multiple transitions', in W. R. Heinz (ed.) *Transitions to Employment in a Cross-National Perspective*, New York: Cambridge University Press.

Thomson, R., Holland, J., McGrellis, S., Bell, R., Henderson, S. and Sharpe, S. (2004) 'Inventing adulthoods: a biographical approach to understanding youth citizenship', *Sociological Review*, 52(2): 218–39.

Valli, L. (1986) *Becoming Clerical Workers*, London: Routledge and Kegan Paul.

Vogel, S. H. (1978) 'Professional housewife: the career of urban middle class Japanese women', *Japan Interpreter*, 12(1): 16–43.

Walkerdine, V., Lucy, H. and Melody, J. (2001) *Growing Up Girl: Psychological explorations of gender and class*, New York: New York University Press.

Weathers, C. (2001) 'Changing white-collar workplaces and female temporary workers in Japan', *Social Science Japan Journal*, 4(2): 201–18.

Westberg, A. (2004) 'Forever young? Young people's conception of adulthood: the Swedish case', *Journal of Youth Studies*, 7(1): 35–53.

Wetzel, P. (2004) *Keigo in Modern Japan*, Honolulu: University of Hawaii Press.

White, J. (1970) *The Sôkagakkai and Mass Society*, Stanford: Stanford University Press.

White, M. (1993) *The Material Child: Coming of age in Japan and America*, New York: Free Press.

Wulff, H. (1995) 'Inter-racial friendship: consuming youth styles, ethnicity and teenage femininity in South London', in V. Amit-Talai and H. Wulff (eds) *Youth Cultures: A cross-cultural perspective*, London: Routledge.

Wyn, J. and Dwyer, P. (2000) 'New patterns of youth transition in education', *International Social Science Journal*, 52(2): 147–59.

Yajima, M. and Mimizuka, H. (2001) *Kawaru Wakamono to Shokugyô Sekai: Tranjission no Shakaigaku*, Tokyo: Gakubunsha.

Yamada, M. (1999) *Parasaito Shinguru no Jidai*, Tokyo: Chikuma Shobô.

Yoder, R. S. (2004) *Youth Deviance in Japan: Class reproduction of non-conformity*, Melbourne: Trans Pacific Press.

Yu, W. (2002) 'Jobs for mothers: married women's labour force re-entry and part-time, temporary employment in Japan', *Sociological Forum*, 17(3): 493–523.

Index